The American Journalists

OUR PRESS GANG, or,

A Complete Exposition of the
Corruptions and Crimes
of the American Newspapers

Lambert A. Wilmer

ARNO
&
The New York Times

Collection Created and Selected
by Charles Gregg of Gregg Press

Reprint edition 1970 by Arno Press Inc.

LC# 73-125723
ISBN 0-405-01706-5

The American Journalists
ISBN for complete set: 0-405-01650-6

Reprinted from a copy in
The Columbia University Library

Manufactured in the United States of America

OUR PRESS GANG

OUR PRESS GANG;

OR,

A COMPLETE EXPOSITION

OF THE

CORRUPTIONS AND CRIMES

OF THE

AMERICAN NEWSPAPERS.

By LAMBERT A. WILMER, (Ex-Editor,)

Author of "The Life, Travels and Adventures of Ferdinand De Soto," "The Quacks of Helicon, a Satire," "Preferment, or Ambition's Ladder," "The American Sibyl," etc., etc.

PHILADELPHIA:
J. T. LLOYD.
LONDON: SAMPSON LOW, SON & CO.,
5 LUDGATE HILL.
1859.

Entered according to Act of Congress, in the year 1859, by
LAMBERT A. WILMER,
In the Clerk's Office of the District Court of the United States, in and for the Eastern District of Pennsylvania.

DEDICATORY EPISTLE.

TO SAMUEL C. UPHAM, ESQ.

My Dear Upham:

Having determined to dedicate this book to you, I reflected that it would be difficult to introduce your name into a work which deals in scarcely any thing else but censure, wherefore I puzzled myself to find something in your conduct which deserves to be condemned. The worst fault with which I can possibly charge you, is your retirement from a profession which cannot well spare any of its honorable members; and this fault of yours was the more inexcusable, because you abdicated the chair editorial at a time when you had abundant reason to be satisfied with your success as a journalist, and with the many "golden opinions" which your excellent management of the press had gained for you. The single offense just spoken of entitles you to a place among the condemned editors; nevertheless, with a just appreciation of your motives, I subscribe myself

Your unchangeable friend,
THE AUTHOR.

June, 1859.

INDEX.

	Page
PREAMBLE	9
INTRODUCTORY NARRATIVE	17
Author's pilgrimage	17
First experiment as an editor	18
Change of location	18
Another removal	19
General Duff Green	20
His quarrel with General Jackson	20
A trial	21
Newspaper project	22
Birth of the Baltimore Saturday Visiter	23
Troublesome copartnership	25
Explosion	26
Settlement	28
Unpleasant predicament	29
The prodigal's return	31
Fate and fever	31
A new enterprise	32
Embarrassments	33
In office	34
Another change	34
A gloomy perspective	36
Brightening prospects	36
Something unexpected	37
The Kaleidoscope	38
New difficulties	39
Back again to Philadelphia	40
Various engagements	41
Organ grinding	42
Another disastrous partnership	42
Troublesome litigation	43
The organ surrendered	44
A recusant editor	45
Other engagements	46
Commentaries	47

SECTION I.

FOURTEEN SERIOUS CHARGES AGAINST THE NEWSPAPER PRESS	50

SECTION II.

PROOFS TO BE GIVEN	54
The culprits	54
Exceptions	55
Military illustration	55
Stubborn facts; truth a libel	56
Confirmation	57
Cause and effect	57
Various modes of operation	57
General character of American journalism	58
Rustic innocence	58
Proofs from all quarters	59

SECTION III.

TYRANNY OF THE PRESS	60
Abundance of newspapers	60
Newspaper authority	60
Our editors; who and what are they?	61
The first charge	62
Tremendous power of the Press	62
C. J. Ingersoll's testimony	63
Testimony of Judge Ludlow	64
Hear the Washington Union	64
Other testimony	64
Usurpation of the Press	65
Is it qualified for dominion?	65
Morals and intellect of the Press	66
SUPPLEMENTARY ILLUSTRATIONS	68
Deportment of the tyrants	68
One of the monarchs	69
The tyrants' masters	70
"Dead heads"	71

SECTION IV.

FOREIGN CHARACTER OF THE PRESS	73
The "accident of birth"	73
Alien editors	74
Hatred of government	76
Mistakes corrected	76
Vagabond editors	77
Recapitulation	78
Examples	79
Foreign editors preferred	80
The newspaper pets	81
Origin of the "Satanic press"	81
Superiority of foreign editors	82
SUPPLEMENTARY ILLUSTRATIONS	84
Madame Lola Montez	84
Editorial corps of N. Y. Herald	84
Tribune and Express	84
New York Times	85
Foreign organs	85
Catalogue of foreign newspapers in the United States	85
Opinions of the foreign Press	88
John Mitchell	88

INDEX.

SECTION V.
Toryism and Treachery of the Press...90
    Excuses..90
    The charge....................................91
    Real traitors..................................92
    The grand mistake........................94
    Detestable doctrine........................95
    Commotion-makers.......................96
    Review of the subject....................99
    Newspapers opposed to their own
      liberty...99
Supplementary Illustrations..........101
    Silly and stupid journalists..........101
    Manufacture of "leaders"............102
    Excitement breeders....................103
    A conscientious seceder...............103

SECTION VI.
Villainous Deceptions of the Press..104
    Example—the negro question.......104
    Origin of the excitement..............104
    The agitation begins....................107
    Progress of the mischief..............107
    The South excited.......................108
    Effects of negro emancipation......109
    Application..................................111
    Cui bono?...................................111
    Entomological comparison...........112
    African fever...............................112
    Incantations................................113
Supplementary Illustrations..........114
    Greeley's history.........................114
    Gen. Houston *vs.* Horace Greeley..115
    Greeley's amiable eccentricities....115
    William Lloyd Garrison...............115
    The apostles of abolition..............116

SECTION VII.
Other Deceptions of the Press........118
    Explanations wanted..................118
    Curious fraternity.......................120
    A national blessing....................122
    Invocation to James G. Bennett.....122
        to Horace Greeley.......123
        to John W. Forney......123
        to Jesper Harding.......124
    A change for the worse..............124
Supplementary Illustrations..........126
    Stupendous robbery....................126
    Money-making...........................126
    One faithful witness....................127

SECTION VIII.
More Deceptions.............................129
    Lola Montez...............................129
    Her evidence..............................130
    The foreign organs......................131
    Commentary...............................134
    The plaudits...............................135
    Facts suppressed.........................135
    Irish citizens..............................136
    A plea for the Countess.............136
    Patrick's picture, by Brougham....137
    Newspaper lies in abundance......139
    German citizens..........................140
    A few words of explanation........141

Supplementary Illustrations..........143
    Discontented aliens.....................143
    Republic-building fallacy............144
    The "accident of birth"..............146

SECTION IX.
**Newspapers colleagued with cheats
and impostors**.................................148
    Swindlers and cheats..................149
    Fraudulent banks........................149
    Knavish insurance companies.....150
    The Yankee showman................152
    Barnum's mermaid.....................152
    Jenny Lind.................................153
    "Starring"..................................154
    The Keane mobbing affair..........155
    Swindling encouraged................157
    Roguish publishers....................157
    "Peter Funk".............................158
Supplementary Illustrations..........159
    "Insurance shops".....................159
    Roback the wizard.....................160
    The swill-milk trade...................161
    Stock gambling..........................164

SECTION X.
Demoralizing Journalism...............166
    Abundance no blessing...............166
    Vicious instructions....................166
    One of the instructors.................167
    Another moral teacher................168
    "The great prize fight"...............168
    The grog business.......................171
    Obscene reporting......................173
    Foul advertisements...................174
    "Respectable newspapers"..........174
    A model civilizer.......................175
    Summary....................................178
Supplementary Illustrations..........179
    An editorial grog-seller...............179
    A lascivious journalist................179
    Sottishness.................................180
    Morality of the New York Times...180
    A marriage in prospect...............181
    Beecher censures the Press..........181
    Editorial preaching....................182

SECTION XI.
Political villainies of the Press.....184
    Official roguery..........................184
    Why is it so?..............................185
    Action of the Press....................186
    The remedy................................187
    Newspaper connivance at public
      frauds.......................................188
    Active assistance of the Press......189
    Colossal robbery........................190
    Official thieves taxed by the Press..192
    Amount of the plunder...............193
    Defalcation a felony...................193
    Editorial sympathy with public
      robbers.....................................194
    The latest modes........................195
    Sale of newspaper influence........196
    Summary....................................197
Supplementary Illustrations..........198
    Frightful state of affairs..............198

INDEX.

	Page
Hear the Rev. H. W. Beecher	198
John Mitchell and his friends	198
Jefferson a prophet	199
Organ-grinders	200

SECTION XII.

THE PRESS ELECTS SCOUNDRELS TO OFFICE..202
Application............................203
Just grounds of suspicion............203
Do official thieves fear the law?...205
Are they afraid of public opinion?...205
Common belief........................206
Corruption funds.....................207
Who makes official rascals?.........209
Damning recommendations.............211
The public persuaded to submit.....212
SUPPLEMENTARY ILLUSTRATIONS..........213
Forney plays Duke of Buckingham..................................213
The virtuous Forney abused.........215
Mr. Buchanan's free entertainments..............................215
An afflictive change................216

SECTION XIII.

THE PRESS DEFEATS THE LAW 217
Judicial opinions....................217
Trials a mockery 218
Newspaper opposition to law........218
Reporting criminal cases............219
Injudicious judges..................221
Prejudiced juries...................222
Professional jurymen................224
Abolition of trial by jury..........225
Escape of criminals 225
Criminals defended by editors 226
Powers of reporters 227
Criminals bribe the Press 228
SUPPLEMENTARY ILLUSTRATIONS..........230
Murder of Helen Jewitt.............231
Case of Captain Mackenzie..........231
of Kirby 232

SECTION XIV.

HORRID EFFECTS OF EDITORIAL INTERFERENCE WITH THE LAW 234
Characteristics of editors.........234
The charge............................235
The great crime......................236
Clamors of the Press...............237
The Typographical tribunal.........237
Terrorism of the Press 238
Editorial mobbing...................239
Murder of Evelina Cunningham...241
of Mrs. Rademacher.........241
Dying declarations..................241
Example 243
Duty of citizens....................244
Summary..............................245
SUPPLEMENTARY ILLUSTRATIONS..........246
Execution at Baltimore.............246
The Sickles' case.................. 249

SECTION XV.

NEWSPAPER SLANDERS 251
A vile habit..........................251
Dastardly slanders..................251
New York Tribune and Times.......251
Slanders of Mrs. J. G. Bennett....251
of Lady Gore Ouseley 251
The common vice of newspapers...252
Unrestricted slandering 253
The ladies defended,................257
Vindication of American character.256
Verbal rebukes insufficient........258
Cudgelling and horsewhipping......258
An editor flogged....................258
The flogging justified.............259
A better remedy.....................260
Infamy of the American Press.....260
The defense..........................262
Home-made opinions.................262
Another objection...................264
SUPPLEMENTARY ILLUSTRATIONS..........265
Confession 265
Mrs. Jackson........................265
" Cheap newspapers"...............266
A specimen...........................266
Mr. Cooper, the Novelist..........266
Insignificance of newspaper abuse.267

SECTION XVI.

EXAMPLES, ETC., OF NEWSPAPER DEFAMATION....................................269
" Black mail"........................270
Libertinism, (editorial)...........271
Anonymous correspondents...........271
Local reporting.....................275
Sundry examples.....................276
Retraction of slanders 277
Flogging the best refutation......280
" Putting people down"............281
Propagation of slanders............282
Principal vehicles of slander.....283
Defamation of the dead.............284
Summary..............................285
SUPPLEMENTARY ILLUSTRATIONS..........286
Case of J. T. Lloyd.................286

SECTION XVII.

EDITORIAL DUELS............................294
Matthew Carey and Col. Oswald..294
Cheatham and Coleman...............295
Graham and ———...................296
Biddle and Pettis...................297
Bynum and Perry....................297
Cummings and McDuffie 297
Cilley and Graves 299
Webb and Marshall..................304
Hickey and Moses....................305
Irving and Gibson 305
Woods and Coleman..................305
Freeman and Smith 306
Frost and Hunt.......................307
Kemble and McDougal................307
Smyth and Thomas....................307
Daniel and Johnson.................308
Gilbert and Denver..................308
Nugent and Hayes...................309
Nugent and Cotter...................309

	Page		Page
Cohen and Wintzell	310	"Old Sands of Life"	351
Carrol and Barbagon	310	A well-ridden hobby	351
Carter and De Courcey	310	Benjamin Brandreth	352
Rust and Stidger	311	Dr. Moffatt	352
Rea and Evans	311	An "unshackled Press"	352
Comments	311		

SECTION XVIII.

FIGHTS AND FLOGGINGS OF EDITORS........312
Webb and Bennett.........................313
Injustice to Greeley.....................314
Col. Webb and Duff Green................315
Dwyer and Lasseter......................316
Case of P. G. Ferguson..................317
"Humiliation of the Press"..............318
A female Avenger........................319
Mrs. Lyons and Henry Frost..............319
Frightful mortality.....................320
Prentice and Durrett....................320
Reed and Walker.........................320
Kate Hastings and Ned Buntline..........321
Blair and Pickering.....................321
Harney and Haldeman.....................322
Forrest and Willis......................322
Problem.................................322
The Press of Philadelphia...............323
A narrow escape.........................324
A besieged journalist...................324
Ricketts and Forward....................325
Beaumont and Poindexter.................325
Note....................................325

SECTION XIX.

AMERICAN INTELLECT DISGRACED BY NEWSPAPERS......326
"Is it true?"...........................328
Debased literature......................329
Unholy league...........................330
Americans grossly misrepresented........332
Who are our slanderers?.................333
The Eleventh Charge.....................334
The Twelfth Charge......................336
SUPPLEMENTARY ILLUSTRATIONS.............336
The Sonntag narrative...................336
Unprofitable studies....................338
An admission............................339

SECTION XX.

THE PRESS LEAGUED WITH PUBLIC POISONERS........340
Frauds of Quackery......................340
Murders of Quackery.....................340
Thirteenth Charge.......................344
Instances...............................345
Another specimen........................346
A delicate puff.........................346
Recommendations of poisons..............347
The editors' profits....................348
Many offenders..........................349
SUPPLEMENTARY ILLUSTRATIONS.............350
An infallible remedy....................350

SECTION XXI.

THE PRESS ENCOURAGES MOBBING, TREASON AND REBELLION......353
Mobs and Mobbing........................353
The people condemn mobs.................354
Danger of popular commotions............355
Opinions of the Press...................356
Rebellion at New Orleans................357
New York Quarantine mob.................358
Barbarous treatment of sick people......358
Appearance of the patients..............359
Agency of the Press.....................360
The Christiana mob......................361
The war of races........................362
The "Native mob"........................363
Riot at New Orleans.....................365
German riot in New York.................365
mob at Cincinnati.......................368
Foreign rioters justified...............369
Riot and murder in Philadelphia.........369
Facts suppressed by newspapers..........370
Rebellion in Perry County, O............371
Explanations............................372

SECTION XXII.

RESULTS OF THE INVESTIGATION............374
Journalism unmasked.....................374
The subject reviewed....................374
Discoveries.............................374
The titles of journalism................376
The Press no part of government.........377
The Press as it is......................377
Duty of Christians......................377
Resist the tyrant.......................379

APPENDIX................................381
Charges omitted.........................381
Editorial associations..................381
Venom of Philadelphia journalism........382
The banking system illustrated..........383
A medical editor........................383
No hope for Americans...................383
Empirical murders.......................384
Arsenic prescribed......................384
Edgar A. Poe vindicated.................385
Incitement to mobbing...................386
Treason approved........................386
A clerical editor.......................386
The devil among the Dutchmen............387
Newspaper persecution, case of Mat. Ward....387
The "Forrest Letter"....................390
Persecution of J. G. Bennett............392
A nut for the naturalizers..............393

PREAMBLE.

WHEN useful but unpleasant truths are brought to light, the man who undertakes to divulge them is often expected to give some explanation of his *motives*. But is this expectation fair and reasonable? It appears to me that when truths are genuine and important, the public has no right to inquire whether they are told maliciously, mischievously, or for the best purpose that can be imagined. With respect to the revelations which are about to be made, it might not be easy to explain my reasons for making them, in a way that would be likely to give general satisfaction. To elucidate my meaning, let us take a familiar incident from ancient history:—

When Curtius leaped into a yawning abyss and sacrificed himself, as it seemed, for the benefit of the public, his conduct might have been variously interpreted by his fellow-citizens. Some might have supposed that he was tired of life, and wished to have a decent pretense for committing suicide. Others might have surmised that an excessive love of praise and admiration, or a yearning after posthumous celebrity, induced him to entomb his living body in that extraordinary manner. Some parsimonious people might have conjectured that he did it to avoid the expenses of a regular funeral; and, in short, every man would have accounted for the action in a manner corresponding with the ruling motives of his own conduct. It is possible that many Roman citizens who lived in the time of Marcus Curtius believed that the young man was really actuated by a noble and unselfish desire to *serve his country*, without any hope of reward or any prospect of plunder. But if Marcus Curtius had sacrificed himself in the United States of America, about the middle of the nineteenth century, I apprehend that the last-mentioned supposition, with a majority of the people, would have been more incomprehensible and more incredible than any of the others.

In some particulars, my present undertaking bears a striking resemblance to the suicidal act of Marcus Curtius. I perceive a terrible gulf—a bottomless abyss of typographical iniquity—standing open in this republic; and, to use a phrase much in vogue with my countrymen, I "pitch into it," with some hope of abating the nuisance. My deed, like that of Curtius, will admit of divers interpretations; it will be called rash, inconsiderate, quixotic, presumptuous, impious perhaps, or almost any thing else, except benevolent and patriotic.

It may be very difficult for some of my fellow-citizens to imagine what motives could impel any man to provoke the wrath of such a powerful "institution" as journalism. The first conjecture of nine-tenths of the American people may be that a pecuniary "speculation" is intended. Such a book as *Our Press Gang*, it may be said, is likely to have an extensive sale, and, in this way, the author will be remunerated for exposing himself to the vindictive abuse of the public journals. But, on the other hand, let us consider that booksellers seldom expect to find a market for their publications without editorial assistance; and it is commonly believed that the efforts of the press can *prevent* the sale of any new book, whatever may be its merit. It is not at all probable that the journalists will be magnanimous enough to recommend "Our Press Gang" to public patronage. The favorable attention of the press will not be solicited in any manner; the book will not be advertised largely in the newspapers; nothing will be paid for editorial "puffs," and no *gratis* copies will be presented to journalists. And so the expedients which are supposed to be *absolutely necessary* to make a book marketable will not, and cannot, be used in the present instance. How, then, is the publication of this book to be made "a good speculation"?

Will it be supposed or pretended that the disclosures made in this volume are demonstrations of malice or revenge? You will find no proof of such an allegation in the book itself. None of the author's personal enemies are carbonized, excoriated, or crucified in these pages. None of his friends are spared, if they happen to be connected with the abuses which are made the objects of attack. The names of persons are introduced only in a lawful and justifiable manner; and, in the most aggravated cases of delinquency, the offenders are treated with a degree of courtesy and merciful forbearance.

Had I been disposed to indulge a vindictive disposition, the opportunity would not have been wanting, and the provocations which I have received would have been sufficient for my excuse. The proscription and persecution to which I have been subjected in this city of Philadelphia, merely because I have ventured to attempt some very desirable reforms, have been the themes of PUBLIC REMARK. In a work entitled "The Dramatic Authors of America" I find the following passage:

"Mr. Wilmer's literary productions have gained him many enemies among those who have writhed under his lash, and the consequence is that he is now suffering a kind of proscription which must affect very deeply both his interests and his reputation as an author."

In the preface to one of George Lippard's novels, it is asserted that certain influential persons connected with the press of Philadelphia have used all their exertions to prevent me from earning a livelihood in this city. I have many good reasons for believing that these intimations are correct; but such is my ardent love of TRUTH, that, for her sake,

> "I weed all bitterness from out my breast—
> It hath no business where she is a guest;"

and there were so many facts of general importance to be discussed in this volume, that no space could be wasted in the exposition of matters which chiefly concern myself.

When I speak of the "disclosures" which I am about to make, I do not profess to be a revelator of profound mysteries or a discoverer of truths which have hitherto been indiscernible. Many of the facts which I propose to exhibit are not unknown to *everybody;* but they will be novelties to the PUBLIC IN GENERAL. These facts are not generally known, because, among the few who have had opportunities to become acquainted with them, it seldom happens that there is an individual who is willing to incur the risks of making them public. That they are published *now* is the effect of a somewhat singular combination of causes. The author of this book expects not to ask any favors from the "sovereign people," and he can therefore venture to do them an important service; he does not believe in the omnipotence of the press, and he is not afraid to awaken its indignation; he *does* believe in the omnipotence of Truth, and he hesitates not to fight in her cause, and to trust to her protection. And, besides, (sinner as he is,) he would rather do good than evil; and when he can be patriotic at no greater expense than the endurance of a little newspaper abuse, he is willing to serve his country.

But the public does not see *all* the risks which are incurred in this undertaking. When I offend the newspaper press I offend all the rascality with which it is confederated; and in this way I may provoke whole legions of powerful enemies, if the shot from my battery should happen to take effect.

I hope and believe that I have done no injustice in this volume. In a work which records so many facts, it is scarcely possible that there should not be some trivial misapprehensions and errors. In a country where the newspapers are the principal sources of information, it is almost impossible to obtain a strictly-correct account of any thing; but, in all matters of importance, the evidence was well sifted and scrutinized before it was admitted into this volume. That there are any considerable mistakes in the book is doubtful; but it is certain that the *whole truth* is not always told; and when any ugly affair is spoken of, the reader may generally guess that the reality was much worse than the description. If this book should prove to be less vituperative than some persons expected, the fault is not mine; it is not in my nature to write or publish scurrility or gross personalties, and I never promised to do any thing of the kind. My object is to strike at great abuses, and not to assail small individuals, no matter how deserving they may be of rebuke or castigation.

In one of the last sections of this work I have endeavored to expose the sophistical pretense, that "newspapers are not accountable for their own misconduct, because they are obliged to mould themselves to suit the requirements of the public." I deny that the press of the United States *is* what the public demands. Instead of adapting themselves to the tastes and requirements of the people, our newspapers endeavor to innoculate the public with their own morbid humors and purulent morality. The American people have a great relish for newspaper reading; but it does not follow that they relish *all* that they read in the newspapers. It would be just as wise to suppose that because certain persons have a strong inclination for theatrical amusements, they must therefore delight in all the obscenities and gross immoralities of the stage. But if the taste of the reading public were really depraved, the conductors of the press would not be justified in ministering to such a taste, and cultivating it with untiring assiduity. The public may *require* brothels and grog-shops, (as well as vicious newspapers,) but the keepers of these establishments are not excusable on that account.

Strange attempts have been made to apologize for the

offenses of American journalism by asserting that the newspaper press of *England* is quite as vicious as ours. If this assertion were TRUE, it would afford a very flimsy excuse, or no excuse at all, for the offending journalists of this country. The journalism of England is much older than that of America, and the oldest institutions are expected to be the most corrupt. To plead for our American newspapers, therefore, by saying that they are no more depraved than the journals of Great Britain, is like attempting to extenuate the faults of your juvenile son Bobby by averring that he is no worse than some hoary-headed sinner. The comparison injures the cause which it is meant to defend.

The author of this work does not propose any restriction on the *liberty* of the press; simply because the newspaper press of America has no liberty to be restrained. Its freedom (as we shall see hereafter) is all a farcical illusion. Our journalism is both tyrannical and slavish; it succumbs to every powerful influence, and it is bold and independent only when it attacks the weak and defenseless.

It is not denied that public journalism is a very good thing *in its place.* In this respect it resembles many other things, which are conveniences or blessings in their right locations, and afflictions or nuisances when misplaced. A very useful kitchen utensil, or an important article of bed-room furniture, might be an unsightly or unpleasant object if placed on your parlor table. The chief design of this work is to show that the newspaper press of America has mistaken its proper office and position. It should be a serviceable drudge—a modest, submissive, civil-speaking, unobtrusive lackey; not a supercilious, domineering, insolent, foul-mouthed major domo. In short, the press should be the people's most humble servant, and not their master.

It is not pretended in this volume that public journalists are naturally worse than other people. Three-fourths of mankind will play the knave or tyrant if they have opportunities to do so, and it is the misfortune of newspaper editors to have *many* such opportunities. Some of the best men that ever I met with are conductors of the press, and their integrity is the more admirable because it resists the strongest persuasions to error. But, as few men are able to withstand strong temptations, the editorial fraternity *in general* is of the quality which I am about to describe.

It would be very unfair to require the author of "Our Press Gang" to find remedies for all the mischiefs which he undertakes to point out. With as much reason you might suppose that every man who discovers a fire is under obligations to extinguish it. I make proclamation of existing evils, and take it for granted that the people and their legislators will know what action is required to suit the emergency.

In justice to myself, I must caution the public against the falsehoods and misrepresentations of the offended parties, if they are rash enough to provoke further exposures. Remember, my countrymen, that nothing is easier than lying, especially among newspaper editors; for it is an art which they have studied, and which they thoroughly understand. They can lie openly, or by implication, or innuendo, or even by keeping silence and seeming to overlook a fact. If they condescend to take any notice of this work, it is impossible at this time to say how they will treat it; and, to confess the truth, my mind is very little agitated with the subject.

It is proper to remark, before I finish this preamble, that I have no *particular* quarrel with the newspaper press of America. My publications have invariably received favorable attentions from the public journals. My last work, "The Life, Travels, and Adventures of Ferdinand de Soto," was especially well treated, until the publisher's petition to Congress (with which I had nothing to do, by the way) provoked three or four of the most infamous journals in the United States to attack it. I do not apprehend that the publication of this book will produce an impression unfavorable to the author on the mind of any public journalist whose good opinion is really desirable; and there are some newspaper-men in this country whose fiercest denunciations have an effect like that which the ancients ascribed to the lightnings—they *sanctify* the object on which they fall. In no other respect do the wrathful censures of bad men resemble the artillery of heaven; they cannot blacken or burn, or prostrate, or crush the mortal at whom they are aimed, but sink into the earth, innocuous, at the feet of their intended victim.

Philadelphia, June 16, 1859.

INTRODUCTORY NARRATIVE;

COMPRISING AN ACCOUNT OF THE AUTHOR'S OWN EXPERIENCE AS A NEWSPAPER EDITOR.

As a prelude to the "expositions" which are promised on the title-page of this book, I propose to give some account of my own editorial experience,—which may serve to introduce me to the reader, and to satisfy him that I have had opportunities to make myself acquainted with the subjects which I undertake to discuss.

For almost thirty years, I have been connected, in one way or another, with the public journalism of the United States. During the greater part of that time, I have been engaged at the editorial bureau, and have written for almost every class and variety of newspapers.

My editorial life, for the most part, has been a very sad and weary pilgrimage. I have passed over many mountains of difficulties and through innumerable valleys of humiliation. I have often plunged into sloughs of despondency; and, more than once, have I been captured by the giant Despair. I have fought with Apollyon in many different shapes, and I have encountered the lions unmuzzled and unchained. But, in the whole of my route, I have met with no silver mines and no pleasant land of Beulah; and the heavy burden which I assumed at the commencement of my travel, stuck to me, with increasing and crushing ponderosity,—to the last stage of my journey.

In several particulars, therefore, I have fared much worse than the pilgrim of John Bunyan,—and that is not at all surprising, —for his was a heavenward route, but mine necessarily conducted me in an opposite direction. A brief recital of my misadventures and tribulations may help to convince the public that the editorial profession is not that "primrose path of dalliance" which it must be mistaken for by the thousands who are constantly endeavoring to crowd into it.

THE FIRST EXPERIMENT.

I began my career as a newspaper writer at the age of nineteen; having previously studied law and prepared myself for admission to the bar. Fate determined that of two rascally avocations, I should be drawn into that one which was best calculated to counteract the excellent moral discipline to which I had been subjected in childhood and early youth.

When about to commence the practice of law in Baltimore, I was invited to take charge of a rural newspaper published at Elkton, Md. The prospect of literary renown induced me to accept this flattering offer. I endeavored to astonish the Elktonians,—who were celebrated for their classical proclivities,—and I succeeded, in some measure, by means of a liberal use of Latin quotations and mythological allusions. But, as we had no Greek or Hebrew types in our printing-office, I could not give universal satisfaction to these erudite villagers.

CHANGE OF LOCATION.

Emboldened by my partial success, I now conceived the daring design of emigrating to Philadelphia and connecting myself, if possible, with the luminous journalism of that city. Philadelphia, at that time, was called the "Athens of America." All the most flourishing literary publications of the country were issued from the press of the Quaker City,—which was therefore supposed to be the very fountain-head of American intellect.

On my arrival at Philadelphia, I presented myself to Mr.

Samuel C. Atkinson, publisher of the *Saturday Evening Post* and *Casket;* the former of which was then the most popular weekly paper in the United States, and the latter was the most widely circulated monthly periodical. Both of these publications were conducted by Mr. Atkinson on the most economical plan and his profits must have been extremely great. He engaged me to write editorials and other matters for his hebdomadal and magazine. The employment was sufficient to occupy all my time, and my salary sufficed to pay my landlady and laundress, "without defalcation," every Saturday night!

In those days, writers for the American newspaper and periodical press were not quite so handsomely remunerated as they are at the present time. A publisher who paid his contributors *any thing* was regarded as a munificent patron of literature, and received as many compliments on that score as did that Roman gentleman to whom Horace dedicated his first ode.

ANOTHER REMOVAL.

Having written myself into an incipient consumption without much improving my worldly condition, I resolved on another removal; and, after some consideration, I concluded to try my fortunes in Washington city. But, in the first place, I was obliged to pass some months in the country, to re-establish my health. I took charge of a rural academy near the Catoctin mountains, where I might have enjoyed a tranquil and happy life, if I could have forgotten that there were such things as newspapers and magazines in existence.

But the spell was on me; the evil genius of Typography had thrown its mantle around me, and I was drawn onward by its irresistible magnetism. As soon as I felt strong enough to resume the duties of the editorial desk, I started for Washington, according to my previous intention. My appearance was that of a raw country lad,—as I still wore the rustic dress which I had used in my late secluded dwelling-place; and when, in this sober garniture, I called on several publishers of the leading newspapers of the national metropolis and made them an offer of my assistance, a glance at my costume was sufficient to make the conference extremely short, and a somewhat supercilious repulse was the invariable consequence.

GENERAL DUFF GREEN.

At length, while canvassing for a "situation," I happened to call   General Duff Green, publisher of the *United States Telegraph*. This paper had been the first organ of General Jackson's administration, and it had been established at Washington for the express purpose of supporting that hero's claims to the presidency. When Jackson quarreled with several members of his cabinet and dismissed them, because (as it is supposed,) their families would not associate with Mrs. Eaton, one of Jackson's favorites,—Duff Green threw off his allegiance to the president and denounced him as a tyrant,—alleging that he had endeavored to force the virtuous wives and daughters of his cabinet-ministers to endure the society of a woman whose moral character was not without reproach.

It is conjectured that General Duff Green was dissatisfied with President Jackson on another account. The former wished John C. Calhoun to succeed to the presidency,—but the latter was using every effort to place Martin Van Buren on the track that would conduct him to that high station. These cross purposes were more likely to produce a misunderstanding between Green and Jackson than any *emeute* among the ladies of the republican court.

The defection of Duff Green took place a short time before my arrival at Washington. I found the *United States Telegraph* playing off all its artillery against the old soldier of cotton-bale celebrity, whom, only a few months before, it had represented to the world as the model hero, patriot, and statesman of the age.

When I first came into the presence of Duff Green, I remember that I was considerably, but not unpleasantly, disappointed. His inelegant monosyllabic name had somehow prepared me for the sight of a small, "dumpy," mean-looking mortal, with no more gentility or intellectuality in his appearance than could be easily expressed in four or five letters of the alphabet.

But my preconceptions were widely different from the fact. On inspection, Duff Green proved to be a tall, slender, gentleman-like man, with a piercing black eye and a highly intellectual countenance. The rusticity of my dress and appearance seemed to make no unfavorable impression on the mind of General Duff Green; and I afterward learned that his own experience had prepared him to look with indulgence and sympathy on the condition of those persons whose stock of wearing apparel was not very elegant or abundant. The gossips of Washington reported, that when General Green first came to that city, he possessed but one pair of pantaloons—(brown cassimere); and, as these required renovation before they could be made presentable in good society, the general was obliged to lie in bed, while his "pants" were in the hands of the scourer.

But government patronage had made vast changes in the worldly affairs of this distinguished journalist. At the time to which my narrative refers, he was living in a style of splendor which had rarely been equaled, even in Washington city; and, according to common rumor, he had given some offense to the household of General Jackson by presuming, in the princely grandeur of his domestic establishment, to eclipse the glory and magnificence of the "White House." It was this ambitious design—as some of the Washingtonians declared—which had made the first disturbance between the President and his principal organist.

A TRIAL.

As soon as I had made General Duff Green acquainted with my desire to assist him in the editorial department of his paper, he acknowledged that he wanted such assistance at that time; but he frankly expressed his fears that my youth and want of experience as a political and controversial writer, would disqualify me for the duties which I would be expected to perform in his office. I replied that it did not become me to recommend myself, but that I could refer him to several eminent politicians, who, perhaps, "could give him a satisfactory account of my abilities and moral character."

There was something Parson Adams-like in the latter part of this speech, and the sagacious newspaper conductor smiled at my boyish simplicity, when I seemed to apprehend that *correct moral deportment* was one of the necessary qualifications of the political journalist! However, General Green made a memorandum of my references, promising to write to the gentlemen designated; but, in the mean time, he proposed to test my polemical talents, by allowing me to prepare a reply to a leading article which had appeared in the newly-established organ of the administration, the successor and rival of the *United States Telegraph.* The article to be answered was, (as Duff Green informed me,) written by one of the members of Jackson's new cabinet; and this information made me suspect that the task imposed on me would prove extremely difficult. To my great relief, however, I found this piece of cabinet-work a very weak and clumsy affair; and though Green had allowed me three days to demolish it, I succeeded, as I thought, in performing that operation within three hours. I knew nothing of the subject treated of, except what I gathered from the article itself; but it was easy enough to show up the absurdities and illogical conclusions of my antagonist, and thus, instead of contradicting him, to make him contradict himself.

My reply to the member of the cabinet's "leader" satisfied Duff Green, which was all that I wished to accomplish at that time, and he immediately engaged me at a salary which more than equaled my most sanguine expectations.

NEWSPAPER PROJECT.

I had been in Duff Green's employment only four or five weeks, when I received a letter from Mr. Charles F. Cloud, who had resolved to establish a new literary paper at Baltimore,—and he proposed to place the editorial management of the intended publication under my charge. After some deliberation, I concluded to accept Mr. Cloud's offer. I consented to forego the somewhat brilliant prospects which seemed to open to me at Washington; I gave up a situation which promised to be permanent and a salary which was sufficient for my decent maintenance; and, by acceding to Mr. Cloud's proposals, I engaged in an enterprise which could not be remunerative at the beginning, and which would probably terminate in loss and disappointment.

Doubtless this choice of mine may appear to be extremely indiscreet; but there were some advantages in the change. With a Julius Cæsar-like ambition, I preferred the position of a principal editor at Baltimore to that of a subordinate scribe at Washington. Besides, I loved literature more than the war of party politics,—and my short probation in Duff Green's office had made this branch of the newspaper business more distasteful to me than ever. Moreover, the terms offered by Mr. Cloud were somewhat alluring, though my remuneration would depend altogether on the success of the undertaking.

BIRTH OF THE "BALTIMORE SATURDAY VISITER."

Mr. C. F. Cloud, (who, by the way, was an old acquaintance of mine,) had lately been married to a young lady with a small fortune of about $6,000,—which sum he proposed to invest in this enterprise. He had purchased a printing-office, comprising all the materials which the publication of a weekly newspaper would require. The terms proposed by Mr. Cloud and accepted by me, were:—1. That I should not be expected to contribute any money to the undertaking, as my services as editor would be considered as equivalent to Mr. Cloud's pecuniary investment. 2. That the clear profits of the paper should be equally divided between Mr. Cloud and myself. 3. The printing materials were to be and remain exclusively the property of Mr. Cloud.

It was afterward alleged that I made a "hard bargain" with this gentleman. But the truth is, I merely accepted Mr. Cloud's offer, and if that was too liberal there was nobody to blame but himself. There was not the least anxiety on my part to engage in this enterprise, as the prospects of success were not extremely flattering; and, for some time, I felt very much inclined to reject Mr. Cloud's offer, notwithstanding its supposed liberality.

However, the preliminaries were settled at last, the partnership was formed, and the publication of the *Baltimore Saturday Visiter* was commenced. The history of this newspaper is sufficiently curious to merit particular notice. As it had been found impossible hitherto to establish a literary paper in Baltimore, the common belief was that the *Visiter* would have but "a short run." The most experienced publishers were of this opinion; and when the Baltimore dailies noticed our first issue, they humanely exhorted us to be prepared for the certain disappointment and ruin which awaited us. Nevertheless, the disappointment was all on their own side, for the *Visiter* prospered exceedingly. At the end of six months, it was firmly established; and not only paid all its expenses but began to yield some profit to its conductors.

About three months before this time, however, the expenses of the business exceeded the income, and the financial affairs of the paper were somewhat embarrassed. Mr. Cloud's money had all been used in the purchase of printing apparatus, paper, etc., and he now proposed to take in a third partner, who could supply the funds which were necessary to continue the publication. By this arrangement, my share of the profits would be reduced from one-half to one-third; but, believing it to be a necessary measure, I consented to it without hesitation. The person whom Mr. Cloud had selected as the third partner was a Mr. William P. Pouder—Cloud's own brother-in-law; and this circumstance did not afford me unalloyed satisfaction. But I waived all my objections on condition that Messrs. Cloud and Pouder should subscribe to new articles of partnership, which were written by myself and in which I took care to express all the conditions of our compact with a precision which afterward proved to be of the greatest importance.

TROUBLESOME COPARTNERSHIP.

Soon after the admission of Mr. Pouder, as a member of our publishing firm, a certain Mr. Hewitt, a teacher of vocal and instrumental music, and the author of a popular song called "The Minstrel's Return," volunteered to write editorial articles for the *Visiter*, without any compensation except the glory of being named as one of the editors. Mr. Hewitt had been connected with the editorial department of a weekly literary paper entitled "*The Baltimore Minerva*," which expired of inanition soon after our Visiter was commenced. This gentleman was not one of "Apollo's venal sons;" he had other means of maintenance besides authorship or editorial labor, and he therefore possessed the manifold advantages of such American writers as can afford to "work for nothing and find themselves."

Mr. Hewitt's proposition to write editorials for nothing,— (or for *glory*, which is pretty much the same thing,) seems to have made my partners suspect that their arrangement with me had involved them in an unnecessary expense. They blamed themselves, no doubt, for agreeing to give me one-third of their profits for the performance of work which another man was willing to do without any charge at all. It appears that Messrs. Cloud and Pouder, believed that I had no just claims on the emoluments of the *Visiter*, and no property in the publication, — because I had contributed no *money* to the establishment of the business. They did not seem to understand that my *time* and *labor* were of some value — though a common opinion was that the success of the paper was owing, in a great measure, to my exertions. The business was now placed on a firm basis, the subscription list was increasing with unexampled rapidity, and the income afforded a considerable surplus over the expenditures. In these circumstances my partners may have considered it useless to keep up those expensive "features," which had been necessary at the outset, while the paper was struggling for notoriety and public favor. Having resolved to curtail their expenses, or to lighten their lading, — Messrs. Cloud and Pouder, unceremoniously threw me overboard. In other words, they published *a dissolution of partnership*,—without any previous conversation with me on the subject, and without giving me the least hint of their intentions.

It may be difficult for the reader to believe (what was really the fact,) that this announcement was made in two or three of the daily papers, for several days, before I knew or suspected any thing of the matter. The advertisement did not appear in our own paper, and as I seldom examined the advertising columns of the journals in which it was inserted, the interesting paragraph wholly escaped my observation, until my attention was drawn to it by the inquiries of some of my friends.

EXPLOSION.

Strangely enough, my name was retained at the head of the *Visiter*, for several weeks after the termination of the partnership was announced by Messrs. Cloud and Pouder. And after their repeated assertions in the *Visiter's* own columns that I no longer had any connection with the paper, the words "*Published by Cloud, Wilmer and Pouder*," still appeared, in conspicuous type, under the title of every number.

The next movement of my partners was to have me bound over to keep the peace, though I had made no threat and exhibited no signs of violent resentment. I expostulated with them, however, in a mild way, and endeavored to make them understand our relative positions; but they appeared to be altogether convinced that the law would sustain them in the very singular course which they had chosen to pursue. I think it likely that they were acting under the directions of some excessively cunning attorney, who had succeeded in persuading them that their behavior to me was legal and justifiable.

In the mean time, my position was very embarrassing and almost indefinable. I continued to write editorial articles for the *Visiter* and to offer them for publication; otherwise I should have seemed to subscribe or consent to my own expulsion from the business. But my written articles were not published; and, as the printing materials were exclusively the property of Mr. Cloud, I could not insist on having my editorials put in type. By this time Mr. Hewitt had begun to exercise those duties which I was not permitted to perform. Moreover, my partners refused to supply me with any money, and plainly gave me to understand that I should never receive another copper from that establishment. Perceiving that they were laboring under a very great mistake, I deemed it expedient to open their eyes at once by asserting my rights in a manner which would bring our affairs to a crisis. I therefore made out several small bills against subscribers in the city, collected the money, and gave the customary acquittances. My partners now published an advertisement, declaring that I was no longer connected with the publishing firm of the *Baltimore Visiter*, and warning all persons not to pay to me, or my order, any moneys due to the late firm of *Cloud, Wilmer & Pouder*. I returned this fire by publishing another advertisement, cautioning all persons indebted to the *Visiter* not to pay any money to Charles F. Cloud or William P. Pouder.

Here was a condition of things which some newspaper customers would be likely to find very agreeable. The patrons of the *Baltimore Visitor* were warned, in effect, not to pay their dues to *anybody;* and I doubt not that many of them strictly obeyed the injunction. The only money that could be collected by Cloud & Pouder was obtained from subscribers out of the city and others who had not heard of the disturbance among the publishers, or who did not understand the true nature of the difficulty. In these circumstances, it was almost impossible for my partners to carry on the business, the necessary disbursements of which required a considerable amount of cash every week. Mr. Cloud now came to me with an offer of an accommodation, proposing that I should resume my place in the office, and that every thing should proceed as if no misunderstanding had ever taken place.

I readily agreed to these terms of composition, but required, as a preliminary, that Cloud and Pouder should retract several very offensive statements which they had made in the columns of the *Visiter*. They had asserted, for example, that my collection of moneys due to the firm was *fraudulent*. I wished them to make a public acknowledgment of their error; and, as they refused to do this act of justice, (as I considered it,) I promptly rejected their overtures of peace.

In the mean time I commenced a suit against them in a court of equity, to test the validity of my rights as a partner. The case was afterward removed into chancery; and, of course, a speedy decision was not expected. While we were waiting for the arbitration of this august but dilatory tribunal, the *Visiter* fell into a decline. The public appeared to be disgusted with the quarrels of the proprietors, and the very favorable impression which the paper had made at the beginning of its career was entirely effaced by its subsequent aberrations.

SETTLEMENT.

The decision of the Chancellor was made sooner than we expected. He fully recognized my rights, and ordered a public sale of all the property in dispute, including the subscription list, outstanding debts, and right of publication; and he directed that the proceeds of the sale should be equally divided among the three partners. Finding that a forced sale of the sinking concern would not be very productive, I consented to receive *five hundred dollars* and relinquish all my claims on Cloud & Pouder, who proposed to settle the vexatious affair by this arrangement. I took their notes, with proper security, for the specified sum; and so this extraordinary newspaper *fracas* was brought to a termination. The effects of it, however, were long and seriously felt by all the parties concerned.

If a good understanding could have been maintained among the publishers of the *Visiter*, the paper would have afforded us all a decent maintenance at least, and perhaps a competency for life. But the disagreement proved very disastrous to all the members of the co-partnership. The *Visiter* soon passed out of the hands of Cloud and Pouder. Some time after it came into the possession of T. S. Arthur, who subsequently transferred it to Dr. J. E. Snodgrass. The last-mentioned gentleman, finding that it would not pay him for his trouble, very judiciously permitted it to expire.

In the foregoing account of my misunderstanding with Messrs. Cloud and Pouder, I make no charge of moral delinquency against those gentlemen. If ever I felt aggrieved by their conduct, I have long since forgiven them, and it is really unpleasant to my feelings to refer to the subject of our dispute. But the facts related form a part of my editorial experience, and, on that account, their introduction into this narrative was unavoidable.

UNPLEASANT PREDICAMENT.

I have reason to believe that I was the principal sufferer by the untimely collapse of the *Visiter*, though I do not charge myself with any participation in the faults which produced that melancholy catastrophe. Soon after my suit in chancery was commenced, I found that the very low condition of my fiscal affairs would oblige me to leave Baltimore and seek employment elsewhere. At this juncture I was absolutely *penniless*. During the whole time of my connection with the *Visiter*,—that is to say, for six or eight months,—I had drawn as little as possible from the funds of the establishment; for the success of the enterprise required that nearly all the income of the paper should be employed in the business itself. At this time my style of living was so extremely economical, that my private expenses did not exceed *three dollars per week*.

But I had not yet learned the art of living on *nothing ;* and, when the *Visiter* ceased to afford me any means of subsistence, I made up my mind to return to Washington and apply for readmission to the office of the *United States Telegraph.* For want of funds to pay the usual traveling expenses, I proceeded to Washington *on foot.* As the distance was only thirty-six miles, I expected to walk over the greater part of the course in one day. Night overtook me when I was about six miles from the metropolis. Having no cash with which to pay a tavern bill, I was indebted to the hospitality of nature for a lodging-place. A green bank, at a short distance from the road, was my couch, and an oak tree was my canopy. I wrapped myself in my cloak, and reposed on the bosom of my mother earth with far more comfort and satisfaction than I have sometimes experienced in more luxurious dormitories.

Before I betook myself to rest, I reflected, (with very little bitterness of feeling, however,) on the great change which had recently taken place in my worldly condition. Only one short month previous to that time, I had been one of the proprietors of a flourishing newspaper business, which might be considered as equivalent to a fortune. Now I was a homeless wanderer, in a more hapless and hopeless condition than that of the common mendicant—for I was "ashamed to beg." During my long walk I had partaken of no food or refreshment, except a few chinquopins and fox-grapes, which I had gathered from the thickets at the side of the road, and I was now about to pass the night on the naked earth! But, while there is no room for self-reproach, and no acute physical suffering, it is possible to be cheerful and happy, in almost any circumstances. On the most careful examination of recent events, I could not discover that any fault or omission of my own had produced that reverse of fortune under which I now suffered. I felt assured that it had been impossible for me to foresee or to prevent the misfortune which had overtaken me. Having thus soothed and tranquilized my mind with "adversity's sweet milk, philosophy," I went to sleep.

THE PRODIGAL'S RETURN.

Early on the following morning I arrived at Washington. I called on Gen. Duff Green, and met with a very friendly reception. He had heard of my misadventure in Baltimore; indeed, that notable affair had been the subject of journalistic remarks in every part of the country. Gen. Green advised me to take comfort; "for," said he encouragingly, "I think you can do something better than publishing a weekly newspaper devoted to light literature." He invited me to resume that situation in his office which I had abandoned about half a year before, to engage in my unfortunate enterprise at Baltimore.

FATE AND FEVER.

I thankfully accepted General Green's offer; but it appears to have been an ordination of destiny that I should not remain in Washington city. Two weeks after my return to the metropolis, I had a severe attack of bilious fever, which was epidemic there at that time, and I was soon reduced by this disease to a condition which made my recovery almost hopeless. I was convinced that nothing but a change of location would restore me to health, and although I was too feeble to walk without assistance, I resolved to travel.

Having sent for a vehicle, I was lifted into it, (my landlady and my fellow-boarders protesting against the movement as an act of suicide,)—and having been conveyed to the stage-office, I took passage for Baltimore. The effect of a change of air was almost miraculous. When I reached Baltimore I was able to walk without help; and having decided on going to Philadelphia, by the way of the Chesapeake and Delaware Canal, I entered a steamboat which was connected with the line of conveyance by that route. The crossing of Chesapeake Bay in this steamboat completed my cure; and, on my arrival at the western terminus of the canal I found or fancied myself almost as well as ever.

A NEW ENTERPRISE.

At Chesapeake city, I happened to meet with an old acquaintance of mine who resided at Elkton. This gentleman was a prominent member of the Whig party, and he informed me that the Whigs of Cecil County, Maryland, wished to establish a newspaper organ, and that they were willing to raise, by subscription, a fund sufficient for the purpose. He proposed, on behalf of his party, that I should become the publisher of the intended paper, and he mentioned the sum of money which the party would supply for the purchase of printing materials and other incidental expenses.

There was something in this proposal which pleased me; and instead of proceeding to Philadelphia, as I had intended, I accompanied my Whig friend to Elkton and had an interview with some of the other leading members of his party. A subscription paper was prepared, and twenty or thirty of the wealthiest citizens of the county affixed their signatures, each pledging himself to contribute a specified sum; and, on the strength of this assurance of pecuniary aid, I purchased, on credit, the printing apparatus of the Elkton Press, ordered some additional materials from Baltimore, and commenced the publication of the "*Cecil Courant.*" Being very young and altogether inexperienced in the ways of politicians, I never harbored a suspicion that the contributions which the signers of my subscription paper had promised and pledged themselves to pay, would not be forthcoming as soon as the funds were required. Yet, as the sagacious reader has probably guessed before this time, scarcely *one-fourth* of the money was ever produced. In the meanwhile, as the political course of the paper did not please a majority of the citizens, the circulation and the advertising custom of the "Courant" were not sufficient to pay expenses. Several large bills for type, paper, etc., were to be paid, and the contributions on which I had relied for the means of payment, were not to be obtained. My embarrassments increased every day and threatened to reach a crisis; my political friends and "patrons," whose delusive promises had drawn me into this predicament, looked with stocial composure on my troubles, and expected me to labor as zealously in their behalf as if their engagements with me had been strictly fulfilled.

EMBARRASSMENTS.

About this time, my suit against Cloud & Pouder, of the *Baltimore Visiter*, was decided, and the five hundred dollars which these men had offered to pay, to avoid a public sale of the property in dispute, was received by me in several instalments. One hundred dollars of this money I paid to my solicitor, and the balance was applied to the liquidation of the debts of the *Cecil Courant*. And so, after all my labor on both papers, I found myself as poor as I was at the beginning. True, I was the nominal possessor of a printing-office; but I still owed a large portion of the purchase-money, and the "establishment" was mortgaged for almost as much as it was worth.

It has been my fortune, on many different occasions, to be placed in circumstances of difficulty from which there seemed to be no possible means of extrication. In the case now under consideration, I was enclosed in a labyrinth from which I could see no chance of escape. Some few of those men who signed the subscription paper had honorably fulfilled their engagements. The money had been expended in the business, and I could not refund it. My obligations to them made it necessary for me to continue the publication of the paper, although every number that was issued plunged me more deeply in debt and made my ruin more inevitable.

I offered the printing-office for sale, but could find no purchaser. I proposed to *give* it away to any man who would assume my obligations; but no one could be found who was willing to undertake the hazards of the enterprise, for it had now become evident that a Whig organ could not be supported in Cecil County. As a last resort, I determined to remove the office from Elkton to Port Deposit, a very thriving town in the same county, where I hoped to meet with better encouragement. As Port Deposit is situated at the head of navigation on the Susquehanna River, it is a place of considerable business; and, on this account, my change of location seemed to be decidedly for the better.

IN OFFICE.

Soon after my removal, some of my Whig friends made application to the Governor of Maryland to have me appointed a Justice of the Peace. Without any effort or solicitation on my part, I obtained the appointment; and, owing to several favorable circumstances, the office proved to be quite profitable. Though there were several other justices in the town, the magisterial business of Port Deposit seemed to be all in my hands, and the amount of this business was very considerable. Indeed, some of my duties were extremely onerous—for I was expected to preserve order in a place which was not at all remarkable for the quiet behavior and tractable disposition of its inhabitants. For a considerable part of the year, Port Deposit was filled with strangers,—a majority of whom were men who passed a large portion of their time upon the river; and people who live much upon the water are apt enough, sometimes, to make themselves troublesome on dry ground. The raftsmen who were engaged in floating timber down the Susquehanna, and the boatmen who navigated the lower portion of the river and Chesapeake Bay, had, for some time, been accustomed to consider Port Deposit as a sort of play-ground, where they could enjoy a perpetual saturnalia. While they sojourned at this place, therefore, their deportment was often exceedingly offensive to the stationary population of the town. The colored people of the neighborhood likewise, —the slaves especially,—had become, in a measure, ungovernable, and often assembled in considerable numbers, making riotous demonstrations and producing a good deal of alarm among the quiet citizens.

Being unexpectedly placed at the head of municipal affairs in this stirring and progressive town, I determined to introduce some reforms which had hitherto been considered impracticable. It was commonly believed that certain laws intended for the preservation of good order could not be enforced in Port Deposit. I have always thought that such laws can be enforced *anywhere* (in the United States), if the persons charged with the execution of those laws have any *inclination* to enforce them. Certain ·I am that it cost me very little trouble to assert and maintain the supremacy of law and order in Port Deposit—though my whole police force consisted of but one constable. The secret of this success consisted altogether in the use of *wholesome severity*. I took care that no offender should go unpunished, and that every offense should meet with *adequate* retribution. This obviously correct policy soon produced the most happy effects.

In the meanwhile, as I enjoyed a monopoly of the magisterial business of that neighborhood, the emoluments of my office soon enabled me to discharge most of those pecuniary obligations to which the publication of the newspaper had made me liable. Being fully aware that the justiceship had been bestowed on me merely to enable me to continue the publication of the *Courant*, I still labored to keep it afloat, though, like a mill-stone fastened to my neck, it was dragging me downward with an irresistible momentum. At length the time came when it was impossible to issue another number—my resources were all exhausted, and I was compelled to class the *Cecil Courant* among the magnificent failures of the age. I had now the best possible excuse for retiring from this field of labor, in which I had toiled for about two years without even the *hope* of reward.

ANOTHER CHANGE.

Rejoicing to find myself once more at liberty, I left my rural location with the hope of retrieving my lost time, as far as that was possible, by making another attempt to establish a literary newspaper or magazine in Baltimore. With reference to this design, Edgar A. Poe and I had had some correspondence. He proposed to join with me in the publication of a monthly magazine of a superior intellectual character, and he had written a prospectus, which he transmitted to me for examination. While this project was under consideration, Poe was invited to assume the editorial duties of the *Southern Literary Messenger;* and, as he immediately obeyed this call, the grand intellectual illumination we had proposed to make in Baltimore was necessarily postponed.

A GLOOMY PERSPECTIVE.

As soon as I returned to the "City of Monuments," I began to confer with some of the printers, hoping to find one enterprising enough to unite with me in the effort to "get up" a new weekly paper. But this design met with but little favor, as the typographical gentlemen of Baltimore were generally too poor to undertake the pecuniary risks of such an enterprise, and it was still believed that Baltimore was not the proper location for a journal devoted to polite literature. The *Visiter* was still in existence—Mr. T. S. Arthur being the publisher; but that paper was generally believed to be "on its last legs;" and its prospective failure was an additional discouragement for all who contemplated similar undertakings.

Months elapsed, and my prospects every day became more gloomy. The newspaper business was at a low ebb in Baltimore, and my chances of obtaining employment as an editor were not at all flattering. I had brought a wife with me from Port Deposit, and I was now threatened with a small addition to my family, and my income was just *nothing at all.* In short, my situation was too wretched to be described, and it is impossible for the reader to imagine any thing worse.

BRIGHTENING PROSPECTS.

About this time General Duff Green removed from Washington to Baltimore, and established in the last-named city a daily newspaper called "*The Merchant*." As soon as General Green commenced business, I called at his office and was cordially received by the veteran publisher.

Without waiting for any application on my part, General Green proposed to engage me as his assistant-editor. The salary offered by him was perfectly satisfactory, for in money matters this gentleman was always very liberal. In compliance with the general's wishes, I took my seat at the editorial desk of the "*Merchant,*" and commenced operations immediately. During the forenoon I learned from General Green that he had a partner in his present undertaking. This partner, as I afterward found, was a practical printer, and he was a man who widely differed, in many particulars, from my good friend, the general.

When I went home to dinner, I was almost intoxicated with joy; and when I made my wife acquainted with our unexpected good fortune, her delight was greater, if possible, than my own. It had been so long since any *lucky* accident had befallen us, that we had begun to consider ourselves secure from any future casualties of that kind. The event of the morning seemed to change the complexion of our destiny. The least that could be expected was a respite from the severe sufferings which we had lately experienced. This assurance alone was enough to make us consider ourselves pre-eminently fortunate.

SOMETHING UNEXPECTED.

In the happiest frame of mind I returned to the office of the "*Merchant,*" where I found Duff Green and his partner in earnest conversation; and I soon learned that the subject of their discourse was deeply interesting to myself. The partner, it appears, was a man of excessively economical habits, and he was now protesting vehemently against the arrangement which Duff Green had made with me in the forenoon. He declared emphatically that no assistance in the editorial department was required, and that the appropriation of money to such a purpose was ruinous extravagance. General Green appeared to be embarrassed and disconcerted. As the partner was one of that kind of gentlemen who express their views, in all circumstances, with little reservation, it was impossible for me not to overhear the debate and to understand its import. There was nothing for me to do, therefore, but to signify my willingness to retire from that position to which I had been so lately appointed, if my continuance therein was not satisfactory to all parties concerned.

My resignation was accepted with seeming reluctance by Gen. Green and with evident delight by his colaborer. If the reader has a keen perception of the ludicrous, he may see something exceedingly comical in this adventure; but I assure him, on my honor, that, at the time of the occurrence, I could discern nothing laughable in the matter. If the disappointment had concerned nobody but myself, I should have borne it, I believe, with perfect equanimity. But the case was different; and as I have no wish to excite compassion, or any feeling akin to it, I will not attempt to describe the state of mind in which I returned to my dwelling-place with the chilling intelligence that all the joyous expectations which had been awakened only a few hours before, had proved to be nothing but illusion and mockery.

THE KALEIDOSCOPE.

A short time after this sad occurrence, I received a visit from two young men,—journeymen printers,—who had conceived the ambitious design of setting up a "Book and Job Printing Office," and publishing a weekly newspaper. They wished me to "edit" the paper,—and they proposed conditions similar to those which had formerly induced me to undertake the management of the *Saturday Visiter*. In lieu of a regular salary, I was to receive one-third of the profits. Having nothing better in view, I accepted their offer, and the publication of a small weekly paper, called "*The Kaleidoscope*," was commenced.

Several circumstances were inimical to the success of this paper. In the first place, the publishers did not understand the newspaper business, and they had neither the tact nor the capital which was required to obtain a good circulation. But, strange as it may appear, the *title* of the paper was, perhaps, the chief obstacle to its prosperity. Our agents reported that many persons refused to put their names on our subscription-lists, merely because they did not know the meaning of the word "*Kaleidoscope*," and they were afraid that the reading matter of the paper would be as hard to comprehend as the title. The patrons of polite literature in the United States are generally shocked at the very suspicion of any thing abstruse or profound in those publications which depend on them for support.

The clear profits of the "Kaleidoscope" might be represented by ciphers,—and as my share was one-third of the sum total, a very little arithmetic will exhibit the precise amount of my compensation. But the remembrance of this stage of my existence is as disagreeable to me as an account of it might be to others; for the comfort and satisfaction of all parties, therefore, I pass speedily over that gloomy tract, which, (after having once traveled it in reality,) I have no desire to revisit, even in memory or imagination.

Suffice it to say, that I wasted more than four years of my life in the vain effort to make myself useful, and to earn an honest livelihood in the only place where I have endured the miseries of extreme poverty—that is to say, in *my native city!*

NEW DIFFICULTIES.

A short time before I determined to bid a final adieu to that city which has made itself so famous for its appreciation of public benefactors, I received a letter from my eccentric friend Edgar A. Poe,—who was then officiating as the editor and critic of the *Southern Literary Messenger*, published at Richmond, Va. In his epistle, Poe gave me to understand that he was preparing to leave Richmond, and he advised me to come thither without delay,—as he was quite sure that I could obtain the situation which he was about to vacate. If I could have safely depended on this assurance, it was wholly out of my power to act in accordance with Mr. Poe's suggestion—for I could not raise money enough to pay for the transportation of myself and my family to Richmond. *Borrowing* was an expedient which I never thought of; and I doubt if any case of urgent necessity could have driven me to that mode of financiering, which, with some men, is a never-failing resource. My principles never would allow me to borrow a dollar, when there was a possibility that I might not be able to refund the money; and, besides, I never could acquire a knowledge of that phraseology which is used in soliciting a pecuniary favor.

BACK AGAIN TO PHILADELPHIA.

A fortunate circumstance enabled me, at last, to remove from Baltimore to Philadelphia. When I first settled myself in the last-named city — A. D. 1839-40—I was constrained to become a regular contributor to the *Lady's Book*, the *Saturday Evening Post*, the *Saturday Chronicle*, and other publications of about the same caliber. At that time, there was no literary paper or periodical in Philadelphia which could pretend to a high order of intellectuality, and I believe there were not more than two or three publications of that class in the United States. It is a notable fact that, at *no period*, has the intellectual character of a magazine made it either profitable or popular in this country. If literary periodicals of genuine merit have ever met with any distinguished success in this part of creation, they were indebted for their prosperity to some "feature" or peculiarity which was scarcely consistent with their claims to superior intelligence. And yet no people in the world are more generally enlightened and more appreciative of intellect than Americans! Here we have a paradox which I will endeavor to explain in another part of this volume.

VARIOUS ENGAGEMENTS.

With Mr. Louis A. Godey, of the *Lady's Book*, I had long been acquainted. He was formerly a clerk in the office of a paper called the *Daily Chronicle*, published by Charles Alexander; and while I was doing the editorial work of the Saturday Evening Port and Casket, the office of the *Daily Chronicle* and that of the *Post* and *Casket* were in the same building, situated at the S. W. corner of Chestnut street and Hudson's Alley. Mr. Godey and I had been neighbors, therefore, and for a long time after my return to Philadelphia we were very good friends. I contributed largely to his magazine, and he paid me for my labor according to his usual terms, which was all that I had a right to expect. Nevertheless, I was compelled to look out for some more remunerative employment.

It was in the year 1840, I think, when I became one of the editors of the *Public Ledger*, a well-known daily paper of Philadelphia, which was published at that time by *Swain, Abel & Simmons*. Although I merely undertook to write literary and miscellaneous articles, critical notices, etc., for the Ledger, I was very often called on to supply "leaders;" —the manufacture of which is the most important duty of the editorial department. According to the best of my remembrance, I remained in the *Ledger* office for somewhat more than a year, and then retired, because the publishers refused to make an addition to my salary.

As soon as I withdrew from the *Ledger* office, I made an engagement with the *Daily Chronicle*,—published by Charles Alexander. It was the second paper of that name which Mr. Alexander attempted to establish in Philadelphia, and both attempts were unsuccessful.

"ORGAN GRINDING."

My next editorial engagement, was with the *Evening Express* — a daily paper, published by M. Hardin Andrews. The *Express* was established by Mr. Andrews, for the express purpose of advocating the re-election of John Tyler to the Presidency. When Tyler became president, "accidentally" (as some of the newspapers expressed it,) by the death of General Harrison, his friends (*i. e.*, the office-holders under his administration,) determined to nominate him for re-election, and in order to make his election sure, it was considered necessary to establish a number of Tyler organs in different parts of the country. The Tylerites of Philadelphia raised, by contribution, a fund sufficient to purchase printing apparatus, and to maintain a newspaper for several months, promising to furnish additional supplies at some future time. Mr. Andrews was chosen to preside over this Philadelphia organ of Tylerism, and he called on me to assist him. The *Express* was a two-cent cash paper. It met with considerable favor, and I doubt not that it would have made a prosperous voyage, if it could have thrown its politics overboard. Tylerism was unprofitable freight, and it was much too heavy for ballast.

ANOTHER DISASTROUS PARTNERSHIP.

My connection with the *Evening Express*, after enduring for several months, to the entire satisfaction of Mr. Andrews and myself, (as I have every reason to believe,) came to a very singular and unexpected termination. A young man, with whom I had had some acquaintance in Maryland, and who was nearly related to an ex-governor of that State, came to our office and proposed to purchase an interest in the *Evening Express*. Mr. Andrews,—who had probably discovered that Tylerism was a failure,—offered to sell all his right and title in and to the establishment for eight hundred dollars. The young Marylander, Mr. V——, agreed to these terms; and, as he wished to secure my services, he proposed to make me a partner in the business. It was understood that he should pay $500 of the purchase-money, and that I should become responsible for the balance. All parties being satisfied with these conditions, Mr. V—— gave Andrews his note for $500, with the endorsement of a well-known and responsible man, who resided somewhere in the neighborhood of Baltimore. At the same time I gave my notes for the balance of $300. Mr. V—— and I were then put in possession of the *Evening Express* and all its appurtenances—Mr. Andrews having announced, in the last number published by him, that the ownership of the paper had been duly transferred to us, his successors.

About a week after I and my new partner took possession of the business, it was discovered that the endorsement on Mr. V——'s note was a *forgery!* My partner was arrested on this charge and bound over for trial, and Mr. Andrews came to me and demanded a restitution of the printing-office, subscription books, etc. I agreed to restore the property to him, provided he would return the notes for $300, which I had given him at the time of the purchase. He could not return these notes, for he had traded them away. I was liable for the payment of these notes when they came to maturity, and I refused to surrender the printing materials, etc., to Andrews while I was still under obligations to pay a considerable part of that sum for which this property had been sold to me and my partner.

TROUBLESOME LITIGATION.

I thought then, and still think, that my course in this affair was perfectly correct; however, Mr. Andrews was advised to have recourse to the law. His attorney, knowing that a civil suit was out of the question attempted to compel me to surrender the property by charging me with a criminal offense. It was alleged that I had conspired with Mr. V—— to "cheat and defraud" Mr. Andrews;—as if I, or any other man of common sense, would be likely to attempt a fraud of that kind, which could not fail to be detected in less than two weeks! The young man who committed this silly forgery, was, in fact, almost an idiot; otherwise he never could have attempted such a preposterous trick.

An examination of my case was made before Recorder Vaux, who immediately dismissed the charge, as there was not a particle of evidence to sustain it.

In the meanwhile, some of the Tyler men, who had contributed their money to establish the *Express*, came to me and entreated me to keep possession of the office, alleging that the property belonged to them and not to Mr. Andrews; and, for certain reasons, they did not wish him to recover it. To this I replied, that if Mr. Andrews would return what I had paid him, (*i. e.*, my notes,) I should feel bound to make the restitution he demanded; as the office had been purchased from *him*, and I could not be expected to know any thing about the private arrangements between the Tyler men and their publisher.

Mr. V—— was committed to answer for the forgery; he renounced all claim to the *Express*, and I became the sole proprietor of a business which could not be carried on without a continual loss; I had enough experience of that kind already, and I called on the Tyler men to provide themselves with another publisher.

THE "ORGAN" SURRENDERED.

Two enterprising young men, Messrs. Severn and Magill, consented to take charge of the paper, which I gladly gave up to them on the sole condition that they should become responsible for the payment of the notes which I had given to Mr. Andrews.

As these young men were both practical printers and very industrious, they were enabled to make a great reduction in the expenses of the business, and the existence of the *Evening Express* was thereby prolonged. The new publishers changed the name of the paper to the *Evening Mercury*, and I was still retained as "the literary and miscellaneous editor." The political department was superintended by Francis J. Grund, who held a fat office in the Custom-House, and was, therefore, bound in honor and conscience to do all he could for the benefit of the administration and its newspaper organ. I presume that he received no compensation for his editorial services, except the salary and perquisites which appertained to his office; but, doubtless, he was exceedingly well paid.

This Mr. F. J. Grund was an Austrian by birth, but he had made himself well acquainted with the English language, and few writers for the American newspapers used that language more correctly than he did. The Tylerites regarded him as a man of stupendous abilities, but his reasoning powers were not of the highest order; and, as a newspaper scribe, he sometimes committed errors of judgment which were absolutely wonderful.

A RECUSANT EDITOR.

Some misunderstanding took place between Mr. Grund and the publishers of the *Evening Mercury*. The former suddenly discontinued his labors, and the latter were left without a political editor. In this exigency, they requested me to exercise my ingenuity in the glorification of John Tyler; and, more to accommodate the worthy publishers than for any other object, I undertook the arduous duty. There was something humorous in the undertaking, which reconciled me to the labor; besides, I reflected that the next president would certainly be John Tyler or a *worse man;* and, on the principle of choosing the lesser of two evils, I felt justified in supporting "His Accidency." Having quieted my conscience in this way, I discussed the subject of Tylerism with as much gravity and zeal as Mr. Grund himself, or any other well-paid officer in the Custom-House, could have done it. In fact, the absence of Mr. Grund from his post was never discovered.

When the presidential election came off, the fate of Mr.

John Tyler was decided, and the *Philadelphia Evening Mercury*, and all the other organs of Tylerism, found it necessary to change their tune. The *Evening Mercury* assumed the title of "*The Daily Keystone*," and became a regular Democratic paper. Soon after this mutation, my connection with the establishment was discontinued, as other arrangements in the editorial department were necessary.

OTHER ENGAGEMENTS.

I find that this narrative is becoming more prolix than the occasion requires, and I must therefore hasten to a conclusion. Since my retirement from the office of the *Evening Mercury*, I have, at various times, assisted in the editorial management of the papers whose names are here appended: The *Daily Sun*, the *National Eagle*, (Native American,) the *American Banner*, (ditto,) *The Temperance Pledge*, *The Daily Pennsylvanian*, *The Philadelphia Sunday Mercury*, and two or three others, which perished in their infancy, and left no memorial of their existence.

I have also, during my residence in Philadelphia, contributed local sketches and other reading matter, to several papers with which I had no connection as *editor*. Among those papers were *The National Gazette*, published by the Messrs. Fry; *The Spirit of the Times*, by J. S. Du Solle; and the *Philadelphia Press*, by John W. Forney. Moreover, I have occasionally supplied the "*Philadelphia Correspondence*" for several journals in New York and Boston. In short, I have had enough to do with newspapers of various classes and kinds to know exactly what they are, and to tell what sins of omission and commission may be laid to their charge. But I wish it understood, that not all, nor even a considerable part of the editorial delinquencies which I am about to record, have come under my observation in those particular offices where I myself have been employed. On the contrary, it has been my good fortune, *generally*, to be associated with journals which enjoyed a much better moral reputation than a majority of those newspapers which are published in our principal cities.

In other respects, my connections with the press have not been very fortunate. Having settled myself in Philadelphia, circumstances compelled me, during the last eighteen or twenty years, to form engagements with the newspapers of this city, very few of which are in a prosperous condition. Some of those for which I worked were, therefore, not able to pay my salary with any degree of punctuality, and, on this account, I left them. Others were too niggardly to afford me a fair compensation for my services; and, in one case, the insolent and overbearing conduct of a publisher led to my withdrawal from his office. This man, in fact, gave me *notice to retire;* but, within less than a week after my departure, he begged me, very earnestly and somewhat abjectly, to *resume* those labors which his ungentlemanly deportment had interrupted.

The circumstances referred to in the last paragraph will show how it happened that I was connected with so many different papers, and why my engagements with some of them were of very short duration. I confess, moreover, that I have often found the duties and position of a newspaper editor extremely irksome, and that, in many instances, I was detained at my post solely by the necessity of providing for the wants of my family. About five years ago, I began to make the most strenuous efforts to establish myself in some other kind of business which would afford me the means of maintenance; and, to my very great satisfaction and relief, I have accomplished this object at last. I am now, (*laus Deo!*) wholly independent of the newspaper press, and could live very comfortably and contentedly, if "that most beneficent institution of the age" were annihilated.

COMMENTARIES.

This is "the chronicle and brief abstract" of my experience as a newspaper editor; and if the reader expected to find in this preliminary sketch any thing like a *penitential confession,* it is probable that he is disappointed. The world has been favored with the published memoirs of reformed gamblers, reformed inebriates, reformed swindlers, reformed prostitutes, and reformed pickpockets; but no biography of a reformed EDITOR has ever been written, nor is any thing of the kind to be expected. Truly, we have the printed lives of James Gordon Bennett, Horace Greeley, and others, but these works (which were doubtless examined in manuscript by Messrs. Greeley, Bennett, etc.) show no signs of reformation, for they are merely laudatory or apologetic; and when people entirely approve of their own past conduct, or find excuses for it, there is no prospect of any change for the better.

My serious opinion is, that such editors as stand in most need of reformation are not likely to be reformed, unless they should happen to be converted under the gallows,—where the most incorrigible offenders often become penitent and resolve to do well, when there is no longer any opportunity for them to do otherwise.

Throughout the whole of my professional career, I have been "indifferently honest," and yet "I have done some things," (as Hamlet says,) "which might make my mother regret that she bore me." I have, for instance, recommended books which I never read, singers whom I never heard, dancers whom I never saw—physic which I never took, itch ointments which I never used—and candidates for Congress whom I would not have employed as cooks or scullions in my kitchen. These inexcusable sins were followed by exemplary punishment. I never recommended a worthless author, a vile politician, or any other undeserving person, who did not afterward rank himself among my uncompromising enemies; and my most relentless persecutors have been those for whose sake I have made the greatest sacrifices of honor and conscience.

I do not ask the *public* to absolve me from the guilt of these transgressions; and, more by way of explanation than apology, I will now mention that these were the errors of my earlier life. I walked in the beaten path of journalism without reflecting that it might be the broad road to infamy and perdition. Nevertheless, there were some operations of the newspaper trade which custom has sanctioned but which I never could be persuaded to adopt. Never did I earn a dollar by any perversion of truth or justice. My editorial recommendations of worthless people were mistaken acts of friendship or benevolence. Never did I make any unjustifiable assaults on private character; never, in the heat of political debate, did I assail the moral reputation of my opponent. Never did I indite a newspaper paragraph which provoked a libel suit or a breach of the peace. Never did I forget that it is possible for an editor to be a gentleman.

I will not say, as Mr. John W. Forney did in his Tarrytown speech, "My honesty has been the only obstacle to my preferment," but I can safely aver that I should have been more successful in my vocation if I had been less scrupulous.

Several years ago, I proposed some reforms in the newspaper and magazine business, and made several attempts to establish a truly independent, plain-dealing but strictly decorous journal, in Philadelphia. Since that time I have been proscribed by a certain editorial "clique," and every attempt that cowardice and malice could devise, has been used to cut off all my resources, and compel me to leave the city. Some evidence of this fiendish and almost incredible villainy will be exhibited in other parts of this volume.

4

OUR PRESS GANG.

SECTION I.

FOURTEEN SERIOUS CHARGES AGAINST THE AMERICAN NEWSPAPER PRESS.

I. I charge the American newspaper press with the tyrannical exercise of power and authority to which it has no just pretensions; and I assert that its usurpation of such power and authority is a daring infringement on the rights and liberties of the American people.

II. I assert that the American newspaper press is controlled and directed, in a great measure, by MEN OF FOREIGN BIRTH; and that many of our most influential public journals are *Anti-American* in feeling and sentiment.

III. I charge the newspaper press of America with practical hostility to our republican government and to all free institutions.

IV. I charge the newspaper press of America with a systematic and continuous effort to mislead the judgment of the public in relation to matters of the greatest national importance.

V. I assert that the American newspaper press is the zealous advocate and interested colleague of every form of villainy and imposture; that it is the abettor and confederate of all who defraud and plunder the people; and that it enables such cheats and despoilers to extend and enlarge their operations, and to carry them on with facility and impunity.

VI. I charge the newspaper press of America with fostering immorality and vice, and with being instrumental in producing that want of sterling integrity which prevails among all classes of the people.

VII. I assert that the newspaper press of America encourages and promotes official corruption and malfeasance; that it uses its influence to secure the election or appointment of bad and irresponsible men to important political stations; and that it persuades the people to submit quietly to the extortions and oppressions which are incidental to all governments whose affairs are administered by agents without honesty or responsibility.

VIII. I assert that the newspapers of the United States unwarrantably interfere with the administration of public justice; that they make it impossible for any man charged with a criminal offense to have a fair trial; that they have often caused the most desperate offenders to be acquitted and turned loose on society; and that many innocent persons, by their unwise or malicious meddling, have been brought to condemnation and punishment. Many guiltless victims of journalistic folly, prejudice, or ill-will are now enduring unimaginable torments of body and mind in our States' prisons, and many others (more fortunate, perhaps) have been brought by the same detestable agencies to a shameful and agonizing death.

IX. I charge the newspaper press of America with invading the sanctuary of private life, disturbing the peace of families, giving extensive circulation to groundless and malicious slanders, calumniating the worthiest and most honorable men and the purest and most innocent women, driving many objects of its detraction to phrenzy and desperation, and making them in reality as vile and worthless as they are represented to be by their malignant and remorseless slanderers.

X. I charge the American newspaper press with provoking ruffianly individuals and the excitable classes of our population to violations of the law; causing many sanguinary duels, many disgraceful cases of assault and battery, and terrible popular commotions, which often lead to bloodshed and the destruction of much valuable property.

XI. I charge the newspaper press of the United States with debasing the literature of our country and making the intellectual character of the American people much less respectable than it deserves to be in the eyes of other nations.

XII. I charge the newspaper press of America with checking the diffusion of useful knowledge among the people, by withdrawing the attention of the reading public from useful, salutary, and legitimate objects of study.

XIII. I charge the newspaper press of America with being accessory to thousands of murders every year by assisting quack doctors, or "patent-medicine men," to make extensive sales of their pernicious compounds.

XIV. I charge the newspaper press of America with exciting rebellion, urging the disorderly rabble of our cities to revolutionary movements, and offering encouragement and protection to rebels and traitors, especially to those of foreign birth.

Many other accusations,—and very grave ones too,—might be brought against the newspaper press of our country;*— but the fourteen charges here produced are sufficient in number and importance, perhaps, to attract the notice of the public; and if I succeed in making it appear that every one of these charges is TRUE, enough will be done, I hope, to open a way for one of the most necessary reformations of the nineteenth century—namely, the reformation of Public Journalism.

* See the Appendix to this volume.

SECTION II.

SHOWING WHAT THE AUTHOR OF THIS VOLUME EXPECTS TO PROVE, AND HOW HE INTENDS TO PROVE IT.

Having charged the newspaper press of my country with several disgraceful and criminal offenses,—I am now under a moral obligation to show that all of my charges have a substantial foundation in justice and truth. But let it be distinctly understood, at the outset, *what* I have undertaken to prove.

THE CULPRITS.

I do not assert that *every individual journalist* in the country, is chargeable with all the misdemeanors and crimes comprised in the foregoing BILL OF INDICTMENT, if I may be allowed to call it by that name.

It is absolutely *impossible* for some of our newspaper editors and publishers to be guilty of all of those offenses. Peradventure their case is similar to that of certain ladies, whose conduct, in one or two particulars, has always been indisputably correct, and whose virtue, therefore, is not liable to any shadow of suspicion. In such circumstances, it would be very unfair to assail the reputation of those ladies, by urging that their want of personal attractions has preserved them from the criminal solicitations of the other sex—and that they have never sinned, merely because they have never been tempted.

It would be equally unjust, perhaps, to represent that some newspaper editors have not committed certain professional misdeeds, merely because they have too little popularity and influence to make their favors a marketable commodity. If they are virtuous in action, we must agree to consider them so in principle.

EXCEPTIONS.

It has been acknowledged, in the preface to this volume, that *some* American journalists, are men whose honor and integrity are above all suspicion. I sincerely wish that it were possible for me to preserve those shining lights of journalism from all that moral obscuration, which the dark shadow of their professional pursuits must cast upon their private character.

If, by any practicable means, I could ascertain who the honest and the incorruptible newspaper men of the United States are, I would have all their names inserted in this volume, and printed in *letters of gold*—if our typographical artists did not shrink from the task. And I should perform this act of justice, without any apprehension that the *length of the catalogue* would encroach too much on these pages, which are specially devoted to the exposition of newspaper rascality—for which duty, of course, a considerable space will be required.

But the plan of this work requires me to treat the American newspaper press as a *unit*—or as one body composed of many members — and the individual cases of exception just referred to, do not properly come under my notice. These exceptions are not numerous or influential enough to require any modification of that censure which is applied to the public journalists as a class.

My fourteen accusations refer to the newspaper press in its collective capacity;—and the strict propriety of *that* application is all that I can be expected to prove.

MILITARY ILLUSTRATION.

In this connection, the newspaper press may be compared with an army which commits many atrocious deeds in a conquered territory. It is quite possible that, in such an army, there are some individuals who take no part in the robberies, rapes, and murders which are perpetrated by their associates, and they may even behold the actions of those associates with feelings of horror and indignation. But when the operations of that army are described, the censure of the historian is applied to the whole body without discrimination, and it is seldom possible to deal with the facts in any other manner. In my account of the misdeeds of the *typographical* army, I am obliged to generalize in the same way, assuming (with strict republican propriety, as I conceive) that a very large majority is a fair representative of the whole.

"STUBBORN FACTS."—TRUTH A LIBEL!

With respect to the kind of evidence which I propose to adduce for the support of this "indictment," a few words of explanation will be sufficient. I agree with one of the wisest as well as one of the wittiest of poets—Samuel Butler—that "there is no argument like *matter of fact;*" and, if circumstances favored the plan, I would resort to no other kind of logic. In the annals of our newspaper literature I could easily find facts enough to make all my predicates as stanch as the pillars of Hercules. But it happens (unluckily, perhaps, for the best interests of truth) that many of those facts are closely locked up by legislative interdictions. It has often been decided by the courts that the *truth*, in some cases, is the most offensive of all libels; and, though this doctrine has lately met with some verbal repudiation, it is still practically maintained in our halls of justice, when a rigid interpretation of the libel law is desirable. And, owing to circumstances which I will be obliged to explain in the sequel, the law of libel is never more stringent in its operation than when the newspaper men themselves—the most remorseless and unscrupulous of all libellers—are the prosecutors!

However, if the law of libel were ten times more severe than it is, it would not be oppressive to me; for I have no inclination to violate any of its minutest injunctions. In my exhibition of facts, I shall confine myself to those which are, in all respects, suitable for publication; although this course will necessarily exclude much of the evidence that could be brought to bear on the subject of this treatise. In the relation of occurrences connected with the history of the newspaper press, I will have recourse to the statements which have been already published, choosing those accounts which I suppose to be most authentic and reliable.

CONFIRMATION.

The candid and intelligent public must decide whether the facts adduced are sufficient to support my charges against the public journals. In the experience of every American citizen, perhaps, there will be found much confirmation of the testimony, and the equity of my deductions or conclusions will, in many cases, be apparent at the first glance.

CAUSE AND EFFECT.

I will invite the attention of my countrymen to certain evil *effects*, which must be obvious to them all. Each of these "effects defective," (as Polonius says,) "must have a cause;" and if the causes which I am about to point out are not the true ones, where shall we find others that are more probable?

These observations refer to the more occult transgressions of journalism; but, in a majority of cases, the most deplorable effects will be *distinctly traced* to newspaper causation, so that no doubt on the subject can possibly exist.

VARIOUS MODES OF OPERATION.

Under this head it may be proper to remark, that some of the vices of the newspaper press have various phases in different locations, and, therefore, we must not rashly conclude that such vices are merely sectional, or confined to particular situations. For example, the malicious and aggressive spirit of journalism, which, in our western and southern States, blazes out in furious and coarsely abusive declamation, may take the form of sly and venomous innuendo in Pennsylvania, and, further to the eastward, it may appear in the garb of puritanical intolerance or blood-thirsty fanaticism.

The newspapers of New Orleans or Cincinnati may openly advise the mobs of their respective cities to resist the execution of the laws, or to take violent possession of the ballot-box. In Philadelphia or New York, similar objects may be gained by faintly exhorting the vagabonds *not* to redress their "intolerable grievances" by a too hasty resort to clubs and brickbats!

GENERAL CHARACTER OF AMERICAN JOURNALISM.

It appears to me that the character of our newspaper press is intrinsically the same in every part of the country. The differences are chiefly in externals, and are merely politic adaptations to the humors and tastes of the neighborhood on which the journal depends for its support. If any favorable distinctions can be made, they certainly cannot be placed to the credit of the newspapers of Philadelphia, New York, Boston, and the other principal cities of our Union, where the highest degree of American civilization, refinement and intelligence is supposed to be discoverable.

RUSTIC INNOCENCE.

Some of the *country* newspapers—like many of the rural maidens—appear to be unexceptionably innocent; but I will not pretend to decide whether this appearance generally proceeds from innate purity of heart, or from rustic simplicity and ignorance of the world. I have observed some meretricious tendencies, however, in papers which were possibly issued from such publication offices as log-huts or hollow trees; and all experience tends to confirm my hypothesis, that the character of American journalism is but slightly modified by local circumstances.

PROOFS FROM ALL QUARTERS.

In accordance with the views just taken, I collect my examples and evidences of newspaper depravity from all parts of the country; and my censures are applied, (as truth and justice seem to require), without any topographical distinction whatever.

An examination of the evidence will be commenced in the next section.

SECTION III.

USURPATION AND TYRANNY OF THE NEWSPAPER PRESS.

Examination of the First Charge.

ABUNDANCE AND INFLUENCE OF NEWSPAPERS.

We learn from competent authorities that there about *three thousand* newspapers and periodicals published in the United States. The aggregate circulation of these newspapers and periodicals is supposed to be at least five hundred millions of copies *per annum*. Almost every inhabitant of the United States, who can read any thing, reads newspapers; and it is rumored that very great numbers of the American people never read any thing else.

NEWSPAPER AUTHORITY.

An immense number of our fellow-republicans have no ideas, no creed, no opinions, except those which are derived from their newspaper reading. Here in Philadelphia, for example, thousands of our population rarely presume to make up their minds on any subject until they have the authoritative decision of their intellectual guide, the *Public Ledger*.

Every American has his newspaper oracle, as every African has his *fetish*, or talismanic counselor. Each has a superstitious reliance on the infallibility of his mysterious director; but neither can give any *reason* for implicitly submitting his judgment to such guidance. How does Mr. Smith, Mr. Brown, or Mr. Hopkins know that the editor of the Public Ledger, or of the New York Sun, or of any other penny paper, or of any *two-penny* one, indeed, is a wiser man than himself? Why should it be taken for granted that a certain man's opinions are worth more than those of other people, because that man is an editor?

I have seen the interior of many newspaper offices,—and I can assure you, my dear compatriots, that I have seldom mistaken an editorial *sanctum* for a temple of Minerva. I have seen many a shallow coxcomb, many a stupid blockhead, seated at an editorial desk; and it is possible that I may have witnessed some such phenomena in the offices of several of those very journals which you are disposed to regard as the most oracular.

OUR EDITORS.—WHO AND WHAT ARE THEY?

The newspaper editors of the United States are often—and indeed, most commonly—men who have not succeeded very well in some other kind of business. They are ex-lawyers, ex-doctors, ex-parsons, ex-blacksmiths, ex-shoemakers, ex-tailors, ex-fiddlers, ex-play-actors, and, (with few exceptions,) excessively common-place and insignificant people. Some of the most able and intelligent editors have been journeymen-printers; for these artistes, (especially the compositors or type-setters,) have many facilities for the acquisition of useful knowledge; and not a few of them really possess a larger fund of general information than some members of the so-called "learned professions."

The lawyers, clergymen, and physicians who abandon their professional pursuits to become conductors of the press, are seldom persons of superior abilities; a fact which may be inferred from their change of occupation; for talents of a high order are more likely to meet with appreciation and encouragement in the practice of law, physic, or divinity, than in the performance of any subordinate duties of journalism.

Of the persons who write for the press in this country, a very large proportion are FOREIGNERS;—Englishmen, Irishmen, Scotchmen, Welshmen, Frenchmen, Germans, etc. Many of these exotics have lived but a very short time in the United

States; and, of course, their acquaintance with American affairs must be very superficial.

THE FIRST CHARGE.

Let it not be supposed that the preceding remarks are digressive or irrelevant. All the observations just introduced have a direct bearing on our subject, and on that part of it which is now under consideration. To make this fully apparent, let us refer, once more, to the CHARGE which it is our present object to substantiate. We find, by analysis, that this charge will admit of four specifications; to wit:—

1. It is alleged, or implied, that the newspaper press of America possesses extraordinary and tremendous powers.

2. It is alleged that the public journalists have *no just claims* to the possession of these powers; that is to say, they have no legal right to them, and no moral or intellectual qualifications which would entitle them, in any circumstances, to assume the direction and control of public affairs.

3. It is alleged that the American newspaper press exercises its powers in an oppressive and tyrannical manner.

4. It is alleged that the newspaper press audaciously encroaches on the *political* rights of the American people.

TREMENDOUS POWER OF THE PRESS.

With regard to the first specification; viz., "That the newspaper press possesses extraordinary and tremendous powers," I suppose that the fact is almost or altogether *self-evident*. But, if any proof be required, we will hear the witnesses; and I will afterward give you, in a few words, very strong circumstantial evidence to corroborate their statements.

I offer you the testimony of Charles J. Ingersol, an ex-member of Congress, and a distinguished politician of the Democratic school. Many of you believe him to be a true patriot and an honest statesman; and I have no reason for believing otherwise. Mr. Ingersol is now in the seventy-sixth year of his age; his political career is finished; he has nothing to expect from the favor of his fellow-citizens, and very little to fear from their resentment. I presume that he is a disinterested witness. His testimony against the usurpation and tyranny of journalism has exposed him to floods and whirlpools of newspaper abuse; and he has been severely censured, on the same account, by some of the journalists of his own party. He must have foreseen these effects of his denunciation of the newspapers, and the fact that he *did* denounce them, regardless of their vindictive fury, proves his sincerity and manly independence. Moreover, Mr. Ingersol's long life, spent, for the most part, on the political arena, has given him many opportunities to become acquainted with the powers and peculiarities of American journalism; and we may suppose, therefore, that he speaks *understandingly* on the subject.

In short, it is impossible to doubt that this gentleman has all the qualifications of a faithful and reliable witness.

CHARLES J. INGERSOL'S TESTIMONY.

Mr. Ingersol has testified to several important matters connected with the subject of our inquiry,—some of which will be useful to us for future reference. At present, we will direct our attention to that part of his testimony which relates to the POWERS of the newspaper press, and its abuse of those powers.

In a letter dated July 5, 1858, and addressed to a committee appointed to make arrangements for the celebration of the Anniversary of American Independence, Mr. Ingersol declares his belief that "newspaper editors are *the real sovereigns of our country;*" and he goes on to say that, "with such monarchs as editors and such aristocrats as corporators, corruption must be one of our national institutions, and virtue, which is said to be the vital spark of republics, must become a mere explosive stench."

This appears to be a very strong declaration to come from an American statesman who is older, by several years, than the Declaration of Independence! But we have something still more energetic:—

TESTIMONY OF JUDGE LUDLOW.

Judge Ludlow, who presides in the Court of Quarter Sessions, Philadelphia, declared in a recent charge to the Grand Jury, that the American newspaper press is "ALL POWERFUL."

HEAR THE WASHINGTON UNION.

I offer you, likewise, the testimony of the *Washington Union*, one of our great national organs, the chief expositor of "Democratic" principles in the United States, and the principal mouth-piece of the present administration. The evidence of the Washington Union, in this case, may be regarded as a *confession*, inasmuch as it tends to criminate that journal itself. In such circumstances, the testimony of the "Union" is entitled to much credit,—setting aside the musty proverb, that "The worst offender generally turns State's evidence."

"The Newspaper Press, (says the Washington Union,) controls the state and the church; it directs the family, the legislator, the magistrate and the minister. None rise above its influence, none sink below its authority. The aggregate matter thrown off daily and weekly in the United States—nearly all of which is read by the American people—is absolutely beyond computation. The newspaper press is the GREATEST POWER IN THE STATE; and, from its very nature, it places every other power, to a greater or lesser extent, in subjection to its laws."

OTHER TESTIMONY.

The Philadelphia Evening Bulletin of July 23, 1858, said —"The power of the Newspaper Press is enormous, it has even alarmed a public man who was once deemed very sagacious,—but it is in vain for him to attack it."

The distinguished American orator and political philosopher, Edward Everett, says:—"The newspaper press of the United States is, for good or evil, the most powerful influence that acts on the public mind,—the most powerful in itself and as the channel through which most other influences act." *Vide* "Mount Vernon Papers," No. xi.

I could offer you the testimony of many eminent statesmen, jurists, clergymen, and authors, all bearing on the same point; but *quis multis*? What signify the opinions of others when you can examine the facts for yourself? Does not your own daily experience teach you that the public mind is controlled and directed by the newspapers? Are not public opinion and newspaper opinion identical? And is not public opinion evidently *manufactured* by the public journals? Did you ever know any sentiment to prevail extensively in this country until it was first eliminated from the newspaper press?

USURPATION OF THE PRESS.

If the newspapers form public opinion, they govern the country; they control the elections and direct the choice of our executive, legislative, and judicial officers; for popular opinion is the instrument by means of which these operations of our government are effected. America, therefore, is governed by an oligarchy of QUILL-DRIVERS! Truly said Mr. Ingersol, (in the letter quoted above,) "this is a most contemptible despotism."

IS THE PRESS QUALIFIED FOR DOMINION?

In the second specification of Charge I. it is alleged that the journalists have *no just claims* to that sovereignty which they have so boldly assumed. For the elucidation of this topic, let us inquire, once more, who and what are these newspaper sovereigns? It was intimated, somewhere above, that a very considerable number of them are ex-lawyers, ex-physicians, ex-preachers, ex-shoemakers, ex-tailors, ex-fiddlers, exotics, and others who are, in no respect, extraordinary people. Five *per cent.* of them, perhaps, are men of good education and superior abilities. Ten per cent. of them, it may be, are men of common sense and common-school education. Fifty per cent. of them, at least, are men *without* common sense and with no education at all—certainly with no education of that kind which would qualify them to become public instructors.

MORALS AND INTELLECT OF THE PRESS.

It may be proper to remark, in this place, that every shallow or stupid fellow who has had the advantages of "a regular college education" is not, merely on that account, to be supposed to be well fitted for the legitimate duties of journalism. There are some kinds of knowledge which are not to be acquired in schools and colleges, and which, to a newspaper conductor, may be indispensable. But let us not forget that WISDOM is of still greater importance to the editorial profession than knowledge of any kind; and wisdom is that very qualification which newspaper editors in general do not possess.

What! are *wise editors* a rarity? Methinks I hear a sound which resembles the laughing chorus in a Dutch opera. Ha! ha! ha! he! he! he! hi! hi! hi! ho! ho! ho! Only to think of a scarcity of wise editors in the United States of America! Have we not Greeley, the proverbial philosopher of the New York Tribune? Have we not Bryant, the poetical sage of the New York Evening Post? Have we not Forney, the subtle politician of the Philadelphia Press? Have we not Prentice, the sententious and epigrammatic scribe of the Louisville Journal? Have we not Mrs. Jane Swisshelm, a "Plato in petticoats"? And have we not hundreds of others who have given irrefragable proof of their wisdom by being successful in business, establishing popular journals, and accumulating large fortunes?

I do not deny that *some* of our newspaper editors are "wise fellows enough," (quoting the words of Dogberry). I grant that many of them have a certain kind of shrewdness, or worldly wisdom which will pass among a majority of my countrymen for the genuine article. But I emphatically deny that many American editors have that kind of wisdom which ought to make their opinions or counsels authoritative, or even respectable. The distinction between shrewdness and wisdom is immediately discoverable, when you consider that there may be such a thing as a shrewd RASCAL; but a *wise* rascal is an impossibility.

I assert that American editors, in general, have neither the moral nor the intellectual qualities which are the least that we should expect from men who claim a right to direct the judgment of a whole nation. Their assumption of such a high prerogative, therefore, is presumed to be an inexcusable act of usurpation; for, except on the score of moral and intellectual superiority, they can have no imaginable claim to the power and authority which they now exercise.

To show you the fallacy and absurdity of their pretensions, I will now offer you a few items of evidence relating to the morals and intellect of the newspaper press; and in other parts of this book I will have occasion to give many other illustrations of the same subject.

James Fennimore Cooper, the distinguished American author, makes use of the following language :—

"As the newspaper press of this country now exists, it would seem to have been devised by the great agent of mischief to depress and destroy all that is good, and to elevate and advocate all that is evil in the nation. The little truth that is urged is usually urged coarsely, and is weakened and rendered vicious by personalities, while those who live by falsehoods, fallacies, enmities, partialities, and the schemes of the designing, find the press the very instrument that devils would invent to effect their designs."

In another place, Mr. Cooper says: "Every honest man appears to admit that the newspaper press in America is fast getting to be *intolerable*. While escaping from the tyranny of foreign aristocrats, we have created in our midst a tyranny of a character so insupportable that a change of some sort is becoming more and more indispensable every day."

Daniel Webster, the eminent American statesman, in his celebrated speech ou the Public Lands, makes reference to public journalism in the United States, and speaks of it as "a polluted and shameless press."

I could fill a volume quite as large as this with extracts of similar import, but it is unnecessary at present to enlarge on this topic, as the folly and wickedness of American journalism will be the themes of much future discussion in this work. If I succeed in convincing you that the American newspaper press is eminently foolish and wicked, you will be satisfied, I presume, that it cannot be safely entrusted with "a voice potential" in the management of our national affairs.

And with respect to the two last specifications of my first charge, viz., "That the American newspaper press exercises its powers in a tyrannical and oppressive manner," and that "it audaciously encroaches on the *political* rights of the people," these points, likewise, will be fully discussed in our following pages. Indeed, you will find that the details of these two predicates constitute the principal part of my argument.

SUPPLEMENTARY ILLUSTRATIONS.

DEPORTMENT OF THE TYRANTS.—The editors and publishers of the more successful papers are apt enough to play the tyrant, professionally and otherwise, on all convenient occasions. They have an extravagant notion of their own importance, and they are disposed to exact a great deal of respect and deference from all who approach them.

The keeper of a boarding-house in Philadelphia, informed me that a foreign sub-editor of one of the daily papers of that city was, for awhile, one of his boarders; and this person's behavior was so arbitrary and overbearing, that the whole household was in a state of mutiny. The habit of domineering which this man had indulged in print, was visible in all his conduct. He assumed the control of the whole establishment, exacting unconditional submission and obedience from every member of the family. He was indeed "the autocrat of the breakfast-table," and if the smallest fault could be found with the toast or coffee, he would pronounce an invective against the landlord with more than Demosthenian energy. Sometimes, if the butter was not unexceptionable, or if any other imperfection was discovered in the provisions, he threatened to bring all the thunders of the press to bear against the offending caterer. The person who made this curious demonstration, pretends to be one of the great intellectual lights of Philadelphia journalism.

The larger number of our American newspaper-men have risen from subordinate positions—they have been in subjection to other tyrants of their own class; and as they know by experience what it is to be treated like slaves, they seldom miss an opportunity to teach others the same lesson. Emancipated slaves are always insolent.

The manners of some of our most distinguished journalists are so offensive, that it is impossible for a man of the least sensibility to remain in company with them for five minutes without feeling himself insulted.

ONE OF THE "MONARCHS."— Several years ago, a well-known and "highly respectable" political paper of Philadelphia, was published by a man whose position among blackguards might be compared with that of Plato among philosophers. I never knew a person, in any rank of life, whose manners were more intolerable or whose general character was more contemptible. He was, by turns, a despot and a sycophant; his insolence passed all bounds, but when properly rebuked, it was followed by the most abject submission. But his lust for giving offense was so unconquerable that, even while he was apologizing for one insult, he generally contrived to offer another.

Unluckily for himself, he left the "Quaker City," and removed further toward the "Sweet South," where he rose so much in public estimation, that some idly-disposed gentleman mistook his value and honored him with a severe horsewhipping.

The journalist here spoken of was the "prince of blackguards," as intimated above; but if there were such a thing as an Aristocracy of Blackguardism,—*many* members of the editorial profession might be called Dukes, Earls, or Marquises, and no titles of nobility would be more indisputable than theirs.

THE TYRANTS' MASTERS.—With all their superb pretensions to sovereignty, our newspaper tyrants themselves are often in a state of absolute bondage. Their position, in this respect, is somewhat like that of the Roman emperors, who, even while they pretended to universal dominion, and claimed not only the respect but the *adoration* of the people, by placing themselves among the gods, were subject to the capricious and insolent dictation of the Prætorian soldiery.

Our editorial monarchs, (as Mr. Ingersoll calls them,) have quite a variety of lords and masters. The slavery of *political* editors is pitiable; they dare not express an opinion or publish a syllable without the approbation of their party leaders. The whole newspaper press of the country, (as I will show in another place,) is subject to the Banking Interest, and in fact, to every other corrupting influence. In many cases, the publishers and editors of newspapers are controlled, in a measure, by persons whom they affect to regard as their subordinates and dependents. The Journeyman Printers' Association exercises great authority over nearly all the papers in Philadelphia, and in other places, and the publishers are often obliged to succumb to their own workmen. This circumstance, however, is not to be regretted, as it may tend to improve the character and conduct of the Press; for many of the journeyman printers are men of fair reputation and *gentlemen*, which many of the editors and publishers are not. I have known the proprietor and editor of a very influential paper to be rebuked for his ungentlemanly and dishonorable behavior, by one of his own journeymen.

Every man who advertises largely in the newspapers is one

of the masters of the press, and the journals who enjoy his patronage would no more venture to give him offense than the newspapers of Paris would venture to excite the wrath of Louis Napoleon. Moneyed corporations, (to which many of the editors are deeply indebted, and which actually *maintain* not a few of them), possess unlimited authority over the "free and independent newspaper press of our country."

In short, there is no reality in the boasted freedom and independence of American editors.

DEAD HEADS.—Every monarch has his *prerogatives*—among those of the newspaper sovereigns are free admission to all the theatres, opera-houses, hippodromes, monkey-shows, picture galleries, dioramas, living crocodile exhibitions, etc.; free passages over railroads and in steamboats; free access to the bars of hotels, wine and liquor stores and lager-beer saloons, and untaxed admission to the tables of sixpenny coffee-houses and shilling refectories. Being unprofitable customers, the gentlemen of the press are regarded by the tradesmen who contribute to their comfort as a sort of spirits or genii who are privileged to help themselves to the good things of this world without making any pecuniary requital; for ghosts having to travel by aërial conveyance, are not expected to burden themselves with pocket-money. On account of their spectre-like habits, editors are known among theatrical people, tavern keepers, steamboat captains, etc., by the title of DEAD HEADS. The supernatural powers attributed to them produce much awe and apprehension among the unfortunate people who are subject to their visitations. These unfortunates feel constrained by sad necessity to submit to all the requirements of the press, knowing or believing that an offended editor could ruin not their business only, but their reputations likewise, merely by throwing out some scandalous hint in his next issue. The tyranny of the press, in its operation on certain trades and professions, is almost inconceivable: no despotism could be more complete. I have heard that beautiful actresses, etc., have been constrained to prostitute themselves to prevent their professional reputations from being blasted by the efforts of a libidinous and resentful editor! Such abuses of editorial power are supposed to be of *frequent occurrence* in America.

SECTION IV.

THE FOREIGN AND ANTI-AMERICAN CHARACTER OF OUR NEWSPAPER PRESS.

Examination of the Second Charge.

THAT the "foreign element" enters largely into the composition of American journalism is a fact which may be proved to demonstration; and, indeed, this fact affords the only explanation of many moral phenomena which present themselves to our daily observation.

In this division of my subject, I will direct the reader's attention to several circumstances connected with newspaper management in this country,—circumstances which must be obvious to every man of ordinary intelligence, and which he will find it impossible to account for in any other manner than by supposing that the prevailing sentiment of our public journals is *Anti-American*.

"THE ACCIDENT OF BIRTH."

IMPRIMIS, it is very evident that the *birth-right* of Americans is ignored by the newspapers in general. It is not admitted by them that native citizens have, or ought to have, any political rights or privileges superior to those of naturalized foreigners. On the contrary, the doctrine almost universally preached by the public journals is, that an alien who has taken out his naturalization papers is, to all intents and purposes, an *American*, and no less an American than any native of the soil. This is newspaper doctrine, but it is not the doctrine of reason or religion,—it is not the doctrine of universal law,—and it is a doctrine which is not recognized by the Constitution of the United States.

Reason and common sense teach us that every man is under peculiar obligations to the land of his birth, and, as these obligations are reciprocal, he has peculiar claims on his native country. He has certain rights which cannot be extended to strangers without manifest injustice to the children of the soil; for it should be understood that the relation in which a man stands to the land of his nativity is precisely like that of a child to its parent. His country may adopt other children, but if she grants them all the privileges which naturally belong to her own offspring, her treatment of the latter is both unjust and unnatural. These are truths which have never been questioned in any other country but America; they are truths founded on the unchangeable laws of nature, and no human legislation can supercede or annul them.

The highest legal authorities declare that it is a principle of *universal law* that a man cannot put off the allegiance which he owes to the land of his birth. (See Blackstone's Commentaries, Book I., chap. 10.) It is impossible, therefore, for an Irishman, a Scotchman, or a Dutchman to become an American; for this change could be effected only by NATURAL REGENERATION,—and that is a miracle which our legislators are not able to perform. This is a topic on which I shall have to speak more at large hereafter. At present, I refer to the absurd and pernicious newspaper pretense, "that aliens, by a certain process of naturalization, are completely Americanized," to furnish my readers with a very good proof that the press which earnestly disseminates such a doctrine must be controlled by some influence which is very much in antagonism with the cherished feelings of the American patriot, who is honestly and laudably proud of his birth-right.

ALIEN EDITORS.

In fact, as I now propose to convince you, the principal disseminators of this doctrine are *not* Americans. It is a fact with which I am well acquainted, and which you can easily ascertain for yourself, that *the most influential newspapers of America are controlled by foreigners,* not a few of whom have resided but a very short time in this country!

Unquestionably the greater number of these men have been taught, from their infancy, to despise popular governments, or to regard them as impracticable; and in spite of all conversions of creeds and changes of circumstances, the religious or political sentiments which men have acquired in childhood and early youth will adhere to them, more or less, through life.

Our foreign editors, in their private conversations, generally prove their assent to the Pythagorean policy of keeping one creed for their own particular use and another for public discussion. Many of these imported scribes are inflexible monarchists, except when the requirements of business compel them to act a different part. We may justly suspect that when such men write in defense of republicanism, their advocacy is jesuitical or *Pickwickian.* Let it be understood, however, that I do not condemn our editors of foreign birth because they are still partial to those institutions which, in their childhood, they learned to love and respect. I do not censure any foreigner for his antipathy to republicanism, when I consider what a repulsive aspect it must often present to strangers who see it hideously distorted by the moral diseases to which it is liable in this country, and who erroneously suppose that it could not exist in any other condition.

I condemn many of the Englishmen, Irishmen, Scotchmen, etc., who are employed as newspaper scribes in America, because they take an unfair advantage of their position and *insidiously* attack our institutions while they hypocritically profess to admire and defend them. It may be said for their excuse that they are merely performing that task which Dr. Johnson considers so extremely difficult—viz. " writing up to the ideas of other people." " They are employed to write republicanism, and in doing so they only perform their part of a contract." But the misfortune is that they do *not* fulfill their contract; for, like many other insincere advocates, they injure the cause which they undertake to defend.

HATRED OF GOVERNMENT.

Lord Byron once avowed himself a republican in principle, "but, (said he,) it is probable that if I lived under a popular government, I should become a monarchist." If Byron supposed that the feeling which prompted him to make this declaration was one of his own peculiar eccentricities, he was greatly mistaken. Men of all classes are apt enough to dislike their *masters*. They are easily displeased with the power which controls them, while that authority which they do not feel or fear has some claims to their favor. For this reason, many people, (like Lord Byron,) prefer any form of government before that under which they live; and, in all their migrations, they show the same disaffection for that rule to which they are bound to render obedience. To bad men *all* governments are irksome. John Milton represents Satan as making strong objections to the government of Heaven, which he regarded as intolerably tyrannical. There is nothing preternatural or superhuman in the old blind man's charactery of his diabolical hero; and the same repugnance to celestial rule which the poet ascribes to that arch-disorganizer would be felt by many *earthly* gentlemen of our acquaintance, if it were possible for them, by any process of emigration or naturalization, to become denizens of the heavenly kingdom.

MISTAKES CORRECTED.

In the application of these remarks to our present subject, we must consider, in the first place, that because a man is, or has been, a bad monarchist, it does not follow that he must necessarily be a good republican. If an Irishman or Englishman, a Scotchman or a Dutchman, has been seditious and ungovernable in his own country, we must not take it for granted that he will become an exemplary citizen of the United States.

If he has become disgusted with the monarchical government under which he was born, we must not rashly conclude that he will be a cordial friend and steadfast supporter of our republican system. A man who has been a rebel, a traitor or a seditious subject in Europe, may become a very troublesome fellow in America, if he has any opportunity to meddle with public affairs; and I have seen many living exemplifications of this truth.

It was said above that nearly all of our *most influential* journals are partly or altogether controlled by foreigners. These imported scribes are presumed to have become disgusted with the governments of their respective countries, and this fact is supposed to be good evidence of their republican proclivities! It would be just as wise to conclude that because a man does not like the taste of aloes, he must necessarily have a relish for wormwood. To some men, (as we have hinted above), *all* governments are very bitter physic; and I have good reason to believe that a majority of the expatriated newspaper writers belong to that ever-dissatisfied class. Like Milton's hero, they would probably be displeased with the government of Heaven itself, and that they would endeavor to overthrow it if they had any hopes of success.

VAGABOND EDITORS.

I have been informed—and my own observations tend to confirm the report—that the greater number of the exotic scribes employed in this country are mere vagabonds, and that very few of them have any claims to respect on the score of intelligence or integrity. It is believed that newspaper writers of character and ability are better encouraged in Europe than in America; for intellect and literary talent are among the indispensable qualifications of a European journalist; and men who possess these qualifications are always in demand on the other side of the Atlantic. When a foreign writer comes to this country, therefore, and is willing to work for such pitiful wages as our niggardly publishers are accustomed to pay, the natural inference is, that such a writer has not the talents and accomplishments which would have made him marketable at home. Or, if he happen to possess good intellectual gifts, we may generally suspect that some moral delinquency, or some political misdemeanor—some offense against the government or the criminal code of his own country—has made it expedient for him to change his place of residence.

Doubtless many European scoundrels—burglars, pickpockets, political agitators, scrubby literateurs and other public nuisances—imagine that they can do just as they please under our free institutions; and when they arrive among us they often give proof that they came hither with such expectations. The behavior of our imported editors, when they have settled themselves in America, seldom fails to make us aware of the causes which have induced them to favor us with their company.

Candor obliges me to make the confession, that America is the only country where blackguard journalists are not only tolerated but generously rewarded; the only country where the greatest rascals of the profession are always prosperous and INFLUENTIAL! This circumstance alone is enough to attract to our shores the vilest class of newspaper scribblers from the various nations of the old world.

RECAPITULATION.

Now let us review two extraordinary facts in connection with each other:

1. The newspaper press is "all powerful," (using the words of Judge Ludlow;) or, in the language of Mr. Ingersol, "newspaper-men are the monarchs of America." Without any exaggeration or hyperbole, we may say that the power of the press is tremendous and almost irresistible. This fact admits of no dispute.

2. This potent engine is controlled in a great measure, by FOREIGNERS; not a few of whom are men of infamous character. Some of them have been traitors to the land of their birth

and others are charged with the grossest immoralities or the blackest crimes

My fellow-citizens of America, I do not, (like many others,) profess to believe that you are the wisest people in the world —but I persuade myself that a majority of you have common sense; and I therefore place these facts in juxtaposition before you, hoping that you will perceive the humiliating and dangerous circumstances in which you are placed. But, before we proceed further, I will endeavour to satisfy you that there is *really* a preponderance of the foreign and anti-republican elements in the composition of our American journalism.

EXAMPLES.

In the first place, I call your attention to the fact that the two most successful publications in America—viz., the most prosperous and influential daily paper and the most widely circulated and popular weekly, are owned by men of foreign birth. Of that weekly paper, I have but little to say in the present connection. The proprietor of it, fortunately, is a moral and religious man; he shows no inclination to be mischievous, but contents himself with catering for the amusement of his five hundred thousand readers. But with the other paper, *videlicit* the *New York Herald*, the case is quite different. This journal is read by people of all classes, and its power and influence are universally acknowledged. Although this Herald is denounced from one end of the country to the other as the most corrupt and profligate journal in existence, its opinions on almost every subject are often quoted as indisputable authority, and hundreds of other newspapers adopt its views and republish its statements without the least reservation.

Many others of our leading journals are partially or entirely controlled by foreigners; to say nothing of those German, Irish or English organs which have been established among us to maintain doctrines or promote interests which are often widely at variance with the true principles of our republican constitution. Every political refugee or fugitive from justice who immigrates to these shores—if he can scribble a paragraph or a line of English—is eligible to the situation of principal or assistant editor of an American newspaper. A French valet, an Irish coachman, or a Dutch hostler will generally be required to exhibit some testimonial of his honesty and capacity before he can obtain employment, but alien EDITORS, (luckily for themselves in most cases,) are never expected to produce any proofs of their professional abilities or of their previous good behavior.

FOREIGN EDITORS PREFERRED.

Foreign writers are often employed by American newspaper publishers in preference to our own countrymen, even when the latter are known to have superior qualifications. The reasons for this preference are various. Sometimes it is found that an editor of foreign extraction will work more cheaply than an American, and the former is generally more submissive and tractable than the latter, and is therefore more available when any particularly dirty work is to be performed. Besides, the literary vagabonds who come to this country in search of em-employment, usually represent themselves as the very Drummond Lights of European intellect, and our newspaper proprietors generally belong to a class of people which is easily imposed on by extravagant pretensions.

In all newspaper offices, therefore, where several editors are employed, one of them, at least, is almost sure to be a foreigner. In some offices the editors and reporters are nearly *all* aliens; and this I believe is the case with some of the principal journals of New York, which pretend to be the leading newspapers of America. Many of the most prosperous newspapers of Boston, Philadelphia, Cincinnati, Louisville, New Orleans, etc., are richly supplied with the same imported commodity.

In short, there is a sufficient preponderance of this foreign material in the composition of American journalism to give the whole of it a foreign tone; and that it really has such a tone you must have discovered if you are in the habit of reading the newspapers. You have discovered, no doubt, that aliens—Irishmen and Dutchmen in particular—are the *pets* of the American press. No fond mother can be more anxious to palliate the misdeeds of her darling boy than our public journals are to gloze over the errors and offenses of these "better citizens."

When reporting the misdemeanors of the Irish and Dutch, the papers are accustomed to keep the nationality of the offenders out of view; and the very *names* of the parties are sometimes Americanized to favor the amiable deception. Our own national character is much disgraced by the strenuous efforts of the journalists to conceal the fact that *three-fourths* of the deeds of ruffianism and crime which are reported in our public prints are commmitted by foreigners, and particularly by the natives of Ireland and Germany.

THE NEWSPAPER PETS.

The partiality of the American papers for aliens is partly explained by the fact that many of the editors themselves are men of foreign birth. But the Irish and Germans are special objects of favor because their numerical strength, together with their ignorance and credulity, makes them the convenient tools of faction and an element of political dynamics, by means of which the rascally demagogues and their colleagues of the press can carry elections and obtain an ascendency over all that is honest, virtuous, and respectable in the country.

ORIGIN OF THE "SATANIC PRESS."

It would be impossible for us to understand some of the mysteries of "American journalism," if we were not acquainted with the fact that much of this journalism is *not* American. The contemplation of this fact produces a mixed feeling of gratification and regret. We are delighted to find that the worst weeds in our journalistic garden are exotics; but it is by no means pleasant to observe that those pernicious weeds have all the advantages of soil, sunshine, and cultivation. It is gratifying to our American feelings to ascertain that the seeds of newspaper rascality were brought to our shores from the other side of the great waters; but it is painful and humiliating to confess that this plant of foreign origin thrives and flourishes on the soil of America, and appears to improve by transplantation, as the potato was improved when transferred to the congenial earth of Old Ireland.

The first paper in America which was ever charged with "black mailing," and some other corrupt practices, was the *New York Herald*, the plan and *modus operandi* of which originated with James Gordon Bennett, a native of Great Britain. When the *Herald* began its erratic career, the newspapers of America generally condemned Mr. Bennett's mode of doing business; but when the other journalists found that the course of the *Herald* met with public favor and the most liberal encouragement, their consciences, which had been crying out so lustily, were all put to sleep, and the plans and expedients of the New York Herald became models for general imitation.

The illustrious Bennett often styles himself "The Napoleon of the American press." Some years ago, he was accustomed to call himself the "Head Devil" of the typographical Pandemonium. On some accounts, he has an unquestionable claim to these titles—for he may be considered as the arch-contriver of our present newspaper system, with all its ambitious, unscrupulous and diabolical peculiarities. To the genius of Bennett we ascribe the *origin* of that infernal system which has enabled many newspaper proprietors to become nabobs in wealth and despots in power; but we hold to the opinion, that some of Bennett's disciples or imitators, in the conscienceless villainy of their operations, have gone far beyond the example of their "Napoleon" or "Head Devil." Bennett himself is astonished at the proficiency of his own pupils.

SUPERIORITY OF FOREIGN EDITORS.

Perhaps it may be asked, whether the ascendency which

foreign newspaper writers have obtained in this country does not prove that they are superior, in some respects, to our own native scribes? This is a very pertinent question, I confess; and, in spite of my national partialities, I am obliged to admit that those imported penmen are really superior, in one or two particulars at least, to a majority of my own countrymen. In two qualities, which enable their possessors to take the lead on almost every occasion, the exotic journalists have greatly the advantage of their American competitors. The qualities to which I refer are ARROGANCE and IMPUDENCE; and I solemnly declare that I never knew any men to possess more of those good gifts than the aforesaid exotics. They are well qualified to make their way through the world, (to borrow Butler's comparison), as pigs force a passage through quickset hedges—*i. e.*, with their faces.

The veriest Cockney or Corkonian cannot be connected with an American newspaper for twenty days before he undertakes to school our statesmen, to instruct our legislators, to direct the judiciary, and to propose amendments to the Constitution. And, as these men speak from the veiled sanctuary of the Press, their most impertinent and nonsensical utterances are mistaken for the oracles of wisdom. Thus are they encouraged to presume more and more, until they make themselves our dictators and sovereigns, assuming the direction of public affairs, and boldly claiming a control over every branch of our government. Gracious Heaven! what a strange condition of things is this! The Constitution of the United States will not permit a foreigner—not even an *honest* and *respectable* foreigner—to be President or Vice-President of this republic, but here is a gang of European rabble—vagabonds at best, and some of them convicted malefactors—who claim powers superior to those of the President himself; and unquestionably these men, in opposition to the spirit of the Constitution, take a larger part in the government of our country and in the management of public affairs, than the chief magistrate, or any legally constituted authority.

The newspaper press governs the country, and this "politic convocation" of base and rascally foreigners controls the press!

SUPPLEMENTARY ILLUSTRATIONS.

MADAME LOLA MONTEZ.—This distinguished lady, in a lecture lately delivered before a Dublin audience, declared that "*half of the most efficient editors and reporters in the United States are Irishmen!*" Madame Montez is intimately acquainted with newspaper affairs in this country. She has been a resident of the United States, and while she was in America her professional pursuits brought her into frequent communication with the conductors of the press. I believe that her declaration quoted above is strictly true.

EDITORIAL CORPS OF THE NEW YORK HERALD.—The New York *Courier and Enquirer* said, in allusion to its neighbor the *Herald*: "This journal is edited by a *band of foreigners*, several of whom have been engaged in writing for some of the most scurrilous papers in Europe."

TRIBUNE AND EXPRESS.—In an altercation between these two New York journals, the *Tribune* said, with reference to the *Express*: "Three quarters of the persons employed about the office are Irish. The reporters are Irish, the small boys are Irish, the pressmen are Irish, two of the *editors* are foreigners, and the whole crowd of agents and news-boys that scatter it about the city are Irish. And yet this same *Express* is the Know Nothing organ of New York city!"

The *Express* denied a considerable part of this accusation, but admitted that *four* of its editors and reporters were foreigners, viz., "one Irishman and three Englishmen!"

If a paper which pretends to be the expounder and advocate of Native American principles can indulge so freely in the imported luxury, what can be expected of those journals which scarcely attempt to conceal their foreign partialities?

I believe that the gentleman who superintends the literary and free-love departments of the *New York Tribune* is an Englishman. It is understood that Mr. Greely himself attends to the Fourierite and Abolition branches of the business. Concerning the other members of the *Tribune corps* I have very little information.

NEW YORK TIMES.—I am indebted to a friend in New York for a list of the editors and reporters who are employed by the *New York Times*, which is presumed to be one of the most influential papers in America. I find that the "foreign element" predominates in that establishment.

The *New York Herald, Times*, and *Tribune*, occupy a prominent position in the ranks of journalism, for which position they are indebted more to their SWAGGERING IMPUDENCE than to any other quality, moral or intellectual. Nevertheless the newspaper press of America takes its tone, in a great measure, from these sheets, which in their very *form*, as well as in their constitution and character, are any thing else but American. Their deceitful advocacy of Republican principles is always opposition in masquerade.

FOREIGN ORGANS.—Of those papers which *make no secret* of their foreign proclivities, there is a very large number published in the United States, as the following catalogue (which is far from complete, however,) will certify :—

FOREIGN NEWSPAPERS PUBLISHED IN THE UNITED STATES.

NEW YORK.
Albion, English.
Courier des Etats Unis, French.
Irish News.
Irish American.
Freeman's Journal, Irish.
Catholicke Kirchen, German.
La Chronica, French.
Echo d' Italia.

Le Progress, French.
Criminal Zeitung, German.
Parish Visitor, Irish.
Staats Zeitung, German.
Y Drych Ar Gwyliedydd, Welch.
Clychggrown Oemdlaethrawl.
Abend Zeitung, German.
Guardian, Irish.
Alliance, do.

American Celt, Irish.
Am. Botzchafter, German.
Atlantische Blatter, do.
Cambso American, Welch.
Churchman, Irish Catholic.
Irish Citizen.
Cometa, Italian.
Crusader, Irish.
Demokrat, German.
Welshman.
Irish Catholic.
Metropolitan Record, Irish Catholic.

STATE OF NEW YORK.
Telegraph, German, Buffalo.
Demokrat, do. do.
Aurora, do. do.

PHILADELPHIA.
Demokrat, German,
Free Press, do.
Wochenblatt, do.
Herald and Visiter, Irish.
Instructor, do.

PITTSBURG.
Irish Catholic.
Courier, German.
Republikaner, do.
Freiheits, do.
Friedlsfreund do.

BALTIMORE.
Catholic, Irish.

CINCINNATI.
Republikaner, German.
Volksblatt, do.
Volksfreund, do.
Telegraph, Irish.

Israelite, German Hebrew.
Apologist, German.
Deborah, do.
Hockwachter, do.
Wachreitsfreund, do.
Zeitsblatter, do.
Turn Zeitung, do.

TOWNS OF OHIO.
Demokrat, Germ. Bucyrus.
Staats Bote, Germ, Canton.
Botschaffer, do. Circleville.
Germania, Cleveland.
West Bote, Columbus.
Volks Tribune, do.
Botschaffer, Dayton.
Intelligencer, Germ. Sandusky.
Unser Flagg, do. Tiffin.

TOWNS OF PENNSYLVANIA.
Des Brudderblatt, Leipsic.
Volksfreund, Lancaster.
Zeitung, Weisport.
Berichter, Aaronsburg.
Freund, Allentown.
Welt Bobe, do.
Patriot, do.
Republikaner, do.
Freidensbote, do.
Berichter, Bellefont.
Express, Germ. Doylestown.
Demokrat, do. Easton.
Schnellpost, do. Hamburg.
Demokrat, do. Harrisburg.
Bechter, do. do.
Der Hirt, Cuttotown.
Volksfreund, Middleburg.
Votschaffer, Milford Square.
Demokrat, Pottsville.
Am. Republikaner, do.
Adler, Reading.

OUR PRESS GANG.

Liberal Beobachter, Reading.
Der Geist der Leit, do.
Der Neutralist, Shirleysburg.
Freund, Sumnytown.
Amerikaner, Germ., Sunbury.
Gazette, do. York.

WASHINGTON, D. C.
Wochenblatt, German.
Citizen, Irish.

VIRGINIA.
Zeitung, Germ. Wheeling.

KENTUCKY.
Auzeiger, Louisville.

LOUISIANA.
Courier, French, New Orleans.
Gazette, German, do.
Le National, French, do.
Creole, do. do.
Standard, Irish, do.
Le Propagateur, French, do.
La Vigilant, French, Donaldsville.
Le Messenger, do. St. Jamesville.
L'Impartial, do. Vermillionville.
Vis-a-Vis, do. Baton Rouge.
Le Pioneer, do. Napoleonsville.
Le National, Plaquamine.
Gazette, German, New Orleans.

MISSOURI.
Auzeiger, St. Louis.
True Shepherd, Irish, do.

Freund, German, Herman.
Wochenblatt, do. do.
Tribune, German, St. Louis.

ILLINOIS.
Auzeiger, Freeport.
Zeitung, Belleville.
Auzeiger, Peru.

INDIANA.
Volksbote, German, Evansville.

IOWA.
Demokrat, German, Davenport.

WISCONSIN.
Den Norske Amerikaner, Norwegian, Madison.
Demokrat, German, Manitowoc.
See Bote, do. Milwaukie.
Phœnix, do. do.
Zeitung, do. Port Washington.
Republikaner, do. Sheboygen.

TEXAS.
Zeitung, Galveston.

CALIFORNIA.
El Clamor Publico, Spanish, Los Angelos.
Journal, German, San Francisco.
Le Pharo, French, do.
Le Messenger, do. do.
Oriental, Chinese, do.

This array looks formidable enough, and the existence of so many national organs in the United States proves that our foreign population is not so easily assimilated and Amercanised as many of our politicians would pretend.

OPINIONS OF THE FOREIGN PRESS.—The papers whose names are comprised in the foregoing registry are entitled to some credit for *showing their colors*. They are not enemies IN DISGUISE, like the Satanic journals of our Atlantic cities and their pupils in different parts of the country. The Irish and German organs usually speak out their sentiments as distinctly as any lover of plain dealing could require. They often express their contempt for the American people and their dissatisfaction with the laws and institutions of our country. For example, the *Boston Pilot*, (an Irish Catholic organ,)—embraces every opportunity to show its scorn for the "accidental" citizens of this country :—

"The Americans," said the Pilot on one occasion "are a people who love to be humbugged. To address them in a spirit of soberness and truth is perfectly ridiculous. You must tell them that they are the greatest people the world ever saw, the smartest nation in the universe, that they possess combined the virtue, intelligence and industry of all the other races of the earth. The success you meet with in humbugging them will be in a corresponding degree with the thickness of the butter you spread on them," etc.

If these were wholesome, medicinal truths, we certainly would not like to have them administered to us by the students of the *Secreta Monita*, or the runaway slaves of Queen Victoria.

JOHN MITCHELL.—This gentleman is an "exiled Irish patriot," and a very good representative of a numerous class of modern political martyrs. If he had left his country *voluntarily*, his patriotism would have been unquestionable, and if he had not made America the scene of his operations he would have had some claim to the gratitude of our republican citizens.

The truth of some of my preceding remarks is exemplified in the deportment of this Mr. John Mitchell. He is as little satisfied with the condition of our political affairs, as he was with those of Ireland,—and he is no less an agitator and commotionist at Washington than he was on the banks of the Liffy. Almost as soon as he arrived in this country he began to publish a paper and to plunge over head and ears, (that is to say, very deeply indeed,) into American politics. His main effort seemed to be to bring the slave question to a CRISIS; and because the Southerners will not consent to have a grand explosion *on the very day appointed by Mr. Mitchell*,—that excellent republican becomes as wrathful as Pelides and threatens to withdraw from the scene of action, thereby leaving the less resolute explosionists to produce the catastrophe, as well as they can, without his assistance!

This behavior would be surprising indeed, if the actor were not a native of Ireland and a political refugee. These circumstances "season our admiration," and enable us to contemplate such a display of extravagant audacity without wonder and with a *modified* feeling of disgust and indignation.

SECTION V.

THE TREACHERY, "TORYISM," AND ANTI-REPUBLICANISM OF THE AMERICAN PRESS.

Examination of the Third Charge.

EXCUSES.

WISHING to deal liberally and leniently with "Messrs. Editors," and to afford them all possible opportunities for exculpation, I am ready to admit that much of their misconduct is the result of their *intellectual deficiencies*. I concede that there is much more of folly than of knavery in some of their most censurable behavior; and this circumstance may serve, in some measure, to excuse their offenses, or to mitigate the severity of that condemnation to which they would otherwise be liable.

But, on the other hand, let it be considered that *all* villainy is nearly allied to folly, and that many other rogues besides newspaper editors might hope to escape from the castigation of justice if defective rationality or a natural imbecility of intellect could always be offered as an excuse for immoral or criminal actions. Society must be protected against the transgressions of knaves and fools *both;* and when people are sufficiently idiotic or insane to become troublesome to the public, it is just as necessary to place them under restraints as if they were accountable agents and capable of criminal designs.

It signifies but little, therefore, in the present discussion, whether the offenses committed by the press are acts of folly or of villainy, if the public is likely to suffer as much in one case as in the other. If my house has been destroyed by an incendiary, it is a matter of little importance to me whether

¹the deed was performed by a man of weak intellect, who should have been confined in some asylum for imbeciles, or by a scoundrel who deserves to be immured in the penitentiary. The case would be no better for me if the fool or maniac who applied the torch imagined at the time that he was doing a noble and praiseworthy action.

The conductors of the press, in many cases, may be regarded as incendiaries. They consider themselves as the torch-bearers of the public—the intellectual illuminators of the age; but their flambeaux, in general, are less luminous than mischievous, being carried in such a way as to produce very little enlightenment, and very great danger of conflagration. Doubtless some of them intend to do well; and even while their reckless conduct endangers this noble fabric, the American Republic—*domus mansionalis libertatis*—they may persuade themselves that their deeds are virtuous, praiseworthy and patriotic.

But, although this misapprehension on their part may acquit them in the court of conscience, we must not give them a license to do mischief because they may happen to do it by mistake, or under a wrong impression, not having judgment or rationality enough to distinguish between good and evil. The press is a somewhat dangerous instrument, even in the hands of the wise and judicious; but when it is controlled by fools or madmen, the hazard is too great to be permitted, if the security and welfare of the public are objects worthy of consideration.

THE CHARGE.

I have charged the American newspaper press with "*practical* hostility to our republican government, and to all the institutions of freedom." I do not deny that the press, with some exceptions, is *speculatively* patriotic; I do not deny that it discourses very largely, and sometimes quite enthusiastically, on such topics as equal rights, republicanism, popular liberty, and so forth; but I assert that its advocacy of these things is specious and fallacious, and that, in relation to all such matters, its *practice* is diametrically opposed to its preaching.

That very POWER, which the journalists boast of, proves that they are not the friends of popular liberty and equal rights. According to the testimony of Mr. Ingersol, and many others, these newspaper men are usurpers and despots; they themselves acknowledge that they control the ballot-box, the legislative halls, and the courts of justice. Can usurpers and despots be the friends and sincere advocates of popular liberty? Can this self-constituted quill-driving oligarchy, which assumes a control over all the functions of our government, and thus overrules the legitimate authority of the people, can it pretend to array itself on the side of republicanism or genuine democracy?

But with the mere *inconsistencies* of newspaper editors I have nothing to do at the present time. The object of this book is to point out abuses which affect the interests of the public. I have no present concern with the private or public *opinions* of the quill-drivers, and I feel under no obligation to examine all the disagreements which may appear between the conduct and the creeds of these gentlemen. I undertake to *describe* their conduct—not to account for it. They may be canting hypocrites or disguised traitors to the cause of freedom, and they may be real aristocrats or monarchists in the penetralia of their own hearts; or they may belong to that numerous class of weak people who *sincerely* advocate one thing and practice another; or they may be too crazy or idiotic to have a settled belief in any thing, or to know when their deeds are at variance with their professions.

I am not bound by the duties I have assumed, to decide whether a majority of our journalists belongs to one of these classes or to another. But, lest the reader should be curious enough to perplex himself with that question, I offer a few suggestions which may help him to escape from the difficulty.

REAL TRAITORS.

My candid opinion is, that many of our newspaper men are

really hostile to republican institutions, and that their antagonism is the result of cool deliberation and a well-defined purpose. This opinion is much strengthened by the facts which have been exhibited in the preceding Section. When we become aware that our newspapers are controlled, in a great measure, by *foreigners*, we may easily conjecture that these publications are, to a high degree, anti-republican in spirit and practice.

I have hinted before that I have no faith in the republicanism of our alien editors ; no, not even in the republicanism of those who have been traitors and rebels to the monarchies and despotisms of the Old World. It is quite possible that a rebel may be a rascal, and the same man who has plotted treason against a tyrannical government may attempt similar mischief against institutions of a very different character. The same incendiary who has fired the Corinthian palace of monarchy may be tempted to apply his torch to the Doric temple of freedom.

Among the assassins, or executioners of Julius Cæsar, there was but one man, perhaps, who was not a greater scoundrel than Cæsar himself. And, among those men who have been expelled from the different nations of Europe for their hostility to the ruling powers, there may be greater rogues and tyrants, *in embryo*, than the corrupt and despotic rulers whom they were so anxious to depose. We Americans, therefore, ought not to be very well pleased, when the political refugees of Europe come to our country to take charge of our public journals and to direct the current of popular opinion.

We want no lessons in republicanism from mendicious or mendacious Scotchmen, blundering Hibernians, and addle-headed Germans. The science of free government is eminently rational, and reasonable men alone can expound its principles or even comprehend them. I do not deny that many persons of transatlantic birth have all the capacity that is required to understand the true policy of our republic ; but I emphatically deny that *such Europeans as are most likely to favor us with their company* are qualified, in the least degree, to instruct us in the duties of citizenship, or to take any prominent part in the management of our national concerns.

Many of our newspaper conductors,—the foreign ones especially,—are evidently not acquainted even with the *rudiments* of our political system. Or, if they do understand the principles of our government, they are the more inexcusable for their constant endeavors to discredit and pervert them.

THE GRAND MISTAKE.

With the newspaper press in general it appears to be an admitted fact that the mob and the people are identical. No discrimination is made between *plebs* and *populus;* and I comprehend that much of the trouble which afflicts this nation, and much of the danger which threatens it, originate in this very remarkable error. I have always cherished the belief that a great majority of the *American* people have none of the characteristics of a MOB, though the contrary is often made to appear by the misconceptions and misrepresentations of the public journals. If the *mob* is predominant in this country, the Republic has ceased to exist—for mob-rule is either anarchy or despotism.

The general deportment of the newspaper press is a practical acknowledgment of mob-rule; and it appears to be the constant effort of journalism to establish that sort of government in this country. Many of the doctrines of the pseudo-democratic press are pre-eminently mobbish, and, in the same degree, *anti-republican.*

Of all misnomers, the term " Democratic party," as applied to the faction which now bears that name, is the most preposterous. The *Ochlocratic* party would be a far more suitable designation. Modern Democracy is no more like the Democracy of JEFFERSON than corrupt Romanism is like apostolic Christianity. So far from recognizing the right of the people to govern, this pernicious faction has actually contrived to keep all the power of the country in the hands of a scrubby minority, —*alias,* a MOB. It has elected several presidents by over-ruling the will of the great majority and transferring the right of choice from the American public to a few corrupt and villainous politicians. A Democratic caucus or convention may be called a *mob* with some propriety, but I do not believe that any such body, in its character or actions, can fairly represent the American people.

The political caucus, or convention system, so strongly recommended and supported by the newspaper press, is altogether an anti-republican contrivance. The plan originated in ancient Rome, after the death of Caligula, when a military caucus, called the Prætorian guards, disposed of the principal offices in the State by putting them up at auction and selling them to the highest bidder.

DETESTABLE DOCTRINE.

Another anti-republican trick of the newspapers is the attempt to extinguish every feeling of *patriotism* in the American bosom. The doctrine that our country is every man's country is exceedingly well calculated to answer this purpose; and when the American citizen is persuaded that he has no *peculiar* ties to the land of his birth, he is less disposed to love and cherish its institutions. The sad effects of these newspaper teachings are seen every day. Our best citizens, having learned from their typographical oracles that they have no country to care for, become, in some measure, the indifferent spectators of public affairs, while the only active politicians are corrupt demagogues, grog-sellers and the lowest order of vagabonds. The people are staved off the course and the track is left in undisputed possession of the Mob!

The *Washington Union*, which is presumed to be the principal organ of Mr. Buchanan's administration, lately asserted that "the only treason which an American citizen can commit is treason to his PARTY!" This is a virtual declaration that the American is under no obligations of duty or gratitude to his country. Patriotism is a virtue which he is not expected to possess; but in lieu thereof, he is bound to acknowledge his allegiance and subjection to a clique of bad men who are supposed to represent his "party." A more detestable doctrine could not be preached, even by the organs of the misnomered "Democracy;" and the man who adopts such a rule of conduct is a more abject slave than any subject of the czar or sultan.

However, this doctrine is a natural offshoot of the favorite newspaper theory that the American soil is the common inheritance of the whole human race, and that BIRTH-RIGHT is a mere "accidental" circumstance, of little or no importance.

COMMOTION MAKERS.

The anti-republican proclivities of the newspaper press are likewise exemplified in the continued efforts of the public journals to produce popular excitements and commotions. An excitable or impulsive people is not qualified for self-government, for such a population is easily led into those excesses which are destructive to all rational liberty. By the efforts of our senseless or treacherous journals, the American public is often worked up to an exhibition of ridiculous enthusiasm, which, in some cases, closely approximates to insanity. Causeless excitement is one of the characteristics of a mob; but the "sovereign people" of America can never appear to less advantage than when they fall into fantastical or maniacal exstacies.

Allow me to remark, my dear countrymen, that I have often blushed for the follies which you have been impelled to commit by the gassy *afflatus* of journalism. That *afflatus*, by the way, is nothing like the "*afflatus ventorum benignus*" mentioned by Pliny, or that to which Cicero refers when he says, "*Nemo vir magnus sine afflatu aliquo divino unquam fuit.*" The journalistic *afflatus* is a pestilential blast—a vaporous, miasmatic exhalation—which produces terribly afflictive epidemics, fevers of a very alarming type, which, at various times, have swept over the whole area of our beloved country. For example, we have had the Fanny Elssler fever, the Jenny

Lind fever, the Dickens fever, the Irish Repeal fever, the Dr. Kane fever, and, latterly, the Atlantic Cable fever; which last, if we may judge from present appearances, is likely to end in a chill of disappointment.

While the Elssler fever was at its climax in Baltimore, some of the infected citizens of that place perpetrated an act of foolery which deserves to be commemorated by *another monument*. They intercepted the "divine Fanny" in the street, took the horses from her carriage, and ambitiously usurped the places of those more intelligent and respectable animals. What a spectacle! We are told that Elssler herself was overwhelmed with astonishment, and uttered that exclamation which has since become proverbial: "Mein Gott, wot a peebles!" The act of indecorum was, indeed, enough to astonish a DANCING GIRL.

But these countrymen of Washington—these citizens of the "model republic"—could never have acted such an absurd part if they had not been the victims of that intellectual malaria—that intoxicating vapor, which a corrupt newspaper press has diffused through the atmosphere of this land of freedom.

Let us hope that our countrymen are not constitutionally disposed to commit such a folly as man-worship, or woman-worship either; nevertheless, the stimulations of journalism have often incited the "Sons of Liberty" to commit acts of idolatry of which no sensible Mongul or Hindoo could possibly have been guilty. We have seen General Jackson idolized; and we have heard, very recently, some talk of *erecting statues* in honor of an estimable but unfortunate naval commander, who made an unsuccessful voyage to the polar regions!

The newspapers often urge our fellow-citizens to make such extravagant demonstrations of affection and gratitude to public benefactors; but it will generally be found that the journalists have some latent designs—some sordid, selfish and mischievous purpose of their own, when they set up a living effigy of human greatness, and call on the people to prostrate themselves before that idol, who is superior, perhaps, in scarcely any respect, to the basest and most insignificant of his worshipers.

All impulsive action is dangerous in republics or democracies. Even when we honor or reward the services of those men who have been the unquestionable benefactors of the nation, we should prove that we are guided by reason and a sense of justice and not by a wild and passionate enthusiasm, which is often as brief in its duration as it is sudden and violent in its action.

It is better and much safer always for republics to be discreetly ungrateful, than rashly and extravagantly remunerative.

In all cases, when the newspapers attempt to "get up an excitement," you may justly suspect, my fellow-citizens, that they are about to fool you, "to the top of your bent." When they require you to become ecstatic in your admiration of any particular man or woman, you may safely conclude that the *papier-mache* idol is about as suitable for adoration as one of your mantel ornaments, or any other toy composed of similar material. True merit or genuine greatness is seldom appreciated by newspaper editors, and if they are compelled to acknowledge it, they do so with frigid reluctance. Do not forget, my countrymen, how you compromised the dignity of manhood and the august character of American sovereigns, by paying extravagant attentions to that overrated singing damsel, Jenny Lind, and that pleasant but superficial tale-writer, Charles Dickens. You cannot easily forget how soon your infatuation on these occasions was followed by shame and repentance. But, alas! the most painful conviction of one error of this kind does not prevent you from committing another. Observe, my misguided compatriots, that your conduct will often discredit your national character while you submit yourselves to the direction of the foreign vagabonds, and other interested excitement-mongers, who have the principal management of your newspaper press.

REVIEW OF THE SUBJECT.

Now let us recapitulate: The American newspapers are practically hostile to republicanism and rational liberty, because—

1. They usurp power to which they are not entitled by the constitution and laws of the country.

2. They endeavor to establish the dominion of the mob in opposition to the rights of the people, and they effect their purpose by giving undue ascendance to villainous minorities.

3. They labor, and not unsuccessfully, to suppress that virtuous *love of country* which is the vital principle of all republican governments.

4. They endeavor to cultivate an excitable disposition among the people—a disposition which often leads the masses to acts of turbulence and outrage—to rebellious or revolutionary movements—to man-worship and other extravagant manifestations of popular feeling—all of which are discreditable and dangerous to the institutions of freedom.

NEWSPAPERS OPPOSED TO THEIR OWN LIBERTY.

My third charge against the newspaper press will admit of various other specifications; but the exuberance of my subject makes it necessary for me to be concise. However, there is one point the mention of which I cannot well afford to omit; and I warn my readers that I am about to make a declaration which may surprise some of them; for nothing, at the first glance, could appear to be more paradoxical.

The newspapers of America are violently opposed to the "LIBERTY OF THE PRESS!"

> "Quoth Hudibras, 'Make that appear,
> And I shall credit whatsoe'er
> You please to advance.'"

Truly, if it can be shown that the journals endeavor, with all their ability, to restrict their own liberty, you may argue, *a fortiori*, that they are the active enemies of free institutions in general. Well, my dear friends, the proofs are abundant enough; but, to economize time and space, let us select a few of them for present consideration.

In the first place, I appeal, Messrs. Editors, to your own experience. Have not some of you been flogged by your brethren of the press for publishing facts and opinions which you believed it to be your privilege and duty to make known to the public? I ask you if many of you have not been caned and kicked by others of your profession, until, to borrow Butler's idea, you could discriminate instantaneously, by the sense of touch, between the several kinds of wood and leather which are used in the manufacture of boots and cudgels? And I ask you if your corporal sufferings have not been often induced by your zealous efforts to diffuse useful knowledge among your fellow-citizens? Mr. Bennett, of the *New York Herald*, to give one example among many, was severely whipped for conscientiously endeavoring to make the sovereign people better acquainted with the moral and political character of Colonel Webb of the *New York Courier and Enquirer*. Do not many of the duels, street fights, and assassinations which take place among editors originate in the efforts of some of them to punish others for publishing unpalatable truths, even when they are such truths as every editor, in a free country, ought to be allowed to publish?

Now, does it not occur to you, Messrs. Scribes, that when you flog, kick, or shoot each other for any legally justifiable publication made in a newspaper, you prove your active hostility to the liberty of the press?

The records of our courts will show that more *libel suits* are instituted by newspaper men than by any other class of people; and they often prosecute each other on this score when they have no reasonable cause of complaint. Those journalists who are most apt to abuse their own powers, the most libellous and remorseless scoundrels of the whole gang, are often the most spitefully vindictive when they themselves become the objects of attack. Possibly I may have occasion, in another place, to give several examples of this kind. Moreover, the "Gentlemen of the Press" often endeavor to stir up *popular indignation* against each other, and those very common occurrences, the mobbings of printing-offices, are often brought about by the efforts of newspaper men to punish each other for claiming and exercising the rights of American citizens, and practically asserting "the liberty of the press."

SUPPLEMENTARY ILLUSTRATIONS.

SILLY AND STUPID JOURNALISTS.

Some allusion is made, near the beginning of this Section, to the "intellectual deficiencies" of editors. In another part of this work it is intimated that many members of the "Press Gang," like the old men of Juvenal, have a "plentiful lack of wisdom." Lest these opinions should be called singular and heretical, I will quote several authorities, not so much to prove that my views of this subject are correct, as to show that they are *not original.*

"Is it possible," asked the *Edinburg Review*, with reference to the intellectual character of some of our leading newspapers, "is it possible that any well educated man in America can read these journals with respect?"

Captain Hamilton, a traveler of some celebrity, says: "I read newspapers from all parts of the United States, in order to form a fair estimate of their merit, and found them utterly contemptible in point of talent."

Similar opinions are expressed by De Tocqueville, the French political philosopher, and many others who have crossed the Atlantic to inspect the social and political affairs of this republic. But these are European opinions. "They come from people who are prejudiced against the institutions of our country." Be it remembered, however, that the most successful and prominent journalism of this country, viz., the "*Satanic Press,*" is not an *American* institution. Any imputatation against it, therefore, is no offense to our nationality.

But those English and French opinions have had abundance of American corroboration, though the tyranny of the press in this country makes it inconvenient and somewhat hazardous for American freemen to offer an unbiased opinion on the subject.

James Fennimore Cooper, our distinguished novelist, certifies that the intellectual, as well as the moral character of the American press, is "villainously low."

"Look around you," says the Boston News,—"and see a thousand successful proofs that no excellence or acquirement, moral or intellectual, is requisite to conduct a press. The more defective an editor is, the better he succeeds. We could give a thousand instances."

"Many editors," says Mr. James Gordon Bennett, "are unfitted by nature and want of capacity to come to a right conclusion on any subject. They pervert every public event from its proper hue and coloring." See *Life of Bennett*, p. 204.

MANUFACTURE OF "LEADERS."—The leading articles of the daily papers sometimes exhibit signs of ability and erudition, but these appearances are generally fallacious. Our ex-shoemaker editors can produce such articles by the score or dozen, merely by re-vamping and heel-tapping paragraphs, cut from European papers or purloined from Dictionaries of the Arts and Sciences. Some of the blunders made in transcribing are excessively ludicrous; but as these articles are but little read, and as the students of newspaper literature, in general, are not very astute critics, the errors of the "principal editor" usually go undetected. It is just as easy to prepare second-hand "leaders" as it is to preach second-hand sermons.

The habit of pilfering from European journals, which prevails to a great extent among our "leader"-writers, will help to account for the fact that many of our journalists seem to devote more attention to the affairs of Europe than to those of our own country. Many anti-republican sentiments are stolen from the foreign prints and repeated in this country by editors who, perhaps, have not sense enough to discover the *drift* of the plundered merchandise. Hence I have charitably supposed that some of the apparent treachery or toryism of our editors may be ascribed to their want of wisdom or common sense. When it is necessary to believe that they are either fools or scoundrels, the supposition of their folly is the best compliment that we can pay to their integrity of purpose.

EXCITEMENT BREEDERS.—Popular excitement is the element in whose "ennobling stir" the journalist feels himself exalted. Whatever disturbs the tranquillity of the public increases the emoluments of the press and magnifies the importance of the editor. To stimulate the rage of factions,—to promote the warfare of races,—to exacerbate sectional jealousies, to inflame and infuriate the passions of the rabble ;—in short, to produce an agitation of some kind, without any regard to the consequences, is now the obvious design,—the AVOWED purpose, of some of our most distinguished, successful and influential journalists.

In this condition of things, the good people of America need not strain their eyes with staring across the Atlantic to discover *the worst enemies of the Republic.*

A CONSCIENTIOUS SECEDER.—It is mentioned in the Life of James Gordon Bennett, "written by a New York Journalist," that an editor in South Carolina sold his paper and seceded from journalism, giving the following explanation of his conduct :—"As a reason for not entering into the violence of party spirit which now exists, I must express my entire disapprobation of the present state of the *American Press*, and my firm belief that, unless a change be effected, it is destined, at no distant period, so totally to overthrow our splendid political fabric, that not one stone will be left on another."

The *name* of this wise and good editor is not mentioned by the "New York Journalist," who devotes five hundred pages to the glorification of James Gordon Bennett!

SECTION VI.

VILLAINOUS DECEPTIONS PRACTICED BY THE NEWSPAPERS.

Examination of the Fourth Charge.

THE specifications of this charge are (to borrow the phraseology of auctioneers' advertisements) "too numerous to mention." *Every* subject discussed in the newspapers is mystified or misrepresented in proportion to the importance which is attached to it by the gentlemen of the press.

EXAMPLE.—THE NEGRO QUESTION.

To exemplify this fact let us take up the *pro-and-anti-slavery agitation*, which appears, at times, to throw the whole nation into convulsions. If you have any philosophic phlegm in your constitution, my good reader, I invite you to join with me in a cool investigation of this matter; and if we can contrive to forget all the information concerning it which we have derived from the newspapers, it is possible that we may begin to understand it.

ORIGIN OF THE EXCITEMENT.

A very little examination will convince us, I think, that all the popular irritation, the bitter animosities, and the mutual aggressions which have attended this unhappy feud between the advocates and the opponents of negro slavery, may be traced to the treasonable operations of newspaper editors and their coadjutors—to wit, certain harmonial philosophers, "strong-minded women," atheistical fanatics, and rascally politicians.

Some of us who are not very old may remember a time when there was little or no abolition excitement in this country. Persons who held opposite opinions on the subject of negro slavery could argue as coolly on that subject as on any other. The rice and cotton growers themselves could listen with a degree of equanimity when their favorite "institution" was condemned. Some of our most eminent statesmen—Jefferson and Clay for example—expressed opinions adverse to slavery, and their popularity in the South was but little affected by this circumstance. An abolition journal was established in my native State, which lies on the sunniest side of Mason & Dixon's line; and this journal was not only tolerated by the slave-holding population, but was pretty well encouraged and supported.

These facts, if you recognize them as such, may convince you that the American people once thought and felt on this subject very differently from what they do at present. How do you account for this remarkable change? "Oh, it was produced by the abolition excitement, of course." This sentence in quotations I suppose to be *your* answer. It is a very common answer to the question which I have just proposed.

Yes, my learned Theban, you have *partly* explained the cause of that political thunder whose astounding detonations have almost frightened the genius of American liberty into hysterics. That thunder *was* produced by a certain mysterious agent which you may call abolition electricity. This explanation, as far as it goes, is well enough; but allow me to tax your philosophical profundity a little further. Tell me, if you can, what generated so much of that electricity? What gave it concentration and fulminating power? What gave it "the rage to roar and the strength to fly?" What armed it with the ability to scorch and burn, and to shake the institutions of freedom to their very foundations?

Abolitionism had existed for many years in a fœtus-like or undeveloped condition. The first American apostles of this "movement" (unluckily for the welfare of the cause) were a few half-crazy old women, some of whom wore pantaloons, and assumed masculine designations; but their fussy anility shone through every disguise. These people held occasional meetings, very thinly attended, in the New England towns. Their orators in petticoats and pantaloons seemed disposed to turn the whole world topsy-turvy. Their principal object of denunciation was negro slavery; but, from that target, their arrows often glanced at the constitution and laws of the United States, the memory of our revolutionary patriots, the institutions of civilized society, the marriage contract, the Christian religion, etc. Their frantic enthusiasm on all subjects was noticed chiefly for the purpose of ridicule. Their seditious, immoral, impious, and blood-thirsty clamors, were excused on the score of their supposed insanity.

Nobody imagined that these wretched lunatics would ever have the ability to do much mischief, as the sphere of their operations was confined chiefly to the "Down East" villages, where GAS of all kinds is too much diffused to be dangerously explosive. But, on some unlucky day, certain excitement-mongers discovered that very good political capital, or electioneering material, might be made of anti-slavery gas; and, immediately after this discovery, newspaper organs devoted to the propagation of abolition principles, were established in different parts of the Eastern and Middle States.

Prominent among these "organs" was the *New York Tribune*, the principal editor of which was Mr. Horace Greeley, whose advocacy of all the fantastical theories of the day had procured for him the ironical *sobriquet* of "The Philosopher." When Greeley began to publish the *Tribune*, he had reached that age, at which, according to Dr. Young, "man begins to suspect that he is a fool;" but it is probable that Horace was never diffident enough to entertain any suspicions of the kind; and his successful maneuvering may lead others to conjecture that folly was worn by him merely as an overcoat or outside wrapper. Nevertheless, there is some truth in that proverbial philosophy which represents fools as the special favorites of fortune. Greeley's *Tribune* soon became the most successful paper in the United States, and the most unscrupulous and mischievous.

THE AGITATION BEGINS.

At the time when Greeley and his colaborers of the abolition press began to "get up an agitation," the slavery question was, comparatively speaking, a matter of very little national importance. In fact, it might scarcely be called a *question* at all. Few reflective men denied that negro slavery was one of America's greatest afflictions, and the expediency of abolishing it gradually, and with suitable precautions, was scarcely a subject of debate. Indeed, the process of abolition had commenced, and the advance of negro emancipation was as rapid as any judicious patriot or philanthropist could desire. Maryland, Virginia, Kentucky, and several other slave states, were almost prepared for the change; and among the Southern people in general the opinion began to prevail that negro slaves are scarcely worth their keeping, as their maintenance commonly exhausts the soil and impoverishes their owners.

The condition of America, at the time to which we refer, resembled that of a patient who is slowly recovering from some chronic disease. The kindly operation of natural causes is effecting a cure, and the evident convalescence of the sufferer relieves the anxiety of surrounding friends. But, alas! the doctor comes in at this moment,—the potion is administered,—the curative operations of nature are interrupted,—a relapse takes place, and the state of the invalid is more hopeless than ever. Thus, by the ignorant meddling of those miserable quacks, the abolitionists, the sickness of poor Columbia has been prolonged and exacerbated. Instead of permitting their victim to recover in an easy and natural way, these empirical rascals,—on pretense of hastening the cure,—must apply their blisters, pour in their fiery Thompsonian draughts, and torment their victim with stimulating injections!

PROGRESS OF THE MISCHIEF.

By grossly misrepresenting the state of popular feeling in the East and North, the abolition newspapers contrived to excite the hostility and intense hatred of the people of the South. The slaveholders were made to believe that the people of the Free States were their most bitter and violent enemies. The tone of the Abolition press convinced the Southerners that their distant countrymen wished for nothing more earnestly than *immediate* abolition; and that, to effect this object, they were ready to incite the slaves to insurrection—to supply them with arms and ammunition, and to produce, on the soil of republican America, a re-enactment of all the horrors of St. Domingo.

THE SOUTH EXCITED.

These vile misrepresentations of the abolition prints were enough to excite the fears and the indignation of the South. Angry and intemperate responses were made by the presses and stump-orators of the Slave States; and thus the seeds of civil war were sown by a few scribbling and spouting enthusiasts, who,—call them fools, philosophers, philanthropists, or what you will,—have proved, in effect, to be the worst of traitors—the most mischievous of all incendiaries.

I assert that all the frightful turmoil, to which reference has just been made, was produced by the efforts of newspaper-men and others to manufacture political capital, and to open a new field for the operations of corrupt journalists and unprincipled demagogues. At the time when the maggots of Abolitionism began to bestir themselves, there was no cause or pretense for a slavery agitation in this country. The evil, as I have mentioned above, was gradually correcting itself, and the wisest statesmen perceived—what experience has since proved to be the fact—that any attempt to *hasten* the liberation of the negroes would certainly act in a contrary direction.

The slaveholders of America were not proper objects of condemnation; for, admitting that slavery is a moral wrong as well as a national affliction, our contemporary fellow-citizens of the Southern States are not accountable for the existence of that wrong, (for it did not originate with them), nor can they be justly required to expose themselves to great inconvenience and danger by immediately suppressing a bad institution, which was forced upon them by the folly and selfishness of a preceding generation.

On the principle that it is allowable to choose the lesser of two evils, our countrymen of the South are morally justifiable in retaining the institution of slavery for a time. Were they to liberate all their negroes instantaneously, they would produce evils of far greater magnitude—evils far more afflictive to the whole nation than slavery itself. The negro slaves of the South, if liberated, would not, without some preparation, be qualified for admission to the rights of citizenship, nor would they even be fitted to reside among freemen on any terms of equality. If it is proposed to give them personal liberty, and to keep them still in a state of political subjection, I cannot see that their condition will be much improved by that kind of emancipation, or that the justice and philanthropy of the white man will be more conspicuous than they are at present. On the score of *natural equity*, a free negro, born in the United States, has a much better right to vote at our elections, and to hold governmental offices, than any "adopted citizen." If you are not prepared to do Sambo full justice, (which, indeed, you could not do at the present time without very great sacrifices), do not be unwise enough to call on your brethren of the South to place him in a position where he might demand and insist on having those natural rights which you are not willing to allow him. What, indeed, could be more inexpedient, at the present time, than to infuse thousands and myriads of emancipated slaves among a population which is already debased and corrupted to the last degree by a copious and incessant importation of political bondsmen, rogues and vagabonds, from every nation of Europe?

EFFECTS OF NEGRO EMANCIPATION.

I am inclined to believe that if the people of the Southern

States were disposed to execute terrible vengeance on their northern opponents, they could not do so more effectually than by a sudden abolition of slavery. The inevitable consequence would be a rush of the colored population to the North—for liberated negroes move in that direction as naturally as Scotchmen are supposed to move southward. In a very short time, I presume, the sympathizing friends of the African would find the constant influx of this sable tide somewhat inconvenient; for these dark-complexioned people—and especially such of them as have once been slaves—have certain peculiarities which prevent them from being desirable neighbors or acceptable citizens.

I once asked a very noisy Abolitionist if he really wished for the immediate manumission of all the southern slaves. After a little hesitation, he honestly confessed that nothing could be more undesirable! If all of the slavery agitators were equally reflective and candid, they would probably make the same confession. What excuse then, in Heaven's name, can they offer for disturbing the peace of the American public with their everlasting racket? They must have discovered, many years ago, that they themselves have riveted the chains of the Ethiop and armed his oppressors with a whip of scorpions. The cause of African emancipation has been made to relapse fifty years at least by the ill-advised meddling of fanatical abolitionists, editorial fools, (or "philosophers,") and scurvy politicians.

I have been striving to convince you that the subject of southern slavery never stood in any need of northern tinkering. The white population of the South were the chief sufferers by their peculiar institution. They had begun to be aware of this fact, and the natural consequence was, that our great national curse was in a fair way to be eradicated by the slaveholders themselves. It was principally their own affair, and the management of it should have been left in their own hands. The Southerners found that they were afflicted with a scirrhous ulcer, they had begun to apply the most suitable remedies, when the northern quacks rushed in and insisted on tearing out the diseased flesh with red-hot pincers! Of course this unsolicited and impertinent interference met with an indignant repulse.

APPLICATION.

In our *Fourth Charge*, the Newspaper Press is made accountable for a "systematic and continuous effort to mislead the judgement of the public in relation to matters of the greatest national importance." The subject of negro slavery is introduced to illustrate this charge. It is a subject which has been "systematically and continuously" misrepresented by the journals; and they have succeeded in giving it a fictitious importance which it did not originally possess. I assert that the African race and its destiny are entitled to much less consideration than the fate of this Republic, the welfare of the American people, and the progress of human liberty in every part of the world. And yet our newspaper-men and many of our statesmen, (alas!) are endeavoring to make us believe that the "nigger question" is the principal subject, if not the *only one*, that deserves our notice.

In order to attempt an impossible act of justice to the Africans, we are advised to provoke an internecine war, to dismember our national confederacy, to construct two antagonistical governments on the ruins of this prosperous republic, to separate the American people into two nations already prepared to be deadly enemies; and by an act of national suicide, to furnish the opponents of popular liberty, throughout the world, with an unanswerable argument, a demonstrative example, to prove that republican institutions cannot be sustained, even in the most favorable circumstances.

CUI BONO?

And when all these sacrifices have been made, what will be the condition of Sambo himself, for whose particular benefit so much has been done and suffered? The results of the great fracas, as far as the negro is concerned, will probably be to prolong the date of "chattel slavery" for two or three centuries to come, and to extend its area from the shores of Chesapeake Bay to Cape Horn!

ENTOMOLOGICAL COMPARISON.

I have heard that there is a singularly mischievous worm, or some minute insect, in the navigable waters near which the American city called Annapolis is situated This animalcule, which is scarcely visible to the naked eye, perforates the bottoms of vessels, even when they are defended by copper sheathing, and the port, on this account, is but little frequented by mariners. The operations of these tiny creatures have been ruinous to the commerce and prosperity of a city. Our Slavery Question agitators are worms of a similar kind; though apparently feeble, insignificant and contemptible, they have given proof of their ability to do immense damage, and our "ship of state" may be sunk at last by their indefatigable efforts.

The public mind must be in a very unhealthy state of excitability when the intemperate disputes of Northern fanatics and Southern "fire-eaters" can produce such violent national spasms as those we have lately witnessed.

> "Oft from the follies of a few
> A land's calamities have sprung.
> Oh, be forbearing, and eschew
> The froward heart and reckless tongue,
> Check ye the despicable fray;—
> A paltry ape may fire the train,
> But desolation's course to stay
> Wisdom and skill may toil in vain."
>
> *American Sibyl.*

AFRICAN FEVER.

It was hinted above that the "African Fever" which afflicts poor Columbia might have proved a comparatively harmless disease if it had been judiciously treated. But the aspect of the case has been very much altered for the worse. The journalists and the other agitators have aggravated the malady until they have succeeded in giving it a malignant character and a fatal tendency. They have forced the North and the South both into positions from which it may be difficult for either to recede with honor and safety. They have made it *necessary* for the slaveholders to enlarge their territory; and this will certainly be done, in spite of all opposition. The agitators have also produced a factitious necessity for such a party as that which is called the Black Republican, —to operate as a check on the expansion of the slave-holding domains. Thus two violent and irreconcilable factions have been instituted, each faction having an apparent basis of reason and justice, though both factions, (paradoxically enough,) owe their existence to an unreasonable and unjust parentage.

The dispute between these factions threatens to be interminable, and God alone knows to what extremities that dispute will be carried. Were I disposed to be a "prophet of plagues," I might easily display a long catalogue of probable calamities which this causeless and bootless quarrel may inflict on our posterity, "even unto the third and fourth generations." To my perceptions, there is something disgustingly bestial in that profound indifference which too many Americans of the present day manifest for all that concerns the peace and happiness of our successors on this stage of existence. Immersed in the sordid pursuit of present objects, we are unmindful of the debt of gratitude which we owe to the Past, and, with still greater culpability, we forget our sacred obligations to the Future

INCANTATIONS.

Writers on magic tell us that it is a comparatively easy task for the necromancer to call up a powerful and malignant demon; but to *dismiss* the fiend, when you have done with him, is the grand difficulty. My countrymen,—you have allowed your wizards, (your typographical ones,) to evoke the potent and infuriated spirit of civil discord. He has obeyed the summons ;—but neither your science nor that of your journalistic magi can send him back to his sulphurous habitation. Some wisdom superior to your own must now be invoked to deliver you from the infestation of your diabolical enemy.

SUPPLEMENTARY ILLUSTRATIONS.

GREELEY'S HISTORY.—Horace Greeley, one of the prime movers in the Abolition disturbance, is a native of Amherst in the State of New Hampshire. He was born on the third day of February, 1811. The precocity of his genius is duly celebrated by his biographers. In his early youth he worked on his father's farm, but afterward became one of the junior assistants in a saw-mill. At the age of fifteen, he began to learn the printing business, in the office of the *Northern Spectator*, a weekly paper published in Rutland County, Vermont. In 1830, (says one of his biographers,) "he was known to fame only as a flaxen-haired journeyman printer, not particularly promising in talent." In 1831, he removed to the city of New York, which city has been his place of residence up to the present time. In 1834, he established a weekly paper, called the "*New Yorker*," which was published for seven years, and, at one time, "reached a circulation of nine thousand." In 1841, Mr. Greeley formed a co-partnership with Thomas McElrath, a lawyer of New York, and began to publish the *Tribune*.

His qualifications as a journalist are thus described by one of his admirers :—"Able and skillful as a logician, he is yet emphatically a *theorist* in the most speculative sense of the word. In the chair editorial, he is the powerful exponent of MOST ABSURD THEORIES, but his *intentions* are always honest."

In a letter to Mr. Bonner, publisher of the New York Ledger,—Mr. Greeley, while defending himself against the charge of writing *poetry*, speaks for himself as follows :—

"I have been accused of all possible, and of some *impossible*, offenses against good morals, good taste, and the common weal; I have been branded as an *aristocrat*, a *communist*, an *infidel*, a *hypocrite*, a *demagogue*, a *disunionist*, a *traitor*, a *corruptionist*, etc., etc., but I cannot remember that any one has flung in my face my youthful transgressions in the way of rhyme."

I cheerfully acquit Mr. Greeley of the charge of writing *poetry;* and if he should ever undertake to defend himself against the OTHER charges, I hope the public will hear him with patience, and judge him with candor and charity.

GENERAL HOUSTON *v.* HORACE GREELEY.—The Washington Union avers that General Houston, in one of his speeches made just before the last presidential election, gave the following description of the New York philosopher:

"Horace is a most remarkable man: he is the *whitest* man in the world. His skin is milk-white. His hair is white, and thin and scattering. He wears a white hat and a white coat; and I must be permitted to give it to you as my candid opinion that his liver is of the same color."

GREELEY'S AMIABLE ECCENTRICITIES.—A newspaper correspondent, who appears to be an enthusiastic admirer of Mr. Greeley, writes as follows:

"Greeley seeks no society, and has none except that of persons who desire to make something out of him. He is the most good-natured, innocent person in the world. All grades of society are alike to him. He will stop and converse with the congressman and the carman alike. His sympathies are with every body. He is not more careless in his dress than in his habits. Money is no object with him. If he goes to a restaurant to dine, he puts down a bill to pay for his meal and never looks at the change. It is said that he is often cheated with counterfeit notes by persons who know his carelessness and unconcern in such matters."

WILLIAM LLOYD GARRISON.—This man is supposed to be

the father, or one of the fathers, of political abolitionism. I was once induced by curiosity to hear a lecture delivered by him in Philadelphia. The subject of his discourse, as announced in the papers, was Southern Slavery; but with that theme he contrived to associate a general review of *religious creeds*, each of which he proposed to subject to a new rule of valuation, by asking the business-like question, "Will it pay?" By means of this test, he appeared to have satisfied himself that all the forms of Christianity were worthless. To exemplify the vanity of religious professions, he told us that he himself had once been a member of the Baptist Church, and was then supposed to be a sincere Christian; but "that was all a mistake." He had never been a believer, and his connection with the church was continued just long enough "to see if it would pay."

I believe that Garrison published an Abolition paper in Baltimore about the year 1826, and this was probably the first attempt to establish an anti-slavery organ in the United States.

THE APOSTLES OF ABOLITION.—I never heard an abolition speech, and never read an abolition paper, which did not contain something offensive to religion, patriotism and good morals. This circumstance is enough, *per se*, to convince me that the present abolition movement is unhallowed, and that it cannot effect any good object. There is a certain class of violent reformers and pseudo-philanthropists; who seem to doubt whether Divine Omnipotence could govern the world without *their* assistance, and such people are apt enough to suppose that they themselves can effect any beneficial change in human affairs without the help or approbation of Almighty God.

Now, it is my happiness to believe that every good work which is done on earth has its origin in Heaven. When it suits the purposes of Divine wisdom to authorize any change in the condition of our species, or of any particular race, such a change is made *possible*, and suitable agents are provided for the execution of the work. When Deity wills that the African slave shall be liberated, a way will be opened for the accomplishment of that merciful dispensation, and the obstacles, which are now insurmountable, will be removed.

It is equally certain that the *human instruments* employed to effect this sacred purpose will be such as infinite wisdom and supernal goodness would select for such a work. The evangelists of a GOOD CAUSE are not self-accused hypocrites, avowed atheists, godless and graceless "philosophers," promoters of strife and hatred among men, clamorers for the effusion of innocent blood, boastful contrivers of treason, and shameless enunciators of blasphemy. No resemblance, therefore, can be traced between the caitiff leaders of the Abolition faction and the accredited instruments of Heaven.

Hence we conclude that' African emancipation is a work reserved for other times and for very different agents.

SECTION VII.

VILLAINOUS AND SHAMEFUL DECEPTIONS PRACTICED BY NEWSPAPER EDITORS.

Further Examination of the Fourth Charge.

EXPLANATIONS WANTED.

HAVE you ever considered, my fellow-citizens, that there is something in your social and political condition which cannot be easily understood ? The available resources of this country are sufficient to afford a liberal and handsome maintenance for all of its inhabitants. And yet we have destitution and pauperism in abundance, at all times ; and not unfrequently there is a season of almost universal distress, when the operations of productive industry are suspended and many thousands of people, who are able and willing to work, are deprived of their regular employments and reduced to a state of absolute starvation.

Have your newspaper oracles ever explained the *cause* of these calamities ? Or have they succeeded in making you believe that your afflictions are imaginary ? Have they quite convinced you that your misfortunes are blessings in masquerade ? It is said that mesmeric operators can make their "subjects" believe that a glass of filthy lager-beer is sparkling champaign or genuine *chateau morgeux.* Doubtless our charlatans of the press can perform similar miracles on *you*, my intelligent and sagacious countrymen. Controlled by their magnetic influence, you are made to swallow many a foul and bitter draught, with as much apparent relish as if you mistook it for the richest product of Gallic or Burgundian vintage.

Your journalists persuade you, my unfortunate compatriots,

that you are rich and happy; but a much better tutor, viz. your own experience, must teach you that you "are wretched and miserable, and poor and blind, and naked."

You are blind indeed, if you cannot or will not see that our republic is sorely afflicted with a complication of disorders, the origin of which is never satisfactorily explained by the newspaper press. You must have observed, for example, that vast numbers of our countrymen cannot obtain remunerative and constant employment; and yet the typographers pretend that it is expedient, desirable and necessary to import whole legions of workmen from England, France, Ireland, Scotland, Germany, etc. You, mechanics and laborers, complain that your work, when you have it, does not afford you a sufficient recompense. "For that trifling inconvenience," says Sir Oracle of the *Herald, Tribune,* or *Times,* you may have a speedy and efficient remedy. "A Protective Tariff will soon make your handicraft occupation yield you a princely income!"

Here we have a capital illustration of our subject. That tariff finesse reminds me of the tricks which are used by some cunning birds to decoy intruders away from their places of incubation. Our editorial fowls lead you on a wild-goose chase after "a sufficient tariff," merely to prevent you from examining those shady retreats where the hens which lay their golden eggs are performing their mysterious duties.

I make no objection to "Protective Tariffs." Pile them on to what elevation you please; let them "o'ertop old Pelion or the skyish head of blue Olympus;" but I earnestly exhort you not to depend on *them* for deliverance from your present tribulations. I am altogether convinced that no protective measures can materially improve the condition of the industrious classes in America, while our monstrous BANKING SYSTEM, that great national vampire, is permitted to exhaust the vitality of the country. For much correct and valuable information on this subject, I refer you to that able exposition of financial frauds which is made by Mr. William M. Gouge, in his "History of Paper Money and Banking in the United States."

CURIOUS FRATERNITY.

There is a certain relationship—you may call it consanguinity—between journalism and banking. They are united by the most tender ties of sympathy and affection, like the twins of Leda; though journalism is supposed to have something divine in its nature, and banking is altogether " of the earth, earthy." Such is the indissolubility of the fraternal league that journalism is willing to forego all that is glorious in its destiny—all that is god-like in its condition—for the sake of perpetuating its disgraceful association with a groveling, corrupt, and scoundrel-like brother.

But when we begin to speak of the connection between the American banking system and the newspaper press, we approach a mine of villainy of such stupendous proportions that we hesitate to apply the match, lest the explosion should shake our republican arch from the keystone to either abutment. Nevertheless the performance of this perilous duty is unavoidable. It is necessary to *shock* our countrymen, occasionally, if we wish to make them believe in the reality of their own danger.

Our venerable statesman and true patriot, (as I believe,) Charles J. Ingersol, shocked the American public not a little when he declared, on a recent occasion, that the country is governed by newsmongers and moneyed corporations. With reference to the well-known confederacy between the public journalists and corrupt financial institutions, Mr. Ingersol speaks as follows:

"Jefferson's life and letters are full of lessons against that despicable despotism of the press which distorts an inestimable blessing into an insufferable curse ; so that when an absolute monarch is said to marshal sabres against types, it is not easy to say which is the worse. What would Franklin, Reed, Mifflin, and other Pennsylvania founders have thought of legislators doing little more, year after year, than legalizing the vilest of all aristocracies—corporations to make and do every thing; conferring vested rights of possession, privileged forever; trampling down liberty's twin sister, equality; so that the upper class are nearly all either corporators or printers?"

Another distinguished American statesman significantly remarks: "There is no law to prevent the banks from subsidizing the press."

"Over the newspaper press," says Mr. Gouge, "the banks have great power. Few journalists can venture to expose the money corporation system in such terms as everybody would understand, without risking the means of support for themselves and their families. The neglect of subscribers to pay up arrears has brought many of the newspaper men in debt to the banks. Others who are *not* in debt ARE SUPPORTED PRINCIPALLY BY THE BANKING INTEREST." (See "Gouge on Banking," Chapter XIX.)

The Hon. John C. Calhoun, in a speech delivered in Congress, A. D. 1816, said, in reference to the state of the currency, "The evil I desire to remedy is a deep one—almost incurable, because connected with public opinion, over which banks have a great control. They have, in a great measure, a control over the press; for a proof of which I refer to the fact that the present wretched state of the circulating medium has scarcely been denounced by a single paper in the United States."

Since this speech was delivered, the alliance between banking and journalism has become more intimate, and the rascalities perpetrated by this shameful confederacy have increased in magnitude, and become infinitely more complicated. The mutual support which banking and journalism afford to each other, and the multitude of abuses which arise from their co-operation, are matters at which it will be necessary for me to glance in another part of this work. At present, I refer to the subject merely to give an example of the manner in which the newspaper press "continuously and systematically misleads the judgment of the public in relation to matters of the greatest national importance."

A NATIONAL BLESSING.

The scribes of the press make the people believe that our American banking system is a great public convenience and a blessing to all classes of the population. If Satan himself had a special newspaper organ in the United States, that Stygian journal could not utter a more diabolical falsehood. Some of the journalists, who are a little more conscientious than others, speak of the banking system as "a necessary evil." "It has some bad effects to be sure, but many kinds of business could not be possibly carried on without it."

There is some truth in this last declaration. Certain knavish speculations could not be prosperously managed without those facilities and "accommodations" which the banks afford to their favorite customers. Some *newspapers*, (as Mr. Gouge intimates,) could not be sustained without the patronage of the bank interest. You may safely conclude, however, that all newspaper-men, and all other business operators, who rely on such support and who cannot live without it, are, (to use an agricultural phrase,) "not worth their fodder." In fact, such gentlemen cannot do their country a greater service than by DYING for it as soon as possible.

The abuses of Banking would afford an almost inexhaustible theme for newspaper discussion. There is scarcely any subject which is intrinsically of more importance to the American people, and yet it is a subject which our leading newspapers cannot and *dare* not touch.

INVOCATION TO JAMES GORDON BENNETT.

I call on you, Mr. James Gordon Bennett,—the bell-wether of our editorial flock,—to give us your ideas respecting the banking business, as it is now managed in this country. Do you think that we should ever have had a "bread riot" in the United States, if we had never had an incorporated bank? Would a considerable number of our working people ever have wanted employment for months at a time, if oppressive financiering corporations had never been tolerated among us?

INVOCATION TO HORACE GREELEY.

I call on you, Mr. Horace Greeley, the model political philosopher of our republic. Will you vouchsafe to illuminate the dark corners of our understandings with the coruscations of your dazzling intellect? Unquestionably your elephantine faculties have sometimes been exercised with sad reflections on the topic to which I now invite your special notice. That you are an adept in the great art of financiering is proved by historical evidences of no very antique date. If any proof of this kind were required, the slightest reference to your connection with the Irish repeal agitation would be sufficient. Relying, therefore, on your intimate acquaintance with the subject, I ask you if fraudulent banking does not produce more human misery on this continent than negro slavery itself? And I ask you besides, if the multitudinous evils of this kind of banking are not *remediable*, and, on that account, more hopeful and suitable matters for editorial agitations than that "southern nuisance" which you and your colaborers have endeavored so earnestly and so *successfully*, I fear, to protract or perpetuate?

INVOCATION TO JOHN W. FORNEY.

I call on you, Mr. John W. Forney, our American Warwick, you who can conscientiously make and unmake presidents, as easily as you can clasp or unfasten your gum-elastic garters (if your own report and that of your admiring friends may be trusted); you, whose stubborn honesty, according to your own declaration, has been the insuperable bar to your preferment, I call on you for a distinct answer to these plain and pertinent questions:—"Is the Kansas issue, your favorite hobby, or the principle which it is supposed to involve, a matter which concerns the people of the United States more than that stupendous system of corruption and robbery which is daily carried on by moneyed corporations in every part of this country? Does not that system make our republican government an illusion and a mockery, by establishing among us a power which is more secretive and irresponsible, and therefore more oppressive and dangerous, than any unlimited monarchy of Europe?

INVOCATION TO JESPER HARDING.

I call on you, Mr. Jesper Harding, publisher of the *Philadelphia Inquirer,* you who have lived for fifty years, like a virtuous salamander, in the midst of a glowing furnace of financial iniquity; you who have witnessed all the miraculous operations of that money-making machinery which depends on the *chiffonier* for its supplies of material, and which, by an easy and rapid transmutation, can change a beggar's discarded rags to a legal equivalent for houses and lands, and whole tons of gold bullion. I call on you, my venerable neighbor, to come forth and expound the mysteries of banking to my victimized countrymen. Have you ever known a newspaperman to sell himself, "soul, body, and breeches," to a bank? Or, to pursue the inquiry in a more general way, is it not a *common practice* for soulless and conscienceless corporations to "buy up" newspapers and to make them acquiescent and accessory to the most wicked and daring abuses that have ever been practiced on a free people?

Now, Messrs. Editors, I have often heard you complain that good subjects for "leaders" are not always accessible. I present you with a large supply of material for this branch of your manufacture. If you are afraid to use it, let us hear no more talk of your "freedom and independence."

A CHANGE FOR THE WORSE.

There was a time when *some* newspaper editors could speak of our banking institutions with a degree of manly intrepidity. In 1835, Blair's *Globe* endorsed the following sentiment: "Of all inventions which have been put in operation in this country to promote the inordinate accumulation of wealth, the most exceptionable are incorporated companies, and the worst of all incorporated companies are Banks."

In 1842, the *Democratic Review* assured the public that "bankers, capitalists, corporators, stock-jobbers, and political traffickers controlled the government."

In 1826, when the Plattsburg Bank exploded, Mr. Flagg, a brave and honest country editor, was prosecuted for libel, because he denounced the villainy of some of the parties concerned in that disgraceful catastrophe.

In 1840, the *Washington Globe* declared that more than *forty-eight millions* of the public money had been lost by means of bank defalcations during the war of 1812.

Even the *New York Herald*, in 1842, was honest enough to denounce some of the swindling operations of the Banks, as the subjoined extract will show :—

"The horrible morals of the financiers of the present day have unfitted the country for any banks, or for any other currency than gold and silver. Within the last few years, nearly one hundred and fifty banks, including the United States Bank, have broken to pieces, and property amounting to one hundred and fifty millions of dollars, or more, has evaporated under the management of the bankers and financiers of the age."

Many other unfavorable notices of particular banks, and of the American Banking System in general, may be found in newspapers published nearly a quarter of a century ago; but, more recently, the gentlemen of the press are expressively silent on this subject; or if they touch it at all, it is with all that nervous caution which old ladies exhibit when they handle their cracked and puttied china-ware.

It is evident that the "Banking Interest" has succeeded in purchasing, not only the connivance, but the active co-operation of the journalists. And the earnest and zealous support which is given to the Bank usurpation by the conductors of the press, convinces me that any imaginable villainy,—any conceivable form of oppression and tyranny,—could secure the same powerful influences in its behalf, merely by a liberal outlay of money. And as

"It is my occupation to speak plain,"

I am constrained to declare my belief that a nation which can be persuaded to tolerate such financial abuses as those which now exist in this country, might be induced to submit to any other tyrannical infliction, if the contrivers thereof were wealthy and corrupt enough to enlist the public journals in their enterprise. If ambition, and not avarice, were the ruling passion of our oppressors, we might have a POLITICAL DESPOTISM instead of a Bank Regency.

SUPPLEMENTARY ILLUSTRATIONS.

STUPENDOUS ROBBERY.—Within a few months a revelation of facts connected with the management of the State Treasury of Ohio, proves that depredations to the amount of $200,000 have been committed in that department. The robbers were the State Treasurers, and their confederates were certain banking institutions and certain newspaper editors. The influence of journalists and bank officers obtained for Breslin, (the principal defaulter,) the management of the public funds. A bank president was his principal surety, and the missing money had been used chiefly in banking speculations. It appeared in evidence that several newspapers had been subsidized by the robbers.

MONEY-MAKING.—During the year 1857, the five Mints of the United States coined $19,426,312 worth of copper, silver and gold, which metallic materials had been legitimately acquired and were intrinsically worth the sums which they represented. In the same year, the one thousand four hundred and sixteen paper-money manufactories of the United States increased their note circulation from $194,847,950 in 1856, to $214,778,822 in 1857; or to the amount of $19,030,872; while the specie in their vaults was diminished from $59,314,963 in 1856, to $58,-349,338 in 1857. Thus, for every metallic dollar coined by the government, the banks issued a paper dollar, and the effect was a corresponding *depreciation* of the metallic currency. It was, in fact, a robbery of every man who had a genuine dollar in his possession.

ONE FAITHFUL WITNESS.—The only honest and truthful remarks on the Banking System which I have seen in an American newspaper within the last fifteen years, were published in the *Philadelphia Pennsylvanian,* a few months ago.

"We would call the attention of the people," said the Pennsylvanian, "to that legislative system which invests numerous chartered companies, all over the United States, with a right so important that every civilized country on the globe, except our own, has jealously guarded it as a prerogative of the government only. Of what avail are higher duties on foreign merchandise to the working-man, when his increased wages are paid in fresh-stamped notes, for which there is no security save the credit of the banks that issued them, and which become worthless the moment that credit is put to the test of liquidation?

"It may be said that the laboring man spends his paper dollars, as he earns them, every week; and so he is not the loser on the day of reckoning. That day is a day of revulsion, followed by years of business stagnation, entailing want and degradation on the industrious classes, and dishonor, perhaps, upon their offspring. It is at such a price that they accept, in return for their hard labor, the worthless, flimsy stuff called bank notes. Nor is this all. Even while the sham prosperity of over-issues of notes lasts, and the laboring classes are employed, *they* are the persons who pay the penalties of a fraudulent multiplication of money. The prices of provisions, clothing, and the rates of rent, in every country, are regulated by the quantity of money in use, or its value or price. If that quantity is doubled by the issue of paper dollars, the prices of provisions, etc., will become double what they were before. Hence the workman, who must give his time and labor for every dollar which he puts into his pocket, gains nothing by increased wages, attended by a proportionate increase of the expenses of living.

"But the corporators of banks, who have millions of dollars printed at an expense of twenty-five cents per thousand notes, and who give no time and no labor to the easy operation, pocket all that money, or the interest made by loaning it to others, as clear profit. They appear in the same provision market with the laboring man; they with a twenty-dollar bill each, the manufacture of which did not cost them one cent, and which they obtain by merely asking for it at the counter of the bank; the laboring man, or his wife, with a one-dollar note, the hard-earned wages of the preceding day. The privileged bank-note coiner, or bank director, is rich; he can afford to pay the highest prices, and he does it cheerfully; but, in so doing, he stimulates the prices of the poor man's vegetables, meats, etc., and so binds a heavier burden on the shoulders of his industrious fellow-citizen.

"It must be clear and obvious to every one, that so long as such an iniquitous system of fraud is carried on and sanctioned by the laws of this country—so long as certain privileged people may turn worthless paper to any amount of money, being virtually subject to no control or restriction—no legislative enactments, no protective duties, can improve the condition of the masses or protect the public at large from the harassing oppressions of a class insignificant in numbers and worthless in character."

These are truths which all the newspaper editors in the country understand, but which scarcely one of them will venture to utter.

SECTION VIII.

OTHER SHAMEFUL AND WICKED DECEPTIONS PRACTICED BY THE NEWSPAPERS.

Continued Examination of the Fourth Charge.

LOLA MONTEZ.

WHO has not heard of Madame Lola Montez, otherwise called the Countess of Landsfeldt? I offer you the testimony of that celebrated lady, and recommend it to your serious consideration; hoping to convince you, as we proceed, that no moral eccentricities which may be imputed to the witness can affect the validity of this evidence.

On the evening of December 6th, 1858, Lola Montez delivered a lecture in Dublin to a crowded and intelligent audience. Her subject was "*America and its People,*" and her discourse, (which was intended for Irish ears and not for American ones,) contained many facts of momentous interest to the people of this country, facts which never, by any accident, could find their way into the American newspapers!

It may be true that the assertions of Madame Montez, standing alone and unsupported, are not entitled to unqualified credence. Madame Montez is a light-heeled lady, and the world has given her credit for some corresponding levity of character. But she *can* be in earnest when she tries; as she proved when she horse-whipped a certain California editor; and that meritorious and virtuous performance is enough, by itself, to redeem her reputation from much of the obloquy to which it has been exposed. The very act of flogging a lying editor seems to indicate a love of truth; and, thus construed, it is an act which may help to establish the credibility of a witness.

But, luckily for our present purposes, the facts which we are about to quote from the lecture of Madame Montez are well proved by other testimony besides that of her ladyship. There are some truths which are recognized as soon as spoken, even when they are presented to our observation for the first time. The truthfulness of the extracts which I am about to give, is obvious enough to be discerned by every intelligent man in the United States. But it is very probable that many of those who derive all their information from the public journals will be surprised, as well as indignant, when they find, by a perusal of these extracts, that they have been, all their lives, "continuously and systematically deceived" in relation to matters of the *highest* national importance.

It is the constant endeavor of our newspaper-men to make their readers believe that FOREIGN IMMIGRATION is an advantage and a blessing to this country. Madame Montez was very intimate with some of our American editors and she has heard their *private* opinions on this subject. She is enabled therefore to give the following correct information to her Dublin audience.

HER EVIDENCE.

"Her ladyship's lecture," says a Dublin paper, "dealt chiefly with the subject of Emigration. The Know-Nothing party, (she said,) had succeeded only in displaying its own impotency, while endeavoring to check the foreign influx. The annual increase of the foreign population in the United States, ranged from thirty to fifty per cent. over the native population; a ratio which must, in a very few years, place the political destinies of that country in the hands of those who had been born in Europe.

"An American statesman had lately declared on the floor of Congress, that the *increase* of the foreign population, in the preceding year, was equal to the entire population of five of the smallest States of the Union."

"By the registry of State servants, it appeared that over one-sixth of the public employees. civil, military and naval, were foreigners ; to whom were annually paid about four hundred thousand dollars. This immense patronage had been bestowed on them by the Democratic party as a reward for their votes; and the faction which opposed the Democrats would bid just as high for foreign support, if it was in a position to do so."

"Foreigners constitute, even now, the balance of power in that country, and it is too late to strive against the influence which they have attained. America ought therefore to direct her attention to assimilating them and melting them down among her own people as speedily as possible. *But that will be a difficult task.* Early associations and ties of kindred are not so easily broken and the laws of domestic affection, operating on the broader circles of the national family, must forever modify the social relations of natives and foreigners in America. These affinities were manifested in the daily advertisements of German, Irish, French, Swiss, Swedish, and many other clubs and organizations."

The facts thus stated by Lola Montez, must be almost or quite *self-evident* to every American reader who has the least acquaintance with the true condition of things in his own country. In *one* particular, I hope that her ladyship is mistaken. I hope that it is an error of judgment on her part to suppose that it is "too late," to strive against the establishment of a foreign dynasty in America. But let us follow the luminous countess a little further :—

THE FOREIGN ORGANS.

"There are, (said Madame Montez,) more than three hundred newspapers in the United States published and edited by foreigners, for the avowed purpose of meeting the wants of the foreign population, and which are constantly appealing to their prejudices. A German paper, published in Kentucky, boasted lately that, within ten years, the country would be entirely controlled by foreigners. The same paper pointed out certain 'defects in the Constitution of the United States, which must and shall be altered by the powerful German organizations,' (Red Republicans); and among other reforms, this bold advocate of Teutonic usurpation called for the abrogation of all laws which require the observance of the Christian Sabbath, the administration of oaths on the Bible, the offering up of prayers in Congress, the exclusion of atheists from legal acts, etc. 'All these,' said the German editor, 'are violations of human rights, and they must and *shall be* abolished.'"

Language similar to this quoted by Madame Montez is in very common use among the foreign newspaper organs of America. The editors of these publications generally belong to the most sanguinary school of republicanism. Compared with them, the French revolutionists were mild and merciful reformers. They regard all the restraints of law and religion as intolerable grievances; and the way in which they would exercise their "human rights" is by inflicting on others all manner of inhuman wrongs. Many of them would not be satisfied with any thing less than a new revolution every month, with the privilege of confiscating the property and chopping off the heads of all who do not subscribe to their own blood-thirsty, anarchical and atheistical principles. They appear to be as little pleased with the constitution and government of the United States as the Parisian rabble of 1790 was with the regency of the Bourbons. But let us have a little more of her ladyship's exposition of American affairs, which proved so grateful and exhilarating to her Dublin audience.

"It would be impossible," continued Lola Montez, "to give any idea of the violence of newspaper writing in the United States, and for this dreadful and growing evil there seems to be no remedy. It is the first muttering sound of the social and political war of races which is inevitable in America. It is a war which always has existed, and always will exist, where separate races and nations are brought together in any thing like equal numbers, and which can end only when one becomes victorious. There is no truth which history more plainly records. It was thus that the Saxons became masters of England and the Franks and Goths of France and Spain. It was thus that numerous Scythian tribes got possession of Greece and the beautiful provinces of Asia Minor. The history of the world shines with lights by which we may read the fate of the American Republic,—seeing that whenever a foreign population flocks into a country faster than it can be assimilated and absorbed among the general inhabitants, the work of national disintegration has commenced. (Applause!) This process has now been going on for ten or fifteen years in America. *The Americans themselves do not see it;* so true it is that nations never perceive the signs of their own decay until the rot has struck to the heart." (*Great Applause!!*)

While her ladyship's delighted Irish audience is exulting over the prospective ruin of our country, let us pause for a moment to inquire why "the Americans do not see it." This inquiry brings us back immediately to that part of our subject which the preceding extracts are intended to illustrate. The Americans do not see the frightful and ruinous effects of foreign immigration because they choose to see nothing except through the *spectacles of journalism,* and these false glasses will not afford them a glimpse of the terrific reality.

This is one of those "matters of the greatest national importance," concerning which the newspaper press of the United States "continuously and systematically misleads the judgment of the American people."

In the course of her lecture, Madame Montez remarked that she had "often conversed with brilliant statesmen in America, who admitted with a painful candor that their country is fearfully threatened with anarchy. Some of them confessed that a form of monarchy would be the only remedy for such a catastrophe, when it should come."

In conclusion, Madame Montez referred to the distinguished part which Irishmen had borne in the advancement of American civilization (! ! !) "At least," said she, "half of the most efficient editors and reporters in the Atlantic cities are Irishmen."

COMMENTARY.

Now, my dear countrymen, I have given you a brief abstract of Lady Lansfeldt's lecture. Let us fairly and impartially consider the value of this evidence. It may be objected that Madame Montez is a woman, and that her testimony relates to matters which few of her sex are supposed to understand. To meet this objection, I am enabled to tell you that her lecture is supposed to have been written, before her departure from this country, by a shrewd fellow enough, viz., one of those foreign editors who are signalized in the lecture itself as having contributed so largely to the "advancement of American civilization."

The lecture was undoubtedly written by a *man*, and by one who was well acquainted with American politics. In this case, the exotic scribe had no motive for deception. Admitting that it was his wish to gratify the foreign audiences, for whom this lecture was intended, by calling attention to the symptoms of decay, the signs of speedy dissolution, which are discoverable in the present condition of our republic, he could not more effectually reach this object than by *truthfully* reporting the effects of that excessive influx of the foreign element which must infallibly make the population of this country unfit for self-government.

Every well-informed and sensible American who reads the preceding extracts must perceive that they have *internal evidences of truth;* and, in such circumstances, it matters very little whether the speaker is a female dancer or a profound statesman—a scribbling vagabond or a sagacious political philosopher. The truth is no less the truth, even when it is spoken by the devil himself.

I expect to convince you that the facts comprised in the foregoing extracts are not *exaggerated* in the least, though your journalistic betrayers may endeavor to make you believe that such is the case. It was unnecessary for the writer of Madame's lecture to deepen the shades of the picture, for the reality was gloomy enough for his purpose. Indeed, it is very evident that he found it convenient to *suppress* some particulars which have an important bearing on the subject, but which were not calculated to gratify the national pride of an Irish audience.

THE PLAUDITS.

Apropos to this topic, let us inquire what was the nature of that impulse which prompted the "brilliant and enlightened" Dublin audience to applaud her ladyship vehemently whenever she referred to the probable overthrow of this model republic? Why should any Christian assembly exult and rejoice in the contemplation of such a disastrous catastrophe? Why should Irishmen—the recipients of so much sympathizing kindness from the people of these States—hail the approach of our national calamities with rapturous acclamations?

The people of Dublin were well aware that the political convulsions which threaten the downfall of the American Republic, will be brought about, in a very great measure, by the agency of their own expatriated countrymen. Their joyous shouts, therefore, may be understood to have expressed their anticipation of a *national triumph*. The destruction of American freedom was recognized by the Dublin audience as an Irish victory.

FACTS SUPPRESSED.

I say that so far was Madame Montez from aggravating, in her description, the pernicious effects of foreign immigration on the institutions of this republic, that she actually *concealed* from her Irish hearers some of the most important facts connected with this subject. There were several particulars which she could not easily introduce to their notice. She could not, (for example), be expected to tell the Dublin gentry that the excessive importation of *Irishmen* to this country is enough of itself to convert the Home of Liberty into something resembling a stupendous PIG-STYE—a most unsuitable dwelling-place for that bright divinity who shrinks from all moral pollution.

Lola Montez told her Irish audience that foreign immigration is ruining America ; but she did not tell them exactly *how* this process is developed. She did not venture to tell the people of the Hibernian metropolis that the population of all our large cities is thoroughly vitiated and corrupted by the foreign ingredient which enters so largely into its composition. She did not tell them that the principal part of that pernicious ingredient is imported from the Emerald Isle. She did not tell the ladies and gentlemen of Dublin that a large proportion of their countrymen who now reside in the United States, and whom we readily admit to the rights of citizenship, are morally and intellectually inferior to the negroes whom we hold in personal and political bondage.

IRISH CITIZENS.

It wou d be impossible, I think, to find on the surface of this green earth a race of men more unqualified for self-government, more unfit to enjoy the rights of republican citizens, than the Irish ; such of them, at least, as are most likely to be incorporated with the population of America. They are credulous, disorderly, capricious, ungovernable, factious, violent, unreasonable ; every thing, in short, that republican citizens ought not to be. They are the most convenient tools that any villainous demagogue could select for the accomplishment of the most ambitious and treasonable objects.

A PLEA FOR THE COUNTESS.

I have undertaken to convince you, my much-abused countrymen, that your treacherous journalists have kept you so deplorably ignorant of matters connected with the vital interests of your country, that a female dancer may be your school-mistress. Do not be offended with Madame Montez because she displays the undraperied truth as liberally as she exhibits her own ankles. Be grateful, rather, for the instruction she offers you, and confess that some of the facts which I have extracted from her Dublin lecture, though they are obvious and indisputable enough, are startling novelties to you, simply because you have never met with them in the newspapers, from which all your information is derived. By them you have been drilled or dragooned into the belief that the muddy tide of immigration is as great a blessing to this land as the inundations of the Nile are to Egypt. You have been taught that the Irishmen and Dutchmen who come to this country in countless swarms, like the locusts of Africa, are the most suitable material in the world for the composition of a batch of good republicanism. The Countess of Landsfeldt deserves your gratitude for exposing the falsehood and treachery of your typographical counselors.

PATRICK'S PICTURE, BY LORD BROUGHAM.

Concerning the Irish ingredient of our republican population, something has been said above.; but, if your knowledge of the Hibernian character does not enable you to recognize the truth of my remarks, I offer you the corroborative testimony of Lord Brougham. This witness is one of the ablest statesmen of our day, one who never delivers an opinion on any subject which he does not understand, and one who can scarcely be suspected of any disposition to do injustice to the character of a people who may almost be considered as his own countrymen.

In some remarks on the sanguinary horrors of the French Revolution, Lord Brougham speaks of "the mischiefs which may spring from popular enthusiasm, when bad men obtain sway over a nation little informed and unable or unwilling to judge for itself, ready to believe whatever is told by interested informants, to follow whatever is recommended by false advisers for their own selfish ends." The natives of Ireland are then cited by his lordship as an example of a people who are "not free from such influences."

"The Irish people," says Lord Brougham, in continuation of this subject, "are excited and moved to action in the mass by appeals to matters of which they do not take the pains to comprehend even the outline, much less to reflect on the import and tendency. They are made, and easily made, to exert themselves for things of which they have formed no distinct idea, and in which they have no real interest whatever. They leave to others, (viz., their spiritual and their political guides), the task of forming their opinions for them, if mere cry and clamor—mere running about and shouting—can be called opinions. They never are suspicious of a person's motives, merely because they see that he has an interest in deceiving them. They never weigh the probabilities of a tale nor the credit of him who tells it. They may be deceived by the same person nine times in succession, and they believe him just as implicitly the tenth—nay, were he to confess that he had willfully deceived them, to suit a purpose of his own, they would consider this only a proof of his honesty, and lend an ear more readily, if possible, to his next imposture. Such a people can be easily moved to witness and to suffer the grossest violations of justice: they would let themselves be hallooed on to the attack of their best friends by any wily impostor that might have gained their confidence, and would suffer men as base and as execrable as *Marat* to usurp the honors of their Pantheon."—*Vide Brougham's Statesmen of the Times of George III. Lea & Blanchard's American Edition, page* 85.

Ah! how different is this photograph from the common newspaper portraitures, which represent Patrick not only as a hod-carrying or pickaxe-handling angel in corduroy-breeches, but as a sterling Republican or "Democrat," and a particularly safe and reliable citizen!

NEWSPAPER LIES IN ABUNDANCE.

On all subjects connected with foreign immigration, the American newspapers, with very few exceptions, lie constantly and with the most reckless audacity. Even the *amount* of this immigration is falsely reported, in order that the people of this country may be kept in ignorance of their own danger. Captain Marryatt says, "I do not believe that the Americans themselves know what the amount of foreign immigration is."

The Philadelphia American Banner of August 17, 1850, said: "There is a concerted effort on the part of certain shipowners, Emigrants' Friend Societies, newspaper editors, and other rascally individuals and associations. to *conceal* the amount and increase of immigration into the United States. The plan of deception is so extensive that not only a majority of the public journals but some of the officers and agents of the United States Government, (too many of whom are foreigners themselves,) lend all their aid to make the treacherous concealment more effective."

The *quality* of our imported population is also villainously misrepresented. It is not true that the emigrants in general, or that even a large proportion of them, are "worthy and industrious people." The statistics of our prisons and almshouses show that a vast majority of our paupers and criminals are foreigners. Of the IRISH people who come to America, I do not believe that one in fifty assists the productive industry of the country. Comparatively few of them engage in manufactures or agriculture. They congregate in our large cities, and employ themselves chiefly in occupations which add nothing to the wealth of the public; and some of their favorite pursuits are eminently mischievous. Many easy trades, suitable for invalids and old women, are usurped by brawny Irishmen. In Philadelphia, New York and Boston, ninety per cent. of the grocers and other shopkeepers are Irish. Strapping Hibernians peddle oranges and roasted chestnuts about the streets, or doze, for uncounted hours, over a tray of molasses-candy or a basketful of shriveled vegetables in the market-house.

It is true that some Irishmen are excellent laborers, when they happen to be inclined that way; they manage the wheelbarrow and spade with unrivaled address, and endure storm and sunshine with heroical fortitude. It often happens, however, that they retire precipitately from more active engagements as soon as they acquire capital enough to set up a grog-shop, or some other "light business." The common remark that our railroads could never have been constructed without the help of Irish laborers, is very questionable and not very complimentary to American energy and industry. But, assuming that the remark is true, and with due regard for the convenience of the traveling public, I would suggest that a republic without railroads might be better than railroads without a republic.

GERMAN CITIZENS.

The German immigrants have a better reputation than the Irish with the public in general, but they are not so much in favor with the newspapers. The latter circumstance is explained partly by the fact that Irish *editors* in America are twenty times more numerous than Dutch ones, and partly by the other fact that Irishmen for *electioneering* purposes are ten times more useful than Dutchmen.

That the Germans, in general, are more *industrious* than the Irish, and better citizens on *that* account, I am disposed to believe. But their stubborn nationality, their distinctive social habits, their peculiar modes of thinking, and the difference of their language, all conspire to make their assimilation with the American people a very tardy and difficult process. Though somewhat less excitable than the Irish, they are no less turbulent and troublesome when their evil passions are aroused; and, although many of them are ultra-republican in theory, their notions of political liberty are so extravagant and irrational that *absolute monarchists* would be much safer and more eligible citizens.

The false valuation which the newspapers place on our "adopted citizens," and the many other errors and absurdities which are scattered abroad by the press to mystify the subject of immigration, are productive of so much evil and danger, that I deeply regret the necessity which compels me to quit this subject before I have given it a tithe of the consideration which it deserves. But, before we proceed to the discussion of other topics, it may be expedient, in this place, to introduce

A FEW WORDS OF EXPLANATION.

It is the common trick of the Anti-American newspaper press of this country to check all inquiry into the subject which I have just been endeavoring to illustrate, by raising the hue and cry of "KNOW-NOTHINGISM;" as if facts could be disproved, opinions refuted, or principles overthrown, by giving them ridiculous names. But in this case the hackneyed exclamation of Messrs. Editors will not answer their purpose. I have nothing to do with the "Know-Nothings," and never was a member of their mysterious association. To this emphatic and solemn declaration I will add, that I do not approve of secret political organizations, unless the necessity for them is very obvious indeed; and I hope the time is far distant when it will be *necessary* for an American patriot to conceal his political belief.

Mine is an eclectic school of politics; I am ready to accept all that is true in the creed, and all that is commendable in the practice of any party. In religion, I would rather be called a Christian than a Presbyterian, an Episcopalian, or a Papist; in politics, I prefer the name of PATRIOT before that of Whig, Democrat, or Know-Nothing. I have nothing to do with factions; and if, in this book, I have acknowledged the truth of some of their principles, that acknowledgment does not make me responsible for any of their errors of faith or practice.

The truths which I have uttered in this book are indisputable. Why then should I apologize for the utterance? Apologize I do not, and only as a matter of courtesy do I offer these explanations.

Plain dealing is not only the course prescribed by justice, but of all modes of action it is the most *merciful*. I am doing an act of kindness to our "adopted citizens" when I endeavor to make them understand their true position in this country. Their mistakes in this matter have caused much trouble already, and unless they are corrected, the same errors will produce much greater troubles hereafter. In opposition to all the teachings of the newspaper press the foreign population of America must learn :—

1. That they can have no political rights in this country except those which are conceded to them by the self-sacrificing kindness of the native inhabitants. Hence their admission to the privileges of citizenship is an act of GRACE, as well as an act of *questionable policy*, on the part of the American people.

2. That the validity of our Naturalization laws may be called in question; because, according to the principles of *universal* law, and of natural equity, one nation cannot legislate for another; and when America "adopts" an alien citizen, she virtually attempts to repeal the law which binds him to the land of his birth. Hence no foreigner can have an *indisputable* title to citizenship in America.

3. That the American people owe no "debt of gratitude" to any foreigner who may choose this country as his place of residence; for, in present circumstances, it is our best national policy to *discourage* foreign immigration; and, of course, those who come hither are less entitled to our thanks than those who stay away.

4. That, in view of the facts just exhibited, our "adopted citizens" ought to be very moderate in their expectations and demands of political favors; and that, above all things, they ought to refrain from those VIOLENT DEMONSTRATIONS to which they have sometimes been moved by the criminal misrepresentations and instigations of newspaper-men and politicians.

In another part of this work, I will undertake to show that

some of the most terrible popular commotions that ever took place in this country were caused by the mistakes into which the foreign population is led, chiefly by the false and pernicious teachings of the Newspaper Press.

SUPPLEMENTARY ILLUSTRATIONS.

DISCONTENTED ALIENS.—Among other gross misrepresentations which are made by the newspapers, for the purpose of reconciling the American public to that torrent of immigration which is pouring in upon us, it is pretended that our alien citizens in general are delighted with the institutions of our country. I am quite sure that this supposition is very remote from the truth. The foreigners themselves are often candid enough to express their discontent, and their national organs continually cry out for innovations on our laws and customs, and for amendments of our constitution. These organs undoubtedly speak the prevailing sentiments of the nationalities which they represent.

Captain Marryatt reports that, in his confidential communications with the Irish citizens of the United States, he generally found them dissatisfied with the present condition of American affairs.

"We have been accustomed," (says he,) "to ascribe the turbulence of the lower classes of the Irish to ill-treatment and a sense of their wrongs; but this disposition appears to follow them everywhere. It might be supposed that, having emigrated to America and obtained the rights of citizens, they would have amalgamated and fraternized to a certain degree with the people; but such is not the case; they hold themselves completely apart and distinct, living with their families in certain parts of the city where there are few American inhabitants and adhering to their own manners and customs. *They are just as little pleased with the institutions of the United States as they were with the government at home.* The fact is, they would prefer no government at all—if, (as

Paddy himself would say,) they knew where to find it."—*Marrayatt's Diary, Second Series. Chapter on Emigration.*

Orestes A. Brownson, the editor of a Roman Catholic organ, said,—"The institutions of this country can be preserved only by Catholicism." To this the *Boston Pilot*, (another Hibernian mouth-piece) added—"We long to have an Irish policy in America."

The German organs sometimes express the opinion that the institutions of the country cannot be preserved without ATHEISM, or something very much like it. *They* long to have a socialistic, anti-marrying, anti-Sabbath-keeping, anti-Bible-reading policy, in America. Whether that is better or worse than the Boston Pilot's "Irish policy" I cannot say,—and, in fact, I do not pretend to know what Irish *policy* is.

One thing is very certain, however; viz., that our imported citizens are generally dissatisfied with the present condition of American affairs, religious and political; and I believe that a majority of them could easily be persuaded to join in any revolutionary movement, having the ruin of this republic for its object. People who easily abandon the land of their nativity cannot be bound by any strong ties of love and duty to the country of their adoption. The child which flies from the maternal bosom to the protection of a stranger, is not likely to be a pattern of gratitude, affection and fidelity.

THE REPUBLIC-BUILDING FALLACY.

It is a bold assumption of the newspaper press that all manner of men (except negroes) are qualified and fully prepared for self-government. This they pretend to take for granted; though, perhaps, scarcely one editor in America would be impudent enough to make the assertion in unequivocal terms. De Tocqueville's opinions on this subject are more complimentary to our countrymen than the slyly-insinuated hypothesis of our own journalists. That French philosopher honestly admits, and proves, that Americans have a particular aptitude and an extraordinary capacity for the maintenance and enjoyment of political freedom ; and, by unavoidable inference, he shows that other nations *have not* the same aptitude and capacity. According to the newspaper theory, the establishment of new republics, "*hic et ubique*," is just as easy and simple a matter as setting up a crockery shop or a cigar factory. Italy, Hungary, Ireland, and heaven knows what other locations, are spoken of as very eligible sites on which republican structures may be erected; whereas the building of a marble palace on the surface of a quicksand or quagmire would be a more practicable undertaking. Let the histories of Corsica, Poland, Switzerland, and modern Greece, show how easy it is to establish independent popular governments in the Old World. The Corsicans and Polanders gave demonstrative proofs of their unfitness to support democratic institutions; and, though Switzerland and Greece are nominally free, the former is controlled by France, and the latter is garrisoned by French and British soldiers !

From the fact that no such thing as a genuine republic can be established in Europe, I infer that no nation of that quarter of the globe is prepared for self-government; and the next inference is, that Europeans are not likely to become good republicans anywhere.

The common newspaper doctrine, (obscurely expressed, but clearly understood,) that all men are republicans by nature, and that one man (if he is not a blackamoor) is just as well prepared as another to exercise the rights of political freedom, is the doctrine which underlies our naturalization system; it is the doctrine which disposes so many of our countrymen to "fillibustering," and persuades them to sympathize and almost to *co-operate* with Irish Repealers, Hungarian patriots, etc. "All the world must be republicanized," is the idea; when, in fact, it would be much easier to change the whole family of man to mathematicians, sculptors, painters, or poets, than to make them republicans.

It requires a great deal of indoctrination and training to make good republican citizens; and, besides, we must have the proper *material* to work with, or the experiment will very rarely be successful. We Americans have not quite succeeded in moulding ourselves to the right pattern, though, (as De Tocqueville supposes,) we have extraordinary adaptations and facilities for so doing. How, then, can we undertake to make America a republican charity-school, for the reception of vagabond pupils from all parts of the earth, promising to board and educate them on the easiest terms, with no extra charge for washing? We must give better proof than any we have lately exhibited of our perfect acquaintance with the principles of virtuous liberty, before we venture to assume the "delightful task" of instructing those who are likely to prove very intractable and indocile disciples.

THE "ACCIDENT OF BIRTH."—According to the teachings of Journalism, it is an accident, and rather an *unlucky* one, to be *born* in America. W. L. Mackenzie, an insolent Scotchman, who committed an act of presumption which might have involved this country in a war with Great Britain, congratulates himself because he is a citizen of the United States "by *choice* and not by chance." John Tyler and Millard Fillmore were reproachfully and contemptuously treated by the newspaper press because they became Presidents "by accident;" and *native citizens* are disparaged on a similar account.

I suppose that *Esau* regarded birth as an accidental and trivial circumstance when he sold his right of primogeniture for a mess of red pottage. He was punished severely, however, for his base and wicked surrender of an inestimable privilege; and perhaps he was thus made to understand that birth-right is not an effect of *chance* or accident, but a gift of Divine Providence. If my fellow-citizens could be persuaded to read their Bibles more and the newspapers less, *they* might attain to a correct understanding of the same subject. "The accident of birth" is a detestably atheistical phrase; and a very *foolish* one, too, if they who use it intend to signify that birth is a matter of *trifling importance*. It is this "accident" which makes one man a prince and another a beggar—one person a genius and another a blockhead. The most momentous affairs of human life often depend on this " accident."

The constitution of the United States makes an unequivocal distinction between native citizens and those of foreign origin ; and, by suggesting the modification of the Naturalization laws to suit future circumstances, it plainly intimates that *other* distinctions between natives and aliens may become necessary. In short, the common newspaper doctrines relating to the subject of birth-right are groundless and untenable.

SECTION IX.

SHOWING THAT IMPOSTORS AND CHEATS OF ALL KINDS ARE ASSISTED BY THE NEWSPAPERS.

Examination of the Fifth Charge.

THE Americans are more plentifully supplied with newspapers than any other people in the world. This undeniable fact is often mentioned by our countrymen as a subject of rejoicing and mutual congratulation. It is understood, of course, that a nation which has an abundance of newspaper literature must be well informed and "enlightened;" but allow me to remark that this is a most fallacious conclusion.

In the preceding pages, I have endeavored to make it appear that, on some subjects of great importance to themselves, the American people are *not* well informed. Permit me now, my fellow-citizens, to open your eyes to the interesting fact that we Americans are more extensively cheated and swindled than any other nation of the world. People who are cheated and swindled repeatedly, and to a great extent, must be either very foolish or very ignorant. I do not charge you with *folly*, my dear countrymen; and I believe that your calumniators themselves are disposed to admit that you have as much shrewdness and worldly wisdom, (at least,) as we usually find associated with a nice sense of honor and incorruptible integrity.

If you are frequently victimized by fraud and imposture, we are forced to believe that it must be for want of correct information; or, to speak more accurately, you are victimized in this way by means of *false information* proceeding from the most corrupt and unscrupulous instructors.

I am convinced that the people of the United States are

annually taxed to the amount of millions of dollars by the fraudulent operations of individual and incorporated rascality. In this statement, I make no reference to the extortions and defalcations of govermental officers. These constitute an account of sufficient magnitude to deserve separate consideration.

SWINDLERS AND IMPOSTORS.

The special subjects to which I would now call attention are the frauds perpetrated by Banks, Insurance Companies and other financial corporations, Stock Gamblers, Theatrical Managers, Showmen, Quack Medicine-makers, Book Publishers, and other scoundrels who derive vast emoluments from the robbery of the unsuspecting public. I assert that the public journalists are, to all intents and purposes, *in partnership* with these scoundrels, giving them the most efficient aid in all their operations, and sharing the profits of their nefarious pursuits.

This theme is much too prolific to admit of any thing more than a brief reference to the particulars.

FRAUDULENT BANKS.

The Banking System of the United States, as I have mentioned elsewhere, is a stupendous imposture. By its operation every citizen of this country is robbed every day of his life; unless, indeed, he himself happens to be connected with the great financiering machine, and so becomes one of the *robbers*. Not one American in five thousand has the least acquaintance with the real *modus operandi* of this machine; because it is the constant endeavor of the newspaper press to mystify the whole matter. Newspapers have been established by banks and maintained by them for years together; and many journals now published in this country could not live without "banking facilities." In the trial of Allibone, president of the ruptured Bank of Pennsylvania, it was proved that he had used the funds of the Bank to "accommodate" the press, without requiring the customary securities for the restoration of the money. In fact, the "loans" which the banks often make to the newspapers may more properly be called gifts, or rather *wages;* the wages of prostitution.

I could fill a volume, larger than this, with the evidences of a villainous confederacy between the newspapers and the banks. Some proofs of this confederacy have already been offered to my readers, but I consider that the course pursued by the newspapers themselves, is a *demonstration* of the fact. The journalists would not cautiously abstain from the discussion of such an important and interesting subject as Banking, unless they had some potent reason for their forbearance. What is that potent reason? All who understand the springs of newspaper action, know that *money* is the only motive-power that can control the operations of American journalism. If these facts, properly considered, were the only proofs we had of a corrupt league between the newspapers and the banks, it would be impossible to entertain any reasonable doubts on the subject. But I tell you, my friends, that the proofs are innumerable and overwhelming; and, if you wish to investigate the subject thoroughly, you will find all the information you require in Allibone's trial, "Gouge on Banking," "W. L. Mackenzie's Life of Martin Van Buren," or the *secret memoirs,* (if they are written,) of almost any distinguished public journalist of Philadelphia or New York.

That well-known confederacy between the newspapers and the banks is one of the facts which I have selected to exemplify my FIFTH CHARGE, which asserts that our American press is the abettor and confederate of all who defraud and plunder the people.

But banks are not the *only* plunderers of the people who are blessed with the sympathy and assistance of the newspapers.

KNAVISH INSURANCE COMPANIES.

The "bogus" Life Insurance Companies, which do a flourishing business in some of our principal cities, will supply us with another convenient illustration. Doubtless there are some substantial and equitably-managed Life Insurance Companies in America, but we are now speaking of the "bogus" ones. Lest the word *bogus* should not be found in your dictionary, I give you a definition of it, according to its general acceptation in America. Bogus is an adjective, nearly synonymous with spurious or counterfeit. A Bogus Insurance Company is one which has no capital and no pecuniary responsibility. Four or five scoundrels colleague together, hire a room for a place of business and furnish it with a writing-desk, a long table covered with green baize, two or three chairs for clients, several office-stools for clerks, a quire of foolscap paper, a pewter inkstand, some metallic pens, a box of red wafers and another of black sand.

These equipments are all that are necessary to enable the "Company" to grant policies of insurance to any amount, to receive deposits of money for *safe-keeping*, and to transact any other financiering business which an institution of the kind might properly undertake. The profligate character and insolvent condition of these Bogus Companies are well known among sagacious business-men, and by no class of people are these companies better understood than by newspaper editors; but the sovereign people in general are not supplied with any information on the subject. On the contrary, there is an evident solicitude on the part of the journalists to maintain the credit of these "swindling shops," and to enable them to carry on their operations unmolested.

Some time ago, the Philadelphia Board of Trade ascertained, by close scrutiny, the rotten condition of several Life Insurance Companies in this city. That Board, with a laudable desire to protect the community against the monstrous frauds perpetrated by these rascally associations, made an accurate report of their affairs, showing that it was impossible for them to meet their engagements. But this salutary exposure was evidently displeasing to the newspapers. It is true that the most notoriously corrupt journal in Philadelphia, pretended in several short paragraphs, to declaim against the fraudulent companies; but this battery was soon silenced, and all who understand the tactics of journalism will easily guess how it was done.

I suspect that not less than twenty or thirty per cent. of the profits of these knavish corporations, and others of a kindred nature, is required to purchase the connivance and co-operation of the press. When an editor becomes restive and begins to discourse in a strain of virtuous indignation, the company administers a sedative, in the form of "a good fat advertisement," or some other tributary offering. The gratitude of the press is manifested not in forbearance merely, but occasionally by strong recommendations, otherwise called "puffs" or "first-rate notices," inserted in the editorial columns and apparently coming from the editor himself. In these gracious paragraphs, the public is advised to have unlimited confidence in the be-puffed corporation. "*We* know that it is sound," (the editor says or seems to say,) "and we consider it a duty to our readers to inform them where they may safely invest their money."

In a puff of this kind which I lately saw in a Philadelphia paper, it was mentioned as a notable fact, and one which was calculated to establish the credit of the Company forever, that it had actually *paid* a certain sum of money for which it had become liable! Paying a debt was quite an achievement in the estimation of this editor; and he appears to have supposed that one performance of this kind, (though it was probably done only for effect,) was enough to atone for a thousand delinquencies.

THE YANKEE SHOWMAN.

In the memoirs or *confessions* of the notorious Phineas T. Barnum—"The Great Yankee Showman"—we have many exemplifications of the ways in which journalism assists imposture and shares its profits. Barnum tells, for instance, how several of the New York papers, at his suggestion, published editorial articles on *mermaids*, discussing the probability of their existence, merely to prepare the way for the exhibition of a marine monster which Barnum had constructed by sewing the tail of a codfish to the body of a monkey! Thousands of dollars were extorted from the credulous public by this miserable artifice, which never could have succeeded without newspaper assistance.

Barnum, like every other successful speculator on the "gullibility" of the American people, was a munificent patron of the newspapers. In one way or another, he paid them liberally for their services; and this is the secret of his prosperity. Having purchased the co-operation of the press, he found that no trick which his conscienceless ingenuity could devise was too extravagant or absurd to deceive the enlightened republicans. Not one of his "speculations" failed to produce a golden harvest, because the newspapers testified that his prodigies were all genuine and well worth the price demanded for a sight of them.

Not the frailties only, but even the virtues and amiable characteristics of the Yankee Nation were used by Barnum and his newspaper colleagues as the means of finding access to that well-guarded sanctuary, the American pocket. Because our countrymen cherish, with filial affection, the memory of Washington, it was thought that the exhibition of an old negro woman, as one who had nursed that illustrious patriot in his infancy, would be "an exceedingly good speculation." I am convinced that there were few editors in the country who did not know from the first that this was a heartless imposition; but I never heard that one journalist took the little trouble which was required to expose the disgusting fraud. Hundreds of editors, on the other hand, appealed to the patriotic feelings of Americans, and earnestly exhorted them not to miss this opportunity for beholding one who had carried their beloved hero in her arms. Of all desecrations, the most detestable is that which attempts to make merchandise of our holiest affections.

When Barnum brought over "The Swedish Nightingale," *alias* Mademoiselle Jenny Lind, his first endeavor was to get up a storm of popular enthusiasm in her behalf; and this object was easily effected by the agency of the newspaper press. Anecdotes illustrative of Miss Lind's generosity, benevolence, etc., were manufactured by Barnum and widely circulated by the journals—each anecdote being, of course, an advertisement in masquerade. By such nefarious means public admiration was raised to fever heat, and many excitable fools were induced to rob their families by paying the unreasonable prices which the "Yankee Showman" demanded for a sight of the "Divine Jenny." No one seemed to realize the utter absurdity of the idea that any thing "divine" would consent to be exhibited by the inventor and proprietor of the Woolly Horse and the Fejee Mermaid. Our countrymen had become phrenzied or intoxicated by "the gassy *afflatus* of journalism;" and when they had been completely robbed of their wits, it was an easy matter to disposses them of their dollars.

"STARRING."

A magnificent game of swindling is carried on by means of a coalition between newspaper-men and the importers of theatrical "stars," opera-singers, ballet-dancers, etc. But I cannot afford space even for an *outline* of these dishonorable transactions. Sometimes there is a dispute or quarrel between the confederates, and then the truth unexpectedly makes its appearance. In this way it has become a matter of general notoriety that every dramatic adventurer, every public singer or dancer, every equestrian performer, every posture-master, juggler or mountebank that comes to this country, must submit to the extortions of the press, or consent to be "damned," as far as newspaper denunciations can accomplish his perdition. The amount of public enthusiasm manufactured for the benefit of any particular adventurer is exactly proportioned to the degree of patience with which such adventurer may submit to the fleecing operations of the editors. Hence we find that the most *open-handed* foreign artists—not the most meritorious ones—always succeed best in their professional tours through the United States.

Forney, the editor of the Philadelphia *Press,* averred that Bennett of the New York *Herald* had grown rich by extorting money from actors and actresses ; and it is generally believed that Bennett was the first "American" editor who succeeded in laying the children of Thespis under contribution. But Bennett's biographer magnanimously concedes that his Caledonian hero was not the original contriver of that "excellent piece of knavery" which has now become incorporated with the regular business of the journalists. If we may believe the panegyrist of James Gordon Bennett, a Mr. Buckingham, editor of the *New England Galaxy,* as early as the year 1825, excited a storm of popular indignation against Edmund Kean, probably because that tragedian would not comply with the requisitions of the press. Because Kean refused to "bleed" metaphorically, he was compelled to do so literally ; for the mob, spurred on by the urgent appeals of the press, assailed him in the most ferocious manner, and, after doing him some bodily damage, forced him to take refuge in the ladies dressing-room of the theatre, from which he afterward escaped in female apparel.

Mr. Buckingham, the editor who is supposed to have produced this excitement, is spoken of by Bennett's "honest chronicler" as "a much respected veteran of the press, whose example as a journalist must have had no little weight on the mind of Mr. Bennett." (What a generous acknowledgment !) But if Bennett was not the first editor who forced histrionic people to contribute to the support of the free and independent journalism of our country, he has an undisputed claim to be considered as *one* of the originators of that tax-levying despotism which compels professional persons, strangers especially, to acknowledge the supremacy of the press by tributary offerings. Dramatic artists are made to understand that any omission of this duty will be punished, not by killing *criticisms* only, but by accusations which will probably subject the offender to the vengeance of an exasperated mob.

Mr. Ullman, who brought over the Italian songstress, M'lle Piccolomini, was strongly commended by a Philadelphia editor for his *liberality;* but it seems that he had not generosity enough, or not *money* enough, to satisfy the whole tribe of typographical Bedouins, for, in the New York Herald of October 9, 1858, Mr. Ullman publishes a long complaint, setting forth the ill treatment which he had received from some of the dissatisfied American journalists:

"There are some of those editors," (says the afflicted Ullman,) " who seize, with the greatest avidity, on any *on dit* or gossip which affects the reputation of a distinguished artist. Such was the case when I brought to America the late Madame Sontag, who was so much shocked with an infamous newspaper attack sent to her on the day of her arrival, that she was on the point of returning to Europe without appearing before the American public."

I apprehend that the "infamous attack" spoken of by Mr. Ullman, was sent to Madame Sontag with an intimation that the fire would be kept up, until she made the usual propitiatory offerings.

Theatrical people seldom receive any fair and honest treatment from the editors. They are the objects of either undeserved abuse or extravagant recommendations, and I believe that those who receive the loudest plaudits of the press are generally the least deserving. Real talent, on the other hand, is apt to meet with a chilling reception from the " Press Gang," and this fact was lately exemplified in the case of M'lle Rachel, the French tragedienne. This lady, in her American tour, relied more on her merit than on her money ; and, of course, she was disappointed.

Many foreign artists who come to this country on "starring" expeditions, are impostors, or something very little better. They are brought over sometimes by speculators on public curiosity, who have previously " made arrangements" with certain " leading newspapers," in order to have a good supply of popular excitement manufactured against the time of the prodigy's arrival. "Many a holiday fool in England," says Trinculo, "who would not give a doit to relieve a lame beggar, will lay out ten to see a dead Indian." In America, the case is still worse. Hundreds of our countrymen, who are in some danger of bankruptcy, will disburse five or fifty dollars, or a much larger sum, for the opportunity to hear a "Swedish Nightingale," or a Norwegian fiddler.

No "starring" imposition could possibly be successful in America, without the help of the newspapers.

SWINDLERS.

Knavish speculations of all kinds are more lucrative than legitimate branches of business. Rascals and impostors, therefore, can better afford to pay for newspaper aid than the most upright merchant or manufacturer. If your eyes are good for any thing, you must have observed that nothing but rascality and imposture is cordially recommended by the public journals. You may find, in the course of your newspaper reading, many complimentary notices of quack doctors, no matter how ignorant and unscrupulous they may be; but the scientific and conscientious physician meets with no editorial applause.

ROGUISH PUBLISHERS.

The worst books and the most worthless periodicals obtain the zealous approbation of many newspapers, and, as a matter of course, they secure a wide circulation. Some of the most prosperous book and periodical publishers in the United States are mere swindlers. They are constantly obtaining money on false pretenses. Almost every book issued by certain "publishing houses" of Philadelphia and New York is, in one way or another, an imposture. All of our most widely-circulated periodicals are "humbugs"—making great pentensions to intellectuality and literary excellence, with little or no genuine merit to support their claims. But the publishers of this nauseating trash enjoy almost a monopoly of the book and magazine market, because they know how to make the newspaper press subservient to their uses. A certain pamphlet novel publisher in Philadelphia boasted that, by means of puffing and advertising, he could make any book *go;* "and I don't care a d——," added he, "whether it has any literary merit or not."

How many thousands of dollars do the American people annually expend for books and periodicals which are absolutely worth nothing! How much of this money could be saved and applied to better purposes if the public would only accept this scrap of good counsel: "*Never buy any thing merely because it is recommended by a newspaper.*"

PETER FUNK.

As a general rule, it is advisable not to expend a single copper, in any way, at the suggestion of a newspaper paragraph. There is *prima facie* evidence of fraud in every such suggestion. In all cases of this kind, the newspaper man performs a duty very similar to that which is assigned to "Peter Funk" at a mock auction in New York. The Peter Funks of Chatham street are certain gentlemen who are kept in pay by the Jewish auctioneers, and who are expected to be in attendance at every public sale for the purpose of advising people, in confidential whispers, to purchase the splendid jewelry, which is manufactured expressly for this trade. Peter assures the artless customer that it is all pure gold; and, as this information appears to come from a disinterested source, many an artless customer is thereby induced to invest his money in the glittering but deceptive merchandise.

The Peter Funks of the newspaper press have a much wider field for *their* operations. Every phase of scoundrelism seeks their assistance and acknowledges the value of their services by the most bountiful remuneration.

As everybody in the United States reads the newspapers, and nine-tenths of the population *believe* them, it is evident that their opposition would fall with crushing and killing effect on any kind of imposture. The very existence of any kind of imposture, therefore, proves that the newspapers do not oppose it. Supposing that our journalists do not love rascality *for its own sake*—supposing that they have not a *natural sympathy* for scoundrelism—they would not permit their fellow-citizens to be deceived and defrauded, as they certainly are every day, without making some demonstration against the abuse, if the success and perpetuation of that abuse were not, in some way, profitable to the journalists themselves. If, therefore, Messrs. Editors were merely *quiet spectators* of the multifarious villainies which are constantly enacted on this soil, we might justly infer that considerations of self-interest kept them inactive. But when we find them earnestly and strenuously engaged in helping the despoilers of the public, we cannot doubt that they belong to the same horde of banditti; and that they are the most dangerous villains of the confederacy, because they assume a disguise which recommends them to the favor, affection, and confidence of their victims.

SUPPLEMENTARY ILLUSTRATIONS.

INSURANCE SHOPS.

The following paragraph appeared in the Philadelphia *American Banner* of November 16, 1850 :—

"Once more we caution the public against fraudulent Life Insurance Companies, some of which, now in operation in this city, are controlled by villains who should have been in the penitentiary ten or twelve years ago, and who make themselves liable, every day, to a criminal prosecution for obtaining money on false pretenses. Have no faith in high-sounding names and the announcement of large capitals—it is all smoke. Some men, pretending to respectability, unaccountably permit their names to be used in connection with these swindles; and, as for capital, some of the "companies" have no more than their office furniture; and that being covered, perhaps, by the landlord's claim, is not subject to seizure for debt. In short, these bubble companies are wholly irresponsible."

These "bubble companies," by advertising liberally in the newspapers, and, perhaps, by gratifying the editors in other ways, were enabled to do a flourishing business for years, and no daily paper in the city, and no weekly one of large circulation, expressed the least disapprobation of their movements. I believe that several of these fraudulent associations are *still* in operation.

ROBACK THE WIZARD.

Doctor Roback, as he calls himself, has practiced the conjuring business in Baltimore, Philadelphia, and New York, for more than fifteen years, occasionally removing from one city to another, and always meeting with the most liberal encouragement "from the press and the public." Roback is a generous advertiser in the newspapers, and his great success in his mystic occupation may be ascribed to that circumstance. He has been arrested several times on the charge of obtaining money on false pretenses, but as his newspaper friends considerately take but little notice of his occasional entanglements with the law, his reputation as an able conjuror is but little affected by these misadventures.

Very lately Mayor Tiemann of New York received a letter from a Mrs. Derby of Belvidere, Illinois, who complained that her husband, Mr. Asaph Derby, had paid Doctor Roback twenty-two dollars, for which sum the Doctor had engaged to use his necromantic skill for the purpose of making Mr. Derby draw a prize of five thousand dollars in a certain lottery. Owing to some miscalculation on the Doctor's part, the experiment did not succeed. Mr. Derby drew a *blank*, and Mrs. Derby, in the bitterness of her disappointment, composed a plaintive epistle to Mayor Tiemann, as aforesaid, and enclosed a letter which her husband had lately received from the conjuror, and of which the following is a copy :—

" MR. ASAPH DERBY.—*Dear Sir.*—Yours of the 3d instant was received, and I was sorry to hear of your disappointment in the lottery. However, I will make it all right, and you shall receive the benefit you expect. I have made a calculation, by which I perceive that you will do better to wait for a while, or to the time mentioned below, and then send again for a ticket, and proceed as follows: Address to F. X. Brennan, Esq., of Baltimore, one dollar; mail the letter on the 5th of April, and tell him to send you in return a ticket for their lottery, with Nos. 5, 47, 68 on it, combined, for the drawing of the 19th of April next; and *this time it cannot fail*, as that day is very lucky for you in this respect.

C. W. ROBACK."

Mr. Derby would have complied with these directions, but his wife, having less faith or more sagacity than Mr. D., gave the information which led to the conjuror's arrest.

It is reported that Roback has accumulated a large fortune by his trade of *conjuring*, which some people have erroneously supposed to be one of the "lost arts." But in America, illuminated by the blazing effulgence of three thousand newspapers, the almost-forgotten science of Zoroaster and Appolonius has been completely revived. I have seen six or eight advertisements of astrologers, soothsayers, etc., in a single copy of the Philadelphia *Ledger*. I am informed, moreover, that astrology is a thriving business in the United States, and that numbers of our most intelligent citizens often hold consultations with the professors of that occult science. Is it possible that we, who bask in the radiance of so many luminaries, (journalistic ones,) can have any occasion to use the feeble light of the stars?

While astrologers, fortune-tellers, and wizards of all kinds, continue to be *good advertising customers*, their mystic arts will never get out of fashion or become unprofitable in a country where the newspaper press is the principal illuminator.

THE SWILL-MILK BUSINESS.

This foul and wicked trade is carried on chiefly by Irishmen;

and Irishmen, as I have remarked elsewhere, are the special "pets" of the newspaper press. Nine tenths of the cows' milk used in Philadelphia and New York is obtained from diseased animals, which are fed on the slops or "swill" procured from distilleries. The Academy of Medicine of New York lately appointed a committee of physicians to examine the quality of the milk thus produced, and Dr. S. R. Percy, a member of that committee, published the result of his investigations; but the startling facts which have been brought to light by this exposure have received scarcely any attention from the public journals. Frank Leslie's *Illustrated News* of New York, and Colonel Fitzgerald's *City Item* of Philadelphia are the only papers in which I have seen any particular allusion to the subject.

Dr. Percy reports that, in order to test the unwholesome quality of the swill on which the cows are fed,—"two of the committee drank some of it, (about a wine-glassful,) and it produced severe griping and purging." The cows which subsist on this swill are always in a feverish condition and their flesh and udders are often in a state of incipient decomposition. Some of them are not able to stand on their feet, and yet they are *milked*, and their milk is sold about the city. The doctors ascertained that children and others who used much of this milk, invariably became diseased and many of them exhibited very alarming symptoms. Dr. Percy gives numerous instances, of which the following are fair specimens :—

"I was called in, (says Dr. Percy,) to examine a child aged sixteen months, whose parents reside in Forsyth street. The child vomited freely; the vomited matter consisting of milk with a little mucus. The countenance of the child was flushed and anxious, the pulse rapid and full, the skin hot and the respiration frequent. The friends were apprehensive of convulsions. I learned that the child had arrived from Boston that morning, that it was accustomed to feed entirely on milk, and until the present time had enjoyed remarkable good health. The mother of the child, who was visiting her sister, had taken from the milkman who supplied the family the usual quantity of milk she gave her child, and put it aside for use. The child had not taken more than usual that day, and had taken nothing else.

"I thought I had a case of simple fever, brought on by the fatigue of travel, and as the child had evidently not entirely unloaded the stomach, I administered an emetic abundantly diluted with warm water. Free vomiting took place of large lumps of curdy matter, which gave the child much relief, and he slept for some time. On awakening he had a large, loose and very offensive evacuation, containing a quantity of undigested curds. I gave a dose of oil with a few drops of laudanum, and directed that the next day the child should use whey instead of milk. By the next evening (Wednesday) the child seemed as well as usual, and the next morning (Thursday) the mother resumed the milk diluted with water. About nine o'clock A. M. I was called again, the child having vomited the milk about an hour after it was taken. It was restless and feverish after it had ejected all the milk. I left it with directions to resume the whey, which it continued until Friday morning, when the mother took it with her to visit another sister living in the neighborhood of the Washington Parade Ground. I saw the child on Saturday morning in West Waverley place; it was then quite cheerful and comfortable, and had taken that morning milk and water without any ill effects. The child remained here some two weeks, entirely recovered its strength, and used milk undiluted, as before its arrival in the city. The mother returned with the child to Forsyth street, and it had not taken the milk supplied to that family an hour when it was troubled with vomiting as before. The mother now insisted that the milk was the cause of the sickness, and would use no more of the milk supplied to the family. Wholesome milk from the country was obtained, and the child was restored to perfect health."

Another child who used the swill-milk was attended by Dr. Percy, who found it in a dying condition, the bowels being extensively ulcerated. And many similar cases are mentioned by the medical committee, the disease in every instance, being clearly traced to the use of the poisonous milk. Hundreds of lives are probably lost every year, by means of the general consumption of this horrible article of food.

The murderous swill-milk business could be easily checked or suppressed by enforcing the laws intended to prevent the sale of unwholesome provisions. But I am convinced that any measure of the kind would be resisted by the Newspaper Press. Frank Leslie's denunciations of this criminal and disgusting trade, were generally condemned or ridiculed. Some charged him with a disposition to persecute "the poor, *honest*, Irish milk-sellers," and others regarded his zeal in this cause as "a very funny kind of *moral quixotism*."

STOCK GAMBLING.—This business, as it is generally managed, is more immoral and mischievous, by many degrees, than the games of faro, poker, *rouge-et-noir*, or thimble-rig; but it is a business which enjoys the countenance and active assistance of the city papers in general, and some of the editors themselves are stock gamblers on the largest scale. The proprietors of one of the most successful Philadelphia dailies have made more money by these "speculations" than by journalism. Newspapers are often used to produce revulsions and convulsions in the stock-market: and it is by the nice management of these spasms that the principal speculators thrive and become opulent. The inflations and collapses of "fancy stocks" are effected chiefly by newspaper agency. The term "gambling," applied to these operations, is strictly correct. The stock-business is not a game of chance, however, nor a game of skill, (properly speaking,) but simply a game of *cheating*.

Dealers in stocks are the special objects of editorial admiration and eulogium. *Harper's Weekly*, (supposed to be one of the most moral newspapers in America,) published an extravagant panegyric on the celebrated Jacob Little, with reference to which panegyric the *Cincinnati Gazette* spoke as follows:—

"According to his own statement, Mr. L. has often exerted himself to inflate fancy stocks, and then, by deliberately conspiring with a PROFLIGATE PRESS to produce a panic, he has destroyed the property of thousands of his fellow-citizens. Yet *Harper's Weekly* presents this conduct as a very commendable sort of thing, and offers the operator as an example of admirable talent and sagacity! We have no comment to make; for we doubt whether the pen of Juvenal could present a stronger satire on men and morals than is contained in this eulogy of a New York journalist on a New York speculator."

SECTION X.

THE DEMORALIZING INFLUENCES OF JOURNALISM.

Examination of the Sixth Charge.

ABUNDANCE NO BLESSING.

YES, my well-beloved countrymen, you have a greater abundance of newspaper literature than any other people in the world; but I have respectfully warned you not to indulge in a jubilation on that account. In the last section, it was proved to your satisfaction I hope that your natural acuteness of intellect and your inherent wisdom have not been much improved by newspaper teachings. I will now, (with your kind permission,) endeavor to make it appear that your *moral* condition has not been much elevated by the same kind of tuition.

VICIOUS INSTRUCTIONS.

Doubtless you have heard of Peter Abelard, an unfaithful instructor, who debauched his pupil, and was punished for his sin in a manner which my bashfulness will not allow me to describe. It is your grievous misfortune, my countrymen, to be placed under the moral guidance of a whole army of Abelards, as corrupt and licentious as the tutor of Heloise, but less learned and more incorrigible; for on *them*, I fear, no kind of mental or corporal discipline could have any chastening and salutary effect.

In one of the earliest divisions of this work, I informed you that the most widely-circulated and influential papers of America are often controlled by men of a vicious and depraved character. It must be evident to your own perceptions that persons of such a character must be bad instructors, and that the *journals* controlled by them must have a vitiating effect on public morals, proportioned to the amount of their circulation and influence. You have observed, perhaps, that vicious people are generally more earnest in their efforts to propagate vice than good men are to disseminate honest and correct principles.

ONE OF THE INSTRUCTORS.

It is undeniable that the most extensively-circulated and the most influential daily paper in the United States, at the present time, is the *New York Herald*. The character of this journal has been pretty correctly delineated in various strictures on the American newspaper press. An acute critic in the *Foreign Quarterly Review* says, with reference to this *Herald*—"There is only one word which can describe the tone of every original sentence which appears in its columns, and this word we must be excused for using—it is *blackguardism*."

This word, however, with all its expressiveness, is not sufficient to describe the crimes and misdemeanors of Bennett's *Herald*, and other publications which belong to the same Satanic school of journalism. A *blackguard*, moving in his proper sphere, may cause but little damage or inconvenience to the public; but a journalist who, habitually and in the most ostentatious manner, insults the moral sense of a whole nation, is a more serious offender, and deserves to be called a *malefactor* rather than a blackguard.

But, as particular mention has been made of Bennett's *Herald*, it may be proper to remark that I am not about to fall into the common error of representing that sheet as the *worst* of its class. The Herald has several competitors in New York, and many humble imitators in different parts of the country, all of which, (according to the measure of their abilities,) serve the devil with as much zeal and success as the reputed founder of their academy.

ANOTHER MORAL TEACHER.

The *New York Tribune*, which, with regard to circulation and influence, aspires to the *second* place in American journalism, is a more hypocritical sheet than the *Herald*, and, on that account, more dangerous. It is the sly and subtle evangelist of all that is false in doctrine and detestable in practice. It has always been the apologist and coadjutor of scheming and corrupt politicians; it revels in popular excitement like a sea-mew in a storm, and is always ready to play "Sir Pandarus" whenever Dame Public shows any frail or libidinous inclinations. The *Tribune*, like many another newspaper of its class, considers it a *duty* to adapt itself to the public's humor in all such cases; and, instead of making any effort to allay the unhealthy excitement of the populace, and to restrain the morbid appetites which are sometimes exhibited by the "sovereign people," this faithful guardian and instructor administers provocatives to its thoughtless pupils, and points out the way to unlimited indulgence. In short, whenever the public is inclined to go on a *scortatory excursion*, (metaphorically speaking,) the *Tribune* and its associates of the Satanic Press are always ready to perform the duties of pimps and pilots.

To show you how these things are managed, I will refer to a matter of very recent occurrence, viz.:

"THE GREAT PRIZE FIGHT"

between Morissey and Heenan, which was, beyond all comparison, the most demoralizing, beastly, disgusting and scandalous affair of the kind that ever took place in any half-civilized country. All that is most abominable in the population of New York, thieves, prostitutes, bawdy-house ruffians, low gamblers and vagabonds of every description, including a fair proportion of newspaper reporters, assembled at the place of exhibition, which was beyond the jurisdiction of the city authorities. Such was the lawless and outrageous character of the mob collected on this occasion, that many persons who had been at tracted by curiosity to the battle-ground, left the spot in dismay, having good reason, as they thought, to be apprehensive of robbery or murder.

The "representatives of the press," however, appear from their own accounts, to have felt quite at home at this scene of ruffianism, prostitution and multiform rascality. While the fight was in progress, a dispute arose in relation to some question of pugilistic etiquette, and the matter was referred to the arbitration of "a gentleman connected with the New York Press," whose scientific blackguardism was taken for granted, and who was permitted to occupy a position inside of the ring, as a token of respect for his honorable and dignified vocation! To the other newspaper reporters was granted the same right of precedence at this grand saturnalia of licentious brutality.

Several of "the most respectable" of the New York journals sent special reporters to the scene of action, exerting themselves to supply the reading public with all the sickening details of the battle.

The *Tribune*, claiming to be the most decent of the "flash" journals of New York, published the longest and most circumstantial account of this fight, devoting no less than *four columns* to that purpose. In order to attract as much attention as possible to the report, it was introduced by the following titular lines in large capitals:

"THE GREAT PRIZE FIGHT!
CONTEST FOR THE CHAMPIONSHIP!!
MORRISSEY THE WINNER!!!
VIVID PICTURE OF MODERN CIVILIZATION."

Then came a characteristically hypocritical introduction, by the editor, in the following words:

"In pursuance of our duty as a faithful recorder of the current events of the day, we are obliged to devote a large space in this sheet to the details of a fight for the *Championship of*

America, between Heenan and Morrissey. No event for years has created so much interest in this city, and, indeed, throughout the country ; a fact most disgraceful to any civilized people ; but, as a fact, compelling us to recognize and record it. We append the detailed account by our special reporter."

There is a falsehood, expressed or implied, in almost every line of this editorial preamble. It is not the "duty" of the Tribune, or of any other paper pretending to common decency, to publish all the particulars of every vicious or demoralizing transaction which may happen to take place in the country, and the *Tribune* was under no "obligation" of any kind to give its readers a "faithful report" of this execrable battle. "The championship of America" is a phrase thrown in by the editor of the *Tribune* to make his hoodwinked patrons believe that this fisty-cuff contest between two wretched vagabonds was an affair of *national importance !* I strongly suspect, and wish to believe, that neither Heenan nor Morrissey is an *American* champion ; and I am quite willing that Ireland, or any other foreign country, should have the credit of breeding them both.

The assertion of the *Tribune* that the people of the United States were generally interested in this pugilistic combat is a monstrous calumny. I do not believe that, even in the city of New York, the more respectable classes of the population concerned themselves much about the matter. Prize-fighting is not an American "institution." The taste for this barbarous and vicious recreation is *exotic ;* and what we find of it in America exists chiefly among our imported population and is cultivated and cherished by our foreign newspaper press.

The deceitful expression of *disapprobation* in the foregoing extract from the Tribune, is, (as was intimated above,) characteristic of that print and of many others, which,—on the supposition that they have *a few* decent and virtuous people among their patrons,—are anxious to keep up some appearance of moral rectitude. Papers which adopt this cautious and insinuating policy are most to be dreaded, for their disguise gives them access to the pure and innocent. The most dangerous bawds and seducers are those who maintain a superficial appearance of virtue and decorum. For days and weeks before the fight took place, the Tribune and other "sensation papers" in New York were exerting themselves to draw public attention to the expected battle and to make it an interesting and exciting subject.

But prize-fighting and every other immoral practice may find resolute defenders and *undisguised* advocates among the newspaper scribes of America. The subjoined extract is taken from a long disquisition on the Heenan and Morrissey fight, written by the editor of a Philadelphia hebdomadal which calls itself a "family newspaper."

"While the rules of the ring," (says this domestic Mentor,) "insist on manly, fair, even-handed contests, pugilism cannot be utterly condemned, nor can the art of self-defense with nature's weapons be scouted. Courage is a quality admired by man and adored by woman; if there is one quality more than any other which a woman despises in a man, it is timidity or cowardice. Every man should exercise his limbs for the purpose of self-defense. A well-delivered knuckled blow from a small man has laid many a big bully on the ground. One word for pugilists:—low as they are collectively, many honorable exceptions have been known. In England, professed pugilists have lived respected and died lamented. (!) Read George Barrow. It is also a positive fact, that the greatest pugilists have been known as quiet, inoffensive men, as the history of the most eminent of the craft will prove." *Etc., etc.*

THE GROG BUSINESS.

Many other vicious practices besides pugilism, (and some *worse* ones undoubtedly,) are fostered by the newspaper press. For example, in many parts of our country, the Liquor Trade has become a moneyed and political power. Wherever this happens to be the case, the interests of this iniquitous trade are sustained by the public journals with the most hearty good will—though a salutary dread of public opinion, or of the Anti-Grog influence, may make the journalist a little cautious in his *mode* of encouraging and promoting the rum traffic. All legislation which could have the least efficacy in checking this traffic is opposed by the newspaper press in general;—and all attempts to enforce the laws which are intended to mitigate the evils of intemperance, are sure to meet with the sarcastic comments or the open denunciations of Messrs. Editors.

It is a common pretense with these gentlemen that *stringent* temperance laws—the only kind of temperance laws that are really useful—cannot be enforced, because "public opinion is opposed to them." The very enactment of such laws is the best proof we can have that public opinion is on their side; for the solemn acts of our legislatures are presumed to be the most legitimate expressions of public sentiment. It is pretended, however, that even here in Philadelphia, and in other places where sobriety and good sense are supposed to be predominant, no efficient laws for the suppression of that vice, which is more afflictive than any other to the American people, would be tolerated!

As three-fourths of the people in the United States have no information on any subject except what is derived from their newspaper reading, it has become a prevalent belief, in many places, that, on the score of *expediency*, the vice of intemperance should not be subjected to any severe legal restraints. The practical results of this false and detestable doctrine may be seen even here in the "Quaker City;" in some parts of which almost every third or fourth house is a grog-kennel, while drunkards are multiplied in our midst, as it were, by geometrical progression.

There is a grog regency in Philadelphia—a regularly-organized association called the "Liquor League," the avowed object of which is to "put down" the friends and advocates of temperance. I do not believe that there is a newspaper in Philadelphia which would dare to utter a word in disparagement of this rum-sellers' association or its objects ; and few, if any, of our journals could be easily persuaded to insert a paragraph in favor of temperance, or any other matter which might possibly give offense to the "Liquor League." Every thing, in fact, which is calculated to injure the traffic in ardent spirits is kept, as much as possible, from the knowledge of the people. For example, though it is generally known to editors that nine-tenths at least of the liquors sold in American taverns and grog-shops are spurious, and composed of the most baleful ingredients, we seldom find any allusion to this appalling fact in a newspaper.

The general course pursued by the public press with regard to the liquor business, is well calculated to make the people believe that no reform in that business is required. This is a practical lie, of course, and a more pernicious one has never been set afloat on the Stygian stream of journalism.

OBSCENE REPORTING.

To give another example of the demoralizing tendencies of the newspaper press, I will refer to the prevalent custom of publishing in the journals a full and minute account of criminal trials, cases of rape, seduction, *crim. con.*, etc., the details of which are often too gross and filthy to be diffused through the atmosphere of a common brothel. If familiarity with vice disposes us to embrace it, (as the most philosophical of English poets avers,) the youth of America, blessed as they are with a luxuriant abundance of newspaper reading, must become adepts in iniquity almost as soon as they leave off their diapers. No narrative of human depravity or crime can shock or horrify an American reader. He has studied every phase of profligacy and flagrant villainy in his early childhood ; and he smiles superciliously, with a consciousness of superior intelligence, when some newspaper scribbler tries (after the manner of the Herald or Tribune) to astonish him with "a full and faithful report" of the latest deed of preternatural atrocity.

FOUL ADVERTISEMENTS.

There is a newspaper in Philadelphia—a *cheap* publication, price one cent—which appears to be the recognized organ of atheism, prostitution, and every thing else that is most perilous and detestable. The advertising customers of this precious journal seem to be under no kind of restriction. All sorts of negotiations are carried on bravely in its columns. Enterprising young ladies and mournful widows willing to be comforted, call on some "kind gentleman" to *loan* them ten, twenty, thirty, forty, or fifty dollars. Gentlemen of various ages announce their desire to "form the acquaintance" of young ladies—sometimes "with a view to matrimony;" but, in general, the language of the advertisement is not so "craftily qualified." Under the head of PERSONAL, "Charlotte" informs "Werter" that she will expect him at half-past nine o'clock on Wednesday evening, when "Albert" will be out of the way; and, in the next paragraph, "Sappho" engages to meet "Phaon" "at the usual place," but hopes that he will be better provided with money than he was at the last interview.

The piquant obscenity of this advertising sheet makes it acceptable, no doubt, with a large class of readers; and, accordingly, it boasts of a great circulation. This circumstance may make us understand that the extensive circulation of a newspaper is by no means a proof of its moral worth and respectability.

"RESPECTABLE NEWSPAPERS."

By the way, my good reader, can you tell what newspaper *respectability* is? In what does it consist? I must confess that it is a thing which I am not able to analyze. A *large* sheet, in general, is more respectable than a small one; and a paper which is sold for two pence per copy is more respectable than one which is sold for a penny. But I do not know that the character of the editor, or the conduct of the publication itself, is a very important item in the account.

Some of the "most respectable" journals in the United States are conducted editorially by knaves and blackguards, fellows in whose society you could not remain for five minutes without a sense of contamination; unless you are reconciled, by habit, to base and profligate companionship.

When I speak of the vitiating and demoralizing influences of the press, do not imagine that I have my eye on such comparatively obscure and insignificant publications as the *Paul Pry*, the *Alligator*, the *Cytherean Miscellany*, etc. These typographical reptiles belong to a class whose power to do mischief is circumscribed within very narrow limits. They burrow in the earth, like scorpions, and when they do happen to exhibit themselves by daylight, you recognize them at a glance and are aware of their noxious character. I bid you beware of more dangerous reptiles than these; such, for example, as those centipedes of journalism which insinuate themselves into your habitations, and, without exciting your apprehensions of evil, innoculate you with their venomous secretions. Beware of those journalistic poisoners who steal upon your hours of fancied security and drench you with their horrible distillments, covering you from top to toe with a moral leprosy, an universal tetter, "most foul and lazar-like."

Let it be observed that the larger number of those newspapers which I denounce as moral pests and intolerable nuisances, are the very journals which many of you, my injured countrymen, regard as unimpeachably RESPECTABLE. That we may come to a better understanding of this subject, I will give you an example of newspaper respectability which immediately presents itself to my notice.

A MODEL CIVILIZER.

Harper's Weekly is, in the estimation of the majority, one of the most respectable newspapers in the United States. It calls itself, *par excellence*, the "JOURNAL OF CIVILIZATION," and I believe that its claims to that superb title are generally allowed. The "Journal of Civilization" must be respectable, and ought to be respected; especially in any region where there is an obvious necessity for moral, social and intellectual culture. Accordingly we find that this faithful chronicler of human progress, (Harper's Weekly aforesaid) is well appreciated in the city of New York, and in some of our western States, where the people have become awakened to a sense of their needs, and are anxious to be civilized by the most rapid and effective process.

The *mode* of civilizing the Americans which the Messrs. Harpers have adopted, is ingenious and sufficiently unique. They are pious men, these Harpers, (Methodists, I believe,) and I dare say they wish to do as much good in the world as is consistent with their pecuniary interests. But they are experienced publishers, and they know very well that, in the present condition of American journalism, "doing a good business" and doing good for the service of the public are two different, distinct and scarcely reconcilable operations. The "Journal of Civilization," therefore, yields gracefully to the force of circumstances and sins on one page while it sermonizes on another.

Two numbers of *Harper's Weekly* happen now to be lying on my table. On the first page of each number there is an engraved portrait and a biographical sketch of a celebrated personage. The two persons selected by Messrs. Harper for pictorial and typographical glorification are "*Arcades ambo,*" and something worse than *Arcades,* if Byron's translation of the term is correct.* One of them is the most infamous editor in the United States, and the other is a notorious stock gambler, who has accumulated a large fortune by means of a thousand fraudulent operations, each of which, separately considered, deserves to be expiated by a life-long penance in the State's Prison. And these pests of civilized society are extravagantly eulogized by the "Journal of Civilization:" their most reprehensible deeds are mentioned with warm approba-

---

* "*Arcades ambo, id est,* Blackguards both."—ENGLISH BARDS AND SCOTCH REVIEWERS.

tion, the biographer being evidently delighted with their ingenious and successful rascality, examples of which are given as evidences of their superior sagacity and aptitude for business.

Gracious Heaven! what must be the effect of such lessons on the minds of thousands and myriads of young people, who are accustomed to regard "the respectable newspaper press" as the most virtuous and infallible of all earthly instructors!

The Reverend Theodore Parker, in a lecture delivered at Concert Hall, Philadelphia, about two years ago, remarked that "the Americans are not an honest people." How, in the name of Heaven, *can* they be honest, when their most acceptable teachers—their very journals of civilization—represent the worst phases of villainy as the brightest exemplifications of human excellence, and propose swindlers and common cheats as models for general imitation?

Sincerely do I hope that the allusion which has been made to *Harper's Weekly* will not be construed as an attempt to show that the paper thus selected for the purpose of illustration is the most mischievous of its class. If it were any thing of the kind I should prove little or nothing against the newspaper press in general, by citing this journal as an example. But if it should appear that *Harper's Weekly* is one of the *least objectionable* of American publications, (as perhaps it is,) then the offenses imputed to it must cast a deeper reproach on our newspapers in general, since they are supposed to be still more guilty.

I refer to *Harper's Weekly* merely to sustain my predicate, that some of the most reputable newspapers in the United States are not irreproachable. I do not deny that the *publishers* of that *Weekly* may desire and intend to do well. Their error consists, perhaps, in delegating the management of their journal to persons who are less pious, less virtuous and less conscientious than themselves. Possibly these publishers may be more injudicious than criminal; but this is an allowance which I am under no obligations to make, for, as I have hinted in another part of this work, a journalist should be held responsible for his errors of judgment as well as for his moral delinquencies. If a newspaper man were allowed to ensconce himself behind his own folly or stupidity, he might have a convenient plea of justification for every offense, and the public would have no safeguard against the evil consequences of his mistakes.

SUMMARY.

The stern necessity which compels me to be concise with every branch of my subject, makes it impossible for me to exhibit more than a small fractional part of the vitiating influences of journalism. Five hundred pages of such a book as this would be insufficient to make the reader acquainted with this single topic. A little recapitulation, however, may enable us to form some faint idea of the extensively deleterious effects of journalism on the moral habits of the American people. Let us bear in mind,—

1. That the *most influential* portion of the public press is controlled chiefly by men of depraved character, who, like Milton's Belial, love evil for its own sake, and delight in the propagation of false and corrupt principles.

2. That editors find it more *profitable*, in a worldly sense, to serve a bad cause than a good one; for their best customers—their most liberal patrons—are the workers of iniquity. Since no kind of rascality—no vicious and demoralizing pursuit—can possibly succeed without the connivance and assistance of the newspapers, all who engage in such pursuits become tributary to the press, and, in one way or another, satisfy the mercenary cravings of the journalists. Interest, therefore, as well as inclination, makes the newspaper press subservient to the cause of vice and immorality.

3. That there is absolutely *no restraint* on the flagitious practices of the journalists. These men exalt themselves above the law, and set legislatures, public opinion and courts of justice at defiance. Therefore the fear of disgrace or punish-

ment which holds other sinners in abeyance, has no restrictive operation on them. They are accessory to thousands of villainies; but, while their less guilty colleagues are often punished, they themselves remain intact. They exert a scathing and pernicious influence on society. The victims of their malign efforts may become wretched, vile and infamous; but they, the authors of so much evil, increase in wealth and honor, power, influence and "respectability."

Consider, *firstly*, that the newspaper press of our country has tremendous powers; *secondly*, that it has strong inclinations and inducements to do mischief; and, *thirdly*, that it is altogether irresponsible and unconstrained in its action; and you may then be able to form some estimate of the vitiating and corrupting influences of American journalism.

SUPPLEMENTARY ILLUSTRATIONS.

AN EDITORIAL GROG-SELLER.—A few years ago, one of the most considerable newspaper-publishers that Philadelphia ever produced, established a grog-shop on a most magnificent scale. It was situated under his printing-office, and, in order to attract customers to his bar he opened a free reading room, in which he filed all his exchange papers. To reach this depository of choice reading, it was necessary to pass the counter where the liquors were sold, and the bar-keeper gave each visitor a glance of expectation as a gentle hint that he ought to refresh himself with a glass of gin or brandy, before he proceeded to satisfy his thirst for useful knowledge. The proprietor of this drinking saloon was, at that time, the most prosperous journalist in the city, and it is hard to conceive what motives could induce him to engage in the liquor trade, unless he had a natural taste for that kind of business.

A LASCIVIOUS JOURNALIST.—A New York Sunday paper gives the following sketch of a certain successful Philadelphia editor. The picture is correct in every particular:

"He could not bear prosperity. His wealth gave development to passions which might have remained under control if he had continued poor. A recent trial has shown that he had two wives and a mistress; or two mistresses and a wife; it is a little uncertain which. One of his mistresses was the wife of a man who is still living. Philadelphia newspapers are generally very severe on New York morals. It would not be amiss for the Philadelphia press to direct its attention to the *practical Mormonism* at its own doors."

SOTTISHNESS.—I have mentioned somewhere that hard drinking is a common vice among editors. This circumstance may help to account for the favorable disposition which they generally manifest toward the liquor trade. The *New York Herald* lately said, with reference to the principal editor of one of the leading journals of Philadelphia :—" He has fallen into the debasing habit of drunkenness, and has thus reduced himself to a condition which makes him a fit subject for some lunatic asylum."

I am informed that two editors attached to the press of Philadelphia made a disgraceful exhibition of themselves at Cape May, last summer. For several days, (if my information is correct,) they were almost constantly in a state of beastly intoxication.

MORALITY OF THE NEW YORK TIMES.—When this paper first published an account of the Key and Sickles tragedy, it severely censured the person who gave Mr. Sickles the first information of his wife's infidelity. According to the notions of the *Times*, the writer of the letter which was intended to put a stop to the adulterous intercourse between Mrs. Sickles and Mr. Key, was " *an enemy to mankind!*" Several other American newspapers expressed the same sentiment in different language, and I observe that the *French* papers generally take the same view of the matter. I know that *crim. con.* in France, like theft in Sparta, is a fault only when it is *detected;* but I did net expect that any *American* journals, (even the most vicious ones,) would dare to insinuate that the man who detects and exposes the sin of adultery is more criminal than he who commits it.

A MARRIAGE IN PROSPECT.—Under this head the *New Orleans Delta*, gives the following rumor, some corroboration of which I have heard from another quarter:—

"There is an *on dit* that one of the editors of the *New York Tribune*, who has distinguished himself somewhat as a poet, is about to commit a matrimonial escapade with a young actress *already married*. (!) She has a pretty, though rather wicked, face, a great quantity of black hair, and is married to a German, from whom she is about obtaining a divorce, in order that she may become *legally* entitled to the devotions of the literary head of the Tribune."

BEECHER CENSURES THE PRESS.—In a late sermon or lecture, the subject of which was the "Sickles Tragedy," the Reverend Henry Ward Beecher introduced these pertinent remarks:—

"The papers are loaded down with this matter. There is not a hamlet or ranche on the continent into which this sore of depravity is not about to drop its ichor. Is it to be taken as a thing settled that our principal journals of news and all of our weekly papers, some of them pretending to morality and religion, are to report the whole news of the criminal calendar and all the shame of corrupt society? What end is gained by a long and minute disclosure of the secrets of iniquity? It would seem that the rivalry of newspapers is not a sufficient excuse for making them the common sewers of human depravity. The prurient details of divorce cases at disgusting length, repetitious columns of news from the prize-fighter's ring, the police-court reports, the details of salacious scandal, and the hateful histories of dissipated life, in which men that are rich, no one knows how, fester in loathsome vices and break forth in disgraceful crimes—must we have this *stream of damnation* passing through our families morning after morning, or else forego all the convenience and benefit of a newspaper?"

The editors of the *New York Tribune* seemed to think that these remarks were *particularly* applicable to their own journal, for they assumed the duty and responsibility of replying to the reverend gentleman's strictures. In their reply, the tone of which was somewhat scoffing and contemptuous, the Tribune editors boastfully proclaimed that they "HAD ALWAYS COMBATTED Mr. Beecher's opinions on this subject." Moreover, they tauntingly gave Mr. Beecher to understand that their blackguard reports were calculated to do more good than his best sermons. In conclusion, they made the scandalous charge, that Mr. Beecher himself was one of their most "constant readers," and that the worthy clergyman never had any appetite for his breakfast until he had first digested the contents of the *Daily Tribune!* Execrable slander!

EDITORIAL PREACHING.—Sometimes the Satanic newspapers undertake to sermonize or moralize, especially in their "leading articles," and when they happen to be at a loss for more congenial subjects. But in these editorial homilies, I generally find something which reminds me of "*latet anguis in herba.*" Some abominable sentiment or some venomous falsehood will probably be discovered under the flowery texture of Mr. Editor's morality. The scribe may offer some good and wholesome suggestions, (filched probably from some other writer,) but, like a cow which gives a good pailful of milk and then kicks it over, the newspaper moralist is very apt to ruin the effect of his salutary discourse by some awkward movement near the end of it.

Thus, for example, a blundering "leader" writer for the Philadelphia *Ledger* lately gave us some remarks on the impropriety of allowing men to redress their own grievances by assassinating the seducers of their wives, sisters, etc., and for awhile, the subject was treated very judiciously indeed. But toward the termination of the "leader," we find it strongly insinuated that the seduction of wives, sisters, etc., is not such a prodigious offense after all, and that public opinion is not much opposed to it, "as is shown by the fact, that if a seducer be put on his trial, in nine cases out of ten, he will be acquitted by the unanimous verdict of a jury." There is enough falsehood and mischief in this single sentence to defeat all the good effect which could be produced by twenty columns of canting, hypocritical, common-place flummery.

It is a common practice with editors, as it is with many other people to

"Compound for sins they are inclin'd to,
By damning those they have no mind to."

Many journalists are strongly opposed to the assassination of seducers and adulterers; and, (without asking what may be the grounds of their opposition,) we must concede that, in that particular, they are altogether right. But it is politic for them to avoid all appearance of *excusing the libertine* while they properly condemn the stern avenger who punishes him by an extra-judicial process.

In all matters appertaining to the science and practice of *morality*, I suspect that the keepers of common brothels would be more eligible instructors than the members of the "Press Gang."

SECTION XI.

POLITICAL VILLAINIES OF THE NEWSPAPER PRESS.

Examination of the Seventh Charge.

COULD I measure the confluent waters of the Atlantic and Pacific with a quart pitcher, could I number the stars in the galaxy as an old huxter-woman counts her eggs in the market, I might undertake to comprise the political villainies of our newspaper press in one duodecimo volume. But my skill in mensuration and arithmetic is not sufficient for such a task. I can show you but a bucketful, as it were, as a specimen of an ocean of iniquity; I can give you but a few algebraic symbols to represent an infinite quantity of typographical rascality.

You will find, by analysis, that my seventh charge against the gentlemen of the press will admit of the following specifications :

1. That the newspaper press encourages and promotes official malfeasance and corruption.

2. That it uses its influence to secure the election or appointment of bad and irresponsible men to important political stations; and

3. That it persuades the people to submit quietly to the extortions and oppressions which are constantly perpetrated by knaves in office.

OFFICIAL ROGUERY.

There are some men who cannot reason, and they of course, cannot understand moral, or even demonstrative evidence. But all men who are not physically or intellectually blind, can *see* what is passing within the scope of their visual faculties. In every case, therefore, when we wish to make people acquainted with the TRUTH, it is better to present it as an *object of sight* than to prove it by the most unerring process of ratiocination.

In the present case, my countrymen, I ask you to use your own eyes. Look at your elected servants; the men who are hypothetically chosen by yourselves to be your agents and ministers in the management of public affairs. Do they faithfully serve *you*, or do they principally serve themselves? Are they honest and trustworthy servants, or is *stealing*, in one way or another, a general practice among them? Are they zealous and industrious in the discharge of their duties? Are they economical in their management of the public funds? Or are they slovenly and negligent in the performance of the required labor, and do they lavish your money in profuse and profligate disbursements?

I assume that your answers to these queries will be nearly in accordance with my own observations; for with respect to visible objects there can be but little diversity of opinion. In short, we all see and know that more than three-fourths of the office-holders in this country are knaves; that very many of them receive salaries for which they render no equivalent services; and that quite a multitude of them habitually commit depredations on the public purse. We see and know that the burden of taxation, in some parts of the country, is doubled—quadrupled, perhaps—by the insane extravagance of fiscal agents, and the plundering operations of official banditti. These are facts of general notoriety;—nobody will or can dispute them.

WHY IS IT SO?

Now, Messrs. Smith, Tomkins, Hopkinson, and so forth, (meaning the public in general,) has it never struck you as something surprising, if not incomprehensible, that the constant perpetration of these monstrous official villainies should be PERMITTED by a nation which boasts of its virtue and intelligence, and which has, in its own hands, all the power that is necessary to put a speedy termination to the abuses under which it suffers ? Is it not a surprising circumstance that the *"organs of public opinion"* never take any decisive stand in opposition to the enormous scoundrelism of the office-holding aristocracy ?

ACTION OF THE PRESS.

When some grand defalcation, or some other remarkable act of official delinquency has been discovered, some of the journals may mention it, perhaps, as an item of news, or as the subject of a wretched jest at the expense of their political opponents, if the delinquent should happen to be one of them ; but seldom, indeed, will any decided condemnation of the offense be found in a newspaper. If the offender is a Democratic " office-holder," his crime may be paraded by the "Black Republican" presses, as an example of Democratic corruption ; and a similar expedient may be tried by the organs of the Democracy if the criminal is a Black Republican.

And thus, for party purposes, the newspapers may expose and condemn individual cases of official malfeasance—but the SYSTEM—the habitual robbery of the public—and other enormities committed by office-holders of *all* parties—is never condemned. The idea held out by the public journals is, that official villainy is a peculiarity of this or that faction ; that it is the ultimation of certain political principles, which constitute the "platform" of a particular party.

But this is a doctrine which is opposed to all human experience ; and, in fact, to divine authority. We know that our official malefactors have been men of every party ; we ought to know that nine-tenths of mankind will do wrong when they are PERMITTED ;—and such of us as have read our Bibles, and believed them rather than the newspapers,—may know that the moral constitution of man is *intrinsically evil.* This luminous truth, ignored by modern philosophers of the Horace Greeley and Joe Barker schools,—was acknowledged even by the heathen moralists of elder times.

The most eloquent and judicious historian of antiquity,— the model of Demosthenes,—while accounting for the extortions, oppressions, defalcations, and other rascalities committed by certain office-holders in some of the Grecian states, says that these misdoings were the inevitable consequences of the removal of legal restraints and allowing "THE NATURAL CHARACTER OF MAN," (ἡ ἀνθρωπεια φυσις,) to develope itself without control.*

THE REMEDY.

As the good old Scotch divine said, when he heard some philosophical coxcomb descanting on "the excellence of human nature,"—"Human nature, sir, is a scoundrel." Newspaper editors ought to be acquainted with this truth, for they commonly have the illustrations very near them; but the obvious remedy for official roguery, which this truth suggests, is never urged on the attention of the public. The journalists never inform us that human nature, and especially office-holding human nature, requires *restraints*, and that the only effective check for scoundrelism is CERTAIN AND ADEQUATE PUNISHMENT.

And why should not an official thief be punished, as well as any other thief? Why should he not be subjected to severer penalties than those which are awarded to the pick-pocket or the house-breaker? All punishment is intended for example, and the most conspicuous and illustrious examples are always the most useful, because they command the most attention. For similar reasons, the crimes committed by a man who occupies a prominent or elevated position, an office-holder for instance, are particularly injurious to public morals, because the evil example is seen by many; and, besides, the vicious actions of a great man are more likely to be *imitated* than the misconduct of an obscure and insignificant person.

In short, there are various reasons why an official rogue should be punished with more certainty and severity than a less distinguished criminal. The "people's servants," (as they are comically denominated,) are favored enough in having

* Thucydides. B. iii. § 82.

honorable and lucrative employments, some of which are almost sinecures,—and they ought to be satisfied without oppressing and plundering their benefactors. I hold that it would be both just and expedient to punish every act of peculation, and every other misdeed committed by an office-holder with a rigor proportioned to the turpitude of the offense. Official malefactors should be indicted like other criminals;—and, if convicted, they can not expect better treatment than more excusable offenders,—(the victims of ignorance and destitution,) meet with, every day, in our courts of justice.

Energetic measures must be used to check the progress of political corruption, or the downfall of this republic is as certain as the dropping of a rotten apple from the twig which supports it. The instinct of self-preservation prompts us to deal rigorously with the traitors and felons who have surreptitiously obtained a share in the management of public affairs. In the present situation of our republic, and in view of the frightfully increasing demoralization of our people, the offenses of public men cannot be too promptly or too sternly rebuked. Every public defaulter, every convicted perpetrator of an official fraud, should find his place in the PENITENTIARY.

Such a politic course, steadfastly pursued, would lead to more than one beneficial result. It would not only restrain public servants from the commission of crimes, but it would also be the means of introducing better men into office. Official situations are now sought by multitudes of bad people, merely for the sake of a good opportunity to "pluck the public goose." But if this operation were made more difficult and dangerous, the crowds of rascals would be less anxious to rush into office, and the management of public affairs would fall into better hands.

NEWSPAPER CONNIVANCE.

To prove that the newspaper men "encourage and promote official malfeasance and corruption," it might be deemed sufficient to show that the press makes no effort to *prevent* these misdemeanors. Mere connivance at crime, is in effect, an encouragement of the criminal. If, for example, you are robbed by a highwayman, while I, having it in my power to protect you, stand by a quiet spectator of the deed, I am morally and in the eye of the law, *particeps criminis*. I am supposed to *encourage* the freebooter by my presence and non-interference. So, when the public journalists make no effective OPPOSITION to the robbery of the people by official bandits, their sympathy with the criminals is evident, and their passive observation of the crimes may be justly construed as permission and encouragement. On this score alone, therefore, the journalists may be properly regarded as the accomplices or accessories of the public robbers. But this is a fact which admits of a great variety of demonstration.

THE ACTIVE ASSISTANCE OF THE PRESS.

You will easily believe, my fellow republicans, that the newspaper men are not merely *indifferent spectators* of the robberies and other outrages which are committed, every day, on the "sovereign people." If you believe that the newspaper press is "omnipotent," as your judges have somewhat injudiciously declared, you must suppose that the journalists *could* check or suppress these abuses, if they were disposed to do so; for omnipotence can do all things. At least, you cannot doubt that the press is powerful enough, if it had the will, to throw serious obstacles in the way of official plunderers. This admitted, it will appear, in the next place, that it must be a very desirable object with corrupt and thievish office-holders to gain the good-will and connivance of the press. And how could this object be gained otherwise than by offering the journalists some equivalent advantage? You perceive that there is a strong motive, in fact a *compulsory* motive, on the part of official delinquents, urging them to propitiate the press. And how could they do this in a more certain and convenient way than by giving the journalists a share of their plunder?

It can scarcely be supposed that any question will be raised concerning the aptitude of the newspaper-men to *receive* this kind of tribute. We learn from Herodotus and Demosthenes that the oracles of Greece and Libya could be bribed by the great generals and other robbers of earlier times. And do you believe, my countrymen, that *your* oracles, your newspaper ones, are more incorruptible than the oracles of Delphos, Dodona, and Ammon? You know that the eager and unscrupulous pursuit of gain is not an uncommon vice in America, and you have no reason to doubt that our newspaper-men are as apt to be infected with this vice as any other kind of people. You see what ADVERTISEMENTS they publish; what appeals from quack doctors, astrologers, grog-sellers, free-love lecturers, impostors and rascals of every class, the pests and nuisances of civilized society; and can you doubt that the men who assist these villains in their efforts to defraud and victimize the public will do ANY THING for money?

Is it hard to believe that a journalist who will publish a knavish, obscene, vicious, demoralizing or blasphemous advertisement for fifty cents, will consent, for a fee of five hundred or five thousand dollars, to whitewash the character and justify the conduct of an official scoundrel? Lest you should be obstinately sceptical on this subject, I will give you such instances as may be conveniently introduced into this volume. But remember, that these are only a few "specimen bricks" from a pile of substantial facts as tall as the temple of Belus.

COLOSSAL ROBBERY.

A few months ago it was discovered *accidentally* that vast spoliations had been made in the State Treasury of Ohio. The matter was investigated by a committee of the Legislature, when it appeared that the persons who had been entrusted with the management of the fiscal concerns of the State had stolen no less than *six hundred thousand dollars* of the public money. It was found that this plundering of the Treasury had commenced in 1847, and that it had continued, without the slightest interruption, through a period of more than ELEVEN YEARS! It was ascertained by the committee of investigation that the State Treasurers were the defaulters. One of them, named Breslin, had embezzled nearly half a million of dollars while he had the control of the Treasury Department; and his successor and brother-in-law, Gibson, was proceeding in the same course when the stupendous villainy of these notable "public servants" was providentially detected. One of the defaulters was a "Democrat," and the other a "Black Republican."

It appeared in evidence before the investigating committee, that it was a matter of general notoriety that both of these men were *poor* when they were first elected to office, and that, soon after they took charge of the public funds, they launched out into a sea of extravagant expenditure. They lived in magnificent style, lent the public money to rotten banks, and engaged in a variety of speculations which required a vast outlay. It appeared in evidence, likewise, that several public journalists must have been acquainted with these proceedings, but it does not appear that any *hint* of mismanagement was published in the newspapers. The silence of the press in relation to a matter of such momentous interest is explained by a part of the testimony elicited in the course of the examination.

It was proved that Gibson, one of the defaulters, had bestowed ten thousand dollars on a public journal called the *Statesman*, (a Democratic organ,) and he acknowledged to the witness, Thomas H. Ford, Esq., that this money was taken from the State Treasury. Mr. Ford expressed his astonishment at this act of "liberality," and Gibson then remarked that the *Statesman* had done him good service by defending him against charges which affected his reputation as an upright and trustworthy public servant!

Mr. Ford, the witness just quoted, further testified that Gibson had often conversed with him on the subject of his (Gibson's) relation to another paper called the *Ohio State*

Journal, which he represented to be under his control; and he told Mr. Ford that he could compel the editors to publish what he pleased. It appears that the defaulters had given this *State Journal* one thousand and two hundred dollars at one time, and probably some other *douceurs,* either to purchase the goodwill of the editors or to pay them for mysterious services which none but the initiated can be expected to understand. The *State Journal,* I think, is an opposition, or "Black Republican" paper. And so it appears that the politic Gibson threw his golden dust on either side, blinding the eyes of both factions, while he disemboweled the fat Treasury of Ohio, as Prince Hal promised to do with the carcass of Jack Falstaff.

Doubtless some other papers in Ohio, especially those published at Columbus, (the State capital,) were subsidized in a similar way by these gigantic defaulters; and I can easily imagine how many charming compliments to the VIRTUE and INTEGRITY of Messrs. Breslin and Gibson were published in the newspapers of that State, at the very time when these men were committing their prodigious depredations.

OFFICIAL THIEVES TAXED BY THE PRESS.

The New York *Courier and Enquirer* said, with reference to Bennett of the New York Herald: "This pest of society holds a poisoned dagger at the throats of certain government officials of this city, who have been compelled to subsidize him into silence. They have been forced by fear of exposure to throw a crust to this troublesome dog."

This was uttered several years ago; and in the mean time, the art of levying contributions on office-holders has been much improved by cultivation;—so that it is now almost impossible for an official thief to steal a single dollar without dedicating half of it to the exacting genius of typography. This heavy taxation on the proceeds of official plunder produces a necessity for larger operations on the part of the plunderers, who are compelled, (in their own defense, as it were,) to filch twice as much as they did in former times,—when they were not obliged to steal for any body but themselves.

AMOUNT OF THE PLUNDER.

The amount of thieving done by official personages in Philadelphia alone is almost beyond computation ; and I am quite sure that Messrs. Editors have their share of the booty. When the claims of any of them are overlooked or ignored, the office-holders are sure to hear of the omission. On this theme, Mr. Forney, in the Philadelphia Press of October 6, 1858, discourses as follows :—

"In the municipal governments, the tax-payer feels most the influence of dishonest servants. It is in these that reckless and corrupt men are most apt to ingratiate themseles. The amount of taxes paid into the treasuries of New York and Philadelphia annually is about *eleven millions of dollars.* What a sum for unscrupulous men to conceal, dissipate or use in corruption !"

Mr. Forney does not tell us how much of this neat sum is appropriated to the support of newspaper literature. I think, however, that at least one half of the journals in New York and Philadelphia would find it very difficult to explain how they are maintained ; unless they are willing to confess that they subsist like maggots in an ulcer, feeding on corruption and aggravating the disease to which they owe their existence.

DEFALCATION A FELONY.

Martin Van Buren, in one of his Presidential messages, proposed to make embezzlement of the public money a felony punishable by confinement in the State's Prison. Mr. Van Buren knew that this is the *only* remedy, and every honest man will admit that it is a remedy which is both just and expedient. The newspaper men generally disapproved of Mr. Van Buren's proposition, though their disapprobation was variously expressed. Some treated it with affected contempt, some considered the measure "too severe," some thought it impossible to enforce such a law, and some,—with the illustrious James Gordon Bennett at their head,—opposed any additional legislation on the subject.

Bennett, it must be confessed, is no *hypocrite*. He does not, like many another journalist, hide his diabolical horns in an old woman's night-cap, or his cloven hoof in a fashionable gaiter. With reference to Mr. Van Buren's proposal to punish defaulters, the Scotch interloper spoke out as follows:—

"Defalcations are no crime. This proposition of President Van Buren is nonsense. Neither party will agree to such an absurdity. Never!" *Vide New York Herald, December* 10, 1838.

If this Caledonian apologist for public plunderers had said that the *newspaper trumpeters* of neither party would agree to Mr. Van Buren's proposal, he would have told the truth. But I hope that a larger and a better class of American citizens will soon see the propriety and the *necessity* of treating official thieves in the manner prescribed by the "Sage of Kinderhook,"—whose counsel, in this instance, is indisputably wise and patriotic.

EDITORIAL SYMPATHY WITH PUBLIC ROBBERS.

Long before the defalcations of Jesse Hoyt were known to the public, Bennett, in his *Herald*, jokingly advised Hoyt to run away, in good time, with the booty he had already secured, hinting that the public, with all its proverbial apathy and stupidity, would soon discover "the errors in Jesse's accounts."

When it was discovered that Samuel Swartwout had embezzled *one million two hundred and fifty thousand dollars* from the New York Custom-House, many of the newspapers defended him, or attempted to extenuate his crime. While Swartwout was carrying on his pillaging operations, his chief clerk and confidential assistant was the near relative of a distinguished editor of New York, who is now *dead;* and, on that account I am unwilling to mention his name. When Swartwout, after the discovery of his robberies, vacated his office and left this country to air his reputation in France, the *New York Evening Star*, and some other journals, became very lachrymose, seeming to consider it a great pity and a burning shame that such "a warm-hearted, *liberal* gentleman" should be driven into exile for such a peccadillo as the theft of $1,250,000.

THE LATEST MODES.

Many papers in the United States are now supported almost entirely by the contributions of office-holders, or office-hunters. Party organs are maintained, in a great measure, by taxes levied on the persons employed in Custom-Houses, Post-Offices, etc.; every one of whom, in some cases, is required to devote a portion of his salary to the support of some worthless and corrupt newspaper. In every department of the public service more persons are employed than are necessary to do the work, and many of the supernumeraries are the sons, brothers, nephews, uncles, cousins, or particular friends of editors, to whose influence they are indebted for their offices. Sometimes editors themselves are office-holders, with liberal salaries, numerous perquisites, and scarcely any thing to do.

The editor of a scurrilous little sheet, published in Philadelphia, lately held an office in the Custom-House, and had so little official business to occupy his time that his principal employment seemed to be the collection and publication of scandal. Multitudes of such people, no doubt, are pensioners on the public revenue, and earn their subsistence by glorifying rogues in office, and calumniating honest men who never expect to have a slice of the public pudding.

Besides having a good share of all the Custom-House and Post-Office plunder, the members of the Press Gang know how to exact tribute or "black mail" from municipal and governmental officers of all grades or classes. Every public functionary who finds that it is easy to descend into the hell of political iniquity, must throw his conciliatory sops to the many-headed Cerberus of the Press.

SALE OF NEWSPAPER INFLUENCE.

The principal journals, especially those of the "Satanic School," have correspondents, agents or *factors*, stationed at the seat of the Federal government during the session of Congress. Among other duties assigned to these faithful ministers is the negotiation of business affairs with congressmen, or with applicants for governmental contracts, or with persons interested in the passage of private bills, or with any others who are supposed to stand in need of newspaper assistance.

Some of these agents boldly offer for sale their own influence and that of the papers with which they are connected, bargaining for the support of such or such a measure, or proposing to "put down" any enterprise, or any rival or opponent for a stipulated sum, half to be paid in advance, and the other half when the proposed service has been duly performed. These newspaper agents are largely engaged in that villianous business called "lobbying," or tampering with the members of legislative bodies, and endeavoring to influence them by various promises and persuasions. One scoundrel of this class, the agent of a Philadelphia paper, was audacious enough to approach the late Senator Benton with overtures which no honest man could entertain. Of course Mr. Benton gave the wretched varlet a suitable rebuff.

When Mr. Lloyd, the publisher of my "*Life of De Soto*," petitioned Congress to purchase some copies of that work for the use of the public libraries, he was besieged by newspaper agents with offers of all manner of assistance. One of these bargainers proposed, for a specified remuneration, to sell Mr. Lloyd the influence of several "leading journals" in New York, declaring that he had been authorized to negotiate for that influence. This agent took care to make the book-publisher understand that Congress would not DARE to hear the petition, much less to grant it, without the *consent and approbation of the Press!*

If Mr. Lloyd had been willing to satisfy the cupidity of these negotiators, his pecuniary resources would not have enabled him to meet their exorbitant demands. He rejected their offers, and immediately his petition was assailed furiously by the *New York Herald, Times,* and *Tribune,* and likewise by several notoriously corrupt papers of Philadelphia. The New York journals just named signified, in terms not to be mistaken, that if any member of Congress presumed to vote for Lloyd's petition, or to show it the least favor, he might expect to be "used up," *i. e.*, to be abused to any conceivable extent. These fulminations had the desired effect, and the petition was quietly laid on the table.

Many of the journals have custom-hunting agents at Albany, Harrisburg, and other State capitals, where money can be made by offering the assistance of the press to any legislative project, whether good or bad; by levying black-mail on official delinquents apprehensive of exposure, and in many another way which the limits of this work will not allow me to particularize.

SUMMARY.

We have been discussing the first specification of my *seventh charge*, in which it is asserted that "the newspaper press encourages and promotes official malfeasance and corruption." I have endeavored to illustrate this subject, as completely as circumstances will permit, by making it appear:

1. That journalism is closely connected with all the machinery of government, and that its consent and co-operation are necessary to make certain abuses of that governmental machinery *practicable*.

2. That the journalists have powerful motives urging them to conceal, extenuate or apologize for, the official misdemeanors of our public men, and that the newspapers *really do* cover up, palliate and defend the worst crimes of the office-holders.

3. That the newspapers strenuously oppose the only mea-

sure, (viz. the infliction of condign punishment on political offenders,) which can reasonably be expected to put an end to the monstrous defalcations, and other villainies, which are constantly perpetrated by men in office.

SUPPLEMENTARY ILLUSTRATIONS.

FRIGHTFUL STATE OF AFFAIRS.—A Philadelphia weekly paper, called the *American Mechanic*, lately remarked :—" Look where we will, we see nothing but the struggles of factions, the strife of demagogues, the increase of licentiousness and corruption. Such, *unfortunately*, are the extent and value of the public domains, the amount of official patronage, the receipts of the revenues and the emoluments of office, that politics have become a distinct profession, looking to success only as a *means of spoliation*. The country is a continual scene of partisan struggles, and parties are formed solely with the hope of pecuniary advantage. We are rapidly degenerating to the sad level of Mexican degradation in all social and political morals."

HEAR THE REVEREND HENRY WARD BEECHER.—" When jobs are so many and lucrative," (said Mr. Beecher in one of his last lectures,) " when the treasury is assailable on every side, when money is poured out like water upon managing rogues and unconvicted political felons, it can scarcely be but that crowds of evil men will haunt the purlieus of national legislation and batten upon plunder. When before did Rumor, almost without periphrasis, charge home upon the *highest members of government* the disgrace of personal corruption and official venality ?"

What else could you expect, Mr. Beecher, in a country governed by soulless corporations and an infamous newspaper press ?

JOHN MITCHELL AND HIS FRIENDS.—The famous " Irish patriot," John Mitchell, became " a sterling Democrat " as soon as he came to this country. He established a Democratic paper, and, in the language of the vulgar proverb, made himself "as busy as a bee in a tar-barrel;" being, all the while, an object of extravagant admiration among his political associates. For a time, the intercourse between him and the other "Democrats" was cordial enough; but those halcyon days have vanished, if we may judge from the following paragraph in a late number of Mitchell's *Irish Citizen:*

"The national Democratic party has disappeared like the morning mist and passed away as a tale that is told! On Wednesday, in the Senate, for the first time this session, our National Democrats ventured to look one another in the face and parted with a shriek of horror and consternation! Such is the harmony of the Democratic party. On every question, *save one*, there are two well-defined and very hostile parties. That *one* question is PUBLIC PLUNDER. That is the great principle which has maintained the harmony of the party for years, but it bursts at last. The Democratic party, from this day, goes straight to dissolution, and the UNION goes with it."

Mr. Mitchell may have "a bit of the brogue, but divil a bit of the blarney," in this instance at least. The truths which he tells his Democratic brethren are wholesome; but whether they will be palatable or not is another question. In one particular, I hope, this excitable gentleman is mistaken. The "Democratic party" may go to perdition as soon as Mr. Mitchell pleases, but I trust that the American Union will survive the wishes and prophecies of its foreign enemies.

JEFFERSON A PROPHET.—Sixty years ago, Thomas Jefferson wrote: "The times will alter—our rulers will become corrupt—our people careless. The time for fixing every essential right on a legal basis is while our rulers are honest and ourselves united. We shall soon be going down hill. It will not be necessary to resort every moment to the *people* for support—they will be forgotten, therefore, and their rights will be disregarded."

Jefferson is often very severe in his denunciations of the political sins of the press, and he often expresses his apprehensions of the mischiefs which corrupt journalism might produce in this country. In fact, he plainly intimates that newspaper influence is likely to prove more injurious than beneficial to American institutions. And remember that, when Jefferson wrote, the "Satanic school" of journalism was not established, and our newspaper press was then, comparatively speaking, in a state of infantile innocence.

Thomas Jefferson was the wisest and most far-seeing statesman that America ever possessed.

"ORGAN GRINDERS."—A paper which avowedly supports the principles of any particular faction is a "party organ," and the editor of such a paper is facetiously called an "organ-grinder." It is one of the supposed improvements of modern journalism to dispense with party organs, or to make less use of them than formerly, trusting for a dissemination of party doctrines to the "neutral" or "independent" press. Like many another boasted *improvement* of journalism, this is a change which is very much for the worse. The party organs of former times hoisted their piratical flags, and all who wished to avoid them could easily do so; but now the buccaneers sail under false colors, and you may come in contact with them without suspecting their real character.

The public should understand that, in reality, there is scarcely any such thing as a neutral or independent daily paper in the United States. Nearly all the diurnal sheets have their political partialities, more or less concealed; but their changes of position are sometimes as sudden, as unexpected and as astonishing to spectators in general, as the whirling over of an iceberg in the Polar Sea. Thus the Philadelphia Inquirer and Colonel Webb's paper in New York opposed the United States Bank on Saturday and came out in its defense on Monday morning. Ironically speaking, it is impossible to account for such phenomena.

The partial discontinuance of the organ-grinding system and the substitution mentioned above, have greatly increased the venality of the American press; for there are now very few daily papers in the country which are not organs in disguise; and the press IN GENERAL is prostituted, more or less, to the uses of the vilest political agitators and the most corrupt factions.

SECTION XII.

SHOWING THAT OFFICIAL SCOUNDRELS OWE THEIR POWER AND ELEVATION TO THE NEWSPAPER PRESS.

Continued Examination of the Seventh Charge.

IF your cordwainer or your tailor is a knave, it is not likely that your boots or your breeches will be excellent articles of their kind; and, in every branch of manufacture, the villainy of the workman will be apt to manifest itself in his works. Now it is generally believed, and with very good reason, that our public functionaries are made by the newspaper editors; and if it should appear that a great majority of these editors are scoundrels, you may reasonably infer that their *manufactured articles* will be worthless and detestable.

I have undertaken to convince you that the conductors of the press, without a great many exceptions, are dishonorable and unprincipled persons; and you have had proof enough to satisfy you that this description does not wrong them. I now ask you to accept, as additional evidence of newspaper villainy, the generally vile character of those public men who are elected to office by the agency of the press.

You will observe, by referring once more to my late comparison, that if one may argue, *à priori*, that because a tailor is dishonest, the garment made by him will probably be a bad one; so, if your breeches, by actual experiment, are found to be villainous and untrustworthy, you may judge, *à posteriori*, that the artist who made them is a rogue. A bad workman and his bad works reciprocally testify against each other. Hence if we can prove that either the office-holders or the editors are scoundrels, and if it should appear in evidence that the former are made by the latter, the scoundrelism of the journalists and the office-holders *both* may become a matter of demonstration.

APPLICATION.

The preceding remarks, which you may mistake for idle joking, are really suggestive of the course which ought to be pursued in the discussion of the second specification of my seventh charge, which asserts that—" The newspaper press uses its influence to secure the election or appointment of bad and irresponsible men to important political stations."

In this part of our inquiry, we must consider, *firstly*, whether our public officers in general, are " bad and irresponsible men ;" and, *secondly*, whether they usually obtain their offices by means of newspaper influence.

JUST GROUNDS OF SUSPICION.

In the first place, I accept the doctrine taught by the Bible, as well as by all human experience, that men are by nature evil ; and that, unless they are subjected to restraints of some kind, they are much more disposed to do wrong than right. Religion is a restraint, (the word is derived from *ligare*, to tie or bind ;) conscience is a restraint, when it is not overmastered by some powerful impulse ; human laws are restraints, so far as their control is acknowledged and their operation is felt ; the dread of public opinion, or of public censure, is a restraint with persons who value their reputations and who desire to have the sympathies of their fellow-men.

Besides these restraints on human actions, there is supposed to be another one, which may be called the *moral sense; i. e.*, a certain intuitive perception of justice and propriety, and a supposed predisposition to *act* in accordance with that perception.

But you will find that this "moral sense" is reduced to a nonentity, when separated from religion, conscience, the fear of the laws and the dread of public opinion. Conceive a man to be not controlled by any of these, and what reliance could you have on his moral sense, or his ideas of what Philosopher Square calls "the fitness of things"? Every reasonable man has moral sense enough, I suppose, to distinguish between right and wrong; but it does not follow that all who perceive the distinction between good and evil, will *do* one or avoid the other. It is one thing to *see* the road which we ought to travel, and another and a very different thing, to walk over it.

I assume that our public servants, like all other men, are sinful by nature; and that, without *some kind* of restraints, they will play the knave at every opportunity. To what restraints are they liable? To those of religion? How many successful politicians or office-holders in this country pretend to act under the influences of Divine grace? How many of them have been regenerated? How many of them are "Israelites indeed, in whom there is no guile?" Genuine Christians, alas! meddle but little with politics in the United States. If the followers of Christ had a better understanding of their duties, the case would be very different.

Some radical changes in our modes of *electioneering* must take place before our public offices can be filled with men who are truly religious or sensitively conscientious. The reverend L. Giustiniani, D.D., formerly a Roman Catholic priest, but recently a convert to Protestantism, reports that a Jesuit missionary, who had been operating in the United States, declared, before an ecclesiastical convocation at Rome, that "almost every political 'head-quarters' in this country is situated in a public-house or tavern, and very often in the *lowest kind* of grog-shops. The politicians are as corrupt as their politics," continued this jesuitical spy and informer, "for without *grog* they cannot advance the interests of their party. Grog is the great lever of Archimedes for the promotion of the ambitious designs of corrupt politicians in America."

Whether this was spoken by a Jesuit or the devil himself, it is the TRUTH; and the truth, even when it comes from a foul source, ought to be acceptable, as a pearl of great price is no less valuable when taken from a rotten oyster. Our most active politicians are grog-sellers, or their best customers, and others whose practices are very much at variance with the requirements of Christianity. These lamentable facts are known to every American, and the inference is that men who obtain offices by availing themselves of the vile modes of electioneering in common use cannot be supposed to feel any of the restraints of religion or conscience.

DO THEY FEAR THE LAW?

To what other restraints, then, are our office-holders subjected? Are they kept in order by a salutary fear of legal punishment? Certainly not; for why should they dread the law or its retribution? What *example* is there to make them afraid? Was any political malefactor ever punished in the United States of America? Did not every attempt to punish Theron Rudd, Jesse Hoyt, William M. Price, and many others, prove abortive? In view of these facts, it appears to be impossible that the apprehension of legal penalties should restrain bad men in office from the indulgence of their corrupt and vicious propensities.

ARE THEY AFRAID OF PUBLIC OPINION?

Do not imagine that, in pursuing this inquiry, we have lost sight of MESSRS. EDITORS. We are now examining their "manufactured articles"; and, in a short time, we shall come to the manufacturers themselves. Expecting to show, in the sequel, that our public functionaries are made by the Press Gang, we are investigating the *quality* of the merchandise, so that we may ascertain how much credit is due to the makers.

It is asked why we should not easily believe that our office-holders are bad men? What is there to *prevent* them from playing the rascal? We have seen that they are not likely to be restrained by religion, by conscience, or by law; and the question now is, "Are they afraid of public opinion?" How is it possible that they can be afraid of this bugbear, if they have enlisted the *manufacturers* of public opinion (*i. e.*, the journalists) in their service? If public defaulters, etc., are enabled, by the connivance and confederacy of the press, to *conceal* their crimes, what reason have they to be apprehensive of public censure? The fault that is hidden is not likely to be condemned.

From all these considerations, it may appear, firstly, that public servants or office-holders have those evil propensities which belong to unconverted sinners in general; and, secondly, that, for various reasons, they are not likely to be withheld from wrong-doing by the restrictive forces of religion, conscience, law, or public opinion. If these two points are admitted, we discover an *antecedent probability* that the greater number of our official people will be evil-doers. In other words, we might EXPECT or suppose this to be the case if we had no positive evidence on the subject.

COMMON BELIEF.

In the next place, I ask you to observe that it is A COMMONLY-RECEIVED opinion among the people of the United States that a majority of the incumbents of public offices are unprincipled and irresponsible men. The "organs of public opinion" themselves admit that there is such an epidemic belief in the rascality of office-holders in general; and the testimony of the press, on this point, is entitled to credit, because the admission criminates the press itself, as we shall see presently. We can have no stronger evidence than the voluntary confessions of the criminal or his confederates.

The Philadelphia *American Mechanic* declared that "Our political managers are continually engaged in contests for supremacy; the ballot-box is profaned by illegal votes, *our offices are occupied by ignorant and brutal incumbents*, disorder marks our municipal legislation, and money is received in the most open manner for the support of local measures by the people's representatives. Any honest man who ventures calmly and decorously to expose the misdoings of the executive department of this plundered city is hunted down as a libeller, indicted, convicted and punished for daring to show how the citizens of Philadelphia are plundered of eight or nine millions *per annum* in the shape of taxes, while ONE-THIRD of that amount would be sufficient to support a better government under an honest administration of public affairs."

CORRUPTION FUNDS.

In a paragraph professing to explain how politicians are elected to office in the United States, the New York Herald of October 27, 1858, says: "The Republicans have a corruption fund of $250,000 for electioneering purposes, and the Democrats have a fund for the same purposes and quite as large." What sort of officers must those be who consent to be elected by such instrumentality?

The Philadelphia Sunday Dispatch, an independent or neutral paper, makes the following charges against the administration of President Buchanan: "The government has descended to a fearful system of bribery to carry out its designs. It has caused many supernumerary and unnecessary hands to be employed at the Mint and Navy Yard, merely for the purpose of bribing men with temporary employment to vote for the favorites of the administration on Tuesday next."

The Washington Union, in allusion to the operations of Congress at its last session, says: "Funds, representing a capital of *two hundred and fifty millions of dollars*, were voted away by the faithful representatives of the people at one fell dash. The objects for which these magnificent appropriations were made were of questionable utility."

In February, 1859, the New York Times reported that C. N. Pyne, United States Marshal of the Southern District of Illinois, had expended for his own uses $7,200 of the public money in *four months*, though his yearly salary is less than $6,000. This charge was preferred against him by his principal bookkeeper, Mr. Martin, who filed his allegations in the Department of the Interior. These facts were brought to the notice of Mr. Buchanan, but that gentleman, "for political reasons," refused to call Mr. Pyne to an account.

If all the defalcations and other villainies committed by "public servants" were published in the newspapers, I apprehend that the largest sheets would scarcely find room for any thing else.

A very sensible correspondent of the Cincinnati Gazette, under the date of April 3, 1859, writes as follows: "It is well remembered when the embezzlement of public moneys, in large or small amounts, by men in high places, caused a thrill of horror and detestation through the length and breadth of our land; but, by FREQUENT REPETITION, though these embezzlements have increased from a few hundreds or thousands to a million at a time, their occurrence now does not even cause surprise, and the perpetrators of these public thefts hardly lose caste in society."

But, without multiplying instances, it is sufficient to say that the newspapers teem with accounts of official rogueries. From the highest to the lowest—from the President at Washington to the policeman at the corner—men in office are the objects of suspicion and distrust, and many of them are charged with offenses which ought to condemn the persons who commit them to the profoundest depths of public detestation.

I say that it is a prevailing belief among the American people, that their political servants, *in general*, are depraved and corrupt. The presumption is, that this sentiment is correct; for the opinion of the majority on all political subjects is incontrovertible. At least this is the theory of our republican constitution. In these circumstances, no affirmative evidence is required to prove the bad character of our office-holders in the mass. The burden of proof rests on those who *deny* that fact which appears to be a matter of general belief. All the additional evidence which has been offered in support of that fact may be considered as *argumenta ex abundantia*. Or, (in plain English,) the proofs of official rascality are so excessively numerous, that we can afford to offer you a few of them when none are required.

WHO MAKES THEM?

We now come to the question which more immediately concerns our present inquiry. Are office-holders *made* by the Press Gang? Do they owe their election or appointment, in a great measure, to newspaper influence? On this topic I will permit some of the editors themselves to speak; begging you, in the first place, to observe, that when the journalists claim to be the manufacturers of such a bad commodity as the office-holders, the claim ought to be allowed. When we see the maker's stamp or ticket affixed to a piece of work which does the artist no credit, we can scarcely doubt that the mark is genuine—for people are not apt to make pretensions to a disgraceful job which they never performed.

The Washington Union, one of our ablest and most conspicuous journals, in a laudatory article on the Newspaper Press, avers that "No party could exist for a year without it. It is a great beneficiary for politicians,—their *main reliance*, and their only means of acquiring public notoriety. It is the ordnance department of politics, the arsenal and magazine from which small minds draw their weapons and ammunition for political warfare. The newspaper press is the greatest power in the State;" etc.

The New York Herald of September 13, 1858, comes to the confessional and speaks as follows:—"The political editor toils, day and night, to mould a piece of ordinary humanity so that it will be received by the people as a superior article. Excuses are found for blunders, palliatives for positive stupidities and encomiums for accidental diversions into the path of duty. The editor exhausts the English language in the praise of his political pet; he is a Cicero in eloquence, a Talleyrand in sagacity, a Washington in integrity."

Bennett, in the same article, proceeds to celebrate the achievments of his neighbor Greeley, who is proposed as a grand exemplar for journalistic politicians. Says the editor of the Herald :—

"It was to Mr. Greeley, more than to any other man, that William H. Seward owed his elevation to the Senate of the United States. It was to Mr. Greeley that Thurlow Weed always looked for assistance in carrying out his Albany lobby schemes, and never looked in vain. And when the leader of the Washington lobby, Matteson, wanted a safe banker for that celebrated thousand-dollar draft, the accommodating breeches pocket of the amiable Greeley was ready to receive and to hold the precious document until it could be passed securely to its ultimate destination. To advance this clique of scheming unworthy, corrupt and ungrateful politicians, Greeley has sacrificed the best part of his life. They were as clay,—and very ordinary clay,—in the hands of the potter. From a small village attorney and a third-rate country politician, Seward, by Greeley's aid, became a Senator of the United States, with a reversionary right to the Presidency if he can get any more Greeleys to help him.

"From a second-rate country editor, Weed turns up as the Colbert of the lobby and the Warwick of conventions. And Matteson,—one of the smallest of rural politicians, is engineered into Congress; and is at the head of a corrupt combination which, if successful, will bleed the country to the tune of ten or fifteen millions of dollars. There was no scheme of corruption, no intrigue in which this precious trio did not engage when they found it would pay, and they always had in Greeley a convenient apologist."

This is James Gordon Bennett's testimony against Horace Greeley; now let us hear the evidence of John W. Forney against Mr. Bennett. Forney is the renowned editor of the Philadelphia Press. In a speech delivered by him at Tarrytown, in the autumn or winter of 1858, he spoke of Bennett and his *Herald* in the following terms :—

"This journal, (the Herald aforesaid,) has grown rich in a career of villainy. Its attacks on personal character, its terrorism over actors and actresses, its reckless intrigues against business men and business interests, had filled its editor's pockets, and Bennett now aspired to a respectable representative position at some foreign court. He applied for such a position to Mr. Pierce; his request was scouted, and he became an assailant of Pierce's administration. He toiled to defeat Mr. Buchanan; he sent agents to Washington and other parts of the country; he sent spies to Lancaster, where Mr. Buchanan resided, to collect scandalous stories and to give them circulation. The Herald expended all its influence and *a good deal of Mr. Fremont's money*, in trying to defeat Mr. Buchanan."

Reciprocating these editorial civilities, Mr. Bennett, after bestowing on Mr. Forney epithets which are better adapted to the columns of the Herald than to the pages of this work, tells how Forney earned the favor of Mr. Buchanan and how he lost it; circumstantially admitting, however, that Buchanan owes his election, in a great measure, to the exertions of Forney in his behalf. This fact is generally conceded by the newspapers of both parties.

In these extracts, we find it plainly asserted that the assistance of some of the most vicious journals in the country is sought after by men who aspire to the highest political stations. Our most eminent statesmen practically acknowledge that their hopes of preferment or aggrandizement are built on the favor and support of such men as James Gordon Bennett, Horace Greeley and John W. Forney!

DAMNING RECOMMENDATIONS.

As libertines seldom pay their addresses to ladies of unsuspected virtue, so licentious politicians rarely solicit the favors of *incorruptible* editors. For the uses of lewdly inclined office-hunters, the prostituted press is always available. On the other hand, it is highly improbable that journals of the meretricious class should be inclined to favor those who do not court their caresses, and hence the pure and virtuous are not likely to be their customers or the objects of their fond attentions.

In fact, the favor and support of some newspapers are enough, *per se*, to damn any politician in the estimation of all honorable men; for the public could have no stronger proof of his rascality When a candidate's name is paraded, with favorable indications, in the columns of the "Satanic Press," his political reputation ought to be damaged as much as his moral character would be by his appearance at the front window of a bawdy-house.

It appears, from the best evidence we can collect, that successful politicians are made by the *worst class* of public journals. Several circumstances conspire to produce this lamentable effect; *e. g.* the most destestable newspapers in America, (as I have mentioned elsewhere,) have the widest circulation and the greatest influence; hence they can make themselves particularly serviceable to knavish politicians; and, being always susceptible of bribery and corruption, they are always available for those who are rich enough, and rascally enough, to use them for electioneering purposes.

It is humiliating and disgraceful enough for *any* public officer in the United States to be suspected of owing his election to the influence of such journals as the New York Herald, Tribune, etc. But when statesmen who aspire to the Chief Magistracy of this great Republic, when the actual occupants of the Presidential Chair, are known to solicit or accept the aid of the most venal and disreputable class of journalists, there is no abyss of hell dark and profound enough to represent the blackness of their infamy and the depth of their degradation.

THE PUBLIC PERSUADED TO SUBMIT.

Only one item of my Seventh Charge remains to be considered; and that may be disposed of with considerable brevity. I think we are now prepared to believe that candidates are elected to office chiefly by the influence of the press, and that it is almost or quite impossible for them to be elected *without* newspaper assistance. We have also discovered that political villains are more likely to be elected by journalistic aid than honest and incorruptible citizens. We have seen that knaves *are* elected to office in a great majority of cases; and we have had indisputable proofs that the newspaper press is the abettor and confederate of these official knaves, accepting their tribute, or hush-money, and a share of their plunder.

The last clause of the Seventh Charge represents that the press "persuades the people to submit quietly to the extortions and oppressions which are incidental to all governments whose affairs are administered by agents without honesty or responsibility."

I suppose it is very easy to believe that the press would persuade the public to endure those abuses which are created, in a great measure, by the agency of journalism itself. When it is understood that the editors have a good share of the "proceeds" of official robberies, it may be expected that the conductors of the press will advise the public to submit patiently to those depredations. And they *do* give such advice as plainly as circumstances will permit. They have taught the people to believe that "defalcations are not crimes;" they speak of them with a levity which implies that they are venial and trifling faults; and they indirectly defend them with the sophistical pretense that because they are "common errors," they are, to some extent, *justifiable!* The same plea would excuse polygamy in the Mormon country, adultery in France and Italy, and cannibalism in some of the South Sea islands.

The "Head Devil of Journalism" openly defended the robbery of the public by alleging that it was "practiced by all parties." The conduct of the press shows that editors generally have adopted Bennett's opinion, though few of them have courage or audacity enough to express it in his unequivocal language.

SUPPLEMENTARY ILLUSTRATIONS.

FORNEY PLAYS DUKE OF BUCKINGHAM.—It appears that, in

the last presidential drama, Mr. Forney played the part of Buckingham to Mr. Buchanan's Richard III. He helped his old friend to the chair of state and was refused the promised reward, because, (like Gloster's perverse favorite,) he became inconveniently conscientious at a time when unscrupulous service was required. This is Mr. Forney's own account of the matter. From his report, it seems that Mr. Buchanan did not request him to commit murder, or any other horrible crime, but merely desired him *to cut off the ears of Mr. James Gordon Bennett!* This, by the way, is the only instance in which Mr. Buchanan was ever known to call for retrenchment, and it is a pity that he could not be gratified. Bennett had violently opposed Mr. Buchanan's election, and some of his abuse was so offensive that Mr. Buchanan, in a conversation with Mr. Forney, a few days before the election, wrathfully inquired, "Why am I to be thus traduced and pursued by this infamous knave? Have I no friends, who will visit New York and punish him as he deserves? His ears ought to be taken off in the public street."

In answer to this intelligible hint, Mr. Forney, (like his prototype, Buckingham,) requested some time for reflection:

> "Give me some breath, some little pause, my lord,
> Before I positively speak in this."

But Mr. Buchanan wished to have it "suddenly performed," and Forney's hesitation gave him great offense. From that time, perhaps, he resolved to find other agents to execute his purposes:—

> "I will converse with iron-witted fools,
> And inconsiderate boys. None are for me
> Who look into me with inquiring eyes.
> High-reaching Buckingham grown circumspect!
> The deep-revolving, cunning Buckingham
> No more shall be the neighbor to my counsels.
> Hath he so long held out with me untir'd,
> And stops he now for breath? Well, be it so."

The editor of the *Herald* was not trimmed off in the manner proposed by Mr. Buchanan, and in allusion to this circumstance, Mr. Forney exclaims:—"I believe that it is owing to my *prudence* and *compassion*, that Bennett is this day permitted to walk Broadway with his long ears on his Scotch head!" (*Vide Tarrytown speech.*)

But the sequel of Forney's account of his quarrel with the President is the strangest part of the narrative. "Soon after he was inaugurated," says Forney, "Mr. Buchanan told me that he wished Mr. Bennett to support his administration! I can now perceive that the man who was thus willing to court the favor of the most abandoned and infamous editor on the face of the earth, was even at that day resolved in his own mind to turn his back on those gallant men in this city and State, who had surrounded him as with a wail of fire, and who had carried him forward into the presidency, after *twenty years* of hard, unremitting and chivalric toil."—*Philadelphia Press.*

THE VIRTUOUS FORNEY ABUSED.—In one of his editorial articles, Mr. Forney says:—" Some of the accusations against me are worthy of a passing notice. The Washington *Union* and the Richmond *South*, have been most fertile in their compliments. Divided between these journals may be found such charges as these: 'The President gave him all the consequence that he ever had; took him by the hand and advanced him, assisted his family, expended money for him and even educated him. And, at the best, Forney's great feat, was the FORREST LETTER, which ought to disgrace him in every man's eyes.' Such, (says Mr. Forney,) is the substance of the personal part of the indictment under which I have been tried, and on which I am now being tried, by these newspaper lawyers."—*Philadelphia Press.*

MR. BUCHANAN'S FREE ENTERTAINMENTS.—In the New York Herald of Friday, August 1, 1856, I find the following paragraph:—

"The *Lancasterian and Intelligencer*, now the home organ of Mr. Buchanan, in 1852 declared that it was notorious that Mr. Buchanan had converted his residence at Wheatland into an unlimited tavern-stand, where all were invited to call and partake of his liquors, the qualities of which he was by no means modest in extolling, free from any charge save the health of Buchanan. In this manner, it adds, has he, night after night, sought by making men drunk, to secure from them, in their drunken moments, pledges to support him. This is positively frightful and gives us a shuddering recollection of Forney's letter to Roberts, touching the Forrest divorce case. The same Lancaster authority further declares that these things have been repeatedly transacted, Sabbath after Sabbath, and defies an honest denial."

The two papers which circulated this statement are now sp cial objects of Mr. Buchanan's favor and patronage! If the story is true, Mr. Forney cannot claim the *undivided* credit of making Mr. Buchanan President; for the "Powers of Grog," seems to have had something to do with that matter.

AN AFFLICTIVE CHANGE.—General Jackson once remarked, "A man who seeks the Chief Magistracy of this country anxiously and by improper methods, will never obtain it." There was a time when this remark was altogether true; but we have lived to witness a distressing change. Large sums of money have lately been expended, for electioneering purposes, by aspirants for the presidency. Mr. S. A. Douglass, it is said, has sold his real estate, or a large part of it, to supply himself with the necessary funds for a presidential campaign; and Mr. Forney, president-maker and editor of the Philadelphia *Press*, is already on his side. But *one* specimen of Mr. Forney's manufacture ought to be quite satisfactory to the public.

SECTION XIII.

SHOWING HOW THE NEWSPAPER PRESS DEFEATS THE PURPOSES OF JUSTICE.

Examination of the Eighth Charge.

ALL that is necessary to establish every particular of this charge has been often enunciated from the judicial bench, explicitly declared in our legislative halls, and admitted by the newspapers themselves.

JUDICIAL OPINIONS.

Judge Ludlow of Philadelphia, in a recent charge to a jury, spoke of the interference of the newspaper press as the greatest obstacle to the adminstration of justice. His Honor admitted that the press is all powerful, but plainly asserted that the tremendous force of journalism is excercised in a way that is calculated to make the trial by jury, and every other beneficent legal institution, totally worthless.

Judge Kent, at a trial of James Gordon Bennett, editor of the *New York Herald,* for libel, remarked, "I can imagine no greater curse to any community than a newspaper so cheaply published as to be brought under the eye of everybody, yet constantly dealing in falsehood and defamation; a paper from the assaults of which neither age, nor sex, nor occupation is exempt; a paper which assails the most sacred professions, and *seeks to bring into contempt the sanctuary of justice itself.*"

With respect to this trial of Mr. Bennett, the *New York Evening Post* made the following remarks:—

"Bennett, the editor of that infamous sheet, the *New York Herald,* was indicted for two gross libels on Judge Noah of the court of Oyer and Terminer. The libeller was convicted. Judge Kent, a man of eminent personal worth and juridical integrity, thought the crime a heinous one, and deserving of severe punishment; but his associates, Lee and Purdy, *through fear of the abuse of Bennett's piratical blackguard sheet*, decided that the punishment should be a small fine; for which Bennett drew his check, and walked out of the Court House snapping his fingers and bidding defiance to courts of justice."

Here we have an instance of the mode in which the decisions of courts are controlled by editorial authority. A majority of the judges favored Bennett because they were afraid of his venomous publications. Courts and juries are *often* overawed in the same manner, knowing that if they venture to give a decision, or to render a verdict which does not agree with the requirements of the press, they will be charged with partiality, stupidity, or corruption, and held up as proper objects of public abhorrence or contempt.

TRIALS A MOCKERY.

The fate of any man charged with a criminal offense is generally decided by the newspapers, even before the Grand Jury has found a bill of indictment. The imposing ceremonies of a criminal trial are little more than a melo-dramatic performance for the entertainment of the spectators; and they are a bitter mockery of the accused party, who has probably read his sentence *in print* three or four weeks before he was arraigned at the bar.

NEWSPAPER OPPOSITION TO LAW.

"Laws," said an American newspaper, "laws are a dead letter where *public opinion* is against them. The Grand Jury have refused to find a bill of indictment in the case of State *v.* Norra and others, for killing a man in a duel, although the strongest evidence of murder, under the laws, was adduced. Laws, we say, are a dead letter where public opinion is against them."

By "public opinion" is here signified newspaper opinion. In America the terms are synonymous, and the things are identical. The newspapers had decided that Norra *et als.* should not be indicted for murder, and they *were not* indicted.

A mob, composed chiefly of foreigners, and calling itself a "Vigilance Committee," in June, 1858, took possession of the municipal government of New Orleans, deposing the legally constituted authorities of the city, and organizing a band of armed ruffians to intimidate the peaceably disposed citizens and the ministers of the law. This was clearly an act of rebellion or high treason, and Judge Theodore G. Hunt, of the First District Court of New Orleans, charged the Grand Jury to that effect. But the local newspapers, in general, took a different view of the matter, violently opposing all legal proceedings against the offenders; and so successful was this editorial opposition that not one of the culprits (if I am correctly informed,) was ever punished, or even brought to trial. The ringleaders of this revolutionary movement richly deserved *hanging*. Their escape with entire impunity produced a feeling of indignation and astonishment,—not in America only, but in many parts of Europe likewise; for this extraordinary transaction, so very disgraceful to republicanism, was a subject of general comment on both sides of the Atlantic.

The circumstance just narrated shows how easy it is for the American newspaper press to control the operations of law and justice, even in the most flagrant cases of culpability, when the offenses committed are productive of national disgrace, and are calculated to make the institutions of our free government contemptible in the eyes of the whole world.

REPORTING CRIMINAL CASES.

In the charge now under consideration, it is affirmed that "the interference of the newspaper press with the administration of justice makes it impossible for any man charged with a criminal offense to have a fair trial." The truth of this allegation will be manifest if you can only be persuaded to open your eyes, and to take cognizance of a few obvious facts.

You know, perhaps, that, as soon as any crime is committed in this country, the newspapers make the public acquainted with all the particulars, as far as they can be ascertained or *conjectured*. Possibly you may know likewise (or, if *you* do not know, *I* do) that it is the common practice of newspapers to MAKE THE MOST of every criminal deed, and of every other startling event that affords a good subject for an interesting report.

In all cases, and especially in locations where there is much competition or rivalship among public journals, it is a grand object with each publication to have the *earliest* and the *most complete* account of any local occurrence which is likely to excite the curiosity of the public. The news collectors or reporters for the press are, therefore, always on the alert when a crime of importance has been committed, each reporter being prompted by a feeling of emulation to obtain material for the best—or rather the *longest*—narrative. Rumors, as well as facts, are incorporated in the report; and, if the thread of the story should happen to be defective in some of its parts, the guessing or imaginative faculties of the reporter are probably called into requisition.

Such, in general, is the process by means of which the public is first made acquainted with the particulars of any notable crime. The newspaper statement thereof must necessarily be more or less imperfect and unreliable; and yet it is on this statement that public opinion is formed; and, in a case of this kind, the first impression which is made on the minds of the public will have a powerful effect on the legal investigation which is to follow.

The report of a "horrid murder" would not be complete— it would not satisfy the cravings of public curiosity—if the reporter for the press should fail to point out some person as the suspected criminal. This he generally does, either in express terms or by unmistakable implication. If the affair should be mysterious, (as, indeed, murder cases generally are,) the reporter, anxious to fulfill the obligations which he owes to his employers and to the reading public, selects a victim of public indignation, and of future punishment perhaps, from among the neighbors, friends, or relations of the murdered party. It must be confessed that this selection is commonly made with some regard to probabilities; for example, if the deceased was an athletic man, and circumstances indicate that he was overpowered after a hard struggle, the suspicion will not be likely to fall on a bed-ridden grandmother, or a wife far advanced in a state of pregnancy. But, in spite of all their caution and sagacity, the reporters often commit irremediable injuries by fastening suspicion on innocent persons.

When the suspected party is arrested and brought before a magistrate for examination, the reporters are in attendance; and every particle of the *ex parte* evidence—and that evidence loosely reported, and often sadly perverted—soon after appears in the newspapers. All the facts of the case, mixed up with more or less fiction, are printed and circulated through the whole country; and this unofficial and unreliable statement is read and *believed* by almost everybody. Every newspaper reader is thus provided with a "foregone conclusion" respecting the merits of the case; and the subsequent verdict of the jury is almost always in accordance with the impressions produced by the first newspaper reports.

INJUDICIOUS JUDGES.

From this view, it may appear that, in all criminal cases, the newspaper reporters and editors are the real judges and jurors both. They examine the testimony, and decide authoritatively on its validity and sufficiency; they render a verdict and pronounce the sentence. The action of the court afterward is little more than a needless piece of formality—a mere official *confirmation* of the views and decisions of the newspaper press.

But the newspaper men are not satisfied with exercising the

functions of judge and jury. Like Bottom the weaver, they are ambitious to play *every* part in the drama, and so become, (as their humor happens to incline them,) either prosecuting attorneys or counsel for the prisoner. Sometimes the whole press of the country clamors for the conviction of accused parties—sometimes the prevailing sentiment of the newspapers is in favor of acquittal. But in *all* affairs of this kind, the course pursued by the public journals is unreasonable, unjust and eminently mischievous—so that, in the language of our Eighth Accusation, "it is impossible for any man charged with a criminal offense to have a fair trial."

PREJUDICED JURIES.

It is impossible, in any criminal case which is tried in the United States, to procure an unbiased jury; for every juror, if he is accustomed to read the newspapers, necessarily forms an opinion before he enters the jury-box. He has prejudged the case, and is therefore *prejudiced*, according to the etymology and true meaning of the word. This evil cannot be remedied by a change of venue; for, as the newspapers penetrate every part of the country, their premature and imperfect reports of criminal cases are read everywhere, and thus the minds of men are biased in one location as much as in another.

In the case of Polly Bodine, (a woman charged with an atrocious murder,) among *six thousand* men who had been returned on the jury lists, no twelve could be found who were not unduly biased, and therefore unfit to try the cause upon their oaths.

At a recent criminal trial, in one of our Western States, every juryman on the panel, except one, admitted that he had formed and expressed opinions in relation to the merits of the case. And, when questioned further, these "good men and true" acknowledged that they had adopted the opinions of the newspapers. Only one of them had not formed or expressed any opinion in relation to the matter at issue; and the reason was, as he honestly confessed, because he "never *read* any of them cussed newspapers." This judicious citizen was sent out of court by the presiding judge; who inferred, (somewhat rashly, as I think,) that a man who does not read the public journals cannot have sufficient intelligence to qualify him for the duties of a juror. It is a question with me whether the citizen who never reads a newspaper is not likely to be a wiser and a better man than one who reads *nothing else* but newspapers, and whose opinions and principles are constituted on this kind of reading.

How is it possible to organize, in this country, such a jury as the law requires? Blackstone asserts that the whole panel or array should be quashed, if there is any reasonable suspicion of partiality or bias on the minds of the jurors, (*Commentaries*. Book iii. c. 23); and every individual juryman who, before the trial, is supposed to have formed an opinion in relation to the matter at issue, ought to be challenged and rejected.

Now here is the grand dilemma: every American who reads newspapers *must* form some opinion respecting the merits of every criminal case; or, if he is incapable of forming any opinion of his own, he adopts the opinion of his newspaper oracle, and so acquires a bias or partiality, which disqualifies him for the duties of the jury-box. On the other hand, if he does *not* read the newspapers, it is presumed, even by judges on the bench, that he lacks that amount of intelligence which every competent juryman must possess. Therefore, all who read newspapers are disqualified, and all who do not read them are *ditto;* and in these circumstances it is hard to imagine where suitable material for the composition of a jury is to be found.

The want of proper stuff for the formation of juries is felt as a very serious inconvenience in Philadelphia, New York, and many other'parts of the United States. In many criminal cases, it is almost impossible for any honest and well-informed citizen to be sworn as a juryman. Such a man, when questioned at the time of trial, must admit that he is acquainted with all the particulars of the case; and, unless he is too much of the philosopher to be biased by newspaper suggestions, he must acknowledge that his judgment has been swayed by journalistic reports. These admissions, according to the rules of criminal jurisprudence, will lead to his rejection; and, in this way, every enlightened and conscientious juryman may be dismissed from the Court.

"PROFESSIONAL JURYMEN."

But, in our principal cities, and probably elsewhere, there are certain idle and worthless fellows, sometimes called "professional jurymen," who hang about the purlieus of the Court House, and are always willing and anxious to be employed as jurors. Many of these are people of very dissolute habits and disreputable character. Being too indolent to engage in any active business, these vagabonds thrust themselves forward when the sheriff is making his *venire;* and being well known to the officers of the court, and always available and convenient, they easily succeed in having themselves impanneled.

Few of these paltry rogues are conscientious enough to acknowledge that their minds have been prejudiced by the newspaper reports; for such an avowal might occasion the loss of the "job," and of the dollar *per diem* which they so much covet. They commonly profess, therefore, to come into court with unbiased judgments; and, as jurors are seldom challenged *propter delictum* in America, these volunteer jurymen, however unsuitable they may be in morals and intellect, are generally accepted by the tribunals of justice; and I learn from very good authority that, in our courts of criminal jurisdiction, the juries are, for the most part, composed of such mercenary and unprincipled persons.

Jurymen of this class, like all other corrupt and unworthy officials, stand in much dread of newspaper censure; for they know that if the press were to do its duty by denouncing them to the public, their nefarious business would soon come to an end. Such jurors as we speak of, therefore, attend to the requirements of the public journals, and their verdicts, with few exceptions, are merely the echoes of what appears to be newspaper sentiment.

ABOLITION OF TRIAL BY JURY.

These are facts which are undeniable, and I have stated them without the least exaggeration. And I now assert without any fear of contradiction, that the action of the newspaper press makes the trial by jury, "that principal bulwark of our liberties," not merely worthless in criminal cases, but absolutely oppressive and dangerous. I do not hesitate to declare my belief that, unless some other remedy for existing evils can be found, the trial by jury ought to be abolished. Admitting that it is "the very right hand of justice," there are circumstances which may make its amputation necessary.

But are we reduced to such a lamentable extremity? Must we surrender one of the most valuable institutions of free government, and practically acknowledge that the morals of our nation are so hopelessly vitiated that public justice can no longer be maintained among us, except by removing its administration as far as possible from the hands of the people. One of two things we shall certainly have to do:—we must either abolish juries or place some restriction on the villainous or idiotic mismanagement of the newspaper press.

ESCAPE OF CRIMINALS.

It is said, among other things, in the Charge now under consideration, that "the newspapers have often caused the most desperate offenders to be acquitted and turned loose on society." Almost every man's recollection will furnish him with some examples of the kind. Villains of the deepest dye are often the objects of editorial sympathy; as we may easily conceive when we reflect that very many of the editors themselves may be classified among the blackest of villains.

Every rogue who is arraigned before a criminal court, may secure newspaper apologists as well as legal advocates, if he is able to meet the necessary expense; for be it understood that newspaper aid is available for every man whose successful knaveries have enabled him to salve the consciences of the editors with golden ointment.

CRIMINALS DEFENDED BY EDITORS.

At Chicago, very recently, a police-officer named Brown, was charged with the scandalous misdemeanor of "levying black mail" on the courtezans of that city, and permitting them to transact their lewd business without interruption, so long as they complied with his requisitions. It appeared in evidence that this caitiff officer had often prostituted himself at the brothels, merely, as he averred, to obtain undeniable proofs of the bad character of the house where these proceedings were allowed. This conduct of officer Brown was openly and zealously defended by the *Chicago Democrat*, the editor of which is an ex-member of Congress! And because the jury in Brown's case did not render a verdict of acquittal in accordance with the views of the *Democrat*, that paper asserted that the jury was packed and that certain officers of the court had been bribed and corrupted.

I bring this example from a remote city, merely to show my readers that the kind of newspaper abuses which are notoriously prevalent in Boston, New York, Philadelphia, and all of our principal cities, are not *confined* to these locations. Wherever the newspaper business flourishes, the laws are more or less inefficient. Criminals who have any political interest or pecuniary ability, can always find journalistic defenders.

In the United States, rum-sellers are generally active politicians; and of course, persons of great consequence, especially at election times. On this account they are the recipients of much editorial favor and respect. Only a few days ago, the keeper of a grog-kennel in Philadelphia, attempted to commit a rape on a female child eleven years old. The little girl was seated in one of the city rail-road cars, which was standing at the terminus of the road waiting for passengers when the scoundrel entered the vehicle, and, finding the child alone, began to take the most indecent liberties with her person. She escaped from the car and flew to a neighboring house for protection. The villain was so confident of security that he made no attempt to escape, but kept his seat in the car, where he was found by an officer who was sent to arrest him. Being engaged in the lucrative business of rum-selling, this wretch could afford to disburse a little money in the purchase of legal and editorial indulgences; and, as an Irishman, he had special claims to the favor and protection of the newspaper press. An effort was made, therefore, "to hush the matter up." I do not believe that the affair was reported in the daily papers of Philadelphia, and all the information I have on the subject, was derived from the Philadelphia correspondent of a newspaper published in New York. The writer of the account declared that the magistrate who examined this case, was induced to go to the parents of the little girl for the purpose of persuading them to withdraw their complaint, which they very properly refused to do.

If this foreign rum-seller could induce a magistrate to make such unusual and unlawful exertions in his behalf, he doubtless understood some kind of rhetoric which would be equally influential with the press. When we consider the eagerness of the reporters to obtain "local incidents," we may justly suspect that their silence has been purchased, when they fail to give the customary attention to a criminal case of such piquant atrocity that it could not be easily overlooked.

POWERS OF REPORTERS.

From what has been said, it may be judged that newspaper *reporters* have a great deal to do with our system of criminal jurisprudence. Their agency is observable at every stage of the legal proceedings. They point out the suspected party, they give the first account of his arrest, his examination and his commitment; and, (without being guilty of absolute falsehood,) **they** may contrive to produce a first impression on the public mind which may be decidedly favorable or unfavorable to the prisoner. The same evidence written out by two different reporters may present two widely different aspects, though it might be hard to fix a charge of pseudology, or even misrepresentation, on either of the scribes. The suppression of a single line, or a single word, of the testimony, may make a momentous difference in its import. The sagacious reader will perceive, therefore, that it behooves a criminal to have the good-will of the reporters, if it can possibly be obtained "for love or money."

CRIMINALS BRIBE THE PRESS.

I suspect that newspaper-men often find the *suppression of facts* more profitable than the publication of falsehoods; for, as it is not *always* a "pleasant thing to see one's name in print," many a gentleman who becomes entangled in the meshes of the law willingly makes liberal payments to avoid newspaper celebrity. And, if the newspapers fail to take any notice of a criminal case, the accused party, whether he be innocent or guilty, has a much better chance of escape.

In a New York paper which is devoted chiefly to criminal intelligence, I lately read: "Great is the talk among the English and Irish *knucks*, (qu. pick-pockets?) of the arrest of Polly Lee and Jim O'Brien, and strong efforts are made to square the case. Three hundred dollars have already been disbursed among lawyers, newspaper-men and others, and still the cry is for more."

Several years ago, the New York *Courier and Enquirer*, the editor of which is the famous Colonel Webb, remarked: "Judging from the history of various parts of the country, for some time past, it is our opinion that, with $20,000, a man may commit any half a dozen crimes that can be named, short of murder; and even that, if he happens to have influential friends."

To this the New York *Herald* adds: "True, every word The list of criminals who have escaped by means of wealth and influence, during the last six years, would astonish everybody."

Yes; and since these candid admissions were made by Webb and Bennett, how many scores of malefactors have gone unwhipped of justice, even in New York city alone, without troubling ourselves to look further? "Any six crimes, short of murder," quoth Colonel Webb, "may be commuted for $20,000;" but he does not tell how the money is to be applied. At least fifty per cent. of the $20,000 must be used to propitiate the newspaper press, for without its concurrence or connivance, I hold it impossible that any conspicuous villainy should go unpunished. In very few cases, could any judge, jury, or prosecuting attorney be induced by bribery to favor criminals, if the press should call for their condemnation.

Our judges, on the bench, declare that the newspaper press is "all powerful," and this, no doubt, is their belief and the belief of all who are connected with the administration of the law. Is it probable, therefore, that any of the ministers of justice should set at defiance this god of their idolatry, this typographical Juggernaut, in whose omnipotence they so steadfastly and so devoutly believe?

Assure yourselves, my countrymen, that the reiterated failure of the law to punish felons of the most execrable classes is caused chiefly by the influences of a corrupt and meretricious newspaper press; influences which, (as I have endeavored to convince you in other parts of this book,) can easily be enlisted in the service of any form of immorality and crime.

In this section, I have endeavored to substantiate that part of my Eighth Charge which asserts that "the American newspapers unwarrantably interfere with the administration of public justice; that they make it impossible for any man charged with a criminal offense to have a fair trial, and that they have often caused the most desperate offenders to be acquitted and turned loose on society." How far I have succeeded in making these truths appear, I will now leave you to judge. But let me assure you that the offenses of the press which we have just been examining, however weighty and worthy of condemnation they may be, will become comparatively trivial and insignificant when we proceed to consider that part of the charge which is reserved for examination in the next Section, where some of the most appalling crimes of journalism will be exhibited.

SUPPLEMENTARY ILLUSTRATIONS.

COMMON BELIEF.—It is commonly believed that the newspapers are often induced by bribes to create public sympathy in behalf of murderers and other great criminals for the ultimate purpose of protecting them from legal retribution. Of course we cannot always have *positive proofs* of this kind of editorial prostitution. Foul deeds are generally done in secret, and with all the precautions that are necessary for concealment. With regard to the illicit intercourse between editors and their seducers for the purposes just mentioned,—

> "It were a tedious difficulty, I think,
> To bring them to the prospect. Strange indeed,
> If any mortal eyes, except their own,
> Should see them bolster. Yet I say,
> If imputation and strong circumstance,
> Which lead directly to the door of truth,
> Can give you satisfaction, you may have it."

The more probable a story is, the less proof is required. This allegation against the editors is so extremely probable, that I defy you, or any other man or woman, to point out any reason why it should be *doubted*. Consider the mercenary character of the journalists; observe what they do for small bribes, and imagine what they might do for *large* ones. They will "puff" any poisonous quack medicine for one dollar, or less money; and in this way they become accessory to many murders. Is it not probable enough that, for a thousand dollars, or a larger sum, they would use their editorial influence to help a criminal at the time of his trial? But perhaps the following items will help to elucidate the subject:—

Murder of Helen Jewett.—Helen Jewett, a celebrated beauty of Augusta, Me., became the victim of seduction, and after being discarded by her relations, she came to New York and fixed her abode at a house of ill-repute, kept by Rosina Townsend. On the night of April 10, 1836, this unfortunate girl was murdered. Suspicion fell on her paramour, Richard P. Robinson; in fact, the evidences of his guilt appeared to be conclusive. It was reported, and believed, that a Mr. Joseph Hoxie had loaned Robinson six or seven thousand dollars to pay the *expenses of his trial*. It is certain that Robinson found a zealous defender in the editor of the *New York Herald*, who, as his biographer declares, "introduced a theory, not without apparent reasons, to show the possibility of Robinson's innocence." The same biographer adds, "From that period, down to the present time, the cry has been iterated, again and again, that the columns of the *Herald* were purchased."

Mr. Bennett denies the impeachment, however, and his biographer says the story is "absurd." Robinson was acquitted.

Bennett was almost the only editor in New York who defended Robinson; but many persons, charged with abominable crimes, have found earnest and resolute editorial defenders in different parts of the country. In numerous cases there seems to be so little reason for the defense that it is impossible to imagine why the journalists should give themselves so much trouble, unless we suppose that they are *paid* for it.

Case of Captain Mackenzie.—This man was the commander of the U. S. brig *Somers*. While at sea, in the year 1842, on the mere *suspicion* that three of his ship's company intended to mutiny, he caused them to be executed at the yard-arm. One of the victims was midshipman Spencer, a son of the Hon. John C. Spencer, Secretary of War. On his return to America, Mackenzie was tried by a court-martial, at the Brooklyn Navy Yard. Before this court, Captain Mackenzie told his own story, and his worst enemy could not have told it more to his own disadvantage. He described the scene and *ceremonies* of the execution, and gave a particular account of his last conversation with young Spencer, who was only nineteen years of age. When he was about to be put to death, the unhappy boy seemed to be concerned chiefly on account of his parents, and expressed his fears that his disgraceful doom might injure his father. "I replied," says Captain Mackenzie, "that it was too late to think of that, and that if he had succeeded it would have injured his father much more. I told him that if his father had the opportunity he would naturally interpos etc save him, and that *for those who had money and friends, in America, there was no punishment for the worst of crimes.*"

No doubt the noble captain believed what he said. He himself had some money, I suppose, and friends too, influential friends, among whom was Colonel Webb of the *Courier and Enquirer*, and several other editors of New York, who succeeded in making the American public believe that the execution of the three men was justifiable; and as public opinion was in the captain's favor, the court-martial acquitted him, of course.

The very poor judgment of commander Mackenzie is exhibited in his own exculpatory narrative, which scarcely shows that there was evidence enough against the three condemned persons to justify putting them in irons. But their summary *execution* was an event which filled all Europe with horror; and the American public would have been still more shocked, if it had not been blinded by the misconstructions and apologies of the New York editors.

CASE OF KIRBY.—In 1842, a man named Kirby murdered a Mrs. Hunter, in Sparta, Tennessee. For some reason or other, this Kirby became a *protégé* of the local newspapers, which resisted every attempt to punish him for the murder. He had money, I presume; enough of it, at least, to purchase editorial friendship among the *Spartans* of Tennessee, though it might have required more cash than he possessed to compound for the murder of a woman in Philadelphia, New York, or Boston, where editorial indulgences are more expensive. Kirby was sentenced to death *four times,* and the supposition is that he may still be alive and merry; for the favorites of the newspaper press are as likely to escape hanging as they are to deserve it.

SECTION XIV.

HORRID EFFECTS OF EDITORIAL INTERFERENCE WITH THE ADMINISTRATION OF JUSTICE.

Continued Examination of the Eighth Charge.

PREPARE your minds, my good readers, for this part of the investigation by recollecting what has been said respecting the moral and intellectual qualities of our Press Gang in general, and of that portion of it, especially, which claims to be the most influential. I have given you to understand that newspaper writers are seldom wise or good men; you have been informed that they are, for the most part, people who have failed in other pursuits, not having learning, talents, or ingenuity enough to make them successful as parsons, lawyers, physicians, blacksmiths, shoemakers, tailors, play-actors, fiddlers, and so forth. You have heard, likewise, that great numbers of them are men of loose morals. Drunkenness and lechery are among the most common vices of the brotherhood; but the sin of covetousness is almost *universal* among them. Persons who have had much dealing with the conductors of the press assert that they will do ANY THING for Money; and this remark, in its application to many of our principal journalists, is unquestionably correct.

OTHER CHARACTERISTICS OF EDITORS.

But the newspapers often appear to be actuated by other motives besides those of avarice. The deportment of the journals sometimes exhibits a degree of FIENDISH MALICE which is absolutely horrifying. At times, the manifestation of such a diabolical spirit is quite general among the scribes of the press. No mercy is shown to the object of newspaper dislike and resentment; nothing less than his total *annihilation* can satisfy Messrs. Editors. The wrath of journalism is like scalding vitriol; it scorches and consumes its victims; it tortures without pity, and exterminates without remorse. In short, the newspaper press literally "plays the devil" when it is disposed to be mischievous. Its rage is truly demoniac; and, like all wrath which has no foundation in reason, it is boundless and implacable.

The irrationality, extravagancy, and ferocity of newspaper wrath, and all the other characteristics of journalism, will be easily understood when it is considered that our "leading newspapers," as they presume to call themselves, are the organs of the MOB; and their position, in this respect, is practically acknowledged in their general deportment. They are, with more or less politic dissimulation, the advocates of a mob regency, in opposition to the rights of the people, the maintenance of law and order, and the general welfare of the republic. In a former part of this work, I endeavored to point out the distinction between the American people and the mob. I hold that the latter is a scrubby minority, and that any attempt on its part to rule over the great body of the public, or to resist the legally-constituted authorities of the country, is, according to circumstances, an act of usurpation, treason, or rebellion.

I have said that the grand mistake of our newspaper press is to confound the people with the mob; and the natural consequence of that mistake is seen in the conduct of the journalists when they adapt themselves, without reserve, to the humors and requirements of the vilest and most vicious classes of the population.

The newspaper men are not only the apologists and defenders of mob rule, but THEY THEMSELVES are the worst kind of a mob, as I shall presently demonstrate.

THE CHARGE.

You will find that the preceding observations will be useful for reference in the discussion which is to follow; and we are now prepared to resume our examination of the Eighth Charge, directing our attention particularly to that part of it which asserts that, "by the unwise and malicious meddling of the newspapers, many innocent persons have been brought to condemnation and punishment."

In the preceding Section it was shown, as plainly as circumstances would allow, that great criminals often escape the castigation of the law by means of the corrupt influences of journalism. It is indeed a heinous offense against the institutions of society to defeat the operations of retributive justice; to offer the greatest possible encouragement to evil-doers by assisting them to avoid the penalties of their transgressions, and by giving malefactors liberty and opportunities to commit new crimes; to deprive our fellow-citizens of that protection which they have a right to expect from the laws of their country. If the delinquencies of the journalists extended no further than this, they would be inexcusable, and deserving of severe condemnation. But I am now about to call your attention to certain misdemeanors of the press, compared with which all the offenses which have hitherto been charged against the depraved journalism of our country are venial, and scarcely deserving of notice.

THE GREAT CRIME.

Could the newspapers commit a more unpardonable sin than that of insisting on the condemnation and punishment of the innocent? That they are justly charged with the frequent commission of this awful crime, is the fact which I expect to make as obvious to your perceptions as it is to my own.

If you accept the truths contained in the preceding pages of this volume, you cannot escape from the conviction that persons charged with criminal offenses are often unjustly condemned and punished in the United States; and an examination of the same evidence, in connection with that which I am about to offer must convince you that the unjust condemnation of those unfortunate people, is the natural and almost inevitable result of newspaper interference with the proceedings of our courts

CLAMORS OF THE PRESS.

Who does not know that, very often, the public journals clamorously demand the conviction of a prisoner at the bar? If I could imagine that any evidence of *this* fact were necessary, I could fill many pages with examples; but, if you are accustomed to read the newspapers you will not require any proofs of the kind. It is quite possible, I admit, that persons whose condemnation and punishment are demanded by the journalists, may be guilty and justly liable to the penalties of the law. On the other hand, it is possible that they may be *innocent;* and, in these circumstances, justice, humanity and common sense require that they should be tried by a rational, reflective and judicious tribunal.

THE TYPOGRAPHICAL TRIBUNAL.

I assert that the Tribunal of the Press is *not* rational, reflective or judicious ; and I protest, therefore, against the iniquity of allowing any man's life or liberty to be placed at its disposal. In order to have a better understanding of this part of the subject, let us reconsider the observation which was made on a preceding page : viz., that "the American Press Gang is, to all intents and purposes, a MOB." Its best actions are impulsive and ill-directed ; it sets itself above the laws, claiming powers superior to those of the legislative, judicial and executive authorities ; its proceedings are informal, irrational, violent and illegal ; and, when it attempts to correct wrongs, to execute justice, or to point out how justice ought to be executed, it never fails to inflict greater injuries and to commit more flagrant acts of oppression than those which it pretends to redress. Mobs, in general, profess to be actuated by *good motives;* they wish to have it understood that they mean to do justice by the speediest and most certain process.

In all of these particulars, the Typographical Mob asserts

its claim to the title we have given it; and in nothing are the mobbish proclivities of the press more conspicuous than in the treatment of persons charged with criminal offenses, whether it endeavors to rescue them from the grasp of the law, or to precipitate their conviction and punishment.

It is a common theme of boasting with the newspapers, that they "control the operations of Courts of Justice." Lest we should suspect that this is mere rhodomontade, we have judicial authority to confirm the triumphant and audacious declaration of the editors. Judge Ludlow of the Common Pleas, Philadelphia, in his official capacity, declares that "the newspaper press is ALL POWERFUL." Similar admissions are frequently made by the dignitaries of the judicial bench. It cannot be doubted, therefore, that the influences of journalism really have a powerful effect on judges, juries, prosecuting attorneys, and all other ministers of law and justice.

But *how* do the journalists "control the operations of courts?" In the same way precisely that all other mobs assert their supremacy over the legitimate authority of the people; that is to say, by INTIMIDATION. The Courts are *frightened* into acquiescence with the requirements of the press.

TERRORISM OF THE PRESS.

"Public Opinion" is the great bug-bear, the Raw-head-and-Bloody-bones, which appals all classes of our countrymen; and those, especially, who hold offices, or who have any expectation of holding them. The newspapers are supposed to manufacture Public Opinion; no wonder, then, that judges and juries, and the public at large, believe in the "omnipotence" of the press. Omnipotence is an attribute of divinity, and of nothing that is not divine. Journalism, therefore, is deified. Judge Ludlow, from the bench, pronounces its apotheosis, in unmistakable phraseology:—"The newspaper press is all-powerful!"

Like the Egyptian god Anubis, Journalism is a dog-headed deity; an impudent, intrusive, snarling, snapping, beastly, monstrous divinity. But what of that? It is no less an object of devotion and worship; because it is "all powerful."

It appears to me that a majority of my countrymen, including Courts and Juries, consider it heretical and impious, in the highest degree, to have any opinion which does not coincide with that of the public; and for the expression of public opinion they look to the newspaper press. From this view, it may seem that, in every criminal case, the decisions of the press are equivalent to the verdict of a jury and the sentence of a court. If Messrs. Editors say that the prisoner is guilty and ought to be hanged, the jurymen, (unless they wish to prolong the job merely for the sake of increasing their emoluments, and that may be a serious object with some of them,) will find it useless to leave their box; and the cruel expedient of locking them up and forcing them to unanimity by starvation will not be necessary. And why should a jury be censured for yielding to the requirements of the press, when the awful voice of judicial wisdom declares that the press is "all powerful?" In such a case, the resistance of the twelve "good men and true," or any attempt to assert their freedom and independence, would be presumption and absolute madness!

EDITORIAL MOBBING.

I have said that the journalists, as a body, constitute a mob "of the worst kind." They are not only a very mischievous mob, but, unfortunately, they are a "respectable" mob, a worshipful mob, a deified mob, and (worst of all,) an irresponsible and *unpunishable* mob. I am convinced that, chiefly by the agency of this *turba sterquilinia*, this fetid editorial rabble, which contaminates all that it touches, our system of jurisprudence is so vitiated that the administration of criminal law, in the United States, is little more than a species of *Lynching;* that system being subjected to the control of a tyrannical, capricious, malignant and pitiless mob; a mob which lacks not reason only, but the very *instincts* of humanity.

It matters little, in practice, *how* a mob effects its designs. It may obtain an ascendency over the laws by the exertion of its own physical force; or, with the same object in view, it may use threats and other means of intimidation; and thereby compel the ministers of the law to act in opposition to their own inclinations and duty.

The mobbing *principle* consists in enforcing the public at large, or its authorized representatives, to submit to the will of a minority. Mobs may accomplish their purpose, *vi et armis*, with guns, pistols, swords, daggers, bludgeons or brickbats; or in an equally effective way, by menaces of slander and abuse; or by employing that terrible engine called Public Opinion, which is supposed to have the power to crush and annihilate; an engine which is more appalling to a majority of our countrymen than cannons loaded with grape-shot, or Paixhan guns or Congreve rockets with the latest diabolical improvements.

The modes of intimidation and compulsion last mentioned are those which are used by the Typographical Mob; and, with this circumstance in view, it is easy to understand how the Press Gang obtains an almost irresistible mastery over the misnomered "Courts of Justice."

Happily the editorial mob is not always *unanimous*. This is the only circumstance of mitigation which presents itself to my notice. If the journalists did not disagree, and debate and quarrel among themselves, their despotism would be complete. Sometimes, however, they act with a degree of unanimity, and so concentrate their forces; and on such occasions, they generally succeed in accomplishing some object which is particularly atrocious and detestable.

If the newspapers generally demand the conviction and punishment of an accused person, it is almost impossible for him to escape; and in making such a demand, the newspapers are just as likely to be wrong as right. In fact, I have often observed that when the press generally unites in calling for the condemnation of a prisoner, the evidences of his guilt are most likely to be defective.

Some years ago, a young lady named Evelina Cunningham was murdered in Cecil County, Maryland. A certain John Connor was charged with the murder; the evidence was merely circumstantial and very unsatisfactory; but the newspaper men generally proclaimed their belief in his guilt and insisted on having him hanged. Connor made a very narrow escape from the gallows. Nine years after his trial, it was ascertained that the real murderer was a certain shoemaker who had been one of the principal witnesses against Connor, and whose dwelling-place was about a quarter of a mile from the spot where the body of Miss Cunningham was found.

Many persons in Philadelphia remember the mysterious murder of Mrs. Rademacher, the wife of a bookseller of that city. A young German cordwainer was charged with this murder. He had no money, nor political influence; and, as a matter of course, no editorial sympathy, no newspaper advocates. It appeared to be a "foregone conclusion" with the gentlemen of the press that he was guilty; and their opinions on that subject were pretty freely expressed. It is almost unnecessary to add that he was convicted, sentenced and executed. I saw a part of his hand, (that very hand which was supposed to be stained with the blood of an innocent woman,) preserved in a bottle of spirits by that celebrated collector of curiosities, Mr. Phineas T. Barnum. I think it not improbable that when that hand is produced at the great Day of Judgment, no sanguinary spot, no indelible stain of murder, will be found upon it. Circumstances which have come to my knowledge incline me to suspect that this unfortunate young mechanic was one of the many victims of newspaper folly and malevolence, and that he really had as little to do with the death of Mrs. Rademacher as I had.

DYING DECLARATIONS.

It is no uncommon thing, in the United States of America,

for persons who undergo the extreme penalty of the law, to make protestations of their innocence with their latest breath. Convicts who have abandoned all hope of escape and who have ceased to make appeals to the justice or to the mercy of mankind; men, who stand on the threshold of eternity and who, mindful of their approaching dissolution, have spent days and nights in preparation for the dread event, have often, *often* I say, at the foot of the gallows, and with the cord about their necks, declared that they were guiltless of the crime for which they were about to suffer.

It is *possible*, indeed, that a desperate criminal may lie, even in such circumstances as these. But it is scarcely credible that a man who knows that the hour of his departure has come, one who evidently realizes all the terrors of his situation and who appears to be concerned for nothing but the salvation of his soul, should, by a voluntary and useless denial of his guilt, annul all his previous work of preparation for death, insult the Majesty of Heaven in whose presence he is about to appear, and forfeit all claims to that Divine mercy which he has sought by day and by night in the gloom of the condemned cell, with tears of sorrow and groans of anguish.

My extensive experience among newspaper editors, has taught me that the habit of *lying*, with some men, is incorrigible; but there are circumstances of coercion which are powerful enough, as I suppose, to restrain the most mendacious of human beings from the utterance of falsehood. I am persuaded that the declarations of the editor of the New York Herald, himself, "the head devil of journalism," would be entitled to much confidence if he were about to expiate his offenses at the gallows and had resigned all hopes of executive clemency.

A dying malefactor may stubbornly refuse to make any confession of his guilt, but very seldom indeed would the most obdurate criminal play the canting hypocrite, or the audacious blasphemer, in his last moments, by steadfastly asserting his innocence and calling on God Almighty to witness the truth of his declarations. A hardened reprobate, at the last scene of his existence, may attempt to play the romantic hero or the blustering bully, but not the sighing penitent or the prayerful saint. It is almost impossible to imagine what motives could induce a man to be hypocritical at such a time. I consider, therefore, that a penitent who is about to be hanged, is generally a *sincere* penitent; and if he is truly repentant, if he is an undissembling suppliant for Divine mercy, his last earthly utterance is not likely to be a lie.

The conclusion is, that when convicted persons are about to be put to death and have no hope of escape, their declarations of innocence are most likely to be true. Such declarations, as I have said above, are *often* made by the subjects of capital punishment, at the time of their execution. In most cases of this kind, the sufferers have been convicted on evidence which, if submitted to an unprejudiced jury, might have been deemed insufficient; but, as I have endeavored to demonstrate, it is impossible for an American jury to be unprejudiced. By the foolish or malicious meddling of the newspaper press every jury is biased; and hence "it is impossible for any man charged with a criminal offense to have a fair trial." The inevitable consequence is, that some accused persons must be unjustly condemned and imprisoned, or executed in obedience to editorial requirements.

EXAMPLE.

Less than two months ago, four men were hung at Baltimore, all at the same time and on one gallows. All of them appeared to be duly concerned for their eternal welfare, and *three* of the four, to the very last, made the most solemn asseverations of their innocence. In fact, there was no sufficient proof of their guilt. It was almost universally believed that one of the sufferers did not commit the act for which he was put to death. These three men were probably murdered by legal process, at the instigation of several of the most influential papers in Baltimore, which clamorously demanded the sacrifice, and resisted all the efforts which were made by some just and benevolent persons to obtain a commutation of the sentence.

DUTY OF CITIZENS.

I select this case for illustration because it is of recent occurrence, and the facts must be within the recollection of all my readers. But the contemplation of the subject is too fearful, too horrifying, to be continued much further. I hope enough has been said to persuade my Christian countrymen to reflect on *their own* accountability in connection with this most flagrant abuse of journalism. Citizens of the United States, while you allow this abuse to be continued, *you* are accessory to many judicial murders; and how can you assure yourselves that the blood of the innocent, which is shed by your permission, will not call from the ground for vengeance on you and your posterity?

But what ought to be done, or what *can* be done, in the premises? This is a question for our legislators to consider. We may be told that the newspaper-reading public insists on having its curiosity gratified by "full reports" of murder cases published as soon as the crime is committed. We are told that the mistakes made by the reporters are unavoidable, and that the comments and opinions offered by the editors are merely the vagaries of "a free and independent press." In this way the public journals commonly excuse themselves for their unauthorized, unwise, and often erroneous publications.

An English satirist gives us to understand that, sometimes,

"Wretches hang that jurymen may dine."

If our views are correct, wretches may be hanged on slighter occasions than this. They may be hanged to gratify a vitiated taste for agonies and horrors, which is supposed to be one of the foibles of newspaper readers in America. Positively, I would not hang a dog to accommodate such an appetite. I would not punish an innocent person with a rap on the knuckles (imprisonment and strangulation out of the question) to humor the depraved tastes of all the newspaper readers in the United States.

The excuses made by the journalists are almost as detestable as their crimes. They prejudice juries, and pervert the course of law and justice, because they are "required to do so by the reading public!" This apology itself is characteristic of American journalism. Nothing could exhibit its baseness, servility, and unscrupulous rascality in a clearer light.

SUMMARY.

That part of my Eighth Charge which we have been examining in this Section avers that "many guiltless victims of editorial folly, prejudice, or ill-will are now enduring unimaginable torments of body and mind in our States' prisons; and many others, more fortunate perhaps, have been brought by the same detestable agencies to a shameful and agonizing death." In proof of these allegations, I have given you facts which all intelligent people in the United Sates must recognize as genuine and true. I have shown you—

1. That many of the most widely-circulated and influential journals of America are controlled by men of defective judgment and loose morality.

2. That the American journalists in general are avaricious and corrupt, malignant and unmerciful.

3. That these injudicious, unprincipled, and pitiless men direct the course of public opinion, and control the action of courts and juries; in fact, that every important criminal case is decided by them before it is submitted to the legal tribunal.

4. That the control which newspapers obtain over courts of justice is precisely like that of a mob—threats and intimidation being used as compulsory measures to enforce the obedience of the legal authorities to the requirements of an incompetent, irrational, extra-judicial, and unconstitutional arbitration.

5. That, in existing circumstances, the trial by jury becomes

a mere nullity, or something worse ; and the decisions of courts are little more than the echoes of a voice which seldom speaks "the words of truth and soberness"—viz.: the voice of the journalistic rabble.

6. That persons judged, condemned, imprisoned, or executed under the direction of the editorial mob, are scarcely less the victims of LYNCH LAW than those unhappy mortals who are sometimes flogged to death or hanged on trees by the infuriated populace, the self-constituted ministers of "speedy and efficient justice," in some of our Western States.

7. That, considering the moral character and intellectual qualifications of these newspaper arbiters, who unjustifiably assume the jurisdiction of criminal cases, we may reasonably expect, and cannot doubt in fact, that, under such a dispensation of justice, the guilty will often be acquitted and the innocent condemned.

The history of our criminal jurisprudence affords many examples to confirm all the specifications of my Eighth Charge. If you feel interested in the inquiry, and do not shrink from the contemplation of such a melancholy subject, I promise you that, by extending your investigations among the records of our criminal courts, you will have abundant proof that innocent victims are often sacrificed to that grim idol—that insolent and exacting Moloch of Journalism which has dared to intrude its blood-stained altars into the temple of Liberty and the sanctuary of Justice.

SUPPLEMENTARY ILLUSTRATIONS.

THE EXECUTION AT BALTIMORE.—Four men named Gambrill, Corrie, Crops and Cyphus, were executed together in the jail yard, at Baltimore, on Friday, April 8, 1859. Henry C. Gambrill, one of the sufferers, was hung for the murder of a police-officer named Benton. Gambrill was about twenty-one years of age; he belonged to a political club called the Plug Uglies, but never had been charged with any crime before the killing of Benton. His family was of the highest respectability and he had an extensive circle of friends, including some of the most eminent citizens of Baltimore. Benton was killed at night, by a shot fired from among a crowd of young men, one of whose companions he had just arrested. After Gambrill's condemnation, a young man named Richard Harris, wrote a letter to Governor Hicks, solemnly declaring that he knew who was the real murderer of Benton and that Gambrill was innocent. Indeed, Harris intimated that he himself was the man who shot officer Benton. But this, and all the solicitations of Gambrill's friends, only induced the Governor to grant a reprieve to the condemned.

Just at this crisis, another police-officer, named Rigdon, was murdered. As he had been a witness against Gambrill, it was presumed that he was killed by some of the members of Gambrill's club. Gambrill knew what would be the effect of this impression, and he published a card addressed to the public, in which he says, "The fearful murder of Mr. Rigdon struck as much terror to my heart as it did to that of his bereaved widow."

The account of the last murder was published in the Baltimore papers with many comments well calculated to excite popular feeling, and public indignation was carried to such a height that, to appease it, it was deemed necessary to hang Gambrill, though he had nothing to do with the murder of Rigdon, and was in jail at the time that deed was committed!

On the night before his execution, Gambrill drew up a long statement, in which he declared that he had not the slightest participation in the murder of Benton, and that he did not even see the pistol fired. His account concluded with these words, "And now, calling God to witness the truth of this, my dying statement, I bid this world, and all its affairs, a final farewell." His behavior, from the time of his condemnation to that of the execution, showed a resigned spirit and an earnest desire to die like a Christian. Gambrill's last words under the gallows were: "Fellow-citizens, I am not guilty of the murder of officer Benton. When you see the drop fall from under me, you will see an innocent man launched into eternity."

Marion Crops, who was hung at the same time, confessed, at the gallows, that he was the murderer of officer Rigdon, who was shot through the window, while he was sitting in his own house. Crops unquestionably deserved hanging.

Peter Corrie, the third of the condemned party, was a young man of twenty-five, whose mother was quite wealthy and much respected. While in a state of intoxication, Corrie was induced to accompany Crops to a spot near the house of officer Rigdon, where Corrie was left standing at the entrance of an alley, into which Crops went to commit the murder. When he was about to be executed, Corrie said, "I never conspired or consented to take the life of Rigdon. He was a stranger to me and I had no malice against him whatever. I was led to the spot while intoxicated, with no thought of committing murder."

John Cyphus, who was hung at the same time, was a negro. He was charged with killing another negro named John King. His last words on the scaffold were, "I was wrongfully convicted and am now to be unjustly punished. Thank God that I have the opportunity to tell you all that I am an innocent man."

These four men were tried and condemned, with many acrimonious denunciations, by the "Court of the Press," before they were arraigned at the bar. *Vide* the Baltimore correspondence of the New York Police Gazette published about the time of the trial. In that correspondence it is alleged that some of the principal journals of Baltimore clamored for the condemnation of the prisoners. And, after the men were sentenced, the same papers are said to have opposed all the efforts that were made to obtain a commutation of punishment for Gambrill and Corrie. I will give one short extract from the Baltimore letter published in the Police Gazette of April 2, 1859. It is brief but significant:

"The papers here seem to have been startled by the unexpected reprieve. They all seem to be alarmed, lest justice should not be done. I am inclined to think that, coupled with the demand for *justice*, is a desire to turn the longed-for execution to account, by selling an extra number of papers containing the horrid details!"

THE SICKLES CASE.—The recent homicide case at Washington affords some very good illustrations of our subject. Daniel Sickles, a member of Congress, discovers a criminal connection between his wife and Philip Barton Key, the District-Attorney. Sickles shoots Key in a public thoroughfare and in the presence of several witnesses.

The fact of the shooting was undeniable, but some circumstances of mitigation, together with a question which might arise concerning the sanity of Mr. Sickles, at the time he committed the deed, and the doubtful and contradictory reports of the affair which were first published, should have prevented any rash adjudication of the case. But, within twenty-four hours after Key was shot, and long before the real facts of the case could be ascertained, the "leading journals" had given their decision; some of them had unconditionally acquitted Sickles and some had found him guilty of murder in the first degree, and plainly informed the court and jury what they were expected to do. These "stern inquisitors" not only convicted Mr. Sickles and decided that "hanging was too good for him," but they even went so far as to implicate *Mr. Butterworth* in the crime; merely, as it seems, because he was a friend of Mr. Sickles and had fulfilled the obligations of friendship by sympathizing with the unfortuate man when he was sorely distressed by the discovery of his wife's infidelity.

I believe that this attempt to make Mr. Butterworth accessory to the homicide originated with the Washington correspondent of the New York Times, who falsely asserted that Sickles had requested Butterworth to follow Key and engage him in conversation, in order that the injured husband might have a better opportunity to shoot the object of his resentment. Supported by no better evidence than the assertion of a gossiping letter-writer, this serious charge against Mr. Butterworth was entertained by two-thirds of the newspapers in America, and Mr. Butterworth's condemnation by these self-constituted arbiters was almost as emphatic as that of Mr. Sickles himself.

Let it be understood that, in my reference to the case of Sickles, I do not produce *him* as an example of innocence unjustly condemned. My present object is to show that even when the newspapers appear to take the most equitable views of a criminal transaction, their conduct is unreasonable and unjust. The facts adduced will illustrate my remark that the Press Gang is, to all intents and purposes, a MOB, and that its *best actions* are impulsive and ill-directed. The entire action of the journalists in relation to the Sickles case was mob-like. Before the coroner's jury had finished their investigations, some of the editorial mob had tried and convicted the prisoner. They assumed the jurisdiction of the matter, appearing to forget that there was such a thing as a regular court of justice in the land, and acting as if the fate of the accused were entirely at their disposal.

Fortunately for Sickles, (if not for the cause of justice,) a majority of the typographical mob, including some of "the most respectable and influential journalists," was on his side. These called for his unconditional acquittal, and he *was* unconditionally acquitted. Certainly. Who could doubt the result?

SECTION XV.

NEWSPAPER SLANDERS.

Examination of the Ninth Charge.

A VILE HABIT.

DEFAMATION is as much a habit of the newspaper press as barking is of dogs, or hissing of serpents. It is very certain, likewise, that this evil habit prevails to a greater extent in America than in any other country. I am under no obligations to tell you *why* newspapers in general are disposed to be defamatory; or why American newspapers are more so than any others. A witness, who undertakes to relate facts, is not obliged to become a philosopher and explain their origin. There are many well-known facts, the *causes* of which admit of no explanation. For example, we know that barking is habitual with dogs in a state of civilization; but we cannot tell how they acquired that habit, or why the dogs of some countries bark more than those of others. In their savage condition they do not bark at all; and it may be that this canine peculiarity, which appears to be a concomitant of civilization, keeps pace with it, and prevails most extensively in those lands where the refinements and elegancies of civilized society are most conspicuous.

Similar observations may apply to the barking of the typographical curs; or, (in less figurative language,) to the slandering propensities of the newspaper press—and of American journalism in particular. Newspaper defamation, like grog-drinking, card-playing, libertinism, etc., may be classed among the disagreeable incidents of civilized life; and, were I disposed to flatter my countrymen, I might add that the superlative malignity and atrocity which appear in the slanderous publications of the American press, are a sad but necessary effect, as well as a strong proof, of the high position which we "Yankees" have attained in the scale of moral and intellectual cultivation.

But, as I am *not* disposed to flatter my countrymen, I will make no paradoxical explanations of the subjects which we are about to discuss. Let the facts themselves be first considered; and, afterward, if the reader insists on any further explication, I will step beyond the limits of the duties I have assumed, and endeavor to give better reasons than those just mentioned for that pre-eminent love of slander which has been assigned to the American newspapers by almost universal consent.

THE COMMON VICE OF NEWSPAPERS.

The whole history of journalism proves that the love of scandal has always been one of its most remarkable attributes. Contemporary with King James II. of England, lived a certain John Tutchin, the publisher of a scurrilous newspaper called *The Observator*. For his numerous slanders, and his constant effusion of profane ribaldry, he was sentenced to be whipped through several towns in the West of England. He petitioned the king for a commutation of his sentence, signifying his willingness to be hanged to avoid the prescribed flagellation. Journalism, at that time, was in its infancy; but even then it appears to have been very far from a state of innocence.

Very recently, the editor of a newspaper in Sweden was sentenced to the gallows for publishing some slanderous charge against a young lady; and his sentence would have been duly executed, had not the young lady herself been merciful and magnanimous enough to plead for his pardon. The severe punishment awarded to this Swedish caluminator proves that the legislators of his country justly estimated the enormity of the crime of which he stood convicted. I have known *American* editors to commit similar offenses, with so many aggravating circumstances, that capital punishment itself would scarcely have been a sufficient expiation of their guilt.

If the stringent government of the English Stuarts, and the somewhat stern legislation of the Swedish monarchy, could not restrain the conductors of the press from unjustifiable assaults on private character, what can we expect in this "free and happy country," where the newspapers are virtually under no restraint whatever?

UNRESTRICTED SLANDERING.

It cannot be supposed that the American press is restrained by the *law*, for it claims to be a power above the law, and this claim is allowed, even by judges on the bench, when they declare that the newspaper press is "all powerful." But it is a common remark that the press, for all its iniquities, is accountable to a certain mysterious tribunal, called "Public Opinion." Oh! the matchless absurdity of that idea!

You have heard of the dying sculptor, who, on being required by the priest to pay his devotions to a crucifix, answered, "Alas! I cannot, for I myself made it!" He could not realize the divinity of his own workmanship. The newspaper men cannot reverence or fear Public Opinion, for it is an article of their own manufacture. They know what stuff it is made of; they understand its composition and its character, and they heartily despise it. How, in the name of all that is ridiculous, can the newspapers hold themselves accountable at the bar of public opinion? Bad men can feel no responsibility where they fear no punishment. Public Opinion never punishes the press for any of its delinquencies; no, not even for its most execrable misdemeanors. The most villainous newspapers in the United States, are the most successful, the most widely circulated, the most profitable, the most popular, the most "respectable." The same crime for which Tutchin, the English editor, was flogged, at a cart's tail, through twenty cities, the same crime for which Lindahl, the Swedish journalist, was sentenced to be hanged, is committed repeatedly and with entire impunity, by some of the most influential journals in the United States of America.

DASTARDLY SLANDERS.

Yes, that most cowardly, wicked, and indefensible species of calumny, the traducing of *female character*, is often practiced by American journalists, without the least injury to their business, or to their REPUTATION! The offense is too common to attract much notice; and, even in extreme cases, when some of the more honorable journalists themselves become indignant and rebuke the offender, the public concerns itself very little about the matter, and the convicted slanderer is, to all appearances, as highly esteemed and as liberally encouraged as ever. So much for the salutary influence of Public Opinion on the decorous and moral deportment of the press.

I have known a newspaper editor in the United States to assert, in print, that a rival journalist had seduced the woman whom he afterward married and that several of his children were bastards. It afterward appeared that there was not an atom of truth in these charges, which almost maddened the lady against whom they were directed; and yet it may be doubted whether the scoundrel who published these calumnies found the profits of his business, or his personal popularity, much diminished on that account.

It is commonly believed that the wife of General Jackson, the seventh President of the United States, was actually *killed* by the slanders of the newspaper press. Not even the advancement of her husband to the highest dignity in the Republic, could recompense that amiable and sensitive woman for the agonies of mind endured by her during the presidential canvass. And yet it does not appear that Public Opinion inflicted the slightest punishment on any of her calumniators.

In the New York Herald of February 21, 1859, I find a long editorial article, under the head of "SCANDALOUS JOURNALISM," which charges the *New York Tribune*, the *New York Times* and the *Albany Evening Journal*, with a simultaneous attack on Mrs. Bennett; which attack (says the Herald,) "was coupled with as much insult as the editors of those papers dared to utter without disgusting the public with the bestiality of the assault." The lady assailed in this way, is the wife of James Gordon Bennett, the editor of the Herald. In his editorial remarks on this subject, Mr. Bennett says, apparently with deep feeling :—

"We have been connected with the American press for more than thirty years, but during the whole of that time, although our criticisms on public men and public affairs may have been acute and occasionally severe, yet no one has ever charged us, and no one can charge us, with ever having, in the slightest degree, lacerated the feelings of women and children, because we were opposed to the principles or policy of the husband or father."

Here I believe Mr. Bennett asserts nothing but the truth ; and though his general course as a public journalist deserves very little applause, he claims an honorable distinction among American editors, by having it to say that he never attempted to blacken the character of an innocent woman.

This one excellent trait in Bennett's newspaper management is enough, by itself, to justify a remark which was made in another part of this work, viz. : that the New York Herald is not, by many degrees, the *worst* newspaper published in the United States.

With reference to the attack on Mrs. Bennett, the *Washington Star* makes the following mild and gentlemanly comments :—

"We regret to see the New York *Times* and *Tribune* compromise their respectability and the dignity of the press by introducing into their columns the names of private ladies in a most unjustifiable manner. The *Times*, in order to have a fling at Mr. Buchanan, makes an indefensible use of the name of the wife of Sir Willaim Gore Ousely, and the *Tribune*, to gratify its hostility to the New York Herald, makes a cruel assault on the wife of its editor. We protest against such delinquency, as being not only unmanly but UN-AMERICAN. The worst enemies of our country and its institutions have invariably admitted that our deference to woman is the redeeming feature of an otherwise (alleged) semi-civilized people; and we put it to the journals in question, whether they mean to rob us of the reputation of that chivalrous trait which has extorted the admiration of our bitterest foreign detractors."

OUR NATIONAL CHARACTER VINDICATED.

The editor of the *Washington Star*, as a mere act of justice to his countrymen, should have exhibited the *cause* of that obvious inconsistency between the "chivalric traits" of our national character and the dastardly conduct of some newspaper editors. The reader has been informed, in another part of this book, that many of the newspaper writers in America are FOREIGNERS, not a few of whom, (as I have given you very good reason to believe,) are persons of very profligate character. There is scarcely a newspaper office in any of our principal cities which does not retain one or more of these vagabond scribblers, whose natural inclination to disparage and defame all that is noble, pure and excellent, is seldom placed under any restriction.

So loosely and negligently is the newspaper business managed in this country, that the publishers and principal editors, in many cases, seem scarcely to know or care what is printed in their own columns. But publishers very often make no *objections* to defamatory articles prepared by their subordinates, if they possess a certain kind of piquancy which recommends them to a large class of readers.

By the publication of slanders, a paper becomes celebrated, or notorious; and infamous notoriety, with most editors, is far preferable to decent obscurity. To my certain knowledge, some of the vilest calumnies ever published in American journals were written by Irish, Scotch, English, and German hirelings, whose extreme willingness to perform such filthy and iniquitous labor, is perhaps the chief reason why they are so often employed by newspaper publishers in preference to the writers of our own country.

It is truly a vexatious circumstance that our national character is often disgraced by the conduct of scoundrels who are not Americans, even by adoption; for, in some instances, our "leading journals" employ writers who have not been in the country long enough to be *naturalized*.

THE LADIES DEFENDED.

In continuation of its very gentle rebuke of a very gross misdemeanor, the *Washington Star* inquires:

"Has the administration of Mr. Buchanan become so invulnerable, or the editor of the Herald so formidable, that the *Times* and *Tribune* are obliged to turn their shafts upon defenseless women, whose only protection against such odious personal assaults is the polite usages of society and the good taste of public writers? Have we so degenerated that our journalists shower their pitiless gibes on shrinking, sensitive women, who are, in no manner, legitimately subject to such attacks?"

"Lady Gore Ousely and Mrs. Bennett have not, at any time, obtruded themselves on public notice, or exposed themselves, in any way, to newspaper comment. Lady Ousely moved, last winter, in the society of Washington with that noiseless, unassuming grace so characteristic of English women of the higher ranks. She was distinguished here for her liberal hospitality, and she was highly appreciated for her undisputed excellence of character and the amiability of her disposition.

"Of Mrs. Bennett we know less; but, if rumor is to be credited, she is a woman of highly-cultivated mind, refined and courteous manners, and extreme kindness of heart. Though she enjoys a large income and is able to command, through the influence of her husband, the flattering attention of the best society, yet she is said to content herself with the quiet attractions of her rural home, and studiously avoids even the harmless publicity of sitting within sight when at the opera. But, were these ladies the opposites of what they are—were they as eager for admiration as the fashionable leaders of the *haut ton*, or were they as ambitious for notoriety as our strong-minded females—yet are they for this to be dragged into print, and are their sensibilities to be coarsely wounded because the *New York Times* has a political spite against Mr. Buchanan, and the editor of the *Tribune* seeks to indulge a personal grudge against the editor of the *Herald?*"

VERBAL REBUKES INSUFFICIENT.

I applaud the feeling which moved the editor of the *Washington Star* to protest against the misconduct of the *Times* and *Tribune;* but I consider it perfectly idle to expostulate, in this gentle way, with the calumniators of female character. The injury is one which cannot be redressed by a verbal rebuke, and the moral constitution of the offender, in such a case, must make him insensible to the keenest reproaches. Severe castigation of some kind—*legal* castigation if possible—is the only proper answer that can be given to such calumniators; and my candid opinion is, that the law of Sweden which *hangs* the journalistic slanderer, is more just, and more MERCIFUL indeed, than the cold indifference of our American legislation, which affords no adequate protection to man or woman from the trumpet-tongued defamation of the newspaper press.

CUDGELLING AND HORSEWHIPPING.

The calumnies uttered by American newspapers are sometimes of such an aggravated nature, and the laws intended for their punishment are so obviously defective, that the use of the cudgel or horsewhip, for the castigation of the offender, has been justified in open court. Counsel, learned in the law, have pleaded the *necessity* of this mode of punishment, and judges on the bench have seemed to admit the substantial justice of the plea.

AN EDITOR FLOGGED.

In June, 1858, Charles Zielinski, the publisher of a paper in Cincinnati, was severely beaten by David Levi. It appears that Zielinski, in an editorial article, had charged Levi with being a gamester, swindler, etc., and insinuated that Levi's wife was too intimate with a certain bank officer. In the excitement produced by these unpleasant imputations, Mr. Levi applied a hickory stick to the back and head of Mr. Zielinski with so much earnestness and effect, that the gentleman of the press was scarcely fit to be seen in public for two or three weeks after this stirring incident.

A suit for assault and battery was commenced by Zielinski, and the case was tried before the Court of Common Pleas in Cincinnati. In the course of this trial, the counsel for the defense cited the authority of Dr. Franklin to prove the equity and propriety of flogging an editor, in certain circumstances, when an atrocious calumny has been published and a retraction of the slanderous charges has been refused.

THE FLOGGING JUSTIFIED.

Judge Oliver, who presided at this trial, remarked that "there are some things which may provoke even an ordinarily good citizen to a breach of the peace. The provocation, in this case, was the publication of newspaper charges of such a nature that the less they were seen or repeated the better. These charges," said the judge, "do not indicate any regard for public morals; but rather evince a delight to revel in publications of a low and vicious character. The defendant, it appears, called on the publisher, stated that he felt himself and family aggrieved, and, in a mild and polite manner, (as the editor admits,) asked for a retraction, which the editor promised to make. But the retraction proved to be nothing more than a repetition, in substance, of the injurious charges. In such circumstances, the result might have been something worse than assault and battery. The state of mind of the accused was to determine the degree of his guilt, and was to be ascertained by the light of the influences under which he acted."

In conformity with these views, the court imposed a merely nominal fine on Mr. Levi, and ordered him to be discharged.

A BETTER REMEDY.

It would be much better, however, if the admitted "necessity" for cudgelling or horsewhipping editors did not exist. If the reputation of our citizens and their families were protected, as they should be, by the laws of their country, a resort to brutal violence, for the punishment of editorial aggressions, would be inexcusable; and the plea that one misdeed is necessary for the correction of another, would be universally rejected as a moral and legal absurdity.

INFAMY OF THE AMERICAN PRESS.

Our American newspapers are celebrated, on both sides of the Atlantic, for their excessive delight in scandal and defamation; and, in this discreditable trait, they are supposed to be unrivaled by the press of any other country. To give you some idea of what is said on this topic by Europeans, I will subjoin a few extracts from sources which are certainly entitled to some attention and respect.—The *Foreign Quarterly Review*, vol. xxix. No. 59, says:—

"The more respectable the city in America, the more infamous, the more degraded and disgusting have we found its newspaper press."

Speaking of one of the "leading journals" of New York the same writer remarks:—" It appears that this journal, by means of its evil gains, has been able to organize throughout the country a very extraordinary, and complete system of correspondence, so that in every chief city of the Union, it has a resident representative. And these are laborers worthy of their hire, being all such reckless libellers of every thing decent, and such impudent dealers in every thing vile, that the 'head devil' himself must be often hard put to it to keep his scandalous supremacy. The cue universally is, 'Spare no one;' thrust yourself into whatever house you can enter, and everywhere leave your slime; let fly at all; the more eminent or excellent your game, the more atrocious the falsehood we want. Never think that a scandal can be too malignant. It is to furnish bitterness for a hundred thousand tongues; and what would be any thing scant or small toward the satisfaction of so many? To *be* satisfactory, say every thing but what is true, and, (above all things), say nothing that is kind."

A late number of *Blackwood's Magazine* says:—" The personalities in which most of the American newspapers indulge are something astounding. One New York paper, during the late panic, published the name of every gentleman who bought a silk dress for his wife or gave a dinner party to his friends."

"In order to form an estimate of their merit," says Captain Hamilton, "I read newspapers from all parts of the Union, and found a great majority of them contemptible in point of talent and dealing in abuse so virulent as to excite a feeling of disgust. *Our* newspaper press is bad enough, (continues this English captain;) its sins against propriety cannot be justified and ought not to be defended. But its violence is meekness, and even its atrocities are virtues, when compared with that system of *brutal and ferocious outrage* which distinguishes the press of America. There the strongest epithets of a ruffian vocabulary are put in constant requisition."

Captain Marryatt says, "The spirit of defamation, so rife in America, is so intimately connected with its principal channel, the Newspaper Press, that it is impossible to consider them separately. Defamation is the greatest curse of the American people; and its effects on society in the United States are most lamentable. The licentiousness of the ·American press threatens the most alarming results, for journalism in that country has assumed a power which awes not individuals only, but the government itself."

"While the American Newspaper Press, (says Charles Dickens,) has its evil eye in every house and its black hand on every appointment, from a president to a postman; while with ribald slander for its only stock in trade, it is the standard literature of an enormous class, who must find their reading in a newspaper or they will not read at all, so long must its odium be upon the country's head, and so long must the evil it works be plainly visible in the republic."

THE DEFENSE.

But for all the expressions of disgust and abhorrence which come from beyond the great waters, Messrs. Editors have a convenient answer.—"These foreign writers (say they) are prejudiced against America and her institutions; and we must not expect to have their favorable report."

This "answer" has not much to do with the main question, which I take to be this: "Is the description of American Journalism given by these transatlantic writers CORRECT?" I *know* that the charges which they bring against our newspaper press are generally TRUE; and, knowing this, I do not trouble myself to inquire with what feeling, or for what purpose, these charges were made.

If an enemy supplies me with a refreshing draught, or a wholesome truth, I am not inclined to question his motives, but feel under more obligations to be grateful than if he were my friend; for he does me an unexpected kindness. But it is the height of folly or knavery to pretend that every European who exclaims against the villainous mismanagement of our public journals is hostile to our glorious institutions. The very reverse is more likely to be the truth; for all who assist in the detection and punishment of newspaper rascality must be classed among the very best friends of our republic.

HOME-MADE OPINIONS.

But if there is any valid objection to imported opinions on this interesting subject, happily we have a few *domestic* ones at your service. For example :—

Recorder Barnard, of New York city, in a charge made to the Grand Jury, delivered on Tuesday, October 5, 1858, made use of the following language :

"It *often happens* that some evil disposed or characterless person establishes a journal, the main object of which is to levy black mail by maligning and villifying people of various ranks in society. In order to make the journal sell more readily, some conspicuous official, or private person, is selected as a target for such calumny, on whom they charge all manner of offenses, and indeed crimes, in order that he may, through dread of continued personal annoyance, and for the sake of purchasing silence in future, consent to have money extorted from him. If, however, he should demand an investigation of the charges made against him, and should he succeed in establishing his innocence, and ask to have the libeller brought to justice, a class of sympathizers is always found asking for his discharge."

The "sympathizers" referred to by the Recorder must be sympathizing *editors*. I do not know what other *class* of American citizens would sympathize with a convicted newspaper slanderer. The *New York Times* replied to this charge of Recorder Barnard with as much asperity as if that paper itself were liable to some of the worthy magistrate's censures. The *Tribune* and *Herald* were more politic on this occasion, and maintained a dignified silence.

Thomas Jefferson, in a letter to John Norvel, writes: "It is a melancholy truth that a suppression of the press could not more completely deprive the nation of its benefits than is done by its abandoned prostitution to falsehood. Nothing can now be believed that is seen in a newspaper. Truth itself becomes suspicious by being placed in that polluted vehicle."

After proposing some improvements in the management of the press, Mr. Jefferson continues: "An editor should set his face against the demoralizing practice of feeding the public mind on slander, and the depravity of taste which this nauseous aliment induces. Defamation is becoming a necessary of life." *Vide Jefferson's Works*, vol. vi., p. 79.

Governor Clinton of New York, in his annual address to the legislature, 1828, referred to the political abuses of journalism as follows: "Party spirit has entered the recesses of domestic retirement, violated the sanctity of female character, invaded the tranquillity of private life, and visited, with severe inflictions, the peace of families. Neither elevation nor humility has been spared, nor the charities of life, nor distinguished public services, nor the fire-side, nor the altar, been left free from attack; but a licentious and destroying spirit has gone forth, regardless of every thing but the gratification of malignant feelings and unworthy aspirations."

ANOTHER OBJECTION.

It may be objected again, that many years have elapsed since Jefferson and Clinton offered the foregoing opinions; and it is possible that, in the mean time, a *change* has taken place in the character and habits of our newspaper press. This supposition is strictly true. Within the last twenty or thirty years, American journalism has changed indeed, and changed very much for the WORSE. All the *improvements* in newspaper management contrived by James Gordon Bennett and his Satanic *colloborateurs* have been added since the times of Thomas Jefferson and De Witt Clinton. The black-mailing system, supposed to have been introduced into this country by the *New York Herald*, has been carried to the highest degree of perfection by the pupils and competitors of that *Herald*, who, like the imitators of Day & Martin's Patent Blacking, have improved on the sable brilliancy of their model.

But to meet all objections, I will find room for one American opinion of a later date :—

"The newspapers," says the *New York Annual Register*, "in conducting their political discussions, set both truth and propriety at defiance. The decencies of private life are disregarded; conversation and correspondence, which should have been confidential, are brought before the public eye; the ruthless warfare is carried into the bosoms of private families; neither age nor sex is spared. The daily press teems with ribaldry and falsehood, and even the TOMB is not sacred from its rancorous hostility."

SUPPLEMENTARY ILLUSTRATIONS.

CONFESSION.—In its celebrated *eulogium* on the Newspaper Press, the Washington Union, like the old Abbot in Scott's *Lord of the Isles*, seemed, for a moment, to be overpowered by a better influence than that under which it usually speaks. The sage of the "Union" was suddenly and unexpectedly seized with an extatic fit of candor and sincerity.

> " He felt within his aged breast
> A power that would not be repress'd;
> It prompts his voice, it swells his veins,
> It burns, it maddens, it constrains!
> O'ermastered by the high behest,
> He spoke, and thus the truth confess'd :"—

"The Newspaper Press," (said the *Union* in this fit of inspiration,) "is the great leveler of the age. That it has disseminated error, immorality and vice; that it has been *a vehicle of slander and malevolence :* that it has fomented pride and vanity; that it has blown up monstrous bubbles and pricked them into ridiculous collapse; that it has fostered speculation and been more or less subservient to schemes of fraud and ambition, NONE CAN DOUBT !"

MRS. JACKSON.—The wife of General Andrew Jackson, and the victim of newspaper slanders, died broken-hearted about the beginning of the year 1829, after her husband was elected to the presidency, but before he was inaugurated. Her *death* was not enough to satisfy the malice of her persecutors; for one of them, the editor of the New York American, proposed the following epitaph to her memory :—

> *Illa vero felix, non tam claritate vitæ quam opportunitate mortis."*

The journal which published this cruel insult to a dead woman, pretended to be "the organ of literature, fashion and good society."

266   OUR PRESS GANG.

CHEAP NEWSPAPERS.—J. G. Bennett's biographer, while explaining the advantages of the "cheap-cash system" of newspaper publication, exclaims with great enthusiasm :—"It is to Mr. Benjamin H. Day, that society is indebted for the successful establishment of numerous daily papers at low prices, in the large cities of the United States. He it was who began to prepare the public for a *profitable* and *civilizing* habit of reading, which has now become fixed and universal. *Even slander was slow in sale* AT SIXPENCE !"

At one penny, or two pence, I suppose this commodity "goes off like hot cakes." To understand the obligations which the public owes Mr. Benjamin H. Day for that "profitable and civilizing" reading matter comprised in those journals which have adopted Mr. Day's "cheap for cash system" of publication, you should examine the advertising columns of the Philadelphia Ledger and the editorial *parterres* of the New York Herald, Times and Tribune. See the next paragraph.

A SPECIMEN.—The author of Bennett's Life, declares that the following spicy address to William Cullen Bryant, the disguished American poet, and the editor of one of the *decent* papers of New York, appeared in the editorial columns of the New York Tribune:

"You lie, you villain! willfully, wickedly, basely lie! The scanty pretext formerly trumped up, by garbling, for this calumny, has been exploded ; and whoever repeats it, is an unblushing scoundrel."

Is it possible that Mr. Bryant could have reported that the editor of the Tribune is a gentleman?

MR. COOPER, THE NOVELIST.—James Fennimore Cooper offended the newspaper men, by giving a somewhat better description of them than they deserved. The following account of the assault on Mr. Cooper, is probably impartial and correct :—" His assailants imagined that they could destroy his literary and personal reputation. The war on this author was determined and furious. His enemies fought strenuously for the liberty of the press, but they seemed anxious to have the whole of it to themselves; for they were enraged at Mr. Cooper's opinions as expressed in his published volumes. They made unjustifiable attacks upon Mr. Cooper's moral character and habits.

" He bore the assaults of the press for *five years,* but finding that the malice of his enemies was inexhaustible, he resorted to legal measures for redress. It is said that he was seriously injured by these attacks. The editors who assailed Mr. Cooper, were James Watson Webb, William L. Stone, Horace Greeley, and some others who were accustomed to *follow the lead* of these journalists."

INSIGNIFICANCE OF NEWSPAPER ABUSE.—Very rarely does any man become the object of a fierce and general newspaper attack, on account of his bad character or conduct. It is true that bad men are sometimes assailed by the press: but if you make strict inquiry, you will find that it is not for their *sins* that they are denounced and persecuted by the editors. Take the case of Bennett of the New York Herald for example. He has been more abused by the newspapers than any other man in America. Supposing that he *deserves* all their abuse, it is probable that he would have escaped nine-tenths of it, if he had not been the most successful journalist in the country. His success, and not his sins, exposed him to the wrath of his editorial competitors. If their *moral* sensibilities had been shocked by his offenses, they would have been less apt than they have been to *imitate* his most objectionable conduct.

Men who become the objects of newspaper abuse, commonly have some kind of merit, and their *good* qualities, not their bad ones, are most likely to expose them to editorial attacks. When a man happens to be a *general favorite* with the press, he is sure to be a worthless fellow, or something worse. Hence we may estimate the value of newspaper popularity. The favorable opinions of *some* editors are of inestimable worth, but with regard to the Press Gang in general, it may be said that their most violent abuse, (if it signifies any thing,) is the best recommendation they can give; and if the *public* so understood it, the slanders of the press would be innocuous.

SECTION XVI.

MOTIVES, MODES, EXAMPLES AND EFFECTS OF NEWSPAPER DEFAMATION.

Continued Examination of the Ninth Charge.

Do you still ask why the newspapers of the United States are more addicted to the vice of defamation than those of any other country? It is explanation enough for our present purpose to say that, besides their *irresponsibility*, which we have already noticed, the American journals have certain inducements to slander, which are peculiar, in a great measure, to the press of this country. For example:—

In consequence of the great super-abundance of newspapers in America, many of them are very indifferently supported, and some of them could not subsist at all on the regular and legitimate proceeds of their business. These starvelings of the press, being unable to maintain themselves in an honorable way, must either perish or betake themselves to prostitution, in one form or another; and, as they often have a natural proclivity in that direction, and quite a genius, as we may say, for the meretricious vocation, they prosper exceedingly, and like the Athenian courtesan Phryne, enrich themselves with the wages of guilt and infamy.

From this outline, you might easily trace the career of many of our "leading journals." Destitution made them prostitutes and prostitution made them opulent; but their old principles and habits adhere to them in all changes of their worldly condition. Prostituted editors seldom become Magdalens; they are inconvertible; and, when they have reached the very pinnacles of affluence and renown, they are the same base, mercenary, abusive, spiteful and profligate reprobates that they were at the beginning of their course of iniquity.

Defamation is a very *profitable* mode of newspaper prostitution. It may be said, in mercantile phraseology, to "pay well." Editors are often liberally remunerated for publishing slanders; and quite as often, perhaps, they are paid generously for *not* publishing them. A man or woman, if distinguished in any manner, and especially if he or she is particularly remarkable for virtues or talents, may be required by Messrs. Editors to *purchase* the inestimable privilege of keeping an unsullied reputation.

BLACK MAIL.

The tribute which is paid to newspaper men by sensitive people who are anxious to avoid the merciless abuse of the press, is technically called "black-mail;" a term which every person who has read *Waverley* will know how to apply. That mode of levying contributions on the public which is called *black-mailing*, originated in the "Land of Cakes," and it is supposed by some to have been brought to America and adapted to newspaper purposes by the Scottish editor of the *New York Herald*. Others contend that this practice of Black Mailing has prevailed among the newspapers of *England* for more than a century; but, as the laws of that country make this practice extremely hazardous, some of the most eminent professors of the art made their escape to America, and connected themselves with the journalism of this republic.

The toleration and encouragement which "The Black-Mailing System" meets with in America, may serve, in a measure, to account for the excessively venomous character of our press. All who refuse to submit to the extortions of the typographical banditti, become the objects of their unrelenting hatred and persecution; and of all modes of executing vengeance, *lying* is the easiest, and, with newspaper-men, the most eligible and effective.

But Black Mailing, like every other kind of robbery, is practicable only against those who have money, or something else that is worth stealing. Now as the poor and miserable are often the objects of newspaper calumny, it must be supposed that there are *other* motives, besides the hope of plunder, which induce journalists to bear false witness against their neighbors.

LIBERTINISM.

I have heard, (and I have no reason to doubt the truth of the report,) that poor actresses, female singers, dancers, etc., are often slandered or denounced in newspapers because they refuse to hear the libidinous propositions of certain editors. A gentleman in whose veracity I have the most perfect confidence informs me that a young and beautiful woman, the wife of an actor of some celebrity, was persecuted by the attentions and insulting conversation of an old lecher connected with the newspaper press of Philadelphia. As this shrivelled satyr would take no repulse, the lady, as a final resort, complained to her husband, and begged him to rid her of the annoyance. But alas! the husband was *afraid* to vindicate his own honor and to protect his wife from the shameful importunities of the ancient libertine. "This man," (said he to his complaining spouse,) "is associated with one of the most powerful presses in the country, and he can easily ruin us both. If we offend him, he will blast my professional reputation and rob me of the means of subsistence; and, very probably, he will take more effectual vengeance by publishing something derogatory to your character as a virtuous woman."

In these circumstances, the timorous husband thought it better for his wife to *temporize* with the old sinner, and the unfortunate woman was obliged to endure his humiliating and disgusting attentions while she remained in the city, her husband, in the meantime, making hasty preparations for her removal.

ANONYMOUS CORRESPONDENCE.

Anonymous letter-writing is one of the most detestable features of American journalism. Nearly all of our daily papers, and many of the weekly ones, have nameless correspondents residing in distant cities, each of whom is expected to supply the paper which employs him with piquant items of intelligence collected in his own neighborhood. The ambition of these wretched scribblers to produce "spicy" epistles is a strong inducement for them to seize on every idle rumor, which by means of amplification and embellishment may furnish the material for a startling paragraph. The more improbable and scandalous the story is, the better it answers the purpose; and, as the writers are unknown, and their identification is almost or quite impossible, they are in no danger or dread of being called to an account for their slanderous publications. In this way, the greatest absurdities of tea-table gossip, the most spiteful inventions of personal enmity, the suspicions and speculations of ill-tempered old women and other scandal-mongers, if they can be made available by a newspaper correspondent, are almost certain to appear in print.

You yourself, my good reader, or your wife, or your daughter, may be the unconscious subject of an amusing, exciting or horrifying anecdote inserted in some remote journal, which is never seen by you or any of your neighbors. The anecdote so especially interesting to yourself, may travel the rounds of the papers for months before it is presented to your notice; and if your own favorite journal should not happen to copy it, you may live and die in blissful ignorance of your own celebrity. You, or the dearest objects of your affection, may be caricatured or calumniated in a widely circulated sheet, published at a distance from your place of abode, and the dastardly villain who concocted the slander may live unsuspected within the shadow of your own mansion. Yes, this assassin of private character, this treacherous spy, who revels in defamation and subsists on the produce of his devilish fabrications, may have access to your fire-side and partake of your hospitality. The popish Inquisition would be more tolerable than this infernal system of espionage.

In view of the condition of things just described, there seems to be much of truth and justice in the following remarks by Captain Marryatt:—"The prevalence of this evil, (newspaper slander) acts most unfortunately on society in various ways It produces a feeling of universal distrust. Society in America appears to be in a state of constant warfare, Indian warfare, where many are crouched, concealed, watching for an opportunity to scalp and tomahawk the reputations of their neighbors."

Our American Judge Kent, in his charge to the jury, when Bennett of the *New York Herald* was prosecuted for libel by Judge Noah, spoke still more to the purpose:—" They, (certain American newspapers,) have their emissaries scattered through the large towns and villages of the whole country, sending their communications to the presses which employ them, like the informations dropped into the Lion's mouth at Venice, disclosing the secrets of the family circle, sparing neither age, nor sex, nor occupation, but assaulting without mercy or remorse, the most sacred professions and the most unsullied reputations."

I do not deny that some few anonymous letter-writers for the press are men of character and honor, indeed I am acquainted with *two* or *three* who deserve to be so distinguished; but I assert that an overwhelming majority of them are ruthless calumniators and conscienceless scoundrels; and I believe that the more unscrupulous one of those correspondents is, the more likely he is to satisfy his employers.

In ordinary cases, it is impossible for newspaper publishers to know whether the statements of their distant epistolary contributors are true or not; and, indeed, they seldom trouble themselves to make any inquiry on the subject. "Every man believes his own judgment and his own watch," says Pope. Just so each newspaper publisher believes or affects to believe his own correspondent. Colonel Webb of the New York *Courier and Enquirer* vouched for the truthfulness of his Washington letter-writer whose evil reports caused the death of the lamented Jonathan Cilley. Colonel Webb was willing to fight a duel, or several duels if necessary, to establish the veracity of this mysterious scribe, who had not manliness or conscious rectitude enough, however, to come forward and assume the responsibility of his own declarations.

Not individuals only, but WHOLE COMMUNITIES are often slandered by the "*nomines in umbra*" letter-writers. Like a majority of their employers, they delight in the disparagement of every thing *American ;* and when they write from cities or towns which are not governed by the representatives of the foreign faction, they almost invariably pretend that those places are suffering all the afflictions of disorder and misrule. The special objects of condemnation with them are magistrates who have not been elected by foreign influence. All the actions of such official persons are misconstrued or misrepresented and their public and private characters are traduced with the most persevering malignity.

The reason why so many newspaper correspondents take this course has been partly explained. It was shown, near the commencement of this book, that the general character and tendency of our newspaper press is ANTI-AMERICAN. Our *principal* journals—those which employ news-collecting and scandal-collecting correspondents—are controlled, more or less, by foreigners, or by foreign influences; and the letter-writers recommend themselves to the favor of their employers, by adopting the opinions and policy of the papers with which they correspond.

The misrepresentations of these epistolary rogues seem intended to make it appear that the only really good citizens of the United States are Irishmen and Dutchmen, and their political associates; and that no peace and good order could be preserved in any of our cities under an American regency, and among the American people, without the chastening and corrective influences of the "foreign element!" The laughable absurdity of this pretense is lost in a feeling of indignation, when we observe how the monstrous slander, humiliating and insulting as it is to our national character, is accepted with apparent favor and relish by the press in general, and, *of course*, by a large portion of the public.

LOCAL REPORTING.

That department of the newspaper business called "local reporting," is nearly akin to the anonymous letter-writing branch of the same business—in fact, it is merely a modification of the same nuisance. I admit that, under proper restrictions, it is a legitimate part of the trade of journalism to collect and report such local events of the day as are suitable for publication; but this kind of work admits of many perversions and abuses; and the reporters, therefore, should be held strictly responsible for their errors and misdemeanors.

The following objections will apply to local reporting as it is generally managed in Philadelphia, New York, and other large cities of the United States:

1. The local reporters, like the letter-writers spoken of above, are *anonymous;* or, if their names can be ascertained, they are often found to be persons without character or property, or any other gage by which they can be held accountable for their misdeeds.

2. These reporters, as well as the letter-writers aforesaid, are expected to produce a certain amount of "matter," and, when the supply of *facts* happens to fall short, they have the strongest inducements to resort to fiction, or to rumors, which, if they are not altogether false, are sure to present the truth in distorted shapes, and with more or less amplification.

3. The newspaper reporters of each city form combinations, or professional associations, to facilitate the operations of their business. Each reporter supplies his associates with a transcript of all the *memorabilia* which he has collected; and, by means of this system of exchanges, the same local news items appear simultaneously in all the journals of a city. And, by means of the same detestable system, any false story, prepared by a careless or malicious reporter, is rapidly propagated; and being published, at the same time, in several different

papers, it appears to have currency and corroboration, and thus obtains undeserved credit with the public.

4. Local reporters are not irresponsible to the public only, but to *their employers* also. The publisher of one of the "most respectable" papers in Philadelphia lately acknowledged that he had no control over his reporter's column. If the reporter is not allowed to publish what he pleases, he may withdraw his services from the recusant paper. In that case, his sympathizing brethren of the Reporters' Association may consider him as an injured person; and, to avenge his wrongs, they may forbid any other member of the society to take his place; and so the offending journal will be left without that indispensable feature, the column of City Incidents. It appears, then, that the local reporter is the irresponsible autocrat of his own department. Of course, he may publish falsehoods and slanders *ad libitum;* and all experience proves that very many reporters are apt enough to avail themselves of this extraordinary privilege.

SUNDRY EXAMPLES.

C. Zielinski, a Cincinnati editor, who was soundly beaten by David Levi, (June 7, 1858,) for publishing a scandalous charge against Levi's wife, attempted to justify the publication by saying that he had *heard* the story, and that, at the time he printed it, he believed it to be true. He had ascertained his mistake afterward, but thought it beneath his editorial dignity to make a retraction.

It appears that Mr. Editor Zielinski did not learn wisdom from the wooden lesson administered to him by Mr. Levi; for, on the 24th of March, 1859, we find him charged with the publication of a malicious libel on Mr. Tucker. In this case, he made his old excuse, viz., that he published the story just as it was related to him; adding that he had no acquaintance with Mr. Tucker and no desire to do him injustice.

"I tell the tale as 'twas told to me,

appears to be regarded by some journalists as an excellent excuse for publishing any slanderous story whatever.

Even in their accounts of local incidents, with the facts of which they might be supposed to be well acquainted, the scribes of the press very often deviate widely from the truth, and, in so doing, commit flagrant acts of injustice.

A little girl, the child of a Methodist clergyman living in Philadelphia, was induced by curiosity to taste some laudanum, a vial of which happened to be left, by a careless servant, within her reach. Nothing serious was the result; but a newspaper reporter, in his ardent pursuit of local intelligence, laid hold of an improved version of the story and published it, much to the annoyance of the parents, whose negligence, (as it appeared from this account,) had caused "Almost a Fatal Accident."

Very lately, a young woman who had some business to transact at a menagerie in this city, had her arm shockingly lacerated by the tiger. From the newspaper account of this affair, it appeared that the sufferer had foolishly exposed herself to danger by attempting to caress the animal. I have since heard that the poor girl was hurt while attempting to rescue her little brother, who had accompanied her to the menagerie, and had incautiously approached the cage of the ferocious quadruped.

An afflictive event often leads to a slanderous newspaper report, which pretends to be a truthful account of the particulars. In this way, the sufferings of individuals and the grief of families are aggravated in the highest degree by the blundering or malignant misstatements of the newsmongers.

RETRACTION OF SLANDERS.

The public should understand that the injury which is done by a newspaper calumny admits of no remedy. The editor, in his next issue, may confess that he was mistaken, or he may be compelled to acknowledge that he lied, but the false report has gone forth into the world, and it will go where no message of revocation can follow it. As John Randolph once said, "A lie will travel from Georgia to Maine while Truth is putting on his boots." Thousands of people who read a defamatory paragraph with interest and relish, will not even glance at the contradiction. Published slanders are like permanent inscriptions in brass or marble; the denial, like words traced in dust, is soon swept away and forgotten. To give you an example:

Some years ago, it was my misfortune to be connected in business with a young man who committed a forgery. He and I were the publishers of a paper called the *Evening Express*. When my erring partner was arrested and committed to answer for his crime, an obscene penny paper of this city announced that the *publishers* of the Evening Express had been sent to prison, charged with forging a promissory note. This item of news was calculated, (and *intended* no doubt,) to make it appear that *I* was charged with forgery as well as my partner. On the same day, the publishers of the penny paper aforesaid sent their reporter to me with an apology and an offer to correct the error. I accepted the apology, and informed the messenger that the correction of the error was a matter which I left entirely to the discretion of his employers. On the next morning the promised correction appeared; and the uninitiated may suppose that full reparation was thus made for the wrong which had been committed.

But that wrong, as I very well knew, admitted of no reparation. The paper which I published supported the claims of John Tyler to the presidency, and every journal in the country which opposed John Tyler, reiterated the statement that the "publishers" of the Express had been arrested for forgery. Some of the papers which copied this interesting item of news, improved it by adding the word *both*, or by using some equivalent phraseology to express the idea that "the *two* publishers of the Tyler organ in Philadelphia" had been charged with an act of felony. When the *denial* appeared, it attracted very little notice, and I do not know that it was copied by a single journal in the United States. But I have not yet come to the end of this pleasant reminiscence. Within the last six months, while looking over a bound volume of a British periodical, I saw the very item relating to the charge of forgery against the publishers of the *Philadelphia Evening Express*, inserted in an article purporting to be a critical examination of American journalism.

Thus, a scandalous report, originally published in a contemptible penny paper of Philadelphia was circulated through the United States, and was finally wafted across the Atlantic, to be incorporated with the standard periodical literature of Great Britain! But the *refutation* of this slander was not repeated, in tones of thunder, by the brazen throat and adamantine lungs of the press; it was an utterance which awakened no echoes, but, "like words congealed in northern air," remained torpid and stationary on the spot where it was first pronounced. Had my *name* been coupled with the infamous charge, that name which no act of mine has ever made liable to reproach, might have gone forth stigmatized in both hemispheres, and no effort which I could have made to stay the progress of the scandal would have been effectual.

Not seldom have I known persons to spend much money and waste much time and labor in the vain endeavor to refute a newspaper calumny. In vain may the victim of editorial defamation publish long, pathetical, and logical advertisements, presenting to the world a demonstration of his innocence. He will find that the world turns a cold and deaf ear to his most touching appeal, and to his most elaborate vindication.

Understand, then, that an editorial caluminator *cannot* retract his charges, even when he is disposed to do so. But editors in general are not *willing* to retract, because retraction is a virtual acknowledgment of an error; and the newspaper press pretends to infallibility. It is undeniable that the confession of a falsehood, or even the acknowledgment of a mistake, greatly affects the credit of a public journal; and this fact alone ought to make the scribes of the press extremely careful in avoiding the *necessity* for such impolitic and humiliating confessions. In all their statements which affect private character, they should be *certain* that they speak the truth. By adhering to this simple rule, I have always been able to avoid that dilemma in which an editor is placed when justice calls on him for a retraction, and the policy of journalism disposes him not to make it.

It often happens that when an editor is compelled by threats of prosecution, or of personal chastisement, to revoke his own declarations, he performs that duty in a way which makes the apology more offensive than the original transgression. This mode of retraction is sometimes the effect of mere stupidity, and sometimes it arises from the anxiety of the journalist to maintain his own credit and dignity, while he makes the required concessions.

FLOGGING THE BEST REFUTATION.

In no circumstances would I recommend any violation of the laws of my country; and I wish to have it understood, that the suggestions I am about to make are not intended to *justify* any act of ruffianly outrage, no matter what may be the provocation. But I mention it as a melancholy fact—and no man can lament it more than I do—that a citizen of the United States cannot repel a newspaper slander in a more effectual way than by inflicting corporal punishment on the slanderer. When the assaults of the press are to be resisted, it may be said, in the language of Æsop's currier, that "there is nothing like leather." When the aggrieved party applies a "cow-hide" to the shoulders of the defamer, that operation makes a deeper impression on the public mind than it does on the flesh of the delinquent; and, (as the public are not always the most accurate of logicians,) when an editor has been flogged for making a particular assertion, the falsity of that assertion is supposed to be as well proved as if the stripes on the sufferer's back were the lines of a mathematical demonstration.

The castigation of the offending journalist is an event which commands attention; it affords a good subject for conversation and debate; and, as editors, like other potentates, are seldom objects of popular favor, the man who humiliates and punishes one of them is regarded as a sort of public benefactor. The very instrument of correction, be it a blue cow-skin or a hickory cudgel, becomes an object of affectionate interest. By general consent, it is considered as something which deserves to be consecrated and hung up, as a precious memorial, in the temple of Justice.

A member of the New York legislature lately attempted to effect the passage of an act to legalize the flogging of editors, in certain cases, with the proviso that no bones should be broken in the operation. It would be a much wiser kind of legislation to remove every pretense for such violent measures, by affording the citizen suitable protection from newspaper abuse; which could easily be done, by placing the slanders of the press on the same plane of criminality with highway robbery, and other felonies of the worst class. Journalists would then understand that the "liberty of the press" does not comprise a license to infringe on the inalienable rights of our neighbors, whose *characters* ought to be as much the objects of legal protection as their persons and property.

PUTTING PEOPLE DOWN.

In one of the Christmas stories told by Charles Dickens, we have an account of a certain Alderman Cute, whose characteristic peculiarity was a perpetual inclination to put somebody down. The same everlasting desire to put people down is one of the idiosyncrasies of our public journalists. Now, it is very evident that the most effective way to put any person down is to slander him. This contrivance is recommended as infallible by the old notary in that wicked opera called "The Marriage of Figarro," and our machiavellian editors often test the utility of the plan by actual experiment.

Sometimes a man is doomed to be put down by the newspapers for reasons similar to those which induced King Nebuchadnezzar to put down Shadrach, Meshach, and Abed-nego. He who refuses to do homage to that brazen idol called Journalism, is deemed worthy of immediate prostration. And, as an American, (if we may believe the organs of "Democracy,") can commit no more unpardonable treason than by refusing to obey his party leaders; so, I suppose, the worst *blasphemy* he can utter is that which affects the divinity of the newspaper press! It was for such impiety as this that James Fennimore Cooper, and Charles J. Ingersol, were anathematized and excommunicated by the Press Gang, with all the comprehensive forms of the popish ritual.

But, although revenge is a very strong motive with the journalists, AVARICE is still stronger. Putting people down by the defamatory process is often a very *lucrative* business. A wealthy politician, for example, wishes to put down a popular rival, or an opulent tradesman desires to put down a successful competitor; in such cases, newspapers are bribed in one way or another, and an irresistible torrent of abuse generally accomplishes the desired object.

PROPAGATION OF SLANDERS.

American newspapers, and especially those of Philadelphia and New York, use a variety of ingenious expedients to give their calumnies an appearance of authenticity and an extensive circulation. Each journalist sends many copies of his paper, hundreds perhaps, to editors in different parts of the country, and receives their publications in return. When the papers which are about to be mailed for editors contain a paragraph which is intended to put somebody down, the mischievous article is marked around with a pen, to solicit the particular attention of those editors to whom it is sent. When a journalist receives a paper marked in the manner described, he considers himself requested either to copy the designated paragraph, or to embody the substance of it in an editorial article of his own. This request is often complied with by editors who expect to ask and receive similar favors in return; and thus scandalous accusations are reverberated from one journal to another, until the object of attack is supposed to be annihilated as effectually as a tornado of newspaper denunciation can do it.

An assault on the reputation of some unfortunate person is often *preconcerted* by several newspapers; and this mode of operation is much facilitated by means of combinations or associations of editors and reporters. The public should distrust all associations of this kind, no matter what may be the pretense for their formation. As the newspaper press is now managed, its "harmonious action" is not at all desirable. It is the very *want* of unanimity and combined effort among journalists which, more than any other circumstance, operates as a check on the tyranny and the complicated villainies of the "Press Gang." Single-handed knavery is mischievous enough, but the evil which may be done by a *confederacy* of rogues is incalculable.

In several of our cities "Editorial Associations" have been formed, the ostensible object of which is "to cultivate feelings of amity and good fellowship among the members of the craft." Some few honorable and guileless men have been drawn into these societies, but the evil tendency of such combinations must be obvious to everybody who understands the moral constitution of our newspaper press. A Philadelphia editor, who is a prime mover in one of these associations, publicly acknowledges that a principal object of the society is to obtain some modification of the LIBEL LAW, "in order to make it less *annoying* to the conductors of the press!" This man wishes to have improved facilities for slandering the defenseless objects of newspaper wrath, as if the license of the press, in this particular, could possibly admit of any extension.

THE PRINCIPAL VEHICLES OF SLANDER.

Say you that some discrimination ought to be made between the "respectable class" of newspapers and those nasty sheets which are supposed to be printed only for the purposes of defamation? Ah, my friends, do not imagine that I would think it worth the while to devote whole pages of censure to such publications as the *New York Alligator* or the *Philadelphia Paul Pry.* The preceding remarks apply to your "respectable" journals, and to them exclusively. The worst calumnies that ever I have seen in print, were published in newspapers which pretend to the highest respectability.

It is doubtful whether the *Alligator* or the *Paul Pry* ever published a false and infamous charge against a dead man or an innocent woman; but it is very certain that female purity and the sanctuary of the grave have been outraged—many times, alas!—by newspapers which are allowed to place themselves in the very *first rank* of American journalism.

Many examples might be added to those which have already been given in this volume, but imperative necessity (as the reader must understand) obliges me to be brief and somewhat *circumspect* in the production of living instances. According to the law of the land, an exposure of the most remorseless calumniator might be an actionable offense. Unpleasant TRUTHS, as construed by legislative wisdom, are the most offensive of libels. One example, however, I cannot afford to omit.

DEFAMATION OF THE DEAD.

The late Edgar A. Poe has been represented by the American newspapers in general as a reckless libertine and a confirmed inebriate. I do not recognize him by this description, though I was intimately acquainted with the man, and had every opportunity to study his character. I have been in company with him every day for many months together; and, within a period of twelve years, I did not see him inebriated; no, not in a single instance. I do not believe that he was ever habitually intemperate until he was made so by grief and many bitter disappointments. And, with respect to the charge of libertinism, I have similar testimony to offer. Of all men that ever I knew, he was the most *passionless;* and I appeal to his writings for a confirmation of this report. Poets of ardent temperament, such as Anacreon, Ovid, Byron, and Tom Moore, will always display their constitutional peculiarity in their literary compositions; but Edgar A. Poe never wrote a line that gives expression to a libidinous thought. The female creations of his fancy are all either statues or angels. His conversation, at all times, was as chaste as that of a vestal, and his conduct, while I knew him, was correspondingly blameless.

Poe, during his life-time, was feared and hated by many newspaper editors and other literary animalcules, some of whom, or their friends, had been the subjects of his scorching critiques; and others disliked him, naturally enough, because he was a man of superior intellect. While he lived, these resentful gentlemen were discreetly silent, but they nursed their wrath to keep it warm, and the first intelligence of his death was the signal for a general onslaught. The primal slander against the deceased bard was published in a leading journal of Philadelphia, the "literary editor" of which had formerly received not only a critical rebuke, but something like personal chastisement also, from the hands of the departed poet.

Since that time, by continued and well-directed efforts, the newspapers of our country have succeeded in giving Poe a character "as black as Vulcan's stithy," and in this hideous drapery, woven by demoniac malice, the unrivalled poet of America is now presented to the world.

SUMMARY.

From the foregoing observations and examples, it may appear that the unparalleled virulence of our American newspaper slanderers does not arise from "too much freedom," as some commentators have supposed, but from a gross misunderstanding of what really constitutes the Liberty of the Press. The policy of the newsmongers is to make the public believe that the abuses I have described are inseparable from the wholesome exercise of those rights and privileges which constitutionally belong to the American journalist.

Our countrymen have been persuaded that it is a dangerous infringement on the Liberty of the Press to place newspaper editors under those necessary restrictions to which, by the terms of the social compact, citizens of every class and condition are bound to submit. In no case does the liberty of one citizen include a privilege to commit aggressions on the rights of another. Under the Constitution of the United States, the conductors of the Press can claim no rights, prerogatives, immunities or exemptions, which do not belong equally to every other class of citizens. You, for example, have as much right to scarify an editor's hide as he has to besmirch your reputation.

The members of the Press Gang would make us believe that it is an abridgment of their "liberty" to prevent them from leveling their filthy batteries against all that is sacred, pure and excellent. With equal reason, you might pretend that it is an abbreviation of *your* liberty to prohibit you from throwing soot, coal-ashes, or the contents of your urinals, out of your front windows into a crowded street.

When the people of America shall learn what that fine phrase "The Liberty of the Press" truly signifies, they will understand that our "national palladium" will not be endangered in the least by preventing depraved newsmongers from playing the pole-cat and making themselves a perpetual nuisance, the toleration of which by the public is not virtuous forbearance but contemptible imbecility.

SUPPLEMENTARY ILLUSTRATIONS.

THE CASE OF JAMES T. LLOYD.—Mr. Lloyd is the publisher of my "*Life and Adventures of Ferdinand De Soto,*" and also of this volume Being an enterprising and energetic man, he successfully established himself in Philadelphia, and was doing an extensive business as a book publisher, when he unfortunately provoked the hostility of the newspaper press, and immediately became an object of the most unrelenting persecution. The press of Philadelphia succeeded in breaking up Mr. Lloyd's business and in exposing him to much undeserved reproach; in fact every exertion was used to blacken his character and to give him undesirable celebrity in every part of the United States.

Of Mr. Lloyd's history before he came to Philadelphia, I know very little. He is the son of a distinguished Temperance Lecturer, now residing at Louisville, Ky., and as far as my own observation extends, his moral conduct is, (to say the least,) as unexceptionable as that of the Philadelphia book-publishers in general. I am under no obligations to Mr. Lloyd, and I have not the least inclination to shield him from any censure to which he is justly liable. At the present time, my observations are strictly confined to his quarrel with the Philadelphia editors, and to the causes and consequences of that quarrel.

Mr. Lloyd's case is a curious one indeed, but it is one which is not new to my experience. I understand it perfectly, and enough has been said in the preceding pages to make the brief narrative, which I am about to give, sufficiently intelligible to the reader. It may be premised, however, that Mr. Lloyd does not *advertise* much in the newspapers; he has discovered other modes of communication with the public, and he is not entitled, therefore, to those special favors which the newspaper men are accustomed to bestow on their best customers.

About two years ago Mr. Lloyd was induced to loan one thousand dollars to the keeper of a boarding-house in Sixth street, where Lloyd and his family made their temporary abode. The boarding-house keeper became insolvent and retired from business; and as the money which he had borrowed from his boarder could not be refunded, Mr. Lloyd was obliged to accept the furniture and "good-will" of the boarding-house in payment of the debt.

Having thus obtained possession of the "establishment," and being under a high rent, Mr. Lloyd determined to carry on the business for awhile until a purchaser could be found to take it off his hands. He kept an excellent table, managed all the affairs of the house in a satisfactory manner, and had as many boarders as he could accommodate.

Among Mr. Lloyd's boarders, there were several gentlemen who were connected with the newspaper press. One of these was the literary editor of a "highly respectable" diurnal, who, as Mr. Lloyd reports, led a very jovial life, and came home almost every evening in a state of bacchanalian excitement. This literary editor kept late hours, and it was his custom to open the front door with a latch-key and to ascend to his dormitory, (not without some noisy demonstrations,) long after all the other inmates of the house had retired to rest.

One night, or rather one *morning*, at half-past two o'clock, the literary editor, after making a clamorous ascent to the top of the stairs, fell backward, rolled down the steps, and falling against the door of a bed-chamber, knocked it open, to the great consternation of the occupant. This happened about the time of the bank "panic" of 1857. Mr. Lloyd's boarders had taken their money from the banks and deposited it in their trunks as places of greater security. The noise made by the literary editor produced a general alarm in the boarding-house; for it was supposed that robbers had effected an entrance, and that all the money would be lost as certainly as if it had remained in the vaults of the banking house.

The chamber into which the literary editor had fallen, was occupied by an old gentleman from California, the happy possessor of ten thousand dollars in gold, which he had drawn from the bank and stowed away snugly under his bed. Pale and trembling, he now appeared at the door of the chamber with a night-cap on his head and a pistol in his hand, and it is possible that the brains of the literary editor might have been blown out, if Mr. Lloyd himself had not fortunately come to the rescue.

Mr. Lloyd declares that the behavior of this editor was, at all times, intolerable. When intoxicated, he was noisy and quarrelsome; and when sober, he was supercilious and insulting. Because his toast was not browned to the proper shade, one morning, he denounced Mr. Lloyd before all the boarders, as a scoundrel and a swindler, and threatened him with the vengeance of the press! He often boasted of his ability to "ruin the establishment" and to bring "all the papers of the city down upon it." His violence frightened the lady boarders, and his offenses were so frequent and so outrageous that Mr. Lloyd was compelled to turn him out of doors. At first, he refused to be dismissed, assuming the right to stay "as long as he pleased," and it was only by resorting to summary measures that Mr. Lloyd obtained relief from his presence.

Mr. Lloyd had another boarder attached to the newspaper press. This was the editor of a small and obscure weekly publication of a somewhat venomous character, and without any *pretensions* to respectability. The editor of this sheet was dismissed by Mr. Lloyd for neglecting to pay his boarding bill weekly, according to the terms of his contract. It is probable that some of the other boarders were delinquent in the same way, for Mr. Lloyd found that the income of his boarding-house was not sufficient to meet the expenses. To provide for the payment of his debts, Mr. Lloyd sold the establishment at auction, and this circumstance afforded his newspaper enemies an opportunity to begin the premeditated attack.

The first assault was made by the little scurrilous sheet, whose publisher had been dismissed from Lloyd's boarding-house for not complying with the prescribed terms of the establishment. One of the editors of this sheet, (as I have heard,) was a reporter, or contributer of some kind, to one of the principal daily papers of our city; and in the reporter's column of that daily paper, the paragraph which attacked Mr. Lloyd was copied from the little weekly, with some slight alterations. This circumstance shows how a journal of the first class may be made accessory to the propagation of a slander which originates in a publication of the most contemptible character.

All the circumstances of this narrative preceding the newspaper attack on Mr. Lloyd were related to me by Mr. Lloyd himself, and I know nothing more of those matters than Mr. Lloyd has told me. But the *newspaper assault* on this man was a circumstance which came under my own observation; and I solemnly declare that I never witnessed any outrage of the kind that was more inexcusable and atrocious. The Philadelphia papers which joined in the attack on Mr. Lloyd were

THREE "RESPECTABLE DAILIES,"

one *not* respectable, and several others whose obscurity and insignificance make them undeserving of notice, even in this connection.

I do not know what *persons* connected with these papers are chargeable with participation in this outrage, or which of the publishers, editors or reporters are blameless in the matter. It is true, however, that some of the Philadelphia editors and publishers cannot control their own columns, and that injurious articles are sometimes published in their papers without their consent, and even in opposition to their wishes. In such cases, the journalists deserve more pity than condemnation. The proprietor of one of our most august dailies acknowledged to Mr. Lloyd that he could not keep a scandalous article out of his reporter's column, and he almost shed tears when he made this humiliating acknowledgment. Another eminent gentleman of the press advised Mr. Lloyd to make his peace with the reporters, "otherwise" (said he) "they will crush you like an egg-shell, for their power is irresistible."

For several days the fire against Mr. Lloyd was kept up; the most opprobrious terms were applied to him freely, and the people of Philadelphia were exhorted to hate, to shun, to abhor him, and to " drive him out of the city." But the only definite charge made against him, with any color of reason or justice, was that some man, living at a distance from Philadelphia, had sent Lloyd an order for some books, enclosing seven dollars and fifty cents, and that Lloyd had " pocketed the money," but failed to send the books. No allowance was made for the possibility that the letter might have miscarried, or for any other accident or delay which might easily occur in an affair of this kind; but because the books were not sent *immediately*, according to order, Lloyd was denounced as a cheat and impostor. It appears that when the order arrived, the first edition of the work which had been ordered was exhausted and a new edition was about to be put to press, for the supply of all demands; and in the mean time, the man who had remitted the order and money, wrote to the Chief of Police in this city to inquire if there was such a firm as Lloyd & Co. doing business in Philadelphia. This letter happened to fall into the hands of one of Lloyd's editorial persecutors, and that worthy gentleman immediately answered it, assuring the person who made the inquiry that Lloyd was a great rogue, that he *never published any books*, but sent circulars all over the country to deceive the people and obtain money under false pretenses! This veracious scribe concluded by advising the man to come to Philadelphia and prosecute the "swindler," intimating that there were persons in this city who would "see him through."

Accordingly, the man who had ordered the books came to Philadelphia and made a complaint against Mr. Lloyd. He acknowledged, in his evidence, that he had received the letter just spoken of and, when closely questioned, he admitted that he never intended to prosecute Mr. Lloyd until he was advised to do so by the Philadelphia editorial letter-writer. He also confessed that he destroyed the letter as soon as he had read it, because the person who wrote it *requested* him to dispose of it in that manner.

Now it is very evident that this charge against Mr. Lloyd was contrived for the express purpose of affording a pretense for newspaper abuse. As soon as Lloyd was arrested, his assailants published the fact with many distortions and aggravations, pretending that his guilt had been *clearly proved*, and that he had been "fully committed" to answer the charge of swindling. All of these false reports were interlarded with the most choice terms and phrases of the "blackguard's dictionary."

The truth is, there was not the slightest evidence of any felonious purpose brought against Mr. Lloyd. He was *not* "committed;" but, being anxious to have the charge investigated, he readily gave bail for his appearance at Court, and since that time he has repeatedly demanded a trial. But the case will never be tried. The object of Mr. Lloyd's persecutors has been gained; they have published him as a felon, and made arrangements to have their accusations scattered over the American continent. His trial before a court of justice would give him an opportunity to prove his innocence; and, besides, it might lead to the detection of a villainous conspiracy, intended to "put him down."

This case of Lloyd, if circumstances allowed me to publish all the details, would afford many fine illustrations of my subject. I could tell you, for example, how Mr. Lloyd was disappointed in his applications for justice; how several magistrates of Philadelphia, on various pretenses, refused to issue warrants for the arrest of the libellers; and how several city aldermen confessed that the power of the press was so tremendous that they were afraid to make any demonstrations against it!

In connection with this case, there is another circumstance which deserves particular notice. The charge against Lloyd, even if it had admitted of any proof, would have been a very trivial affair, (in a pecuniary sense,) compared with sundry cases of swindling and imposture which, almost daily, come under the observation of the press. But Lloyd's affair produced as much commotion and excitement among the editors and reporters as if it had been a defalcation to the amount of five hundred thousand dollars. Some of the Philadelphia journalists must have troubled themselves to have the charge against Lloyd *extensively copied;* for almost every village newspaper in the United States joined in the outcry against "the swindling book publisher of Philadelphia." The consequence was that, for a time, Mr. Lloyd's business was seriously interrupted; and some of the *real* "swindling book publishers of Philadelphia" rejoiced perhaps at the prospect of his downfall. But a man who has moral courage and energy of character enough to publish such a book as "OUR PRESS GANG," will not be extinguished so easily by dark conspiracies, envious rivalship, or any other Satanic influence.

If James T. Lloyd had been the worst man in America, and not the useful citizen which he certainly is, the treatment which he has received from the Philadelphia journals would be wholly unjustifiable. Let the guilty be punished, and punished *severely*, if you please ; but let them have JUSTICE, at least, if no mercy. When a man really offends against the laws of his country, let his punishment be such as the law prescribes, and let it be inflicted in a regular and rational manner, and not by demonstrations of brutal violence or fiendish malice. Breaking up a man's business by means of false reports, starving his family, or driving him out of a city, are not punishments recognized by the laws of this republic, nor by the customs of any civilized nation. If a man is really a sinner, it is not necessary to *slander* and *defame* him to make his conduct sufficiently odious ; and, in no case, should punishment be inflicted by incensed and vindictive parties ; such, for instance, as literary editors who have been ejected from boarding-houses for their troublesome behavior, and angry reporters who expect to be propitiated by gift-offerings or humble applications for mercy.

NOTE.—On glancing over the preceding account, I find that it does not do Mr. Lloyd justice, for some of the *worst* conduct of his persecutors has been passed over without notice. I regret that it is not in my power to place all the particulars of this case on record, for it is an example of oppression and injustice which deserves to be incorporated with the history of the Republic, as a proof that the negligence and indifference of the people may allow the most contemptible usurpation to become formidable and dangerous. When the press can do such things as I have described, the boast of liberty, equality and security is ridiculous.

SECTION XVII.

EDITORIAL DUELS.

Examination of the Tenth Charge.

It is proposed, in this division of our work, to investigate that part of the Tenth Charge which asserts that many sanguinary duels are caused by the intemperate conduct of our newspaper editors. I believe it is a well-ascertained fact that more than two-thirds of the single combats which have taken place among civilians in the United States originated in newspaper disputes. And I think it will appear that more duels have been fought, in this country, by public journalists than by naval and military officers; though fighting is the trade of the latter, and public opinion seems to exact from them a nicer observance of the "code of honor" than is ever required of men who are engaged in more pacific avocations.

Franklin, Bradford, Keimer and other founders of American Journalism, managed to transact their business, I believe, without any resort to pistols or rifles. The first editorial duel which took place in America was fought by

MATHEW CAREY AND COLONEL OSWALD.

In the year 1785. Each of these gentlemen was the editor of a political newspaper in Philadelphia, and a controversy between them, which began in type-metal was terminated with leaden bullets. In this combat Mathew Carey, the challenger, received a severe wound; which, according to the ideas of duellists, was "ample satisfaction." It is mentioned as a "curious coincidence," that Mr. Carey commenced his career of authorship by writing an essay on Dueling. There is nothing very wonderful in that circumstance, as Mr. Carey seems to have had a taste for the sport, and it is very natural for a man to write on a subject with which he is practically acquainted. Thus Mark Anthony composed an essay on Drunkenness, and Brougham the pugilist wrote a treatise on Boxing.

CHEETHAM AND COLEMAN.

James Cheetham and William Coleman, two political editors of New York city, made some arrangements for fighting a duel in the year 1804. Cheetham was the editor of the *American Citizen*, a Democratic organ, and Coleman conducted the *Evening Post*, a Federal paper of great influence. The quarrel originated in an acrimonious debate which had been carried on, for some time, in the columns of the two papers. Cheetham challenged Coleman, and the latter was so anxious to accept the invitation, that his warlike ardor blazed out in the next issue of his journal. The affair being thus made public, the friends of both parties called in the aid of the civil authorities and so put a stop to the valorous proceedings.

After a while, it began to be whispered that Coleman's "indiscreet" publication of his intention to fight, was really a sensible expedient to evade the battle, without any disparagement to his honor. This rumor was industriously circulated by a certain Captain Thompson, Harbor-Master of New York, who did not hesitate to affirm publicly that Coleman was too much of a Christian to resent an affront by shooting the person who offered it. To rebut this slander, and to prove conclusively that he was not a Christian, Coleman challenged Thompson to deadly combat. Thompson accepted the challenge. The parties met on a dreary winter's night, the cold was excruciating, a storm of snow and hail prevailed at the time, and all circumstances combined, (as one of the seconds quaintly remarked), to make the affair "uncomfortable." The falling snow and the obscurity of the night prevented the parties from seeing each other at the distance of ten paces ; and a cruel necessity compelled them to reduce the intervening space. Several shots were fired on each side. "At last," says the narrator to whom I am indebted for this account, and who appears to have been an eye-witness of the scene, "Thompson was heard to exclaim 'I've got it!' and he immediately fell to the ground, mortally wounded."

The surgeon who officiated on this occasion exacted a promise from the dying man, that he would not reveal the names of the parties who had been engaged in the affair. Thompson gave the required promise and faithfully adhered to it, refusing to give any information on the subject of the duel, though he lived forty-eight hours after the reception of his wound and some of his friends were anxious to obtain a statement of the particulars. His only reply to their questions was that he "came to his death fairly." The secrecy of the transaction prevented Coleman from being held responsible for the murder, and many years elapsed before the particulars of the combat were generally known.

GRAHAM AND ——————

The name of one of the parties in this duel is not given by my authorities, and I am not disposed to make any troublesome inquiry in the premises. Mr. W. G. Graham was an associate editor of the New York Inquirer, which was then published by the celebrated Mordecai M. Noah, sometimes called "Judge of Israel." Mr. Graham, it seems, "was distinguished for the easy style of his writings, which were devoted chiefly to expositions of what is called 'Good Society.'" His antagonist was the son of a physician of Philadelphia, and the quarrel arose while the parties were engaged in a game of cards. The duel was fought at Hoboken, November 28, 1827. Mr. Graham fell and died on the spot. The other persons engaged in the affair buried the body secretly; but after a while it was disinterred and subjected to the mockery of a coroner's inquest. The verdict was, that Mr. Graham died of wounds inflicted by some person or persons unknown; but the truth is, (says the narrator,) "every body knew who fired the fatal shot and who was responsible for Mr. Graham's death."

THOMAS BIDDLE AND SPENCER PETTIS.

These men were not editors, but as their quarrel began with an intemperate newspaper controversy, which should not have been permitted by the publishers of the journals in which the dispute was carried on, I conceive that the case may be properly introduced to exemplify the mischievous tendencies of an ill-conducted and irresponsible press.

Pettis was a member of Congress elect from Missouri; Biddle was a Major in the army of the United States, and a brother of Nicholas Biddle, the celebrated banker. The weapons were pistols; and as Biddle, the challenged party, was near-sighted, he stipulated that the distance should be only five feet, by which arrangement the weapons of the combatants were brought into actual contact. Both of the duellists were mortally wounded. They exchanged forgiveness before they were conveyed from the battle-ground. Pettis died on the following morning, and Biddle on the third day after the duel. The quarrel commenced in the papers of St. Louis, Missouri, during an election canvass.

BYNUM AND PERRY.

Mr. Bynum, editor of the *Greenville (S. C.) Sentinel*, and Mr. Perry, editor of the *Greenville Mountaineer*, fought a duel in the year 1832. Bynum was mortally wounded and died in great agony. A violent newspaper dispute led to this catastrophe.

CUMMING AND M'DUFFIE.

A duel was fought, in the year 1822, by Col. Cumming of Georgia, and George McDuffie, a celebrated politician of South Carolina. The affair comes under our notice, because the quarrel began in the newspapers, and because many of the editors labored strenuously to exacerbate the angry feelings of the parties and to procure a renewal of hostilities after Mr. McDuffie had been badly wounded in the first encounter. The newspaper controversy was anonymous at the beginning; but, when the disputants began to indulge freely in personal abuse, Cumming made inquiries and ascertained that his antagonist was McDuffie. A challenge immediately followed this discovery, and arrangements were made to end the controversy by an appeal to arms. Some of the conditions of the proposed battle were unusual and slightly ridiculous. Cumming requested that the fighting costume might be round jackets and drilling pantaloons. McDuffie contended for frock coats, but was willing that each party should clothe his lower extremities as he pleased. When the gentlemen appeared on the ground, both were arrayed, somewhat fantastically, in habiliments which appear to have been made for the occasion. Cumming was dressed in a *blouse* and loose trowsers composed of a light cotton material, and McDuffie, (more aristocratically inclined,) wore garments of similar form, but made of *silk*. It was afterward asserted by some of his political opponents, that this luxurious apparel was padded or quilted in such a way as to make it almost as impervious to a bullet as the hide of a rhinoceros or alligator; but the event of the battle is a sufficient refutation of this slander.

Either the intentions of Mr. McDuffie were not very sanguinary, or his skill in the use of the pistol was very imperfect, for when his weapon was discharged, the bullet entered the ground only four feet from the toes of his own boots. The gunnery of Mr. Cumming was more successful, for his ball penetrated the back of his antagonist, just below the short ribs, and inflicted a wound from the effects of which McDuffie never recovered.

Although McDuffie's wound was very serious and, for many weeks his recovery was doubtful, the newspapers were clamorous for the effusion of more blood. A paper called the *Chronicle*, published at Augusta, Georgia, pretending to give an "authentic account" of the duel, intimated that McDuffie had taken unfair advantage in the battle, and charged him with cowardice, or something like it, because he was satisfied with one wound and did not demand a continuation of the fight. These absurd charges, with various aggravations and insulting comments, were reiterated by many other journals, with the evident design of urging the belligerents to consummate the murderous work which had been left unfinished. Messrs. Cumming and McDuffie were wise enough, however, to disregard these blood-thirsty requirements.

JONATHAN CILLEY AND WILLIAM J. GRAVES.

The cause of that unhappy feud which terminated in the death of the lamented Cilley, may be traced to an indiscreet publication made in the columns of the *New York Courier and Enquirer*, of which the somewhat celebrated Colonel James Watson Webb was editor. The subjoined statement of this extraordinary case is derived from the most authentic sources.

On the 12th of February, 1838, Mr. Wise, Member of Congress from Virginia, called the attention of the House of Representatives to a publication in the New York Courier and Enquirer, which charged one of the representatives with corruption. This charge was made on the authority of an anonymous correspondent of Webb's paper, who wrote over the signature of the "Spy in Washington." Mr. Wise moved a resolution for the appointment of a select committee, with power to send for persons and papers, to investigate the truth of the charge. "For, (said Mr. Wise,) the character of the authority on which the charge is made, is vouched for as respectable and reliable by Colonel Webb, the editor of the *Courier and Enquirer*, in which paper this charge appears, and the House is called upon to defend its honor and dignity against such a disgraceful allegation."

Mr. Jonathan Cilley, a representative from Maine, objected to the resolution, and remarked, "I know nothing of this editor, but if he is the same journalist who once made grave charges against an institution of this country, (the United States Bank,) and who afterward, according to report, received facilities to the amount of $52,000 from the same institution, and then gave it his hearty support, I do not think that his charges are entitled to much credit in an American Congress."

A committee of Congress, which was afterward appointed to ascertain the causes of the duel, declared that "these words spoken by Mr. Cilley in debate were strictly in order; that they were pertinent to the subject then under discussion ; that they did not exceed the limits of his duty ; and that, although they implied a doubt respecting the unblemished honor and good character of the person alluded to, Mr. Cilley was justified in the use of them by a report of a Committee of the House of Representatives, appointed on the 14th of March, 1832, to inspect the books and examine the proceedings of the Bank of the United States. A report made by a majority of the Committee, and published by order of the House of Representatives, declares, that for sixteen months the New York *Courier and Enquirer* was warmly opposed to the Bank of the United States; that on the 26th of March, 1831, and within nine months thereafter, the bank made three loans, amounting to the sum of $52,975, which consisted of notes drawn and endorsed by the editors only ; and that on or about the 8th of April, 1831, the said *Courier and Enquirer* changed its course in favor of the Bank.

It was in reference to the facts contained in this report, and published to the world by order of the House of Representatives, that Mr. Cilley spoke the words which I have quoted ; and for thus alluding to facts put forth in the published documents of that body of which he was a member, he was called to account by the editor of the *New York Courier and Enquirer.*

On the 12th of February, James Watson Webb addressed a note to Mr. Cilley, requiring him to explain or apologize for the language recited above. Webb's note was conveyed to Mr. Cilley by Mr. William J. Graves, a representative from Kentucky. Mr. Cilley refused to receive any communication from Colonel Webb, and Mr. Graves was pleased to consider himself aggrieved by this refusal, though Mr. Cilley, in the correspondence which was commenced between him and Mr. Graves, declared, more than once, that in declining to receive Webb's letter no disrespect to the bearer thereof was intended. This explanation ought to have been satisfactory to Mr. Graves, but it appears that nothing less than *an acknowledgment favorable to the character of Colonel Webb* would satisfy Mr. Graves, and such an acknowledgment Mr. Cilley steadfastly refused to make.

In this state of affairs, according to the notions of "men of honor," a duel between Mr. Graves and Mr. Cilley appeared to be unavoidable. On the 23d of February, Mr. Cilley received, by the hands of Mr. Wise, a formal challenge from the zealous defender of Colonel Webb's reputation, and this challenge was immediately accepted by the high-spirited representative from Maine,—whose previous conduct, throughout the whole affair, had been unexceptionable ; but who now, by consenting to fight in such a quarrel, exhibited a deficiency of sound judgment and of moral courage altogether unworthy of his general character.

The arrangements for the duel were made by Mr. Wise of Virginia, on the part of the challenger, and General G. W. Jones of Kentucky on the part of Mr. Cilley. All who participated in this murderous enterprise, principals and seconds, were members of Congress,—statesmen and legislators! The right of choosing the weapons, according to the laws of the *duello*, belongs to the challenged party. The implements of murder chosen, in this instance, were *rifles*. The selection of these very effective weapons was made, no doubt, by Mr. Cilley's second, General Jones, who, being a Kentuckian, was willing to conform with the usages of his own State, where the practice of duelling presents some of its most unfavorable aspects.

The excessive heroism of General Jones was displayed in the choice of the weapons. The magnanimity and extremely accommodating disposition of Mr. Wise, (the second of Mr. Graves,) were shown in his ready acquiescence with the propositions of General Jones. In his written answer to that gentleman, Mr. Wise says, "your terms of battle, though *unusual* and *objectionable*, are accepted, with the understanding that each rifle is to be loaded with a single ball, and that neither party is to raise his weapon from the *downward horizontal* position until the order is given to fire."

The parties met, by appointment, on the Marlborough road, near the division line between the State of Maryland and the District of Columbia. Mr. Cilley was accompanied by his friend and second, General Jones, Mr. Bynum of North Carolina, Colonel J. W. Schaumberg, and Dr. Duncan of Ohio. Mr. Graves was attended by Mr. Wise, as his second, Mr. Crittenden, Senator from Kentucky, Mr. Menefee a Representative from the same State, and Dr. Foltz of Washington. The two medical gentlemen were on the ground, I presume, not as friends of either party, but merely as surgeons. Besides the persons just mentioned, Mr. Calhoun and Mr. Hawes, (Congressmen from Kentucky,) and two other gentlemen, viz. Grafton Powell and James T. Brown, were present as disinterested spectators! Two cab-drivers were also curious observers of the scene; which, considering the unusual number of people in attendance, might almost be regarded as a public exhibition.

Messrs. Jones and Wise performed their duties as seconds with all that zeal and alacrity which seconds are apt to exhibit on similar occasions. They expeditiously marked off the ground, loaded the weapons, and placed a rifle in the hand of each combatant. The line of fire was at right angles with the rays of the sun. The distance was about ninety-two yards. The choice of position fell by lot to Mr. Wise, and the duty of giving the order to fire devolved on General Jones. At three o'clock, P. M., all the preparations having been finished, the parties exchanged shots, without effect.

An attempt was then made by the seconds and the other

gentlemen present to effect a reconciliation; but this rational and humane object was defeated by the persistent demand of Mr. Graves that Mr. Cilley should "disclaim all exception to Colonel Webb as a gentleman and a man of honor." Mr. Cilley firmly refused to make a concession which, considering the circumstances of the case, could not reasonably be expected from him; for it would have been equivalent to a denial of his own words spoken in congressional debate. General Jones, after consulting with his principal, reported that "Mr. Cilley reasserted the ground which he had assumed in the correspondence; he declined to receive the note of Colonel Webb, because he chose to be drawn into no controversy with him, and he neither affirmed nor denied any thing in regard to Webb's character." Mr. Cilley went further by declaring that he entertained "for Mr. Graves *the highest respect and the most friendly feelings.*"

The friends of both parties, and all the other gentlemen on the ground, appear to have been convinced that enough had been said and done to satisfy Mr. Graves; but that gentleman (according to the testimony of Mr. Wise, his second) insisted on having another shot. Accordingly the rifles were again loaded, the parties resumed their stations, and the two weapons were discharged almost at the same instant. Mr. Cilley was shot through the body. He dropped his rifle, beckoned to the physician, said "I am shot," fell on his face and expired within two or three minutes.

A gentleman who was well acquainted with Mr. Cilley says: "He was a man of chivalrous feelings, and seemed never to forget that he was of ancient and honorable lineage; that his grandfather was a general officer in the Revolution, and that his brother led the charge of the gallant Miller at the battle of Bridgewater, in the war of 1812."

From the preceding narrative it appears that this estimable man was sacrificed to preserve, in all its unsullied purity, the reputation of Colonel James Watson Webb, editor of the New York Courier and Enquirer. The beginning of the quarrel, which terminated with the death of Mr. Cilley, is clearly traced to an anonymous communication written by the Washington correspondent of Webb's paper. Colonel Webb vouched for the honor and veracity of that correspondent; but such is the general character of the gossiping news-collectors at Washington, that even the unimpeachable certificate of Colonel Webb is scarcely sufficient to establish our faith in the statements of one of those ingenious but unscrupulous writers. I think it highly probable, therefore, that Colonel Webb was mistaken, and that his Washington correspondent's assertions, which produced this fatal quarrel, were false and slanderous.

WEBB AND MARSHALL.

Colonel Webb, of the New York Courier and Enquirer, fought a duel with Thomas F. Marshall, on the 25th day of June, 1842. In this combat, which was fought with pistols, Webb received a slight wound in the leg, just below the knee. He was afterward imprisoned for a violation of the laws which had been made to prevent duelling. While he was in prison, Bennett of the Herald, (who had been flogged by Webb once or twice,) magnanimously sent his old enemy a box of the best cigars to comfort him during his incarceration. Webb declined the courtesy by kicking the box and its contents out of his apartment. Bennett, however, was the first to sign a petition for Webb's pardon. In one of his editorial articles in the Herald he referred to Webb's discourteous reception of his present in these terms:

"If Webb will apologize, like a reinstated gentleman, and if he will smoke one of those cigars, as the Indian does his calumet, we will go to Delaware, where he is imprisoned, and obtain his release, or throw a wet blanket over the length and breadth of that State that will bury it in a thick fog until the Day of Judgment comes, on the 23d of April, 1843, according to Prophet Miller."

"This," (says Bennett's biographer,) "may certainly be regarded as one of the prettiest specimens of wit and humor known to the American press!!"

HICKEY AND MOSES.

In the year 1849, Colonel Hickey, editor of the *Vicksburg Sentinel*, was killed in a duel by Joseph Moses. The particulars of this affair have not been published.

IRVING AND GIBSON.

In the same year, a duel was fought in Arkansas by C. Irving, editor of the *Memphis Inquirer*, and William E. Gibson. At the first fire, Irving was badly wounded in the abdomen; but he survived, and afterward became reconciled to his adversary.

WOODS AND COLEMAN.

Israel Woods was the editor of the *Arkansas Democrat*, published at Little Rock, and he was one of the most distinguished bullies of that half-civilized region in which he flourished. Woods was a man of prodigious personal strength, and he had taken a part in many sanguinary duels and street-fights, from all of which he came off triumphantly.

Levi Coleman was a young minister of the Methodist Church. He occasionally contributed to the columns of the Arkansas Whig. His character and deportment were mild and inoffensive, and in all respects suited to his sacred profession. An article on *Dueling*, published by Coleman in the Whig, some time in July, 1839, so greatly enraged Woods that he made an assault on Coleman in the street, kicked him, pulled his nose, and spat in his face. But all these insults were borne by Coleman with the most Christian-like patience.

Soon, however, the preacher found himself contemptuously avoided by all the inhabitants of Little Rock, and even his own congregation deserted him! Worse than all, he was coldly dismissed by a young lady, to whom he was engaged to be married. Soured and irritated by the unjust scorn heaped upon him by his fellow-citizens, Coleman withdrew from the ministry, and, soon after, published in the Arkansas Whig, over his own signature, a most scathing article against Woods. The result was a challenge from the editor of the Democrat, who was considered the most death-dealing duelist in America. Coleman accepted the challenge, and chose pistols for the weapons. The meeting took place, about sunrise, September 8, on the shore of the river, about half a mile above Little Rock. The distance was ten paces. In those days, an Arkansas duel was almost always a public spectacle, but an unusually large concourse assembled to witness the "passage of arms" between the ex-preacher and the editorial bravo. F. Noland, the author of "Pete Whetstone," accompanied Coleman, and a prominent Democrat, named Elias Wharton, appeared as second for Woods. The signal was given, both parties fired, and Wood's bullet passed within half an inch of his adversary's head. But Coleman's ball entered his antagonist's right temple, and the much-dreaded Israel Woods dropped to the earth, a corpse.

This affair at once elevated Mr. Coleman among the "first society" of Little Rock, and he was now much more respected by the inhabitants of that enlightened place than he had been while a faithful and conscientious minister of the Gospel. He became one of the editors of the Arkansas Whig, and distinguished himself as a bitterly sarcastic writer and as an adept in the use of the pistol. Several years ago, he became one of the victims of an epidemic disease which prevailed in that neighborhood.

FREEMAN AND SMITH.

These combatants were both "Generals." They were rival candidates for office in some part of Mississippi, A. D. 1851. General Smith, it appears, wrote and published in one of the newspapers, a letter full of scurrilous accusations against General Freeman. Five shots were fired on each side, and, at the fifth discharge, General Smith was slightly wounded. The two generals then shook hands, complimented each other on the heroism which each had displayed in the battle, and mutually pledged themselves that all future disputes between them should be carried on *viva voce*, on the stump or rostrum, and not in the columns of the "rascally newspapers."

JOHN W. FROST AND THOMAS HUNT

John William Frost, a native of the State of Maine, was one of the editors of the *New Orleans Crescent*. This paper was an organ of the Whig party, and the editor, Mr. Frost, was an able and spirited writer. In 1851, the Whigs of Louisiana had a large majority in the second Congressional district, but could not agree in the selection of a candidate. Two gentlemen, Colonel T. G. Hunt and Mr. I. N. Marks were presented for the suffrages of the party. The editor of the *Crescent* espoused the cause of Mr. Marks, and assailed his rival, Col. Hunt, with considerable acrimony. Hunt challenged Frost. Both gentlemen were arrested and gave bonds to keep the peace. But from the office of the magistrate who had caused them to be arrested, they proceeded directly to a convenient spot in the neighborhood of the United States Barracks, where they made hasty preparations for battle by sending for two double-barreled guns and two gentlemen to act as seconds. The distance was forty paces. At the second fire, Mr. Frost was shot through the left breast and died within half an hour. He had a daughter, fourteen years old, who, by this sad event, was deprived of her only remaining parent, and was left among strangers without any earthly protector.

KEMBLE AND M'DOUGAL.

A duel was fought in California, A. D. 1851, by E. C. Kemble, editor of the *Alta* newspaper, and a Colonel M'Dougal. They were both arrested on the field of battle before any serious damage in person or apparel was sustained by either party

SMYTH AND THOMAS.

Mr. Smyth, whose "Christian" name (if he had one,) is not

given, was the associate editor of a newspaper published at Augusta, in the State of Georgia. In the year 1851, he fought a duel with Dr. Thomas, a South Carolinian, who wrote editorial articles, and very abusive ones it is said, for a paper which was opposed in politics to the journal with which Mr. Smyth was connected. Smyth was severely wounded at the third fire.

J. M. DANIEL AND E. W. JOHNSON.

Messrs. Daniel and Johnson were editors of political newspapers, of opposite sentiments, published at Richmond, Virginia. From violent abuse they proceeded to "villainous saltpetre." They fought in the year 1852. After an exchange of shots, the seconds interposed and the principals were persuaded to shake hands. No blood was shed in this battle. Daniel fought a duel, in 1851, with a Mr. Scott, member of the Virginia Legislature. It was the singular good fortune of this Daniel to come out of all his duels as scathless as his namesake did from the lions' den; but it is doubtful whether the good angels had any thing to do with the escape of the Virginia editor.

GILBERT AND DENVER.

Edward Gilbert was a Californian editor and an ex-member of Congress. It is said that he was the first man who ever established a public journal beyond the Rocky Mountains. General Denver was a member of the State Senate. The origin of the quarrel between these gentlemen is explained as follows:—

In 1852, the Legislature of California passed a bill to provide for sending relief to the overland emigrants who might be in a destitute condition or exposed to danger from hostile Indians. This measure was opposed by Mr. Gilbert in his editorials, and a newspaper controversy on the subject was commenced between him and General Denver. Much ill-temper was exhibited on both sides until a challenge was sent by Mr. Gilbert and accepted by the General. The parties met; Mr. Gilbert fell at the second shot, and expired in less than five minutes.

The weapons used in this duel were rifles. Mr. Gilbert was only thirty-three years of age at the time of his death

NUGENT AND HAYES.

John Nugent was editor of the *California Herald*. Hayes was an assistant alderman of San Francisco. Some editorial remarks made by Nugent, in 1852, provoked a reply from Hayes, who published a card, in the *San Francisco Whig*. The language of this card operating on the delicate sensibilities of Mr. Nugent, incited him to send a challenge to Alderman Hayes, and that excellent conservator of the peace promptly accepted the invitation. In the duel which followed, Mr. Nugent was severely wounded at the second fire.

NUGENT AND COTTER.

The hero of the preceding narrative, Mr. John Nugent, editor of the *California Herald*, though badly wounded in his fight with Alderman Hayes, was not cured of his pugnacious propensity. His wound was scarcely healed, when he was engaged in another quarrel, and (strangely enough,) with another alderman. Possibly it may have been the design of Mr. Nugent to exterminate all the supporters of law and order in California. In this instance, his antagonist was Alderman Cotter. The battle was fought in the presence of a large concourse of spectators; in order, I presume, that the example of the worthy magistrate might have its due effect on the minds and morals of the public. As soon as the parties came on the ground, and the spectators were comfortably provided with seats, the distance was measured, (ten paces,) and the pistols were placed in the hands of the combatants. Two shots on each side were fired without effect, and Mr. Nugent was about to cock his pistol for the third discharge, when the alderman being too quick for him, fired and wounded the chivalrous journalist in the left thigh. The ball produced a compound fracture, which will cause Mr. Nugent to limp through the remainder of his earthly existence. It appears that this gentleman of the press was not very popular among the Californians; for it is said that when he fell, a "yell of exultatation" arose from the crowd of spectators.

COHEN AND WINTZELL.

Mr. Cohen, editor of the *Staats Zeitung*, and Dr. Wintzel, editor of the *Deutsche Zeitung*, (both Germans,) fought a duel in Louisiana, A. D. 1853. This battle took place on *Sunday*, near the city of New Orleans. The conditions of the fight were, that the parties should draw lots for the first fire, which was to be made at the distance of fifteen paces. The man who fired was then to advance ten paces and receive the fire of his antagonist at the shortened distance. By this arrangement, the person who won the first fire was almost sure of death if he failed to shoot his antagonist at a distance which made that performance somewhat difficult. Mr. Cohen was unlucky enough to win the first fire. He fired accordingly and advanced ten paces. Wintzel raised his pistol, but lowered it again. The hope thus raised that he did not intend to fire was disappointed; for he presently raised his pistol once more, fired, and struck Cohen on the right side, just below the ribs. The wound was supposed to be mortal.

CARROLL AND BARBAGON.

E. T. Carroll, editor of the New Orleans Crescent, fought a duel with J. M. Barbagon, A. D. 1852. The weapons were rifles. After the first fire, the affair was amicably settled.

CARTER AND DE COURCEY.

Mr. H. De Courcey was editor of the *Calaveras (California,) Chronicle*. The particulars of his quarrel and combat with Mr. Carter are not on record; but, as we are told that Mr. De Courcey was shot through the body, it is probable that the wound he received was fatal.

RUST AND STIDGER.

In the year 1853, Colonel Rust, editor of the *California Express*, fought a duel with Judge Stidger, near the city of San Francisco. Stidger was slightly wounded.

REA AND EVANS.

Mr. Rea was an editor of Mississippi. Evans was a lawyer. They fought in the year 1854. At the third or fourth fire, Rea was shot through both of his thighs.

COMMENTS.

This registry might be continued to a much greater length; but the examples I have given are sufficient to show that DUELING is a common effect of newspaper licentiousness :—if it can be supposed that such an obvious truth requires any illustration whatever. In the preceding catalogue our attention has been strictly confined to those regular " affairs of honor" which are supposed to be derived from the usages of ancient chivalry, and which deserve to be classed among the savage and unreasonable practices of our benighted ancestors.

The practice of Dueling, however, with all its sinfulness, barbarism and fantastic foolery, may be called a *gentlemanly* vice ; and this circumstance, perhaps, makes it less in vogue than it otherwise would be, with our American journalists. Unmitigated ruffianism and brutality are among the most conspicuous characteristics of our newspaper press; and the quarrels and battles of editors, (as I propose to show in the the next Section), are generally conducted without any regard to the rules and principles of equitable warfare.

SECTION XVIII.

FIGHTS AND FLOGGINGS OF EDITORS.

Continued Examination of the Tenth Charge.

THE newspapers are now charged with causing many disgraceful cases of assault and battery and disturbances of the public peace. Editorial fights and floggings are matters of such frequent occurrence, that they have ceased to attract much notice, except when the circumstances attending them are particularly tragic, melo-dramatic, or farcical. It is probable that an editor is flogged, in some part of the United States, almost every day in the year; and many journalists who escape castigation certainly *deserve* it.

In the estimation of some editors, however, floggings are no misfortunes, but rather the evidences of superior merit. I have heard a newspaper conductor boastfully acknowledge that he had been the recipient of six or eight cudgellings and horse-whippings, and he thought this experience was enough to establish his reputation as a fearless and independent journalist. "An editor who never earns a flogging," said he, "must be timid and irresolute in the management of his paper."

Similar notions are attributed by Captain Marryatt to the editor of the *New York Herald*. Says the Captain :—

"He has been horse-whipped, kicked, trodden under foot, spat upon, and degraded in every possible way; but all this he courts, because it brings money. Horse-whip him, and he will bend his back to the lash and thank you; for every blow is worth so many dollars. Kick him, and he will remove his coat-tails, that you may have a better mark. Spit upon him, and he prizes it as precious ointment. On the day after the punishment, he publishes a full and particular account of how many kicks, tweaks of the nose, or lashes he may have received." *Vide Marryatt's Diary, Second Series, Collins' Phila. edition, page* 58.

The Englishman's account is somewhat aggravated perhaps; but it is very evident that the "Napoleon of the Press" does not "mistake a basting for a blemish," for in the *Herald* of January 21, or 22, 1836, Mr. Bennett publishes a circumstantial account of a drubbing which he had received on the preceding day, from Colonel James Watson Webb; and he gives the details with a self-satisfied and compendious brevity, worthy of Julius Cæsar himself.

WEBB AND BENNETT.

"While I was passing along Wall street, yesterday afternoon, at twenty-five minutes past three o'clock," (says the precise Bennett,) "I was assailed by J. Watson Webb, who came up behind me, and with an oaken cudgel cut a gash in my head, one inch and a half in length and through the integuments of the skull. The fellow, no doubt, wanted to let out the never-failing supply of wit and good humor which has created such a reputation for the *Herald*, and appropriate the contents to supply the emptiness of his own thick skull. He did not succeed, however, in rifling me of my ideas, as neither my cranium nor its enclosure sustained any serious damage. My ideas, in a few days, will flow as freshly as ever, as Webb will find to his cost."

Nearly a column of the *Herald* is occupied with Mr. Bennett's own account of the fracas, every particular of which is accurately narrated. Mr. Bennett's biographer says, with apparent glee and exultation, that nine thousand extra copies of the *Herald* were sold, merely on account of this touching narrative, and the implication is that the journalist was well remunerated for the trifling inconvenience of a broken head. It appears that Bennett provoked this assault by publishing a paragraph which charged Webb, (the editor of the Courier and Enquirer,) with lending his editorial assistance to the operations of certain stock-jobbers in Wall street.

Mr. Bennett is not one of those "cowards and poltroons," who (as Butler says,) "are satisfied with a single beating." He "dares adventure to a second," and, accordingly, he gives Col. Webb occasion for another display of his prowess, only three months after the exhibition just described. The thrilling event took place in Wall street, very near the spot where the same parties encountered each other before. It was on a fine morning in May—but let Mr. Bennett speak for himself:

"As I was leisurely pursuing my business, yesterday, in Wall street, collecting the information which is daily disseminated in the *Herald*, James Watson Webb came up to me on the northern side of the street, said something which I could not hear distinctly, then pushed me down the stone steps leading to one of the broker's offices, and commenced fighting with a species of brutal and demoniac desperation characteristic of a fury.

"My damage is a scratch, about three quarters of an inch in length, on the third finger of the left hand, which I received from the iron railing which I was forced against, and three buttons torn from my vest, which any tailor will reinstate for sixpence. His loss is a rent from top to bottom of a very beautiful black coat which cost the ruffian forty dollars, and a blow in the face which may have knocked down his throat some of his infernal teeth, for any thing that I know to the contrary. Balance in my favor, $39.94." *Vide New York Herald, May* 10, 1836.

INJUSTICE TO GREELEY.

Besides his two rencounters with Colonel Webb, the editor of the *New York Herald* has been the passive hero of several other engagements, which his too negligent biographer appears to have overlooked.

It is a notable circumstance that the principal editor of the *New York Tribune* has received but *one* flogging! Certainly he has met with great injustice, in this particular, if we admit the truth of the hypothesis that frequent castigations are the best proofs of an editor's courage and independence. In his writings, Greeley is brave and independent enough, and I question whether Bennett himself could be more resolute or reckless in giving offense.

COLONEL WEBB AND DUFF GREEN.

Colonel James Watson Webb, the famous editor of the New York *Courier and Enquirer*, is the hero of many fights; and his valor and prowess have been so often crowned with success that his brows may be said to resemble a whole forest of laurels. If Bennett is the "Napoleon of the Press," Webb may be called the *Wellington* of journalism; though his conquest of the imperial Scotchman is not, by any means, his most signal triumph.

One of Colonel Webb's most extraordinary feats of heroism was his attempt to chastise General Duff Green; for Duff Green himself was a man of warlike note, and had been victorious in several contests with other gentlemen of the press. Conquering *him*, therefore, would have been as glorious an achievement as the victory of Ivanhoe over Brian de Bois Guilbert.

The quarrel between Messrs. Webb and Green originated in the violence of political debate. In May, 1830, Colonel Webb went to Washington for the express and avowed purpose of inflicting corporal punishment on General Green; having declared his vindictive purpose, in the columns of the *Courier and Enquirer*, just before his departure from New York. On his arrival at the national metropolis, he met Duff Green in the Rotunda of the Capitol, and was about to begin the operation of *caning*, when Duff Green drew a pistol, and seriously advised Colonel Webb to abandon his project. The Colonel was rational enough to accept this wholesome advice; and, after making an accurate survey of General Green and his pistol, he sat out on his return to New York.

The intrepidity of Colonel Webb throughout the whole of

this trying affair was proved afterward by the calm and business-like manner in which he described, in an editorial article, his interview with General Green. He appears to have been so much at his ease, at the time when Duff Green held him at bay by presenting the pistol, that he was able to observe, and afterward to describe, with the greatest precision, all the peculiarities of the little instrument. From the Colonel's account, it appeared that the stock of the pistol was made of mahogany, the length of the barrel was eight inches, the percussion lock was of fine steel with a slight blue tinge, and the mountings were of brass, fastened on with screws of the same metal. I afterward learned from General Green that every item of Colonel Webb's description was perfectly correct.

DWYER AND LASETER.

The soldier-like coolness and composure displayed by Colonel Webb on the occasion just referred to are scarcely more admirable than the perspicuous and impartial account which another gentleman of the press, Joseph H. Dwyer by name, gives of a disastrous battle in which he was lately engaged. Mr. Dwyer is the editor of a paper published at Portland, Oregon, and his antagonist, Mr. Laseter, is a member of the Legislature of that State. I hope my readers will not smile at the minute details given by Mr. Dwyer, albeit his constant preservation of the editorial plurality *is* somewhat ludicrous. He says:

" Laseter repeated and *re-repeated* that we were a liar and a blackguard, whereupon we did take our inkstand from our desk and hurled it in his face, intending it as a rebuke of his gross insults. Respecting the fight which immediately ensued, we may say that Laseter did not injure us much at the time, and did not gather many laurels.

" More than half an hour had intervened when, as we were quietly passing down the principal street, we were met by Laseter, who seized us by the throat, at the same time planting a heavy blow upon our forehead, and rushed us into the door of a store, where we both fell upon some open shoe boxes, Laseter on top, still grasping our throat. After a few blows, he inserted the thumb of his right hand into our socket. At this time, by a desperate or superhuman effort, we released his grasp from our throat and his thumb from our eye, and fell flat upon the floor.

"Laseter then seized us by the hair and attempted to gouge out our other eye, which we prevented by turning our face close to the floor, and locking our fingers and pressing our hands close to our eyes. After several fruitless efforts to insert his thumb in our right eye, he commenced pounding us on the head with his fist. While this was going on, a large crowd of cowardly ruffians and dogs gathered around and prevented our friends from rendering us any assistance.

"When we supposed that he might be satisfied with the beating he had given us, we requested that he might be taken off; which was done, as we learn, by those kind and humane hands which had kept our friends from interfering, and who supposed, no doubt, that one or both of our eyes had been gouged out of their sockets, and that ample justice had been done to gratify their revenge."

CASE OF P. G. FERGUSON.

P. G. Ferguson, an Irishman, was one of the editors of the St. Louis Herald. In June, 1855, he published a scandalous poem, or piece of doggerel, which was very insulting to the family of Mr. William Bennett, a respectable merchant of St. Louis. Bennett gave Ferguson a severe horsewhipping, and promised to repeat the punishment unless Ferguson should make a sufficient retraction and apology in the next number of his *Herald.* On Sunday, July 1, Ferguson published the following "card" in the St. Louis Republican:

"I hereby certify that Mr. William Bennett called on us and demanded a retraction of the article headed 'High Life in St. Louis,' which retraction I promised to make in the *Herald* of this morning. I did give the retraction in my daily, but, by an oversight on my part, it did not appear in the Sunday Herald, which was contrary to my intention, and my promise to Mr. Bennett was thereby violated.

"I am the author of the poem which gave Mr. Bennett offense; and, not knowing the NERVE of the party alluded to, I now see that I have presumed too much. There was not the least truth in my allusions, and my sole object was to promote the sale of my paper. Therefore I hereby retract the offensive allusions and pledge myself that, hereafter, nothing shall appear in the *Herald* derogatory to the private character of any citizen of St. Louis. This statement I make in justice to Mr. Bennett and from the fear of consequences, and as I know him to be a man who will do all that he has promised, I hereby retract what I admit to be an attempt at slander. I pledge myself further that this shall be published in my next daily, and in the next Sunday Herald.

"P. G. FERGUSON.

"P. S. Mr. Bennett called on me at my room, to-day, at 10 o'clock, P. M., and assured me that he came to give me a *cowhiding*. I have begged that he would not do it, though I admit that I am deserving of even more, as I have assailed his family without cause, willfully and maliciously. P. G. F."

"HUMILIATION OF THE PRESS."

Under this head, the *St. Louis Republican* of July 3, 1855, made the following remarks with reference to the case of Ferguson:

"We publish, to-day, a card which shows, in a two-fold aspect, the humiliation of the press; first, in the spectacle which it presents; and, secondly, in the gross outrage on all decency which made such an apology necessary.

"The family so grossly slandered is known far and near as one of the most hospitable in our city, with ample means to entertain, with warm hearts and kind regards for those who are numbered among their friends, with more than the usual desire to make the sojourn of strangers in our city agreeable and pleasant. Their house has been open on many occasions during the year; but not on these occasions alone have they been conspicuous. Whenever relief has been wanting for the poor and unfortunate, whenever influence and exertions were called into requisition, we have always heard them spoken of as most reliable in such times of pressing need.

"The press has sunk low indeed, it has become degraded and aggressive beyond all forbearance, when, for the avowed profit of a few dollars, the good name of a whole family can be assailed, and upon no other ground but that which has been mentioned. We confess the abasement which we feel at the degradation of the press, as exhibited in this instance; and hope never to see another such example of newspaper prostitution."

A FEMALE AVENGER.

A newspaper paragraph published in January, 1859, says: "There was a great excitement at Omaha, Nebraska, on the 12th instant, occasioned by the wife of Mr. William G. Brown cowhiding the editor of the *Nebraskian* in the post-office. The sufferer had published something offensive to Mrs. Brown; and it was generally admitted that she gave him less than he deserved."

Other American ladies have punished editors in a similar manner for offenses of the same kind.

MRS. LYONS AND HENRY FROST.

In September, 1858, Mrs. Lyons, the wife of a lawyer of Cincinnati, cowhided Henry Frost, the publisher of a weekly paper called the "Town Talk." The husband of Mrs. Lyons had entered a complaint against Frost for the publication of a libel, which was probably directed against Mrs. Lyons. The magistrate who heard the charge was afraid of the influence of the press, perhaps, and refused to hold Frost to bail. Rejoicing at his lucky escape, Mr. Frost, after being discharged, was leaving the magistrate's office, when he was encountered by Mrs. Lyons at the door and received thirty or forty lashes before he recovered enough self-possession to make a hasty retreat.

FRIGHTFUL MORTALITY.

Five editors of the *Vicksburg Sentinel* were killed, in street fights, within ten years. For a time, shooting editors seemed to be the favorite amusement of the Mississippians. Recently, however, these people have become less wasteful of their ammunition, and find it more economical and convenient to *flog* their journalists, when some kind of discipline is necessary.

PRENTICE AND DURRETT.

In the summer of 1857, George D. Prentice, the brave and witty editor of the Louisville Journal, with or without "poetical justice," made an assault on Mr. R. T. Durrett of the Louisville Courier. Prentice pursued Durrett three or four times around a grocery and liquor store, (reminding the classical spectators of that strange event recorded in the Iliad, the chase of Hector by Achilles,) when Durrett, as a last refuge, ran up an alley and into a back yard surrounded by a board fence eight or ten feet high. Finding himself still closely pursued by the swift-footed Prentice, the desperate fugitive made a flying leap and passed over the fence without touching it. This was mentioned in the Louisville papers as a serious fact, and it was added that a more extraordinary leap was never witnessed in that part of the country. One account states that Prentice fired a pistol at Durrett while the latter was soaring over the wood-work, but, (not being accustomed to shoot at game on the wing,) he did not succeed in hitting him.

The cause of the quarrel between these Kentucky editors is not mentioned.

REED AND WALKER.

Judge Walker was editor of the Cincinnati *Commercial*. Mr. Henry Reed was one of the editors of the *Enquirer*, of the same city. These gentlemen, it is said, abused each other very severely in their editorial columns. In August, 1857, they met in the street, and Walker gave Reed an inconsiderable caning. Some days after this interview they met again, and Reed, at this time, being provided with a large pistol, presented it at Walker, merely to frighten him, as we may suppose, for no attempt was made to fire the weapon. Walker knocked Reed down with his fist; and this is the last account we have of the doings of these belligerents.

KATE HASTINGS AND NED BUNTLINE.

Several years ago, a celebrated lady of Nashville, called Kate Hastings, attempted to inflict personal chastisement on that gifted gentleman who uses the *nom de plume* of Ned Buntline. She did not quite succeed in her undertaking, for Ned evaded the instrument of correction by taking refuge in a bar-room. Buntline is a remarkably bold editor, and he has made some extraordinary escapes. It is reported that he was once actually *hanged* by an infuriated mob; but his better destiny prevailed, and he was cut down in time to preserve his valuable life. At another time, when pursued by an incensed crowd, he saved himself by leaping out of a third-story window, nearly thirty feet from the ground. I do not doubt that a history of this gentleman's life would be as interesting to the public in general as the thrilling adventures of Othello were to the fair Venitian.

BLAIR AND PICKERING.

Loring Pickering, editor of the *St. Louis Union*, in November, 1849, published some articles which gave great offense to his fellow-citizen, Judge Blair. Soon after, these gentlemen met in the street, and the Judge, poising his umbrella, ran the sharp end of it into Pickering's eye. In answer to this civility, Pickering drew a pistol and shot the Judge in the leg. The event of this battle, on the Judge's part, was very unfortunate, for his wounded limb proved unserviceable to the end of his life.

HARNEY AND HALDEMAN.

In April, 1846, Colonel Harney, editor of the *Louisville Democrat*, undertook to beat Mr. W. N. Haldeman, editor of the *Louisville Courier*. Haldeman was coming out of a confectioner's shop, eating a piece of *gingerbread*, when Harney sprang upon him, and clasped him in a rude embrace, which pinioned both of his arms close to his sides.

> "Now brave Kentuckian, hold thine own,
> No maiden's arms are round thee thrown;
> That desperate grasp thy frame might feel,
> Through bars of brass and triple steel.
> They tug, they strain; down, down they go,—
> Harney above, Hald'man below."

This poetical description is literally correct—(may the spirit of Scott pardon me for the slight alteration I have made in his verses,)—both gentlemen rolled on the ground, raising a cloud of dust, and attracting a crowd of spectators. "Mr. Haldeman," says the newspaper account, "made a snap at Colonel Harney's nose, got it between his teeth, and held it fast until the Colonel hallooed 'Enough!' The city marshal then came up and parted them."

FORREST AND WILLIS.

Edwin Forrest, the tragedian, made an assault on Nathaniel P. Willis, a popular American poet, and editor of the *Home Journal*. This rencounter took place in the Park, at New York, in May, 1851. Willis gave the provocation by publishing some remarks in the *Home Journal*, alluding to the divorce case which was then pending between Mr. Forrest and his wife. When the gentlemen met in the Park, Forrest knocked Willis down, and struck him several times with a small cane or whip. Willis sued for damages, and recovered $2,500.

PROBLEM.

"Why is there less flogging of editors in Boston, New York,

and Philadelphia, than in some other parts of the country?" This question will admit of two answers, only one of which is true. Some of my newspaper neighbors *have* answered the question by asserting that the tone of the press in the Atlantic cities has been improved; that the editors of those cities have become more courteous, dignified, etc.; and that, as a matter of course, they give less provocation and seldom *deserve* flogging."

Ah! well, this is one answer to the query; now let us have the other. The flogging of editors may happen to be less in fashion, or more inconvenient, in one place than in another. Here, in Philadelphia, for example, the popular sentiment is opposed to violence, owing in a measure, perhaps, to a small remnant of Quakerism, which still exists in the moral constitution of our city. There are *various* mollifying influences which dispose the people of the Atlantic cities to be patient under great provocations, and even to tolerate some of the worst offenses of journalism.

THE PRESS OF PHILADELPHIA.

Some years ago, there was a journalist in Philadelphia, namely Mr. John S. Du Solle, who was assaulted twice at least; once by a physician, at the door of a theatre, and once by a dry-goods store-keeper, in an oyster-cellar. I do not know why Mr. Du Solle was thus distinguished. Certain I am that he gave less provocation than some other gentlemen attached to the daily press of this city. The Philadelphia editors boast of their superior courtesy. Do they really believe that they are the Chesterfields of journalism? I could give them some choice extracts from their own columns to convince them that very few of them have learned even the rudiments of politeness or common decency. But that is not my business at present. I am speaking of editors who have *received* castigation not of those who deserve it.

A NARROW ESCAPE.

Some years ago, I happened, on a certain bright summer's day, to enter an editorial *sanctum* in Philadelphia. The principal editor was engaged in conversation with another person, a visitor, who had come unmistakably for the purpose of applying an ominous-looking instrument which he held in his hand to the back of the trembling journalist, whose appearance and behavior were so abject that I could scarcely persuade myself to say a word in his behalf. However, I did succeed in recommending him to mercy; and, in less than six months after that event, I had my reward in the shape of a spiteful newspaper attack written by that very editor

A BESIEGED JOURNALIST.

Some twenty-five or thirty years ago, a paper called "The Weekly Observer," was published in Baltimore. The editor of this sheet was so exceedingly "free and independent," that, on every Saturday afternoon, as soon as his paper made its appearance, he was sure to receive one flogging at least, and sometimes as many as two or three castigations in one day. He found it necessary, at last, to have a high fence or barricade built across his publication-office, to protect himself from the invasion of his enemies. Behind this barricade he fixed his editorial chair and no visitor was admitted, on any pretense, within that sacred enclosure. One day a stout gentleman, who had " particular business with the editor," called at the office and finding the journalist inaccessible, requested him to "come out and be flogged." This Mr. Editor ungraciously refused to do, and his guest, taking a seat, declared his determination to wait for an opportunity to execute his design, if he remained there two weeks. Meanwhile the journalist sat at his table, writing spicy editorials, and seeming to be oblivious of his friend on the other side of the barricade. Night came, the editor lighted his lamp and proceeded with his "arduous duties." At last, seeming to recollect himself suddenly, he arose, and throwing two or three cigars over the fence, desired the visitor to "take a smoke and make himself comfortable."

This hospitable behavior seemed to change the avenger's purpose, for he started up from his chair, and after pronouncing some maledictions, to which the editor was well accustomed, he raised the siege and departed.

RICKETTS AND FORWARD.

Mr. Ricketts was the publisher of a Democratic paper in Elkton, Cecil County, Md. Mr. Forward was a young lawyer, and wrote editorial articles for the Whig paper, in the same town. Some time in 1854, Ricketts published an article which Forward construed as a personal insult to himself. He attempted, therefore, to inflict corporal punishment on Ricketts, but the latter being provided with one of Colt's "revolvers," fired several times at his assailant. and inflicted two or three wounds, each of which by itself would have been mortal. Forward died about twenty-four hours after the rencounter.

BEAUMONT AND POINDEXTER.

Mr. Beaumont is the editor of the Nashville Banner, a "Republican" organ. Mr. Poindexter is the editorial manager of a "Democratic" paper published in the same city. About ten days ago, Mr. Beaumont, in an editorial article, used the word "traitor" in a way which gave offense to Mr. Poindexter. Since that time, no less that *three* street fights have been enacted by these gentlemen.

Battle I.—Mr. Poindexter, meeting Mr. Beaumont, charged him with falsehood. Mr. B. asked Mr. P. if he were prepared to defend himself at that moment. Mr. P. answered affirmatively. Mr. B. then struck Mr. P. A scuffle ensued—both parties fell. Mr. Beaumont overpowered Mr. Poindexter, and was in the act of inflicting blows, when he was pulled off and the parties were separated.

Battle II.—This battle must have been fought in some place where there was "a cane-seat chair," for we read that, after an angry altercation, Mr. Beaumont seized a chair of that kind and made a blow at Mr. Poindexter. Mr. P. drew a pistol and attempted to fire, but failed. Mr. B. "seized and turned him," when some person who was present took away Mr. P.'s pistol. Mr. Beaumont struck him several times, and was again pulled off.

Battle III.—" Subsequently, (says the newspaper narrative,) both parties met on Cedar street, in front of the Capitol. Mr. Beaumont approached Mr. Poindexter from Vine street, the latter sitting near the steps leading to the Capitol grounds. As soon as a mutual recognition took place, both parties approached to within about thirty steps of each other. Mr. Beaumont requested Mr. Poindexter to change his position so as to get out of range of some laborers working in his rear which request he complied with.

The parties continued to approach, until they were within about fifteen steps of each other, when they halted, and the firing commenced. They exchanged three shots apiece, almost simultaneously. The second shot from Mr. P. took effect in the calf of the leg of Mr. B., inflicting a slight and simple flesh wound. After the third shot Mr. B. attempted to advance, when his leg gave way, and he sank into a reclining position. The firing immediately ceased. Mr. P. laid down his weapons and approached Mr. B., shook his hand, expressed his regret for the whole occurrence, and his pleasure that it was no worse, and thus the affair ended."

NOTE.

In my Tenth Charge it is asserted that the mismanagement of the newspaper-press often excites ruffianly persons to acts of violence, and causes many disgraceful cases of assault and battery; I have given you a few instances, (but quite enough I hope for the purpose,) carefully avoiding those cases which I deemed too brutal, horrifying and disgusting to be introduced to the notice of a civilized public. Few events connected with the history of journalism are of more frequent occurrence than the castigations of editors.

SECTION XIX.

AMERICAN INTELLECT DISGRACED BY THE NEWSPAPERS.

Examination of the Eleventh and Twelfth Charges.

It is possible for people to suffer for want of water where water is most abundant; namely, on the bosom of the wide ocean. In like manner, we may suffer for the want of information where the groaning press throws forth its sheets by millions. The mass of our literature is not more suitable for mental improvement than sea-water is for drinking. Its *abundance*, therefore, is no blessing; but, on the contrary, a very great disadvantage; for it is that very abundance which, (like the multitudinous waters of the ocean,) is the isolating and insurmountable barrier which makes our situation most distressing. We have *too much* literature of the WRONG KIND; and the consequence is that we can have none of that kind that is most needful.

OUR INTELLECTUAL REPUTATION.

Will my countrymen pardon me for disclosing a fact which, if generally understood, might tend, in some measure, to clip the plumes of our national vanity? Consider what motives induce me to make the disclosure. Like all other Americans, I have a sensitive regard for the reputation of my country. I earnestly desire that our Republic should be respectable in the eyes of all the world. I know that it is *entitled* to the respect of mankind in general, and I know that the only reasons why it is *not* respected, is because some of our national characteristics have been grossly misrepresented, and because the powers of American intellect are strangely diminished, in appearance, by the peculiarities of our national literature.

The unpleasant secret to be disclosed is this:—our INTELLECTUAL REPUTATION abroad is, (to use the phraseology of the stock-market,) quoted at a very low figure. It is decidedly below par; or, to be still more precise, it is rated at a discount of about seventy-five per cent., supposing the intellectuality of Europe to be the integral standard.

To show you what reports of our intellectual condition they make in the "old world," I quote a few passages from a British periodical of lofty pretensions and high authority; and you may venture to believe that these extracts express opinions which are very generally entertained in Europe:—

"The American," says the *Foreign Quarterly Review*, "is horn-handed and pig-headed—hard, persevering, unscrupulous, carnivorous, ready for all weathers, with an incredible genius for lying, a vanity elastic beyond comprehension, the hide of a buffalo and the shriek of a steam-engine. He is a regular 'seven-foot fellow, steel-twisted and made of horse-shoe nails, the rest of him being cast-iron with steel springs.' Can anybody imagine that *literature* or *intellect* could be nourished in a frame like this?"

"Whenever men of more than ordinary intellect have risen in America," (says the same authority,) "they have adapted themselves to the over-ruling exigencies in which they found themselves placed. Instead of venturing on the dangerous experiment of endeavoring to elevate their countrymen to their own height, they have sunk into the arms of the mob. Hence the judges on the bench constantly give way to popular clamor, and law itself is abrogated by the law-makers and constantly violated by its functionaries. Hence the ascendancy of Lynch-law over State law; hence assassination in the day-light in the thronged street; and hence that intimidation from without which make legislation itself a farce. The ablest men in America have bowed down before these demoralizing necessities. No man in America stands clear of this rotten despotism. The orator is compelled to address himself to the low standard of the populace; he must strew his speech with flowers of Billingsgate, with hyperbolical expletives and a garnish of falsehood, to make it effective and rescue it from the chance of being serious, intellectual, or refined. The preacher must preach down to the capacities of his congregation, or look elsewhere for bread and devotion. The newspaper editor must make his journal infamous and obscene, if he would have it popular; for never let it be supposed that the degradation of the American press is the work of the writers in it, but of the frightful eagerness of the public appetite for grossness and indecency."—*Vide Foreign Quarterly Review*, No. LXIV.—*Leading Article.*

IS IT TRUE?

The general estimation of American intellect among Europeans is nearly in accordance with the views expressed by this severe critic. The assertions of the British writer are not absolutely false, nor altogether true. In describing *effects*, he is generally correct; but I think it will appear that in his search after *causes*, he is not entirely successful.

It is true that there is such a thing as an UNINTELLECTUAL DESPOTISM in America; but that is not the despotism of the people, (as the reviewer surmises,) but a despotism of the Press. It is true that "Lynch-law is ascendant over State law, and that intimidation from without makes legislation itself a farce." I have asserted the same things in this book, and I have endeavored to show that the American *people* are not chargeable with these deplorable effects; or that they are chargeable only so far as they have it in their power to *prevent* these abuses, and still permit them to be continued.

The reviewer is mistaken in supposing that American orators are obliged to descend to a very low intellectual plane to meet the requirements of their auditories. The most *popular* orator in this country is Edward Everett; and it is doubtful whether intellectual England herself can exhibit his superior. It is true, (as the reviewer intimates,) that some of our most celebrated, or notorious, public journals are infamous and obscene. But it is not true that there is an absolute necessity for editors to be puerile, or depraved, or vicious, or profane, in order that they may be supported. Where is there a more irreproachable newspaper in the world than the New York *Journal of Commerce?* And yet that paper is well sustained, albeit it is published in a city whose moral reputation is inferior to that of the American people in general. There are a few other newspapers in various parts of this country, which, on the moral or intellectual scale, will bear comparison with some of the best publications of Europe; and deserving newspapers sometimes meet with very good encouragement in America. It is admitted that our newspaper press in general is unwise and vicious, and that some of our most successful journals are *particularly* worthless and degraded; but I do not believe that the American public is stupid, silly and vile enough to insist on having its journalism of this character.

DEBASED LITERATURE.

It is obviously true that "the intellectual character of the American people is much less respectable than it deserves to be in the eyes of other nations." Nothing else could be expected, when it is understood that our intellectuality is estimated abroad by the quality of our literature and the characterestics of our journalism.

I confess, with shame and sorrow, that the literature of America is *not intellectual.* Our own countryman, Dr. Channing, discourses feelingly and truthfully on this subject: "Do we possess," he asks, "what may be called a national literature? Have we produced eminent writers in the various departments of intellectual effort? Are our chief sources of instruction and literary enjoyment furnished from ourselves? We regret that the reply to these questions is so obvious. The few standard works which we have produced, and which promise to live, can hardly, by any courtesy, be denominated a national literature."

A candid writer in one of the Philadelphia papers, speaks as follows: "For twenty years past, it appears to have been the earnest endeavor of both publishers and newspapers to annihilate the literature of our country; and they have pursued the very best course for the attainment of that object. The Sangrado system of practice has been applied to our national literature, which our American critics themselves admit to be in a sickly condition. The patient was first reduced to the lowest stage of existence by starvation; then bled by the thriving publishers, who, vampire-like, have drawn all the vitality from the attenuated carcass; and, finally, floods of nauseating trash, which may be likened to luke-warm water, are poured into the suffering invalid, to make recovery from its debilitated condition, utterly hopeless."

A lately-published catalogue of the "New York Publishers' Association" contained a list of twenty-four different biographies of notorious highwaymen, burglars, and pickpockets, and fourteen stories of "New York Life," or that phase of it which is seen at the Five Points, and other resorts of prostitution and infamy. These are called "the most salable books in the market," and that fact appears to be the only one which the conscientious publishers regard as worthy of their consideration.

From these facts and opinions, we may judge what are the peculiarities of our literature in the mass; and is it strange that the people of other lands, when they examine what is supposed to be our favorite reading, should entertain very unfavorable notions of our morals and intellect both?

UNHOLY LEAGUE.

In one of the preceding extracts, it is truly intimated that the efforts of certain classes of book-publishers and journalists are well calculated "to annihilate the literature of our country." At all events, it seems to be their earnest desire to make our literature contemptible and mischievous.

We have ascertained that "the newspaper press of our country is colleagued with every form of villainy and imposture." The book-selling trade, as it is sometimes conducted, is a vile imposition; and the natural law of affinity brings the scoundrels of the book-business into close connection with the rascals of journalism. The union is confirmed by ties of mutual interest, and it is to this pernicious combination that we are indebted for the utter abasement of our national literature.

The newspapers obviously endeavor to cultivate a popular taste for the lightest or most frivolous kind of reading. Their best advertising customers in the book-trade are the publishers of pamphlet novels, etc.; and of course, these are the works which are most cordially recommended to public favor. The flimsiest kind of magazine literature, for similar reasons, is blessed with the warm approbation of journalism, and the consequence is that no periodical of a very high intellectual order has ever been permanently established in the United States. The more worthless a magazine is, the more certificates of merit it is sure to receive from the newspaper press. Thus the Fashion-plate magazines of Philadelphia have been more strongly "puffed" than any other monthly publications in America. I have known *Graham's Magazine* to be styled the "organ of American intellect," and Peterson's "the best periodical in the world!" In short, the most brainless productions of authorship and the most trashy issues of the periodical press are the particular objects of editorial regard, and thus, by newspaper influence and exertion, the most despicable literary productions of America are made the most popular.

The dealers in "Gallows Literature," (as it has very properly been called,) are most solicitous for newspaper favor, and they invariably obtain the largest share of it. The connection of these conscienceless men with the newspaper press is sometimes very intimate indeed; in fact, the duties of the editorial desk are occasionally undertaken by these gentlemen themselves. Sometimes their brothers, cousins, uncles, or nephews, are employed as sub-editors; and as they work in the dark, (or anonymously,) they are enabled to do their relations good service by extravagantly "puffing" every book that comes from their family manufactory. The bookseller is often assisted by his editorial ally in another manner. If he happen to have a successful competitor, who ought to be "put down," or "starved out of the city," (to use a phrase of frequent recurrence in Philadelphia,) the friendly sub-editor can accomplish that object, perhaps, by charging the "unloved-one" with swindling, highway robbery, or some other serious offense.

But many of the tricks of the bookselling trade are indescribable, and some of the assistance rendered by the editors is of such a nature that the public would be more shocked than edified by any description I could give of it. Suffice it to say, that the efforts of these confederated rogues have given currency and popularity to those literary productions which exceedingly disgrace the intellectual character of our country.

AMERICANS GROSSLY MISREPRESENTED.

The foreign scribblers, who have the chief management of our journalistic machinery, have gone still further in their efforts to discredit American intellect and morality. It is from THEM that the editors of the *Quarterly Review* learned that "the degradation of the American press is not the work of those who write for it, but of the frightful eagerness of the public appetite for grossness and indecency!" The Satanic journals of New York and Philadelphia have often made similar assertions, and the *Reviewer* quotes one of our own poets, (some newspaper editor, undoubtedly,) to confirm his scorching imputation:

> "Not theirs the blame who furnish forth the treat,
> But ours who throng the board and grossly eat."

As the distich is not very good English, it is possible that it may be Scotch; and perhaps Bennett of the New York *Herald*, or Mackenzie, the sub-editor of Forney's Philadelphia *Press*, is the author. I hope the British reviewer is mistaken in calling it the production of an *American* poet, for the lines transgress, even beyond the limits of poetical license, by asserting a falsehood, which is more derogatory to our national character than any thing which has ever been uttered by our trans-Atlantic detractors.

If the American newspaper press is just such a press as Americans require, we are indeed a nation of blockheads and blackguards, and the people of Europe are justified in speaking of our morals, manners, and intellect in a tone of contemptuous pity. But I assert that there is a misunderstanding in this matter. Our tastes and morals have been misrepresented, and our intellectual reputation has been most vilely and falsely aspersed.

WHO ARE OUR SLANDERERS?

Our Satanic Journalists, to excuse their own obscenity, malice, profanity, and stupidity, pretend that they are *compelled*, (in opposition to their own nature and inclination,) to make their papers what they are, in order that they may suit the tastes and requirements of the American public!

Thus the New York *Tribune*, when it publishes "full and faithful" reports of a brutal prize fight, or copious details of a foul adultery case, does it merely to accommodate its expectant readers, who would be quite dissatisfied and indignant if a single item of this useful intelligence were omitted. Every "fact" requires publicity, and the more shocking and disgusting a fact is, the more completely and circumstantially it should be exposed to public observation! This idea reminds me of a joke of Voltaire, which, unhappily, cannot be translated into plain English. The *Tribune* has some thousands of readers, and it infers from this circumstance that its editoral management meets with the entire approbation of the public in general!

A Boston paper endorses the following sentiment from Massey's History of England: "To say that the press was, in these days, chiefly sustained by libel, is merely to repeat that the taste of society was depraved. Slander and satire being called for, are produced as readily as low dresses and short peticoats are produced when called for by the arbiters of mantua-making.

To praise or blame the morality or immorality of journalists, therefore, is to fall into the common error of mistaking effect for cause!

The "New York Journalist" who wrote the biography of James Gordon Bennett, says, in reference to the New York *Herald*, "it was made to *suit the public*, and the public would not support a paper of much loftier tone. The *Herald* was never written up to the capacity of Mr. Bennett, but quite up to the demands of its readers."

This is the common pretense of imbecile and diabolical journalism; it is "just what the American public wants, and it could not possibly be any thing better." The press of Europe accepts the explanation,—the vapid and vile character of our newspapers is accounted for, our journalists themselves are excused,—and the American people are incontinently damned for their gross, depraved, and beastly appetites, and for their inability to appreciate any thing noble, elevated, refined, or intellectual.

THE CHARGE.

In my Eleventh Charge, it is asserted that "the Newspaper Press of this country debases the national literature, and makes the intellectual character of the American people much less respectable than it deserves to be in the eyes of other nations."

The facts, I presume, are incontrovertible, except the single circumstance implied in the charge, that we Americans *deserve* a higher intellectual reputation than our newspaper editors will allow us to possess. I admit that certain indications may, with some appearance of reason and justice, be construed as evidences of a low condition of intellectual development in the United States. For example, if it should clearly appear that our newspaper press is precisely what we require, it would be in vain for the Yankee Nation to make any pretensions to superior intelligence. But I positively deny that my countrymen, in general, have more natural taste than the Europeans themselves for vicious, corrupt, and stupid journalism. Much of the relish for this kind of stuff which exists in America is *acquired*, like the relish for coffee, tobacco, claret, brandy, and other articles, which are never palatable when first tasted, but which habit may make agreeable and almost necessary.

Besides, the vicious and mischievous journals which have acquired a large circulation in this country are not patronized chiefly on account of their vices and imperfections, but rather on account of some virtues, or GOOD qualities, which they are *supposed* to possess.

It is strange, but true, that the large circulation of an American newspaper is no proof of its popularity. I suspect that the Philadelphia ———— is the most *unpopular* newspaper in the United States, and yet it is one of our most widely-circulated dailies. People buy it and read it, or read a part of it, because it is cheap, or because its reports of news are tolerably complete, or because it is the advertising sheet in which situations for cooks, hostlers, and wet-nurses are registered, and rewards are offered for the recovery of stray poodles and runaway apprentices. Its readers may even adopt some of its opinions; but on the whole, it is, (as I have said above,) extremely unpopular; and yet I can scarcely believe that it is so because its moral or intellectual tone is too high for public appreciation.

The New York Herald is presumed to be a good NEWSPAPER; and it is extensively patronized on *that* account, I suppose, and not because its editorial articles are sometimes abusive, indecent, or blasphemous. In short, it does not appear that any worthless or mischievous journal in the United States is acceptable with the public merely because it deals largely in obscenity, slander, and the various indecencies and immoralities which characterize American journalism.

I contend, therefore, that when certain editors apologize for their foolish and blackguard conduct by asserting that the American public compels or requires them to act as they do, they grossly slander my countrymen, and "make the intellectual character of Americans less respectable than it deserves to be in the eyes of the world."

THE TWELFTH CHARGE.

The close connection between the Eleventh and Twelfth Charges will be apparent to the reader. On account of that connection, and to economize space, I have undertaken to discuss these two Charges together. In the Twelfth Charge it is alleged that "the newspaper press of America checks the diffusion of useful knowledge among the people by withdrawing the attention of the reading public from useful, salutary, and legitimate objects of study." Owing to the exertions of the Press Gang, the reading of the American people at large is confined almost exclusively to newspapers, magazines of *very* light literature and nonsensical romances, none of which are "useful, salutary, and legitimate objects of study." As the newspapers cause the attention of the public to be absorbed in this kind of reading, to the exclusion of every thing else, it is very evident that the fountains of useful knowledge are virtually shut up, and genuine information cannot be much more generally diffused than it was before the art of printing was invented. Hence the newspaper, magazine, and novel-reading population of America is *not* well informed. The ignorance of the masses is shown by various significant indications, some of which I have pointed out in this volume. And I hold that it is impossible for the people to be well instructed while they have no better teachers than novel writers, periodicalists, and daily or weekly newsmongers, who will not permit their pupils to learn any thing which is not taught in their own academy.

SUPPLEMENTARY ILLUSTRATIONS.

THE SONNTAG NARRATIVE.—In the winter of 1856, a bookseller of Philadelphia brought to me a certain manuscript which purported to be "A *Narrative of the Grinnell Exploring Expedition,* written by August Von Sonntag, Astronomer to that Expedition." The bookseller informed me that he had purchased this manuscript from Mr. Sonntag's wife; that Mr. Sonntag was then traveling in South America; and that he left the papers with Mrs. Sonntag with a request that she would sell them to provide herself with the means of subsistence. I was told, likewise, that after the bookseller had bought the Narrative, he discovered that it was written in such "bad English," that it was impossible to publish it without having it rewritten or translated into some intelligible language. At the request of the bookseller, I prepared the papers for publication, by making such corrections as I thought were necessary. While I was engaged in this labor, I discovered that some person had undertaken the same task before; and that, apparently, he had abandoned the undertaking in despair. This person had made some improvements on Sonntag's work, by giving much better descriptions of Arctic scenery, etc., and I was induced to adopt these improvements, having some reason to believe that one of Sonntag's fellow-voyagers had made the additions, at Sonntag's request.

I flattered myself that the work I undertook would be beneficial and satisfactory to all parties concerned. I supposed that Sonntag himself would rather have his narrative published in English, than in a strange and uncouth mixture of English and German. I was informed that Mrs. Sonntag had agreed to have the manuscript corrected and prepared for the press. The bookseller was anxious to have this work done, and I could not imagine that any other person in the world had any right or reason to trouble himself about the matter.

However, soon after the book was published, it was assailed in the most violent manner by several newspapers in Philadelphia. It was called a spurious production, an "ingenious literary forgery!" Sonntag, (it was affirmed,) had never written any work of the kind. The book was all "fiction and falsehood." The publisher obtained a certificate from the Messrs. Harpers of New York, showing that Sonntag *had* written such a book, and that he had offered the narrative for publication in their Magazine. Messrs. Harper had seen the manuscript, handled it, and returned it to Sonntag because it was "unfit for publication." Mrs. Sonntag likewise made oath that she had sold the manuscript to the bookseller. Harpers' certificate and Mrs. Sonntag's affidavit were published in the Ledger and some other papers, but this evidence produced no effect whatever. It was still proclaimed by several daily papers that the book was spurious. This charge was copied from one paper to another, and circulated through the whole country.

In the meanwhile, the book had begun to sell rapidly, as it was the *cheapest* narrative of Dr. Kane's expedition that had been published. It was retailed at 50 cents per copy, while Dr. Kane's own book was sold at $5. Many people who could not afford to buy Dr. Kane's book, (published by *Childs & Peterson*,) bought Sonntag's narrative, and thus, at a moderate expense, learned how seals are skinned and eaten by the Esquimaux. But the newspapers, it seems, are opposed to having the people instructed *too cheaply*. They made the people believe that the Sonntag book was a "humbug." The sale of it was stopped, the publisher was "put down," Mrs. Sonntag, (who had been allowed a per centage on the profits,) was reduced, as I am informed, to a state of great pecuniary embarrassment, and she *died soon after, in very straitened circumstances!*

Were I disposed to tell the *whole* of this story, it might produce a feeling of indignation in the public mind which the venal and persecuting presses of Philadelphia should be prudent enough to avoid.

This case may help to show that the newspaper press, in *some* cases, is opposed to "cheap literature" and the general diffusion of useful knowledge among the people.

UNPROFITABLE STUDIES.—The intellectual condition of a community devoted to newspaper reading, is shown in a somewhat ridiculous light by a very intelligent English traveler, Mr. G. W. Featherstonhaugh, in a book on America. We may find something to believe and reflect on in the following extract:

"In Little Rock, (Arkansas,) with a population of six hundred people, there are no less than three *cheap* newspapers, which are not only read, but devoured by every body. It seems impossible that there should be any time or inclination for Bible reading, where this kind of cheap poison gets into the minds of human beings. You might as well expect to find a confirmed Chinese opium-smoker engaged in the solution of the problems of Euclid. In this part of the country, it has struck me as the worst of all signs that I have never seen a Bible in the hands of any individual, not even on Sunday." *Vide Harper's edition, page* 97.

Since the cheap newspaper system has been in vogue, Bibles, and all other useful books have gone out of fashion with the multitude. I remember a time when young milliners read Milton's Paradise Lost, Young's Night Thoughts, Thomson's Seasons, and many other things that were tolerably intellectual. I have seen apprentice boys in America studying History, Natural Philosophy, or Metaphysics; but *not lately*. Nothing is read now by young people, but pamphlet novels and the New York weekly papers.

AN ADMISSION.—James Gordon Bennett himself inadvertently admits that cheap newspaper reading debases the literature and intellect of a nation. A letter written by Bennett from London, under the date of July 12, 1847, was published in the New York Herald. It says:

"The cheap newspaper press of London is destined to achieve as great a victory as the like system has done in New York and Paris; but while newspaper literature is in the midst of a great and important revolution that must elevate it to the highest condition of intellectual power, the *general literature* of the day seems to be sinking lower and lower all the time. Indeed the literature of England seems to have degenerated into mere gossip. Hardly a book is published that is worth reading," etc.—*Bennett's Life, page* 397.

SECTION XX.

SHOWING THAT THE NEWSPAPER PRESS IS LEAGUED WITH PUBLIC POISONERS.

Examination of the Thirteenth Charge.

THERE is scarcely any kind of business carried on in the United States that is more extensive and lucrative than the manufacture of "Patent Medicines." Millions of dollars are expended annually by the American people in the purchase of cathartic pills and medicated syrups, composed of unknown ingredients, and manufactured, generally, by people who have no knowledge of chemistry, pharmacy, or therapeutics.

THE FRAUDS OF QUACKERY.

The Quack Medicine Trade is always fraudulent, in one way or another. It is a fraud for any man who has no knowledge of physic, or of the human constitution, to set himself up for a "doctor." It is a fraud to pretend that one medicine will cure many different diseases. It is a fraud to pretend that *all* diseases can be cured by medicines of any kind. It is a fraud to prescribe the same physic for everybody, without any regard for the physiological peculiarities of different patients. It is a fraud to make the public pay one dollar for a bottle of medicine which costs the manufacturer only five or six cents.

There are some other frauds in the "patent medicine" trade which will become discoverable as we proceed.

THE MURDERS OF QUACKERY.

It is commonly suspected, and with very good reason, that *regular physicians*—inexperienced ones especially—sometimes kill their patients by the indiscreet use of powerful drugs.

Apothecaries, whose geniusses have been cramped for many years over the pestle and mortar, sometimes make disastrous mistakes, (how often, Heaven only knows,) and great suffering or death itself, is sometimes the consequence.

Now the question is, whether physicians and apothecaries who have *some* acquaintance with their trades, though they may not be adepts, are not much less likely to commit fatal errors in the dispensation of medicines than men who know *nothing at all* about the matter?

One of the most successful patent doctors in Philadelphia was formerly a tailor in New Jersey, and I doubt whether he ever read a medical book in his life. Another prosperous physic-maker of the same class was, at one time, a horse-doctor in Delaware; and it is rumored that he gave dissatisfaction to his customers in that State by drenching his quadrupedal patients too copiously. He is a *strong* practitioner, however; and his medicine, if not always safe, is presumed to be EFFECTIVE.

It is a common mistake with the public to suppose that the drugs used by quack doctors in the composition of their syrups, panaceas, etc., are generally of a mild and harmless character. There are few articles in the *Materia Medica* which are absolutely harmless, if they are indiscreetly used; but some of the ingredients of the popular medicines are perilous enough, even in the hands of those who are well acquainted with their properties. One of the consumption-curing preparations manufactured in Philadelphia contains antimony, a mineral which is scarcely less poisonous than arsenic itself. The very name of this drug is significative of its character. Report says that it was once used for medicinal purposes in a certain monastic institution, and that it caused the death of many of the monks who took it. Hence it received a name which may be freely translated *Monk's-bane*. Now, the supposition is, that "monk's-bane" is very similar in nature to "rat's-bane," and perhaps it is equally deleterious.

The "Magnetic Sugar," which acquired a sudden but very

short-lived popularity, several years ago, must have contained some potent ingredient, if its common effects have been correctly described.

The various preparations of *Cannabis Indica*, which have lately had a very extensive sale, must have produced a good deal of execution, if they are *genuine* preparations of that dangerous drug.

Thousands of children are put to death by being dosed with patent vermifuges and carminatives. Pink-root is often used in the composition of worm medicines, and it is a strong vegetable poison. When this anthelmintic is prescribed by regular physicians, they consider it necessary to use a purgative medicine immediately afterward, but the quacks seldom or never trouble themselves to recommend the same course.

Some of the cordials, "carminative balsams," etc., which are recommended by their manufacturers as "certain cures for all diseases of the bowels," must almost infallibly prove fatal, if they are administered to young children in the early stages of acute dysentery. I once, (experimentally,) asked the proprietor of one of these nostrums if his physic might safely be used in such cases. He promptly answered, "Yes, in *all* cases." And yet one of the principal ingredients in this medicine is OPIUM!

It is known that fatal consequences have followed the use of a certain patent embrocation which was recommended for the cure of erysipelas. A liniment, warranted to cure gout, rheumatism and several other diseases, was once very much in vogue, and many certificates of its efficacy were published. But it was discovered that in many instances this article produced violent inflammation, ending in extensive gangrene. Several deaths, resulting from the use of this liniment, were *ascertained*, and doubtless there were other victims, (who can say how many?) whose fate is not a matter of general notoriety.

But, without going further into details, let me ask if any thing could be more probable, or more certain in fact, than the frequent sacrifice of human life by ignorant quacks who make a free use of the most dangerous drugs in the composition of nostrums, which are administered, without any possibility of discrimination, to patients widely differing in the state of their health, and in their constitutional peculiarities? Consider how much of this perilous physic must be sold when many of the manufacturers of it become MILLIONAIRES; and supposing that only *five per cent.* of the patent-medicine takers are drugged to death by the merciless empirics, (which is a very moderate calculation I think,) the annual destruction of human life must be immense.

THE THIRTEENTH CHARGE.

In this Charge it is asserted that "the newspaper press of America is accessory to thousands of murders every year by assisting quack doctors, or patent-medicine-men, to make extensive sales of their pernicious compounds."

According to a rule laid down in another part of this work, "we can have no better evidence than the voluntary confessions of the criminal, or of his confederates."

In this case, the quack doctors are the accused parties, and the journalists (as we shall see presently) are their self-accused confederates. I am about to offer you the testimony, or confession, of the "New York Journalist" who wrote the Life of J. G. Bennett, and who appears to be thoroughly acquainted with all the shady recesses and tortuous pathways of journalism. Says this faithful biographer:

"The press is EXTENSIVELY used, and, *horribile dictu*, it is used EDITORIALLY, in some cases, by the proprietors of patent medicines, until the evil is about to be checked by a resort to legislation. Certainly the people suffer severely from heartless imposition, where they rely upon the valuable properties of some of these popular compounds; and the sooner the evil is abated the better it will be for society. Most assuredly the press should be inflexible in its determination to give no *editorial* aid to compounds which cannot bear analysis and commendation."

As far as this testimony tends to implicate the journalists, it is very good evidence, as mentioned above; but when Bennett's chronicler tells us that "the evil is about to be checked," we are not bound to accept that declaration without scrutiny. It is true that a bill was brought before the New York Legislature making it a penal offense to manufacture or vend any medicine the component parts of which are not designated on the envelope. But if this bill had become a law, it would not have placed the makers of quack physic under any sensible restriction, for they might easily have evaded its requirements. Who, for instance, could tell whether the ingredients mentioned on the envelope were the true ones, or whether they were *all* of them? The proprietor of "Ayer's Pectoral" may intimate that the root or bark of the wild-cherry tree is the principal or the only ingredient, except molasses and water, in his syrup. If the preparation is so simple, why is it sold at one dollar per half-pint bottle, when the expense of making that quantity could not exceed half a dime?

If quack doctors should give a wrong account of the composition of their medicines, it would be impossible in many cases to detect the fraud. Besides, the law mentioned by Bennett's biographer was not intended to prevent the newspapers from hiring out their editorial columns to the quack doctors; and this kind of villainy is practiced *now* to a much greater extent than ever it was before.

INSTANCES.

Here is an "editorial" article from a "highly respectable" newspaper of Philadelphia:

"EXPECTORANTS.—Medical compilers assure us that there are no less than *twenty-nine hundred* expectorants offered for sale at the present time, and that but *one* of them is worth any thing, which is the expectorant of Dr. ——. This is an important fact. It serves to guide uninitiated sufferers in the breast in the purchase of remedies. Doctor Smackenbulger, of Vienna, and Count Paradi, of Berlin, the two most eminent physicians of Europe, have drawn up a memorial to be presented to the German Diet for the untaxed admission of ——'s Expectorant into all the German States."

Do not laugh, my dear friends; the affair is too serious for ridicule; and yet there are some passages in this disguised advertisement which are enough to disturb the professional gravity of Dr. Smackenbulger himself. But let us have

ANOTHER SPECIMEN.

The following unsuspiciously-disinterested editorial "notice" is from a very genteel newspaper published in Boston:

"It is a fact that, in the minds of many persons, there is a prejudice against what are called Patent Medicines; but why should this prevent you from resorting to an article that has such an array of testimony to support it as Hobsketter's Stomach Bitters? Physicians prescribe it; why should you discard it? Judges, usually considered men of talent, have used it, and do use it in their families; why should you reject it? Let not your prejudice upset your reason, to the everlasting injury of your health. If you are sick and require a medicine, try these bitters."

A DELICATE PUFF.

The subjoined extract is from the editorial column of a paper published ("with all the modern improvements") in New York:

"THE ACME OF PERFECTION.—This (and we do not write it in a spirit of puffery) has been achieved in the manufacture of Gaiety's Medicated Paper for the *water-closet*. (!) Nothing that was ever presented to the public has accomplished a more complete revolution in its favor than this wonderful article." And in this strain the editor proceeds, being apparently carried away by his sympathy for Mr. Gaiety's brilliant invention; and, after a long, tasteful, and eloquent appeal in its behalf, he concludes by assuring his readers that nothing but an earnest desire to serve the public, as "a faithful journalist," induces him to recommend this "admirable article" to the favor and patronage of his fellow-citizens.

RECOMMENDATIONS OF POISONS.

The preceding examples of editorial "puffing" are taken at random from newspapers which happen to be at hand while I am writing. I have no knowledge of the "medicines" recommended in these extracts, and according to the maxim, "the greater the truth, the greater the libel," it might be unlawful for me, perhaps, to call them worthless or mischievous. Indeed, my candid opinion is, that much *worse* articles are constantly and earnestly recommended to public favor by the newspapers. Those journalists who prostitute their *editorial* columns for the benefit of the quack medicine trade, use no discrimination in the matter, except by regulating the strength of the puffery according to the amount of the compensation.

I have seen some very dangerous preparations earnestly recommended in this way; and indeed *any* physic composed by an ignorant quack, must be more or less dangerous. Nearly all the drugs which belong to the pharmacopœia are poisons, and some of them are very active ones indeed. Medical writers of high repute have admitted, that the free use of medicinal drugs, even by the most scientific practitioners, is somewhat perilous; and Dr. Forbes, an allopathic physician of Edinburg, plainly expresses his belief that lives are oftener sacrificed than saved by the drugging system, even when it is managed with all that caution and discrimination which the science of medicine enjoins on its professors.

But imagine the fearful risks to which people are exposed when they are dosed by hostlers, farriers, journeymen-barbers, essence-pedlers, and others who are too ignorant to understand the hazards of their business, and too reckless or too rascally to concern themselves about its consequences. One of the popular quack medicines of Philadelphia was invented and manufactured by a *boy*, and a very roguish one too, as some passages in his history may certify. The *most successful* quack doctor in this city is a very illiterate fellow ; and, in fact, I never knew any patent-medicine maker who had learning or medical skill enough to qualify him for the duties of an apothecary's shopman.

Formerly the compounders of quack nostrums were conscientious or prudent enough to confine themselves to the use of mild and comparatively powerless medicaments. *Then* their physic was, in a measure, harmless, and their principal knavery consisted in defrauding the people of their money. But recently these villains have become more daring and unscrupulous, and, not satisfied with pecuniary frauds, they have began to sacrifice the health and the very *lives* of their victims, (as I firmly believe,) in their eager pursuit of gain.

The *effects* which are often produced by the administration of quack medicines, the great nervous excitement or the prostration and lethargy which have been known to follow the exhibition of these suspicious remedies, show that some of the ingredients must be *powerful;* and, beyond all possibility of doubt, the greater number of these empirical preparations are more or less poisonous. It is impossible to say how much incurable disease, or how much loss of life, is caused by these widely-dispensed "medicines." When sick people die, it is seldom ascertained whether they are killed by the disease or the physic. If the certificates published by quack doctors only contained an account of those patients who are *murdered* by patent medicines, as well as those who are supposed to be cured by them, whole columns or pages, perhaps, would be required to contain the registry, and the emoluments of the journalists, derived from this flourishing business, would be still greater than they are at present.

THE EDITOR'S PROFITS.

However, it is plain enough that the newspaper men are extremely well paid for their efforts to promote the sale and consumption of poisonous quack nostrums. I once asked a "patent doctor" how he could have the conscience to charge the public one dollar for a bottle of physic which cost him but six cents. His answer was, "It is true that the medicine and the bottle cost me no more than the sum you mention, but I calculate that what I have to pay for advertising and *editorial puffs* brings the cost up to SIXTY-FIVE cents at least!"

Supposing this man's estimate to be correct, it may be inferred that more than *fifty per cent.* of the profits of the quack medicine trade falls to the share of the Public Journalists. It is a magnificent reward, such as traitors and assassins usually expect; but weigh, in the other scale, the guilt and infamy of the bargain, the conscious degradation, the self-abhorrence and the stings of conscience, which even the most obdurate sinner cannot always escape. Verily the well-paid confederates of the Public Poisoners are not to be envied.

MANY OFFENDERS.

The charge of collusion with the Quack Doctors will apply to very many journalists in the United States. I think that half of the American newspapers, at least, allow their *editorial* columns to be used by the quacks; and at least three-fourths of the *other half* publish quack advertisements without any discrimination or restriction. By the way, it is a prevalent belief among newspaper men that their advertising columns "belong to the public;" and some of them seem to question whether they have a right to refuse an advertisement of any kind, "if it is *paid* for!" Bennett's biographer, (as might be expected,) takes this view of the subject, and he censures the *Journal of Commerce* for conscientiously refusing to publish theatrical announcements. He even goes so far as to insinuate that such a refusal on the part of a journalist, ought to be made an actionable offense!

What curious notions respecting the Liberty of the Press this biographer must have! The veriest drab that walks the street may reject a customer if she chooses, but prostituted Journalism considers itself bound to take all the custom that offers. This is a very convenient rule of action for avaricious scoundrels, but the universal recognition of such a principle would make it *quite* impossible, (it is almost so now,) for any good or honorable man to be the publisher of a newspaper.

With regard to the publication of quack advertisements, I think there can scarcely be two opinions among men of common sense and common honesty. If the advertisers are believed to be impostors, (and newspaper men seldom believe quack-doctors to be any thing else,) it is base, dishonest and wicked conduct on the part of the journalist to give ANY KIND of assistance to the imposition.

SUPPLEMENTARY ILLUSTRATIONS.

AN INFALLIBLE REMEDY.—The sudden popularity of a patent medicine is sometimes scarcely more surprising, than its rapid decline or instantaneous suppression. Both effects often proceed from causes which are apparently trivial and inadequate.

A certain pill, which commanded an extensive sale throughout the United States several years ago, became altogether unsalable within the space of two or three weeks, merely because the inventor and proprietor of the successful medicine had hanged himself!

Another instance of popular fickleness, which is less unaccountable, however, occurred within the scope of my recollection. A pulmonary syrup which had long "sold well and paid handsomely," on a certain day went out of the market instantly, and not a bottle of it could be sold afterward. The reputation of this physic was founded on the widely-published statement that it had cured its proprietor of consumption in its most hopeless stage; and this declaration was repeated, and the truth of it vouched for by the newspaper editors, until the gentleman who had been so miraculously and completely restored to health, actually *died* of that very disease for which his medicine was proposed as an infallible remedy. As soon as his death became known to the public, the sale of the medicine stopped; and in this instance the liberal patrons of medical quackery appear to have acted with more than their customary discretion.

"OLD SANDS OF LIFE."—This is the nick-name applied to the person who audaciously pretends that he discovered the medical properties of *Cannabis Indica*, or Indian hemp, which has been in common use as a remedial agent for five hundred years. The pretender to this antique discovery usually began his advertisements with—"A physician whose sands of life have nearly run out," etc.; but it has been ascertained that he is a gay, dashing young fellow, who is likely to live long enough to discover other uses of hemp besides those curative ones which are mentioned in his advertisement. Report says that "Sands of Life" has realized an immense fortune by means of his "new-found old invention," and his zealous allies, the gentlemen of the press, have earned many thousands of dollars by giving him their support.

A WELL-RIDDEN HOBBY.—Consumption, though a lean hobby and generally a slow one, (albeit we sometimes hear of galloping consumptions,) is one of the principal hacks on the turnpike of medical speculation. It is true that the regular medical army have denounced it as an unmanageable jade, and so turned it out of their service, but the "patent doctors" find it to go exceedingly well, with the right kind of harness. Several gentlemen in Philadelphia have made very large fortunes by curing the consumption, or, (what answers their purpose quite as well,) by making the public believe they can cure it.

It is "a good business," in one sense of the phrase, to sell a bottle of physic which costs six cents, bottle inclusive, for one dollar; but it is not so good to speculate on the hopes and apprehensions of people who are dedicated to a speedy death. The exaction of a dying man's last dollar, though a bad affair enough to be presented at "the recording angel's black bureau," is not, *per se*, of as much importance as the delusion of a wretched patient with vain hopes of recovery, or inducing him to neglect means of cure which might be available, and to waste time in experiments which cannot possibly do him any good. The press must be used to further the sales of poisonous medicines, or the "quack doctors" would starve. Now and then, when a really invaluable medicine is placed before the public on its *own merits*, without any regard to "*editorial* puffs," it is attacked by the papers *indiscriminately*. For instance, where can you find a better medicine than *Dr. Brandreth's Universal Vegetable Pills?* and yet the press have done their worst to stop the immense sale of this valuable medicine, because they require no "puffing" to sell. Dr. Brandreth's pills are not made of mercury or other poisonous ingredients, which invariably leave the patient broken in health and constitution; therefore these pills require no recommendation of the "PRESS GANG." They sell faster than they can be made, and hence the coffers of the editors receive nothing from Dr. Brandreth for "puffs." This may account why, for years, the press has done its best to stop their sale; and so it is with any business that requires no aid from the papers—it is assailed most venomously.

DR. MOFFATT.—This man is the proprietor of "The Celebrated Life Pills." He was once the occupant of a small shop in New York, but he is now the possessor of a million of dollars. *He* was indebted for his prosperity to the newspapers, so says the "New York Journalist" who has written the Life of the "Head-devil of Journalism," and who promises to give us another volume to celebrate the achievements of "that most glorious and powerful institution of republican government—an *unshackled press!*"

The definition of an "unshackled press" is a press that enables penniless young men and small shop-keepers to become millionaires and bank presidents by selling quack medicines!

Many other patent medicine-makers have become immensely rich in the United States, and all by the same means; the "unshackled press" being their principal auxiliary in deceiving, swindling, and slaughtering the sovereign people.

SECTION XXI.

SHOWING THAT THE NEWSPAPER PRESS ENCOURAGES AND JUSTIFIES MOBBING, TREASON AND REBELLION.

Examination of the Fourteenth Charge.

WE have now reached the last stage of our investigation; and if the companions of my travel have been good observers along the route, they will find nothing very surprising or incomprehensible in the final subject which presents itself for examination.

We have learned, on the way, that the newspaper press of our country is controled chiefly by foreigners; that many of the Journalists are practically hostile to republican institutions; that great numbers of them are vicious and ill-disposed persons; that our newspapers, in general are the organs of the mob, and that the Press Gang *itself* is, to all intents and purposes, a mob of the worst kind. If these truths are accepted, and I protest that they are undeniable, we shall have but little occasion for facts or arguments to prove that the American newspapers are apt enough " to excite rebellion, to urge the disorderly rabble of our cities to revolutionary movements, and to offer encouragement and protection to rebels and traitors, especially to those of foreign birth."

These are the offenses which are imputed to the journalists in my Fourteenth Charge.

MOBS AND MOBBING.

It is a mistake of the largest kind to suppose that a mobbing spirit is any thing like the spirit of a free people. A populace which is disposed to be turbulent is so far disqualified for the enjoyment of civil liberty. Rioting is a slavish vice; no people are more inclined to it than the Southern negroes, when they are not held in awe by the overseers' cowskin. Under a popular government, there is no occasion for mobbing, no pretense for it; for if a mob is supposed to represent the people, a republican mob is a practical absurdity. It represents the people fighting against themselves and resisting the laws which they have solemnly enacted and pledged themselves to maintain. Under a free government, where any abuse can be rectified at the ballot-box, and where all legislation is done by the citizens or the representatives they have chosen, it is a most unreasonable thing for the people to attempt to redress by brutal force any grievance under which they are supposed to suffer.

But, (as I have hinted once before,) it is another grand mistake to suppose that a mob *does* represent the people. It does not do any thing of the kind. A mob is a discontented minority; and a minority in a republic never represents the people. A mobbing minority resists, insults and defies the law-making and law-sustaining majority. Now it is well understood that in a republic, all that defies and resists the majority is anti-republican; and therefore a mob is of this character. Mobbing is an attempt of the few to govern the many; a measure which is directly opposed to republican freedom; for the essential characteristic or distinctive trait of republicanism, as hinted above, is the predominance of majorities. Whoever aims a blow at this feature, must be, in principle and practice, an enemy of popular liberty, whatever pretension he may make to be a redresser of wrongs and a champion of the oppressed.

THE PEOPLE CONDEMN MOBS.

I have never known a mobbing affair in this country which did not meet with the condemnation of the PUBLIC, *videlicit*, the majority. Every citizen who deserves the name wishes to see such tumults suppressed; for every good and discreet citizen sees the absurdity and wickedness of the thing, and he knows that it is much better to submit to a temporary inconvenience, or even to a wrong, rather than to seek redress from the operations of a wild, lawless and inconsiderate pack of vagabonds.

But to show that the newspaper press does not always sympathize with the people, and that it is not *always* the true exponent of Public Opinion, it may be proved that all the serious popular disturbances which ever took place in the United States have been caused by indiscreet, intemperate or malicious newspaper publications. And I never knew a mobbing affair in this country, unless it was supposed to be a *Native American* riot, which was not directly or indirectly excused or justified by the press. Let the reader examine for himself, and he will find that this has always been the case. In the meanwhile, a few examples will presently be given to refresh his memory.

THE DANGER OF POPULAR COMMOTIONS.

Remember that some of the most disastrous and sanguinary revolutions that the world ever knew began with popular disturbances which, at the commencement, were almost contemptible. We want no revolutions in America, I suppose, at the present time; and yet, whenever a mob makes a demonstration against the laws or government, it may be regarded as an incipient revolutionary movement. It is always prudent and politic for the supporters of law and order to take this view of the matter, and to act accordingly.

With reference to the policy of dealing with mobs promptly and decisively, Lord Brougham makes the following remarks, which are as true and as applicable to our purpose as if one of our own republican statesmen had spoken them:—

"It is not merely the activity of agitators that arms them with force to overpower the bulk of the people; their acts of *intimidation* are far more effectual than any assiduity or address. We see how a handful of men leading the Paris mob overturned the monarchy, and then set up and maintained an oligarchy of the most despotic character that ever was known in the world, all the while ruling the vast majority of a people that utterly loathed them; ruling that people with an iron rod, and scourging them with scorpions. A rabble of ten or twelve thousand persons, occupying the capital, overawed five hundred thousand men as robust and as brave, perhaps, as themselves.

"The tendency of turbulent multitudes is two-fold—their numbers are always exaggerated, both by the representations of their leaders and by the fears of the spectators. The rabble of Paris was infuriated; the Parisian burghers were calm, they had shops, and wives, and children, and they were fain to *be still*, in order that no outrage should be committed on their persons or property."

Now, my American countrymen, consider your shops, *your* wives, and *your* children, and never allow your mobs to obtain such ascendency that the only chance of security for your persons and property will consist in the mouse-like expedient of "being still."

OPINIONS OF THE PRESS.

One of the most common opinions among newspaper editors seems to be that mobbing is much more allowable in a democratic country than in lands governed by monarchs or aristocrats. According to the views I have taken, the very reverse may appear to be the truth. It has been suggested that, under our popular government, mobbing is absurd and inexcusable; and, in a majority of cases, it is treason or rebellion. The late Judge Kane ventured to express a similar opinion—for which he was severely censured by almost all the newspapers of Philadelphia. Some of them devoted whole columns of abuse to the Judge on this very account. Another prevalent notion among the conductors of our press appears to be that it is *impossible* to commit such an offense as rebellion or treason in the United States. The experiment was lately tried, in a very determined manner, at New Orleans. Some of the best lawyers thought it was successful, but the newspapers decided otherwise.

REBELLION AT NEW ORLEANS.

It is almost impossible to ascertain the true history of this extraordinary and disgraceful affair ; for the only accounts we have of it came originally from journals whose conductors probably took a part in the movement, and who were therefore strongly inclined to palliate or excuse it. We have little more than *ex parte* evidence. It appears, however, that there was a struggle for supremacy between two factions ;—one of which triumphed at the municipal election in May, 1858. The other faction objected to the election as fraudulent, alleging that the majority was on its own side, and that if matters had been fairly conducted, the opposite party would have been defeated.

Acting on this assumption, the unsuccessful faction appointed a "Vigilance Committee ;" that committee organized and armed a large force, intimidated the citizens, deposed the lawfully elected public officers, and assumed the government of the city! Scarcely any newspaper in the United States ventured to condemn this movement in such terms as it deserved.

The "Vigilance Committee" had garrisoned one of the public buildings, obviously for the purpose of resisting the lawful authorities. One night the troops in garrison fired on a party of their own men, by mistake, and several were killed or wounded. These killed and wounded were taken to one of the city hospitals, and it was then ascertained that they were *nearly all foreigners!*

Fearing that their position was not altogether safe, the usurpers attempted to legalize their acts by holding a new election, which they promised to conduct in the most equitable manner. They announced that the result of this election would prove the fraudulent character of the preceding one, in which their opponents had triumphed. But when the trial was made, the usurping party was once more signally defeated. This test proved that they were a minority, and that the deposed authorities were the true representatives of the people.

The rebels now became alarmed, as some of the tardy citizens began to show a disposition to hold them accountable for their deeds. Several of the traitors fled, but a large majority of them, as I am informed, remained in the city, being advised to do so by some of the newspapers, with the assurance that they should not be punished!

I have heard that certain officers of the law attempted to bring these rebels to justice, and that the attempt was ridiculed by some of the New Orleans papers, and violently opposed by others.

An account of this strange affair was published in many European journals, and the case was cited to exemplify the weakness and insecurity of our republican government.

THE NEW YORK QUARANTINE MOB.

In August, 1858, a brutal mob attacked the Quarantine Station on Staten Island. They broke open and burned down six brick buildings occupied by the boatmen, the dwelling-houses of Dr. Wallin and Dr. Bissel, and the hospitals.

The New York Evening Post of September 2 says: "The sick, some fifty or sixty in number, were removed from the hospitals by the mob, and are still *lying on the grass*, exposed to the weather and to the public gaze! The houseless physicians and nurses are still in attendance, and strive to make the patients as comfortable as possible. Some of the poor wretches complain that their sores have not been dressed, and that they have received no medicine within the last two days, but their attendants are as busy as possible.

"A man named Milk, assistant engineer of the steamboat Philadelphia, died last night, just after being brought out of the doomed hospital. His body still lies on the grass.

"Three sick men from the ship Liberty of New Orleans are lying on the pier, as it was impossible to provide them with shelter. The loss of property is estimated at $300,000.

"The reason given for this horrid outrage was that the quarantine hospital was a public nuisance."

Another New York paper says: "Many of the rioters were

Irish and Dutch; a big pot-bellied, lager-bloated specimen of the latter nationality, with a fireman's cap, was a ring-leader. The hospital was set on fire in three or four places; but the combustion was most rapid in the centre near the great stairway. The draught upward soon carried the flames to the cupola, which was in full blaze before the wings were well under way. There was a gang of fellows whose particular delight was the smashing in of the windows. They were provided with short clubs, and when they reached the doomed building, they first began by breaking out the windows. While this was going on, others entered the place; one carried a half-gallon measure filled with camphene, which he poured out liberally on the pile of inflammable material already prepared by his comrades, and then the whole was set off with a match.

"*Appearance of the Patients.*—Entering through a breach in the west side of the wall, a large party came down to the women's hospital, and began to remove the patients. The scene was horrible. The poor creatures, in every stage of suffering, some delirious from fever and others in a dying state, were taken out upon their reeking mattresses and placed, one after another, on the green sward, in an angle formed by the two walls. One who had just died was placed in the covered bier and set down close by the others. One was just expiring. The gaunt features and sunken eyes of the poor wretches, as they lay scattered over the ground, were perfectly visible in the light of the burning hospital.

"In the coffin-house, behind the women's hospital, there were twenty or thirty coffins, all of which were destroyed.

" The sick men and women, in their night-clothes, just arisen, weakened with illness and dreadfully excited, were thronging about Dr. Bissell on the open grounds adjoining the building, crying aloud and beseeching him to save them. 'Will they burn us?' 'Will they burn us?' they would repeat, clinging to the physician. The medical gentlemen said and did all they could to tranquillize the poor creatures."

The destruction of the public buildings by this savage and

pitiless mob was unquestionably a hostile demonstration against the government. It was, therefore, an overt act of treason and rebellion.

AGENCY OF THE PRESS.

It cannot be doubted that this treasonable and rebellious movement was excited and *authorized* by the Satanic Journals of New York. On this subject, a Philadelphia paper, dated September 4, 1858, makes the following truthful remarks:—" The New York papers pretend to be highly indignant at the conduct of the mob, and now preach very good doctrine about the supremacy of the law. But the mischief done by the mob is the legitimate fruits of the teachings of these newspapers. They have been preaching for a long time of the necessity of Vigilance Committees, to reform evils which the laws do not reach; and they have often asserted that the people possess the power at any time, " to assume their natural sovereignty ;" which means that any mob may assume to be the people, and to set the laws established by the whole people at defiance.

"This doctrine has led to a great many mobs in New York," (yes, and in other places too,) "and probably will cause a great many more. The Anti-Renters based all their acts on the same kind of teachings, and the Staten Islanders think that they are doing a very worthy act when they declare that hospitals are nuisances which the State has established, and show their public spirit by burning them down. The journals of New York do not seem to be pleased with the practical results of their own teachings."

The only mistake that can be detected in the preceding extract, is the intimation that the preaching of mobbish doctrines is a *peculiarity* of the press of New York. That sort of villainy is practiced by newspapers in every part of the United States; yet, as New York is the fountain-head of Satanic journalism, it must be expected that all infernal doctrines will find strenuous advocates in that city.

When it was found that the horrid barbarities of the Staten Island mob had shocked the sensibilities of the public, some of the more hypocritical papers of the diabolical school began to make exclamations of pity or remorse. But the "Head Devil" was more consistent, and boldly apologized for the misdemeanors which his counsels had helped to produce. In the New York Herald of September 4, 1858, we find the following editorial comments:—

"The acts of the people of Staten Island was not the result of sudden passion; it was not the outrageous license of a crazy mob, but the execution of a calm, well-settled determination. We do not defend mob-law, but experience shows that when the constituted authorities attempt to force upon the people a tyrannical enactment, even an *illegal* check on the part of the sufferers will be excused by a large portion of the community."

This language proves that the Scotch editor of the Herald, though he has been connected with the American press for more than thirty years, has not yet learned even the gamut of harmonious republicanism. What an absurd notion to suppose that the constituted authorities of such a government as ours could "*force* tyrannical enactments upon the people !" If the people choose to elect tryrannical legislators, it is their own fault; and their error must be corrected at the ballot-box, and not by mobbing or rebellion.

THE CHRISTIANA MOB.

On Thursday, September 11, 1851, a fatal mobbing affair occurred at or near Christiana, a small town in Lancaster County, Pennsylvania. A Mr. Gorsuch of Maryland, accompanied by his son and several officers of the law, came to Christiana for the purpose of reclaiming some fugitive slaves. Mr. Gorsuch was protected by the laws of his country, and in the attempt to recover his slaves he acted strictly in accordance with legal requirements. But he and his party were assailed by an armed mob, composed of white men and negroes;

and, in the skirmish which followed, Mr. Gorsuch was killed, several other persons were wounded, and the officers of the law were compelled to retreat.

Some of the ring-leaders of the mob were arrested and indicted for treason. The case was tried in November, of the same year, before the United States District Court at Philadelphia, Judge Kane presiding. The charge delivered by the Judge, on this occasion, was very offensive to the newspaper men in general, who, according to their usual practice, sympathized with the rebels; and, indeed, would not allow them to be called by that name. In one Philadelphia paper, I saw Judge Kane denounced as a "second Jeffries" and an "Old Fogy," because he defined treason against the United States to consist " in levying war against them, and in adhering to their enemies, giving them aid and comfort." Mr. Editor did not seem to know where that definition came from, but stigmatized it as "a relic of Gothic barbarism."

The Christiana rioters or rebels were acquitted, in obedience to the requirements of the newspaper press.

THE WAR OF RACES.

Some of the most fearful popular commotions that ever took place in this country, originated in national antipathies, fomented by public journalists and other agitators. The mixture of different races in the population of the United States is a calamitous circumstance, and the misfortune is very much aggravated by the folly and wickedness of typographers and politicians.

The press has been the chief instrument employed by artful and unprincipled men to prevent the assimilation of the various elements of our population, and to intensify those national dislikes which are always apt enough to break out into open hostility. The numerous organs of different nationalities which have been established among us, are always sowing seeds of discord and endeavoring to make the "adopted citizens" who read them, discontented with their social or political position in our country. It is impossible to satisfy some of these foreign "organists," or even to guess at what they require.

The newspapers *in general* deceive and mislead the alien population by teaching them to believe that they are the "better citizens," and the benefactors of the public. By these indiscreet flatteries, they are made insolent and exacting; and very slight provocations, sometimes, will make them turbulent and rebellious. On account of their clannish habits and numerous organizations, the foreign population of this country may be considered as a *standing mob*, always ready for action. Several serious collisions between the native and foreign populations have already occurred; and it will be wonderful indeed if the jealousies, dislikes and mutual aggressions of natives and aliens do not produce much greater troubles hereafter.

"THE NATIVE MOB."

I have heard of a "Native American Mob" in Philadelphia, but I do not recognize it by that title, though I happened to see some of its operations. The real nature and origin of this mob have been much misrepresented and greatly misunderstood. It can scarcely be denied, however, that the disturbance arose from an angry and intemperate political discussion carried on in the newspapers.

One person who undertakes to give an account of this terrible and disgraceful affair, asserts that Mr. Lewis C. Levin, editor of a penny paper called the Philadelphia Sun, was the author of the mischief. On the other hand, Mr. Bennett of the New York-Herald, who is a Catholic by the way, declares that Bishop Hughes and his newspaper organs produced that agitation which led to all the Anti-Catholic riots in America. The bishop thus denounced by Mr. Bennett as a political agitator and disturber of the public peace, is supposed to be the principal American agent and representative of the Sovereign Pontiff. This Philadelphia mob is commonly believed to have been a collision of the Irish Catholics and Native Americans.

Actual hostilities were commenced on the evening of May 6, 1844. On that evening a Native American political meeting was held in Kensington, a district of Philadelphia, which contains many Irish Catholic inhabitants. Among the speakers who addressed the assemblage was Mr. Levin, the editor of the Philadelphia Sun, a native American organ. While this gentleman was speaking, a party of men, supposed to be Irish Catholics, rushed in among the audience and attempted to break up the meeting. The natives stood on the defensive, and a terrific combat ensued, in which stones, brick-bats, and other convenient implements of mobbish warfare were freely used by both parties. The persons who attempted to break up the meeting must have been provided with fire-arms, for several men on the side of the natives were shot, and, I think two or three were killed and several others were badly wounded.

From this account it appears that the Irish struck the first blow, and their attempt to interfere with the right of free discussion shows how little they understood the principles of political liberty. But the war being now begun, was carried on for several days with deadly animosity. A mob, supposed to be composed of Native Americans, attacked some of the Catholic churches, partially or entirely destroyed them, tore down or burned many dwelling-houses inhabited by the Irish; and, Philadelphia, for the first time, experienced all the horrors of civil war. Some of the Irish, while attempting to defend their churches and habitations, were killed; and some of the opposite party met with the same fate.

A letter written from Washington city, and published in a Philadelphia paper several days after the disturbance had ceased, takes a view of the subject which appears to me to be nearly correct:

"For my part," says this letter-writer, "I blame far less the poor deluded people infuriated by the arts of demagoguery and journalism and set on to disorder for other people's profit, than the folly of our own laws and the criminality and cowardice of those who feel that they ought to be changed, but forbear to make any movement toward that object. The fraudulent, the unprincipled naturalization of large bodies of foreign voters, utterly unfit to exercise the right of suffrage and capable only of becoming the dupes of the bad and the instruments of disorder, has grown up into a serious and daily-increasing evil.

"I look for other commotions, for other scenes of carnage, in every quarter where large numbers of ignorant and excitable foreigners are mixed with the native population. I warrant you that the hireling press will be prompt enough to make party capital of this awful event which, as a national misfortune, should sadden every honest man's heart."

This prognostic has been fully realized. The "hireling press" *has* made political capital of that sad event, and in doing so, it has excused the *Irish* rioters and their more criminal instigators, and thrown all the blame on the native citizens of America.

RIOT AT NEW ORLEANS.

A fight between Irishmen and native citizens took place at New Orleans on the 10th of September, 1851. Pistols and guns, (says the newspaper report,) were freely used. The disturbance was kept up for several days and it was reported that three or four men had been killed. The Mayor ordered out the entire police force and the National Guard. This measure intimidated the rioters and compelled them to disperse. The narrator adds:—"The first onslaught, *as usual*, was made by the Irish." But, from the accounts published in some of the New Orleans papers, you might have judged that the harmless and unoffending Hibernians were assailed in the most barbarous and cowardly manner by the "ruffianly natives."

GERMAN RIOT.

On the fifth day of August, 1850, there was a great disturbance among the Germans in New York. About three hundred men assembled in the Sixteenth Ward and assaulted several persons who had given them some offense, the precise nature of which could not be ascertained. It was reported, however, that the greater number of the rioters were tailors, and that they were "striking" for higher wages. They were addressed by several orators in their own language, and the speeches, judging from their effect, must have been highly inflammatory. The following is given as a literal translation of a fragment of one of these stirring harangues:—

"My brethren, my friends, my fellow-citizens, *revolution* is the word! We must have a revolution; we cannot go on and submit any longer. Revolution! Revolution! Revolution! [Here one loud, unanimous, long-continued shout of applause burst from the dense crowd, with continued cries of *Bravo!* bravo!] Think you that we can get our freedom by *peaceable means and gentle remedies?* No indeed!—we must meet force with force. So only can we be free! Let us have our *rights.*"

At two o'clock, P. M. intelligence reached the 16th Ward Station House that there was a dreadful riot in Thirty-Eighth street. Captain Freeman and a party of his men proceeded to the spot, and there found a number of Germans attacking the house of Frederick Wartz. This man, it seems, had offended the German organizations by working for less than the prescribed wages. The mob had broken the windows, entered the house, driven out Wartz, beaten him severely and torn the clothes off his back.

The chief of police arrested a German named George Schott, who appeared to be the leader of the mob. Schott resisted violently, the mob came to his assistance, and a fierce battle ensued. The policemen retreated but succeeded in carrying their prisoner a little way; they were followed however by a large body of the rioters, and the prisoners were rescued. A large reinforcement of policemen arrived at this moment. Schott, the rescued prisoner, was recovered and several other arrests were made. Some of the Germans when arrested had their pockets full of stones; volleys of these missiles were hurled at the officers of the law, and many of the rioters assailed them with knives, daggers clubs and pistols. Squads of Germans were collected in many different places, and stones were thrown at the policemen as they approached. The whole ward was in an uproar and the greatest consternation prevailed among the inhabitants.

The police were engaged in one uninterrupted battle with the Germans, for the distance of nearly a mile, and several of the officers were severely wounded, some with stones, some with slung-shot, and some with knives or daggers.

A New York paper said, "This appears to have been a more terrible riot than that of the Astor House." The reader may remember how much was said and printed about the Astor House riots; how the facts in their largest details were published in the papers, scattered about the country, and transmitted to Europe, making the conduct of certain theatrical rowdies a recorded scandal to the American people. And it will be remembered, especially, that although the persons actively engaged in the Astor House riot were probably less than half as numerous as those who took a part in this German outbreak, the military were promptly called out in the former case, and efficient measures, (which I highly approve,) were used to quell the disturbance.

But be it observed that a military force is seldom, if ever, called out to check the audacity of *foreign* rebels, although the police may be overpowered, their lives jeopardized and their persons seriously injured.

The Philadelphia American Banner of August 17, 1850, has the following editorial remarks on this German riot:—

"The accounts of this disturbance which were published in most of the newspapers, were *softened down because the rioters were aliens*. Had they been Americans, we should have heard awful accounts of their proceedings; but it is the constant practice of many American newspapers to slur over every outrage perpetrated by foreigners. We had no idea of the magnitude and audacity of this German riot until we read an official account of it, which only one paper in New York had independence enough to publish."

The same paper adds:—" Let the American people consider that if the German tailors alone can get up such a serious outbreak in New York, what might be done if the whole foreign population of America, or any considerable part of it, should be called into action against the peace and security of our country. And let Americans consider further that this foreign population, (composed chiefly of such materials as made up the alien mob in New York,) increases on us at the rate of *three hundred thousand per annum!*"

MOBBING AFFAIR AT CINCINNATI.

German and Irish riots are frequent occurrences in America, and they are often much more serious matters than you would be led to believe by reading the accounts of them in the newspapers.

In December, 1854, a German mob in Cincinnati menaced the Pope's nuncio, Bedini, with violence and death. They were proceeding toward his place of abode, shouting "Hang Bedini!—Kill him," etc. Some policemen ordered the crowds to disperse, which they refused to do, and set the officers at defiance. An attempt was then made to arrest several of the most noisy and abusive among the rioters; the mob resisted and assaulted the officers with great fury. The assembly must have been a large one, for it is said that they formed a long procession as they marched toward the house occupied by Bedini. Many pistols were fired by the Germans, and two or three of the officers were shot, but not dangerously wounded. Several other policemen were hurt with clubs, slung-shots, stones, etc.

The accounts of this affair published in the papers did not state the *facts* of the case. The particulars just mentioned were obtained from the evidence given in at the trial of some of the rioters.

The newspapers, in some instances, openly justified the mob

and condemned the interference of the city authorities. The following editorial article appeared in a New York paper.

"Our first view of the *difficulties* at Cincinnati proved to be correct. That the Germans were right and the Mayor and his myrmidons were wrong, appears to be the popular sentiment at Cincinnati. The police were the true rioters, as we have contended from the first. The whole case is as plain as the nose on a man's face, and we hope the offending parties, (*i. e.* the police!) will be made to feel the force of the law which they have outraged," etc.

Repeatedly have I seen police-officers censured in a similar manner, (and that by newspapers pretending to respectability,) for endeavoring to do their duty to the public by checking the tumultuous misbehavior of the foreign rabble. With regard to the German riot at Cincinnati, the deportment of the newspapers may seem to be a little mysterious, if we suppose that riot to have been an *Anti-Catholic* demonstration. Hostility to Catholicism is not by any means a trait of American Journalism; on the contrary, the Romish church, with its meddlesome hierarchy, obtains ten times more favor and indulgence from the press of our country, than any other religious establishment. The chief objection to the so-called Native American mob, was, that it was Anti-Catholic, "bigoted," "intolerant," etc.

The Dutch riot at Cincinnati was not a *protestant* demonstration, and I am happy to have it in my power to make this statement. If I am correctly informed the Germans who meditated an attack on Bedini, were the members of an Atheistical Red Republican association, calling themselves *Freemen,* and some *political* offense of Bedini exposed him to their resentment. This mob was incited to action, undoubtedly by the inflammatory appeals of the pestilent German newspapers published in Cincinnati.

RIOT AND MURDER IN PHILADELPHIA.

The subjoined report is taken from a Philadelphia daily paper, dated September 12, 1853. The paragraph is craftily constructed to answer a particular purpose :—

"ANOTHER BLOODY RIOT.—On Saturday night, between eleven and twelve o'clock, as the Franklin Hose Company were returning from a fire, they passed the Hibernia Hose house, at which time pistols and a volley of bricks were discharged at them, which were promptly returned by a discharge of pistols from the Franklin company. An Irishman named Hugh Murtha, was shot and killed instantly. Lieutenant McNally of the Marshal's Police, captured twelve of the rioters, who were taken before Alderman Cloud, and committed for trial."

The affair, as stated in this article, does not appear to be *very* serious, but hear another account, in which there is no attempt at concealment :—

"ANOTHER IRISH RIOT AND MURDER.—On Saturday night another deliberate attempt to murder American citizens was made by the Irish members of the Hibernia Hose Company of this city. The Hose House of that company was garrisoned by a band of foreign ruffians, provided with fire-arms, and those weapons were discharged, without any just cause or provocation, at the members of the Franklin company as they were passing the house. Fortunately none of the members of the Franklin were hurt, but a stray shot struck an Irishman named Hugh Murtha, who was walking on the opposite side of the street, and killed him instantly."

In the first account quoted above, it is not mentioned that the murderously-inclined rioters were Irishmen ; nor is it stated that the discharge was made from the windows of the Hibernia Hose House. The phraseology of the story might lead the readers to believe that the Irishman, Hugh Murtha, was killed by some member of the Franklin company, whereas he was shot, unintentionally, by his own countrymen, in the hose house. Other important particulars are omitted in the narrative;

obviously for the pupose of shielding the foreign "pets of journalism" from the censure they deserved. All the rioters who were arrested were Irishmen, as their *names* alone, (if they had been published,) would have certified. The behavior of these men, after they were committed for trial, is thus described:—

"It might be supposed that men proceeding to prison with such charges pending against them, would be somewhat subdued in spirit. But such, we regret to say, was not the case with this gang, for, while passing the Hibernia Hose House, they attempted to give three cheers. They succeeded in cheering once, but were promptly checked by the officers before they could succeed in finishing their expression of triumph."

REBELLION IN PERRY COUNTY, OHIO.

The following dispatch appeared in the Columbus *State Journal*:—

"ZANESVILLE, September 7, 1853.

"Advices from Somerset, Perry County, O., give us intelligence of a terrible riot in that place. The origin we cannot learn precisely. The Irish laborers on the railroad have taken possession of the fire-arms belonging to the county! They marched to the armory, and seized two hundred stand of arms, ammunition, and a six-pound cannon. They then set the public authorities at defiance, and fired at several persons who had given them offence. One citizen was shot in the abdomen and died on the spot.

"The government telegraphed to the sheriff of the county to retake the State arms at all hazards. Captain Graham's company of one hundred men from Zanesville, and the Lancaster company tendered their services, and were dispatched to the scene of action. The ringleaders were arrested, and all is now quiet."

This was a clear case of rebellion—and a very aggravated case too—but, as it was described in many of the public journals, you might have taken the affair for a mere outburst of Hibernian jollity. The State armory was broken open, the arms seized, the laws were set at defiance, and a citizen murdered; but these deeds of matchless audacity called forth no thunders of denunciation from that faithful supporter of law and order, that reliable guardian of our republican fabric—the Newspaper Press!

EXPLANATIONS.

Forty volumes, I believe, would scarcely contain all the proofs and exemplifications which might be brought to the support of my Fourteenth Charge. It is sufficient for our purpose if we have ascertained that American Journalism really sympathizes and co-operates with seditious and dangerous agitators; that it excuses, in one way or another, the disorderly and rebellious movements of the basest class of the population; and that it endeavors, especially, to conceal or apologize for the audacious deportment of the foreign rabble. To explain *why* the newspaper press acts in this manner does not come exactly within the scope of our inquiry; and yet, if we are disposed to extend our researches in that direction, we may find explanation enough in the undisputable characteristics of American Journalism. For example :—

The insolent, presumptuous, and law-despising character of the press, which has been fully illustrated, must be expected to produce a congeniality of feeling with mobs of every kind, and a consequent disposition to favor and protect them.

The fact that popular commotions, and exciting events in general, add to the importance of journalism and increase its profits, may explain why the journalists themselves are apt to be agitators and disturbers of the public tranquillity, and why they are inclined to regard other offenders of the same class with indulgence or approbation.

The foreign composition and character of our journalism, concerning which much has been said in this volume, will account for that sympathizing kindness for aliens which inclines the press to extenuate or to hide, as far as that is possible, the vicious and lawless conduct of the foreign population.

And, besides all this, it may be observed that the American Press in general has begun to take a part in political discussions, which, in former times, were carried on chiefly by a small number of journals called "party organs." This change has brought a majority of our newspapers under the influences of corrupt factions which court the favor of the mob, and of the *foreign* mob especially, because they are supposed, (and not without some reason, alas!) to be the real electors to whom the American people have left the choice of their rulers. Here we discern another reason why the journalists use and recommend so many concessions to the TURBULENT POPULACE, assuming falsely that it is the American public and endeavoring to defend, and even to *legalize*, its most outrageous and treasonable actions.

SECTION XXII.

GENERAL RETROSPECTION.—RESULTS OF THE INVESTIGATION.—RESISTANCE TO NEWSPAPER TYRANNY RECOMMENDED.

My task is finished! Journalism is a "Veiled Prophet" no longer. I have torn away the shining drapery which concealed its hideous aspect; and this idolized Mokana, this base and cruel impostor, stands naked and undisguised before its shuddering worshipers!

REVIEW.

Let us make a retrospection of our labors. What revelations have been made? What truths have been brought to light? What errors have been rectified? What deceptions have been exposed? What crimes have been detected? All of these questions may be answered by comparing the ideal, superbly decorated, self-exalted, and universally-adored Journalism of yesterday, with the real, unmasked, dismantled, disgarnished, disgraced, disgusting, unsightly, and unadorable Journalism of to-day. Look, then, on this picture, and on this. See the flattering portraiture of Journalism, drawn by itself, and compare it with the faithful and uncomplimentary delineation which is now given you. In the difference between these two portraits you may find the result of our investigations.

OUR DISCOVERIES.

The truths which we have discovered in these investigations compel us to discard and repudiate the notion that the newspaper press is the "lever of education," the "great reformer and illuminator of the age," the "mirror of intellectual improvement," and the "driving engine of human progress." These and many other high-sounding titles, applied to it by its eulogist of the *Washington Union*, are meaningless and absurd.

We have discovered that the light emitted by the newspaper press is the thickest of all darkness. It is the darkness of ERROR, and that is a worse kind of obscurity than ignorance itself. What has journalism to do with *education?* Who are its pupils, and what have they learned? What *could* they learn besides atheism, obscenity, contempt and defiance of law, the arts of the seducer, the mysteries of brothels, the practice of pugilism, the tricks of swindlers, the operations of house-breakers, the excusableness of adultery, and the legality of assassination?

Such (as we have ascertained) are the moral instructions of journalism. And what are its intellectual teachings? False theories of all kinds, absurd notions of political economy and civil government, mistakes in science, misrepresentations of facts, crude opinions on every subject, monstrous political doctrines, morbid sentiment, and an occasional glimmer of truth surrounded by a nebulous mass of falsehood and stupidity.

We have discovered the fallacy of the common editorial pretense that journalism is a check on official knavery and venality. So far is the press from restraining the corrupt and villainous inclinations of public men that it *encourages* and *promotes* malfeasance in office, and accepts a share of official plunder. Hence we have designated the journalists as the accessories and copartners of the public robbers.

Our examinations have enabled us to detect the utter absurdity of the newspaper pretense that the press exercises a salutary influence on the courts of justice. It has been proved that most deplorable effects are constantly produced by newspaper interference with the administration of the laws.

It appears from our investigations that the newspaper press discourages the productive industry of the country by upholding oppressive paper-money-making corporations, and encouraging the influx of pauper laborers from Europe.

We have detected many ludicrous or execrable mistakes in a somewhat celebrated panegyric on the newspaper press pronounced by the able editor of the Washington Union. It is impossible now for that hyperbolizing scribe to make us believe that the newspaper press is—

    "A Statesman,"   "A Clergyman,"
    "A Lawyer,"   "A Teacher;"

for we have found, by inspection, that the statesmanship of the press is devoted to the service of corrupt factions, and to the aggrandizement of knavish, office-hunting demagogues.

We have proved that, as a legal counselor, the press instructs its clients that when it is inconvenient to obey the law there is no great impropriety in breaking it. And we have ascertained that,

As a religious instructor, the press informs its congregations that one religion is as good as another; or, that the best religion is the one that is least restrictive, or most "liberal." Among the theologians of the press, the prevailing opinion seems to be that the most liberal religion is that which is furthest from orthodox Christianity.

Our investigations have made us understand that the newspaper press of America is *not qualified* to instruct the people in statesmanship, religion, science, or morality.

Instead of those fine names bestowed on the Newspaper Press by the Washington Union, we have learned to apply some others. For example, we find that Journalism is—

    A Disorganizer,   A Swindler,
    A Rebel,   A Liar,
    A Traitor,   A Slanderer,
    A Rioter,   A Thief,
    An Impostor,   A Murderer.

And many other things that are not pretty and amiable.

THE PRESS IS NO PART OF THE GOVERNMENT.

In the course of our investigations, we have ascertained, I think, that the newspaper press is no part of the regular machinery of government. It is a public convenience, but not a national "institution," as that word is generally understood. The wire-telegraph, or any other contrivance for spreading the news, is as much an "institution" as journalism.

We have ascertained, likewise, that the newspaper press is not a "palladium," as it would fain make us believe. The palladium of ancient times was a mythological representation of WISDOM. It is true that the wisdom of our newspaper press is a MYTH; but in one important particular, journalism differs widely from its supposed prototype, it *endangers* the Commonwealth instead of making it safe.

THE PRESS AS IT IS.

Our inquiries have led to the discovery that, in its present condition, the Newspaper Press of the United States is a powerful agent of mischief; or, as Mr. Cooper says, "it is the very instrument that devils would use to accomplish their designs."

We have learned, also, that it is only as vehicles of *news* that the public journals are unquestionably useful. All of their other pretensions to utility are either hypothetical and doubtful, or obviously false and absurd. The absolute *necessity* of newspapers does not appear. Society has existed without them, and it is possible that it might do so again. I am altogether convinced that if the newspaper literature of America were reduced to one twentieth part of the present amount, the change would be eminently beneficial.

From all the examinations that we have made, it appears that the baneful influences of Journalism are so manifest that all good men should unite in the effort to abate the evil.

DUTY OF CHRISTIANS.

Have the Christian inhabitants of the United States ever

seriously reflected on their *political* responsiblities ? Do they consider themselves obliged, in *all* temporal matters, to regulate their conduct by the example of the early apostles ? Has it never occurred to them that the *position* of Christians in America is very different from that of the earlier followers of Christ in the land of Judea ? The latter had but little to do with the government of their country; they had no political power; and, of course, they were not responsible for such abuses as the criminal negligence of the government permitted to exist in that region. The Christian people of America *have* political power; it is a talent which God has given them, and are they not responsible for burying it in the earth, or for not using it ? Among other great evils which exist in this country by their permission, are the monstrous abuses of the newspaper press. In what part of the Bible have they learned that the toleration of sin is any part of a Christian's duty ? Where have they learned that it is allowable for Christians to strengthen and support the special agencies of the devil ? The God of the Christians is insulted every week in the columns of an advertising sheet of Philadelphia—and yet the followers of Christ encourage that impious journal with their patronage. Announcements of sermons and prayer-meetings are made in close proximity with indictable enunciations of blasphemy !

If the newspaper press is, as many judicious people suppose, the great battery of Beelzebub, I sincerely wish that the whole artillery of the church could be employed against it. Though I am connected with no religious society, I earnestly desire to see the power of the pulpit arrayed against that of the press—since there is no other power in the land bold enough to contend with this diabolical enemy.

The newspapers continually exclaim against the mixture of religion with politics, (unless they happen to make an exception in favor of Catholicism,) but it appears to me that *any* mixture whatever would improve the present condition of American politics—for any change therein must be for the better. I am not afraid of an infusion of Christianity (without sectarianism) into our government. All the editorial prattle about "blue laws," etc., is nonsense or knavery. Blue laws, or even black laws, are better than no laws at all; or no *observance* of them, which is precisely the same thing. Sectarian despotisms have existed—but CHRISTIANITY never played the tyrant.

If we had a Christian party in politics, we might hope for some legislation which would make journalism a *tolerable* grievance,—if any greater improvement in it is out of the question.

RESIST THE TYRANT.

I earnestly exhort my countrymen of all classes and conditions to withstand the tyranny of the press. Fear it not; it is only a monstrous phantom, like the shadowy forms which frightened Æneas at the gates of Erebus. The author of this book may venture to hope that his sincerity will not be questioned when he expresses his belief that the newspaper press is *not quite* "omnipotent." It is powerful only because the people believe in its potency. Yes, it is your erring faith, my countrymen, which clothes this idol, made by yourselves, with the attributes of divinity. Give it only the estimation which it deserves, and you take away half of its ability to do mischief. It is not entitled to your devotions, your reverence, or your obedience. Do not shrink and shiver in its presence, like children before a frowning pedagogue. Regard not its commands, its menaces, or its maledictions. Believe its reports with extreme caution, and never accept its counsels unless you are well acquainted with its designs.

Never regard the press as an impersonality; but remember that when the Times, the Tribune, the Herald, etc., deliver their oracular utterances, the voice may really belong to some Sawney McGregor, Phelim McShane, or Teague O'Flaherty, whose opinions, if they were orally expressed in your presence, you would not suppose to be worth the rind of an Irish potato.

The press would make you believe that it is a grand enchanter; despise its pretensions, and it becomes a pitiful juggler. It appears in the character of a mighty potentate, but if you take no part in the performance, and do not choose to be seen among its retinue, you may contemn it as a scrubby play-actor, in spite of all its majestic strutting and all its regal garniture. The despotism of the press is easily resisted; if the public resolves to pay no homage to its power, it is reduced at once to a state of impotence.

APPENDIX.

I. CHARGES OMITTED.

IN addition to the fourteen charges against the newspapers which are discussed in this volume, there were *six* others in the original manuscript, which were excluded merely because the discussion of them would have made the work too voluminous. Hence it appears that *all* the delinquencies of journalism are not told, and the words, " a *complete* exposure of the corruptions and crimes of journalism," which, by an oversight, were retained on the title page, may seem to promise too much. However, the disclosures which are made in this book will perhaps throw enough light on the character of Journalism to make all its sins discoverable, if the reader is disposed to pursue the investigation.

II. EDITORIAL ASSOCIATIONS.

Some attempt was recently made to establish a new editorial association or confederacy in Philadelphia. It appears that the editors of the *Public Ledger* were not invited to become members of this honorable body, and the omission brought out the following truthful denunciation of the whole movement.

" Some editors and writers for the Press, (says the *Ledger*,) have been holding a convention in this city, for the purpose of improving the newspaper press, and elevating its tone. We have no objection to the individuals who feel that they are guilty of editorial indecencies holding such conclaves and resolving to reform. There is considerable room for improvement in some of them. If association, or any other proper moral restraint can exercise any corrective influence over such newspapers, conventions may possibly do some good. It is not, however, by meeting together, and tickling each other's vanity, that gentlemanly propriety is to be attained. Without the proper instincts of gentility in the individual, little benefit can arise from conventions, no matter how often they are held. It is probably because some newspapers find, from the effect on their business, that their tone is considerably less 'elevated' than the tone of the public, that they begin to feel that some reform is necessary."

To this unexceptionable paragraph, a writer in the Philadelphia *Press*, supposed to be Mackenzie, the Scotch sub-editor, made the following angry response:—

"The more creditable portion of the city press are members of this editorial association; not so the Ishmaels and Bohemians of the craft; and it is amusing to see one of these, a penny worth of small type on discolored straw paper, attempting to sneer at a companionship to which it does not belong, daintily prating of the proper instincts of gentility in the individual who conducts a journal. We should like to know what instruction there is in indecent advertisements, in announcements of cheating fortune-tellers, or in assignations proclaimed to society under the 'personal' head."

Editorial quarrels are useful things, sometimes. They bring out the truth when nothing else could possibly do so.

III. VENOM OF PHILADELPHIA JOURNALISM.

Not by conventions, or confederacies, or any thing else, can some of the venomous editors of Philadelphia be prevented from doing each other damage. They may eat, drink, and get drunk together, and pretend to cultivate social and fraternal feelings in every possible way, but, metaphorically speaking, they will certainly stab each other in the dark, at the first opportunity. The journalists of this city like spiders shut up in a bottle, have preyed upon each other until there is very little left to show that Philadelphia is able or willing to maintain a public press.

This circumstance, more than any other cause, has injured the commerce and prosperity of the city. The New York journals have ten times more influence than the papers of Philadelphia, and they use that influence for the benefit of the island metropolis, and for the disparagement of the city of Quakers. The newspapers have made Philadelphia a city of dark conspiracies, and brought affairs to such a condition that there is very little unity of purpose or harmony of action among its inhabitants.

IV. THE BANKING SYSTEM ILLUSTRATED.

The effect of an over issue of paper money in depreciating the value of the currency is strikingly illustrated in St. Domingo. The government has issued $55,250,000 in paper. The value of it, at this time, is just one cent on the dollar. Such, in effect, is that financiering system which is upheld by our newspaper press.

V. A MEDICAL EDITOR.

A newspaper paragraph declares that S. Hankinson, M.D., *alias* Bland, publisher of the New York Journal, has been arrested by order of Mayor Tiemann. The charge against him is that his "Journal" is an obscene, indecent, and scandalous paper, and that it is used by the said Hankinson for the purpose of swindling and cheating the community, and sapping the morals of the youth of both sexes. The paragraph containing this account is headed, "More war on the swindling doctors."

VI. NO HOPE FOR AMERICANS.

The Irish editor of Harpers' Weekly lately made the tri

umphant declaration that "political Americanism" is at an end. This sad catastrophe is accounted for by the Scotch editor of the New York Herald in his paper of October 27, 1858. Says Bennett: "The Republicans of New York have a corruption fund of two hundred and fifty thousand dollars, (to purchase newspaper influence and other electioneering material,) and the Democrats have a fund for the same purposes and quite as large, but the Americans have only the SANCTITY OF THEIR CAUSE and the purity and fitness of their candidates. They can neither buy venal presses, nor employ mouthing orators to stump the State. Of course they will be left in the background."

The Caledonian scribe *can* tell the truth when he has no particular reason for hiding it.

VII. EMPIRICAL MURDERS.

Sir Robert Walpole, Lord Bolingbroke and Winnington were killed by quack doctors. But quackery never flourished in England as it does in America, and the murders perpetrated by the public poisoners in this country are not likely to appear in print. The number of the victims, therefore, is incomputable. Bennett's biographer boasts that the American quacks owe all their prosperity to the public journals.

VIII. ARSENIC PRESCRIBED.

"The newspaper press is a physician," said the Washington Union. Several years ago, the Philadelphia Ledger, in one of its leading articles, prescribed small doses of arsenic to ladies who wish to "increase their flesh, and give roundness to their limbs." The writer of the "leader" intimated that the peasant girls of Austria are accustomed to *fatten* themselves by the use of this mineral!

In allusion to this very indiscreet and dangerous recommendation, the New Orleans Picayune expressed its disapprobation in this mild and playful manner:

"Arsenic eating! what a pleasant practice! The Ledger does not say how the mineral is to be taken; but we presume that it comes in with the dessert after dinner—perhaps as an arsenic tart, or, maybe, to give flavor to an apple-dumpling!"

IX. VINDICATION OF EDGAR A. POE.

Several years ago I published the following article in a Philadelphia weekly paper:

"EDGAR A. POE AND HIS CALUMNIATORS.—There is a spurious biography of Edgar A. Poe which has been extensively published in newspapers and magazines. It is a hypocritical canting document, expressing much commiseration for the follies and 'crimes' of that 'poor outcast;' the writer being evidently just such an one as the Pharisee who thanked God that he was a better fellow than the publican. But we can tell the slanderous and malicious miscreant who composed the aforesaid biography, (we know not and care not who he is,) that Edgar A. Poe was infinitely his superior, both in the moral and in the intellectual scale. The writer of this article speaks from his own knowledge when he says that Poe was not the man described by this anonymous scribbler. Some circumstances mentioned by the slanderous hypocrite we *know* to be false, and we have no doubt in the world that nearly all of his statements intended to throw odium and discredit on the character of the deceased are scandalous inventions.

"We have much more to say on this subject, and we pledge ourselves to show that the article we speak of is false and defamatory, when the skulking author of it becomes magnanimous enough to take the responsibility by fixing his *name* to his malignant publication."

I do not know that this *vindication* was copied by a single paper; whereas the whole press of the country seemed desirous of giving circulation and authenticity to the slanders.

X. INCITEMENT TO MOBBING.

A Boston paper, dated May 9, 1855, said: "There is no little excitement in this city, at the present time, with regard to the enforcement of the liquor law. It is rumored that nineteen hundred men are leagued together and sworn to resist it, if needs be, at the point of the bayonet."

This pretended "rumor" is only *advice* in disguise, and the English translation is this: "We recommend all the rum-sellers and grog-drinkers in Boston to arm themselves with death-dealing weapons, and to resist the execution of the anti-liquor law to the last extremity. Turn out, ye jovial subjects and soldiers of King Alcohol; murder all the sober inhabitants of Boston, and establish as many temples of Bacchus in the 'City of Notions' as they have in the 'City of Brotherly Love.'"

The law *was* enforced, however, but the "nineteen hundred men," with their bayonets, did not appear. In this instance the stimulus of journalism happened to be unsuccessful.

XI. TREASON APPROVED.

A Southern stump orator lately said, in one of his pestilent harangues: "We must dissolve the Union if they effect any of their aggressive purposes—tariffs, banks, or tampering with slaves."

With reference to this burst of eloquence, the Louisville Journal says: "The *whole speech* is characterized by a manly candor and gleams of practical sense!"

XII. A CLERICAL EDITOR.

The Louisville Journal thus describes Parson Brownlow, the editor of a Western paper: "Brownlow is the 'fighting parson,' renowned throughout the nation. He is a rare genius, and a powerful one. Possessing strong sense and strong passions, he writes with all his might, sparing no one that dares to cross his path as an enemy. He assails his foes with the pen, and thunders at them from the stump and the pulpit; and if they want any thing more of him, he shrinks not from encountering them with fist, or knife, or pistol." (! !)

It seems that clergymen themselves are be-deviled when they become editors.

XIII. THE DEVIL AMONG THE DUTCHMEN.

In August, 1858, the Sheriff attached the goods and chattels of Stephen Mollison, editor of the Cincinnati Volksblatt, to await the result of a suit for libel brought against him by Joseph A. Heman of the Volksfreund. Some articles published in the Volksblatt contained the alleged libels for which Mr. Heman claimed $20,000 damages. Many of the German papers are terribly libellous.

XIV. NEWSPAPER PERSECUTION.—CASE OF MAT. WARD.

Everybody in America was horrified, some years ago, by the newspaper details of the unprovoked murder of a school-master, near Louisville, Ky., by Matthew Ward, the son of a wealthy gentleman residing in that neighborhood. The following is, perhaps, the first *true* account of that affair that has ever been published:—

Willie Ward, a boy of twelve years, was sent to school to Mr. Butler, who had formerly been a tutor in Mr. Ward's family. Butler promised that Willie should not be whipped in school, and that, when he committed a fault, he should be sent home to his father for correction. After this agreement, Willie was severely whipped by an assistant teacher, named Sturges. Mr. Ward called at the school-house, on the following day, and repeated his request that the boy should be sent home for punishment, which Mr. Butler again promised should be done. A short time after this, another boy accused Willie, (falsely, it is said,) of giving him chestnuts in school time, and when young Ward denied it, Butler called him "a little liar," and gave him a very severe beating with a large leathern strap, so that he was bruised black and blue all over.

Willie came home crying, and requested his elder brother, Matthew F. Ward, to go and remonstrate with Mr. Butler. Matthew was a sickly young man, and had been recently going on crutches, in consequence of a bad attack of rheumatism. His physician testified at the trial, that he was under medical treatment at the time to which we now refer. At the request of his mother, Matthew took with him his brother Robert, aged about sixteen. He was also accompanied by Willie, who said to him, while they were on the way, "You know, brother, that Mr. Butler is a stronger man than you are, and Mr. Sturges has a big stick in the school-room." Matthew replied, "I apprehend no difficulty; for I believe Mr. Butler to be a just man, and I shall say nothing to give him justifiable cause of offense."

On arriving at the school-house, Matthew and Robert civilly accosted Mr. Butler, and inquired why he did not send Willie home, according to the agreement. Butler refused to give any explanation of his conduct, and there was an angry dispute between him and Matthew, in the course of which the latter called the teacher "a liar." Mr. Butler then grasped Ward by the cravat, pushed him up into a corner, and struck him two or three times at least, when Matthew drew a pistol and shot him. (Owing to the state of society in that neighborhood it is a common practice, and in some degree an excusable one, for people to carry weapons for defense.) Several witnesses testified that, at the time of the shooting, Butler had Ward "crushed back against the wall, in a corner, as far as he could get, and bent down." Robert Ward took no part in the affair, except, that when Sturges, the assistant teacher, advanced toward Matthew, as if for the purpose of joining in the attack, Robert drew a bowie-knife, and bade him stand back.

It is said that the Louisville *Courier* and the *Democrat* had been spiteful to the Ward family ever since Matthew's sister was married to a son of Abbott Lawrence. George D. Prentice, of the Louisville Journal, was the only editor who was invited to the nuptials, and it is surmised that the other journalists of Louisville thought themselves slighted.

Before the beginning of Matthew's trial, the offended papers published the most inflammatory articles against the Ward family, and endeavored, especially, to make Matthew an object of popular resentment. The passions of the rabble were so stirred up by these influences, that it was necessary to place a guard about the jail where the prisoner was confined to prevent the mob from taking him out and hanging him. The same ill-disposed journals misrepresented all the facts of the case, and succeeded in making the people believe that Butler was altogether blameless, and that Matthew Ward had entered the school in a furious manner and shot the teacher without allowing him any opportunity for defense. All the Northern papers repeated the same story, and to this day very few people know the true history of the affair.

When the day of trial came, no jury could be found who had not decided in their own minds that the prisoner was guilty of deliberate murder, and a change of venue was thus made necessary. The Hon. John J. Crittenden, seeing how Ward was persecuted, volunteered to defend him, and thus raised a storm of indignation against himself. Slanderous charges against Mr. Crittenden were circulated all over the country, and there were threats of mobbing him.

The two papers which took the most active part in this persecution are the same which, in the next year, (1855,) excited the great riot in Louisville by advising the foreigners to go to the polls armed, and to "shed blood freely if necessary."

On finding that a change of venue had been obtained, these journals made a slanderous attack on the judge and jury of Hardin County Court, where Ward was to be tried.

Matthew Ward was acquitted on the ground that he had

acted strictly in self-defense, and that his feebleness of body made a resort to weapons necessary to protect himself from the assaults of a strong man like Mr. Butler.

After the acquittal, the jury was burnt in effigy by a mob. The elder Ward's house was set on fire by the infuriated populace, his garden and plantation were laid waste, and Matthew Ward narrowly escaped being lynched. He saved his life only by making a hasty retreat from the neighborhood.

XV. "THE FOREST LETTER."

Some mention of this celebrated epistle has been made in another part of this volume. It is a topic which I would gladly avoid if possible, but, for fear that the reader might imagine something worse than the reality, I insert the letter itself, (or the most authentic copy of it which I have been able to obtain,) and I would gladly add any explanations which have been made by Mr. Forney if I knew where to find them. In one of his stump orations or editorial paragraphs, (I really forget which,) Mr. Forney speaks of the allusions which his political enemies make to this letter as "nonsensical," but I do not know what he intends to signify by that term. Does he deny that he wrote the letter? and is it his intention to say that it is absurd and ridiculous to suppose that he *could* be the author of such a piece of composition? If this is his meaning, I really wish that he had expressed it in language which would admit of no misconstruction. The letter itself is not "nonsensical." It is full of significance; and, if it is genuine, it must have been written for a serious purpose, which every reader will comprehend.

Mr. Forney, it will be perceived, is quite enthusiastic in his admiration of Edwin Forrest, and he appears to have sympathized deeply with that eminent tragedian at the time when Mr. Forrest made application for a divorce from his wife Catharine. The letter purports to have been written about the time when the Forrest divorce case was pending. The subjoined copy was taken from a newspaper report of the trial, and the letter was produced in court, I suppose, to show that some extraordinary means had been used to obtain evidence against Mrs. Forrest. The person to whom the letter is addressed is Mr. George Roberts, former editor of the Boston Times, and now one of the proprietors of the " Constellation."

" *Philadelphia, January* 25*th*, 1850.

" [*Private.*]—Our friend Forrest is now here, and is about to apply for a divorce from his wife. He has had for eighteen months the proofs of her infidelity; but has chosen to keep them quiet, and would have done so still but for her folly in censuring him in leaving her. It is really astonishing how he has kept these proofs to himself, from all his friends, for all that time, but it is so nevertheless.

"The facts are these, eighteen months ago, while playing in Cincinnati, he caught Mrs. F. in a very *equivocal* position with a young man in his own parlor. She protested innocence, and he let it pass by, loving her as he did profoundly. They passed on to New Orleans, and so home to New York. After they reached home, and had been there for some time, he found one evening on his wife's table a billet-doux in the hand-writing of, though not signed by, this young man, in which she was alluded to in terms the most amorous and unmistakable. The language alluded to her "white arms that wound about his neck," to the "blissful hours they had spent together," and the letter had been kept as a memento until it was quite well worn. Upon this evidence, with other confirmatory proofs, he intends applying to our Legislature for a divorce; but you are now in a position to serve him *in a manner he never will forget*. The person who wrote to Mrs. F., and in whose company she was detected, is Geo. Jamieson, now playing in New Orleans. If you don't know him, you can, as the *editor* of a leading paper, soon make his acquaintance.

" What Forrest now desires to clinch the nail is to obtain in some way an *admission* from Jamieson. I named you to him as a safe, steady, and intelligent friend, and he never will forget whatever you may do for him in this, to him, most vital matter. He suggests that you might institute intimate relations to J., and then induce him, either in your presence or in company, to *admit*, as a thing to be proud of, his connection with Mrs. F. He is fond of a glass, and possibly, in a convivial mood, might become communicative. No harm will come to him, as he is too small game for Forrest, and any admission he may make may be important only as aiding an injured man in getting relieved from a now hateful bond. Can you manage this thing, my friend? It will require skill and caution, and, if successful, will warmly endear you to Forrest. He is nearly crazy at the idea of being placed in his present position, but he will spend half he is worth to be relieved from it. This matter must be kept secret. Above all, do not name me in connection with it. Excuse me for troubling you in regard to it. My ardent attachment to glorious Forrest must be my excuse. Now, won't you help to relieve him?

"It would help in the matter to know that John Greene, the actor, now in New Orleans, is the warm friend of Forrest, and may know Jamieson well.

"You can use your own discretion in letting him know the facts and invoking his aid. This letter is addressed to you with the knowledge of Mr. Forrest.

"Please write as soon after receipt as you can have opportunity to look about you."

XVI. PERSECUTION OF J. G. BENNETT.

The irrational and barbarous manner in which newspaper mobs sometimes attempt to inflict punishment on the objects of their jealousy or hatred is shown in the effort which was made by some of the New York journals to force the proprietor of the Astor House to eject Mr. Bennett *and his wife* from that establishment. In August, 1840, Mr. and Mrs. Bennett (soon after their marriage) took lodgings at that excellent hotel, when an outcry was raised by some half a dozen journalists, (not one of whom perhaps was any better than Bennett himself,) for the purpose of compelling Mr. Stetson, the host of the Astor House, to turn the newly-married couple out of doors. In order to facilitate this measure, which would have been so gratifying to their malice, the persecuting editors published a report that Bennett and his bride had already been dismissed. Mr. Stetson compelled the malicious scoundrels to retract this falsehood, and firmly resisted all their endeavors to make him the instrument of their vengeance.

Though there is very little to admire in the conduct of James G. Bennett, there is not the shadow of an excuse for an attempt to punish him in the manner described. But what had *Mrs. Bennett* done to deserve the same vindictive treatment? The whole affair may remind us of the course which is sometimes pursued by Asiatic despots when they punish an offender without any legal formality, and include his wife and children in the same retribution.

XVII. A NUT FOR THE NATURALIZERS.

While this book is on the press, I have discovered that General Cass, the venerable Secretary of State under our present Democratic Administration, has officially confirmed some of the opinions respecting the rights of aliens to American citizenship, which were expressed in one of my first sections. In a letter dated Washington, May 17, 1853, and addressed to Mr. Felix Legure, an adopted citizen of Tennessee, Mr. Cass writes as follows:

"It is understood that the French Government claims military service from all natives of France who may be found within its jurisdiction. Your naturalization in this country will not exempt you from that claim if you should voluntarily repair thither."

This is sound doctrine, and I am glad to find that General

Cass had independence enough to maintain it, in spite of all the newspaper scolding to which the position he takes may make him liable. The opposite ground taken by our Government in the "Kosta affair" might have involved the United States in a troublesome war, if Austria had been bold enough to resist a claim which every lawyer and statesman KNOWS to be untenable; though Mr. Marcy, and some others, may affect to believe otherwise.

XVIII. THE CALIFORNIANS SHOCKED.

The proprietors of a paper called the *Evening Bulletin*, which is printed in San Francisco, California, were lately prosecuted for publishing the filthy details of the Sickles trial, which they copied *verbatim* from the papers of New York, Boston, and Philadelphia. This circumstance produced some ribald jesting among the journalists of the last-named cities, who thought it "quite ridiculous" for the Californians to pretend to be more decent and moral than the people of the Eastern and Middle States! However, the facts speak for themselves, and the evidence is irresistible:—the Californians will not endure an obscene and vicious press, and the Bostonians, New Yorkers, and Philadelphians will seldom encourage a press of any other character. The world will be apt to interpret these signs in accordance with their most obvious import, and in a manner which the press and people of the Atlantic cities cannot be expected to relish.

THE END.